Soil Forensics

Series Editor

Patrick Randolph-Quinney, Department of Applied Sciences,
Faculty of Health and Life Sciences
Northumbria University, Newcastle-upon-Tyne, UK

Soil Forensics aims to provide a transdisciplinary overview of all relevant forensic fields which interact with the soil environment and Earth-system processes. This includes disciplines such as forensic archaeology, forensic taphonomy and anthropology, geophysics and remote sensing, forensic geology and soil science, forensic ecology, and environmental forensics. Volumes in the series are intended to stimulate multidisciplinary and transdisciplinary approaches at the interface of forensics and the many sub-disciplines in Earth Sciences, Archaeology and others, such as traditional soil science, palynology, geochemistry, biogeochemistry, sedimentology, field archaeology, archaeological prospection, and taphonomy. The series will include investigation into:

- Human taphonomy and experimental decomposition studies
- Experimental standards development and validation
- Violation of the environment (chemical exposure, pollution, illegal mining)
- Search, detection, identification, and recovery of human remains in soil context
- New methods and techniques in soil forensics such as proteomics, magnetic surveys, electrical imaging techniques, and UAV-based spectroscopy and remote sensing
- Application of AI and Machine learning approaches to complex forensic issues
- 3D and 4D modelling, visualization, and spatial analyses (including the use of Geographical Information Systems)
- Stratigraphy, stratification and soil context
- Linking research-based knowledge to the community of action, with a focus on knowledge transfer and practice-informed research
- Degradation studies of organic and inorganic anthropogenic materials in soils.

The *Soil Forensics* Series was originally developed by the late Professor Henk Kars from the Institute of Geo- and Bioarchaeology at VU University Amsterdam. The current Series Editor and Editorial Board will continue to adhere to the interdisciplinary interplay between the sciences and humanities that distinguished Professor Kars' academic career.

Pier Matteo Barone • WJ Mike Groen
Editors

Forensic Archaeology and New Multidisciplinary Approaches

Topics Discussed During the 2018-2023 European Meetings on Forensic Archaeology (EMFA)

Springer

Editors
Pier Matteo Barone
American University of Rome
Rome, Italy

WJ Mike Groen
Netherlands Forensic Institute
The Hague, The Netherlands

ISSN 2214-4293 ISSN 2214-4315 (electronic)
Soil Forensics
ISBN 978-3-031-86307-3 ISBN 978-3-031-86308-0 (eBook)
https://doi.org/10.1007/978-3-031-86308-0

This Springer imprint is published by the registered company Springer Nature Switzerland AG
The registered company address is: Gewerbestrasse 11, 6330 Cham, Switzerland

Foreword: Forensic Archaeology, Past and Present: A Global View

Past

For several decades, crime scenes (CSs) containing bodies have been par excellence the natural place of the so-called "Scientific Police," "Criminalists," "Crime Scene Investigators" (CSI), or "Scene of Crime Officers" (SOCOs), depending on the country being discussed. For the judicial authority, it is natural to request the police to assist to a CS for the recovery of a body and the evidence associated with it, and to present a report of what was observed and recovered, and to have a first, factual, version of what happened.

This happens, and continues to happen, in every country in the world that has a criminal investigation system, and where a body is found on the street or inside a home, for example.

But little by little, and with more complex scenes than those described, it was necessary to call to other specialties not usual in the field of criminalistics and forensics, such as Forensic Archaeology, Forensic Geology, Geophysics, or Architecture, to account for more complex scenarios that somehow exceeded the capabilities of the scientific police. There are times, for example, where a CS is in rural areas, and knowledge of the landscape, climate, flora, fauna, rivers, etc. becomes indispensable for investigators.

Mass disasters with multiple victims, massacres committed during conflicts, bombings of villages, terrorist attacks in cities, and hiding of corpses in clandestine graves are just some of these so-called complex scenes, which need a differential approach on the part of investigators.

At the same time, the number of bodies and their level of fragmentation and mixture make the participation of Forensic Anthropologists, specialists in human osteology and bone trauma analysis, indispensable. There are occasions, such as the terrorist attack on the Twin Towers on 9/11 in New York, where the bodies of the victims were found in a restaurant's areas, and it took the assistance of forensic anthropologists to make a separation on the ground about which bones were human and which were not.

On the other hand, the search for bodies is no longer carried out only with police walking the area or dogs trained to detect odors, but now satellite images, drone images, geophysical searches, Light Detection and Ranging (LIDAR), and intelligent analysis with Geographic Information Systems (GIS) models are used.

Judges and prosecutors usually follow the advice of the police to carry out all these field tasks; normally, they do not know the contributions that other scientific disciplines or academics such as universities can make.

At the same time, the police often believe that it is not necessary to incorporate civilian scientists into their forces for these cases, or they directly think that with a short course in Forensic Archaeology they are already qualified to act as Archaeologists.

What these produces are incomplete recoveries, fragmented bodies with postmortem damage, little understanding of the context of the case, problems in the search for bodies, recovering non-human remains, and in conclusion, a waste of all the information that an EC can provide.

Present

Of the 195 countries that exist today in the world, recognized by the United Nations, a large number have Archaeology programs in Universities, Institutes, and Museums, among others. Even countries that have suffered many years of conflict such as Iraq, Syria, Sri Lanka, Afghanistan, Ethiopia, Mexico, and Colombia, with thousands of missing and buried, have a long and rich tradition of prehistoric and historical archaeology. However, the justice systems of these countries rarely know that there are archaeologists and what they would be for.

On the other hand, in countries such as those mentioned, getting involved in police and investigation tasks can be dangerous, exposing oneself to situations that are not frequent in academic life.

At the same time, the transition from classical to forensic archaeology is not easy. It is not the same to deal with academic colleagues and archaeological sites as it is to deal with police, judges, and the press, with much shorter times, and with the consequences of our forensic reports.

However, important advances in some regions of the world had been happening during the last decades, such as the United States, England, the Netherlands, and Latin America, where Forensic Archaeology ceased to be something related to Indiana Jones, or mummies, in the popular imagination, and becoming a de facto scientific discipline in forensic services.

At this point, it is important to clarify that the concept of "Forensic Anthropology" is not understood in the same way throughout the world. For example, in countries like England, it is a different specialty from Anthropology, Forensic Archaeology; while in the United States and Latin America, anthropologists do Archaeology and Anthropology at the same time.

During the 1990s, different documents and practices began to expand at international level, on the use of Forensic Archeology in the criminal investigations. For example, since 1996, the International Tribunal for the Former Yugoslavia (ICTY) had been using Forensic Archaeologists as a fundamental part of their multidisciplinary teams in the recovery of thousands of bodies buried in mass graves.

Also at international level, the new version of The Minnesota Protocol on the Investigation of Potentially Unlawful Deaths (2016), the so-called "Minnesota Protocol," and the one of the two United Nations (UN) forensic document recommended by UN, explicitly mention Forensic Archaeology as a key discipline in the multidisciplinary teams.

Since 2004, the International Committee of the Red Cross (ICRC) with the creation of her Forensic Unit recognizes also Forensic Archaeology as one of the most important forensic disciplines to document cases of human rights violation.

At a country level, Colombia is the country in the world, after United States, with the highest number of forensic anthropologists, 142, working full-time in the official forensic services provided by different institutions of the Colombian State. In the case of Chile, Peru, or Mexico, for example, it is common for forensic anthropologists to go to the CSs, and they are recognized by society as a whole.

Also in Latina America, the 1980s and the 1990s saw the creation of independent forensic teams, in Argentina, Chile, Guatemala, Peru, Uruguay, Mexico, mainly composed by Forensic Anthropologists, to investigate whereabouts of the disappeared for political reasons.

In this regard, one of the most thriving associations is the Latin American Association of Forensic Anthropology (ALAF), created in 2003, with more than 120 members, which organizes a congress every year and began 12 years ago and 1 years ago, respectively, processes of Certification in Forensic Anthropology and Forensic Archaeology.

As for the outlook in Europe, it is not homogeneous for all countries. In Spain, for example, forensic archaeologists have been especially dedicated to cases related to the Civil War (1936–1939) and the Franco Dictatorship (1939–1975), but there are very few forensic archaeologists working with the police who oversee the CSs.

On the other hand, several European countries, such as England, France, or Germany, among others, have Forensic Archaeologists within their programs for the recovery of the bodies of soldiers who died during World War II.

Finally, it is important to note that it was only in 2023 that INTERPOL recognized for the first time in its DVI guides the value of incorporating Forensic Archaeologists into its teams.

But for what is useful a Forensic Archaeologists, ask very often a judge or a police officer?

At the end of the day, this is the first question that a judge or a prosecutor is going to ask. Even a policeman when he no longer finds a body.

If we remember the mains principals at the CS: define and secure areas that may contain evidence; examine and document the scene; collect physical evidence; and preserve, package, and submit the evidence to the laboratory for analysis, we will see that are not so different than the phases followed by an Archaeologist in a pre or historical site. Of course, the context and the purpose are different, but the steps are very similar. In both cases we are taking about human behavior, and to reconstruct what happened there.

Beyond the stage of recovering a body when it is buried, the work of the Forensic Archaeologist can go beyond that.

To mention just a few areas:

1. *Analysis of the geographical area where the victim is supposed to be:* type of soil, stratigraphy, climate, rainfall, flora, fauna, behavior of rivers, lakes, and sea are some of the matters where the Forensic Archaeologist is trained to provide an opinion.
2. *Search for bodies:* application of Geophysics procedures, LiDar, satellite and aerial images, thermal changes, among others, are some of the methods that the Forensic Archaeologist can apply in the search.
3. *Spatial distribution of objects and taphonomic processes*: by formation, Forensic Archaeologists are trained to describe the spatial location of objects (in this case, bodies and objects), and try to make sense of what these associations are attributed. By taphonomic processes, we mean all the post-mortem changes, natural and human, that affect a body.

Is it possible for SOCOs and forensic archaeologists to work together?

Definitely yes. Knowledge is not the property of a single scientific discipline, and today multidisciplinary work is indispensable.

But in this multidisciplinary work we must ensure that the Forensic Archaeologist is at the same level as a SOCO, not under it.

At the same time, the scientific police forces incorporate full-time Forensic Archaeologists among their services, and not just call them incidentally.

The judicial authority, judges, and prosecutors also must understand that today the application of science to the investigation of crime is a multidisciplinary field and is not enough with the traditional approach based only in police knowledge.

Finally, we believe that incorporating Forensic Archaeologists to outdoor scenes is an advantage for the CSI team, as we can provide a different view on the processes that lead to a criminal act. From survey of big areas with non-intrusive methods to understand the stratigraphy of a burial site, we complement the work of the CSI team, augmenting the possibilities of having a better comprehension of what happened on that place.

Independent Consultant, Buenos Aires, Argentina
Former Director of the Argentine Forensic Anthropology Team, Córdoba, Argentina
Former Head of the Forensic Unit of the International Committee of the Red Cross, Buenos Aires, Argentina

Luis Fondebrider

Preface

It is with great pleasure that we present this new edition of "Forensic Archaeology and New Multidisciplinary Approaches: Topics discussed during the 2018–2023 European Meetings on Forensic Archaeology (EMFA)." This volume brings together the latest research and developments discussed at the EMFA conferences, highlighting the challenges, advancements, and innovations in the field over the past five years.

Since its inception, the EMFA has been a vital forum for forensic archaeologists, forensic anthropologists, forensic scientists, law enforcement professionals, and related specialists across Europe. These meetings have provided an essential platform for sharing knowledge, methodologies, and experiences, fostering a collaborative environment that drives the field forward. This volume stands as a testament to that collaboration and the rich, multidisciplinary nature of forensic archaeology today.

The journey of EMFA began in 2012 with a conference in The Hague, organized by the forensic archaeology unit of the Netherlands Forensic Institute (NFI) and the forensic archaeology expert panel of the British Chartered Institute for Archaeologists (CIfA). Over the years, the EMFA conferences have grown in both scope and attendance, reflecting the increasing importance and recognition of forensic archaeology. The most recent conferences, held from 2018 to 2023, have continued to build on this legacy, bringing together diverse perspectives and expertise from Europe and beyond.

This edition is divided into three main parts, each addressing critical aspects of forensic archaeology and its multifaceted applications:

Part I: Forensic Archaeology Out of Crime Scenes explores cutting-edge methodologies and their application in various forensic contexts. Chapters cover a range of topics, including homicide reconstruction, the use of forensic light in fieldwork, and the practical implementation of forensic archaeology by law enforcement agencies in different countries.

Part II: Forensic Anthropology and Humanitarian Investigations delves into the study of human remains and the application of forensic archaeology in humanitarian contexts. It offers insights into the latest research in forensic anthropology, taphonomy, and the role of forensic entomology in forensic archaeological investigations. This section emphasizes the significance of interdisciplinary approaches in solving complex forensic cases and highlights how forensic archaeology contributes to investigating mass graves and searching for missing persons from historical conflicts, providing closure to families and communities affected by past atrocities.

Part III: Heritage Crimes addresses the growing concern of crimes against cultural heritage. This section examines the role of forensic archaeology in investigating and preventing the illegal trade of artifacts, as well as the destruction of cultural heritage sites. It underscores the importance of preserving our shared heritage and the ethical responsibilities inherent in forensic archaeology.

This volume mainly features contributions from EMFA presenters but also includes additional insights from professionals outside the conference (but always part of the EMFA community), further enriching and strengthening the book's aim and purpose. The authors represent a diverse group, including early-career researchers, established scholars, forensic practitioners, and law enforcement officials. Their collective work showcases both theoretical advancements and practical applications, illustrating the current state-of-the-art in forensic archaeology.

We extend our heartfelt gratitude to all contributors who have made this volume possible. Their dedication and expertise have significantly enriched this publication. We also thank the Springer publishing team, particularly Gonzalo Cordova, for their invaluable assistance in bringing this volume to fruition.

As we look toward the future, we hope that this volume will not only advance the field of forensic archaeology but also foster continued collaboration and communication among professionals worldwide. The challenges we face are complex and multifaceted, and it is through our combined efforts that we can make significant strides in the pursuit of justice and the preservation of our shared heritage.

The Hague, The Netherlands — WJ Mike Groen
Rome, Italy — Pier Matteo Barone
January 6th, 2025

Contents

About the Authors

Pier Matteo Barone is an accredited criminalist, professor, and consultant in Forensic Science, expert in Forensic Geo-Archaeology with a focus on geophysical prospecting (Ground Penetrating Radar (GPR), in particular), remote sensing, Geographical Information System (GIS), and archaeology applied to crime scene investigations, missing persons, and heritage crimes collaborating with several universities (such as Centre universitaire romand de médecine légale (CURML) Lausanne in Switzerland, Nottingham Trent University in UK, American University of Rome, University of Roma Tre in Italy), institutes (Istituto Nazionale di Pedagogia Familiare (INPEF) in Italy, International Red Cross Committee-Switzerland), and national and international police forces. He has been Senior Lecturer in Forensic Science and Director of the Master of Forensic Science program at Nottingham Trent University. He is Chair of Forensic Archaeology and Co-Chair of the Scene of Crime Group (SoC WG) of the European Network of Forensic Science Institutes (ENFSI) and is appointed Crime Scene Adviser by the IUGS Initiative of Forensic Geology. He is Co-founder of Geoscienze Forensi Italia®-Forensic Geoscience Italy and a member of ANCRIM (National Association of Criminologists and Criminalists), CIfA (Chartered Institute for Archaeologists), and Conpef (National Coordination of Forensic Experts). In 2017, 2018, and 2023, he won the Italian Investigation & Forensic Award for Excellence in Forensic Archaeology and Innovation Technology. He is a member of the Management Council of the Italian Association of GPR and a member of the International Response Team—Blake Emergency Archaeology and Anthropology Services. He has published more than 100 books and articles in mainly international and peer-reviewed journals and is on the Editorial Board of several international journals.

WJ Mike Groen is a certified forensic archaeologist and anthropologist employed by the Netherlands Forensic Institute (NFI) and staff member at the Amsterdam University Medical Centers (Amsterdam UMC, location AMC), Department of Medical Biology. His practitioner experience covers approximately 20 years of searching for, recovering, and analyzing human remains from places of incident, crime scenes, and conflict zones. He is Dutch DVI national point of contact for Forensic Anthropology, teaches both undergraduate and postgraduate courses in forensic archaeology and anthropology at several Dutch universities, and is responsible for the forensic archaeology and anthropology module at the Dutch Police Academy. His past academic and professional experience relates to GIS modeling, field archaeology, human taphonomy, and biological anthropology. He is responsible for the introduction of forensic archaeology in the Netherlands in 2005, for co-organizing the first European Meeting on Forensic Archaeology (EMFA) in The Hague, Netherlands, in 2012, and for the creation of the Forensic Archaeology group within the European Network of Forensic Science Institutes (ENFSI) in 2013. Since 2022 he is heading the Forensic Anthropology and Archaeology unit at the NFI. His current research interest cover field recovery protocols, skeletal age estimation, GIS predictive modeling, human taphonomy, and scene of crime science.

Part I
Forensic Archaeology Out of Crime Scenes

Chapter 1
Cutting-Edge Methodologies for Searching Missing Persons

Pier Matteo Barone

Abstract The search for missing persons is a complex and multifaceted process requiring both traditional methods and innovative technological solutions. This chapter explores cutting-edge methodologies such as geographic profiling, geographic information systems (GIS), drones, ground-penetrating radar (GPR), and remote sensing (RS). These technologies enhance efficiency by narrowing search areas, predicting likely locations, and leveraging spatial data for real-time decision-making. Key approaches include geolocation techniques, predictive modeling, and advanced geospatial analyses like locus operandi, tailored specifically for missing person cases. By integrating these tools with traditional search efforts, search and rescue operations can improve their success rates, particularly during the critical "golden hours." Emphasis is placed on interdisciplinary collaboration, ethical considerations, and the necessity for specialized training to maximize the potential of these innovations in forensic investigations.

Keywords Missing Persons · Geographic Profiling · Search and Rescue (SAR) · Remote Sensing (RS) · Ground-Penetrating Radar (GPR)

1.1 Introduction

The search for missing persons is an intricate and multifaceted challenge that has traditionally relied on ground-based methods, including search parties, canine units, and community volunteers. While these methods are invaluable, they possess inherent limitations such as human endurance, the vastness of potential search areas, and environmental challenges. Recent advancements in technology have introduced

P. M. Barone (✉)
The American University of Rome – Geoscienze Forensi Italia® Forensic Geoscience Italy, Rome, Italy
e-mail: p.barone@aur.edu

P. M. Barone, WJ M. Groen (eds.), *Forensic Archaeology and New Multidisciplinary Approaches*, Soil Forensics, https://doi.org/10.1007/978-3-031-86308-0_1

new methodologies that enhance the efficiency and effectiveness of search operations. This article explores cutting-edge technologies and their integration into search methodologies, with a focus on geographic profiling, geographical information systems (GIS), drones, ground-penetrating radar (GPR), and remote sensing (Barone et al. 2021; Congram 2016; Fyfe et al. 2015; Morewitz and Sturdy Colls 2016).

The practical and operational approach must be not only contextualized to the disappearance but also, above all, must involve contributions from top-tier professionals and experts with international experience who professionally know and use cutting-edge technologies. Unfortunately, Italy, for example, remains static in this regard, bogged down by outdated procedures and regulations, failing to keep pace with most foreign nations that invest significant time, economic resources, and personnel in the SAR (Search and Rescue) of missing persons (Commissario straordinario del Governo per le persone scomparse 2024). These nations achieve incredible results during the so-called "golden hours," the first 48 h of the search following a person's disappearance, with a success rate approaching 90% in countries like the United Kingdom (Biehal et al. 2003).

Technophobia, the fear of utilizing expert professionals in the field (even those external to law enforcement), and a lack of knowledge of new methodological approaches cause undeniable harm to the sector of missing person searches. This situation leads to alarming numbers and exacerbates a complex, dynamic, and multidimensional phenomenon that highlights a serious social issue requiring constant analysis and deep commitment.

To combat this phenomenon, innovative technological interventions are being implemented internationally to minimize the time between the missing person's report and the search action and to maximize the result with the possible discovery within the "golden hours" after the disappearance. Geolocation is of primary importance in this area. Geolocation, in general, means being able to locate people, animals, vehicles, and objects in real time and with excellent precision. Synonymous with RTLS (Real-Time Location Systems), geolocation not only triggers traceability and retraceability that provide valuable and strategic information for management support but also creates new value-added services in the field of searching for missing persons. Cell phones, social networks, and even car keys with transponders are all systems that enable precise geolocation of a person. Some applications can track switched-off or out-of-service cell phones using only three words (https://what3words.com/) or through what is called geographic profiling (see the work done by Grampian Police and the University of Glasgow in Scotland, for example) or through satellite image analysis. Let's look at them in detail below (Gibb and Woolnough 2007; Stevenson et al. 2013).

To work with geolocation, one must have knowledge of remote sensing, geophysics, GIS, and geoarchaeology, as well as a good understanding of the territory and related computer and digital tools. In cases of searching for still-living people, the approach that might be most promising is the one termed geographic profiling. While this technique is known in forensic environments as a method for preventing serial crime (see what D. Kim Rossmo has published on the subject), it has never been applied to the search for missing persons (Barone et al. 2022a, b; McKinley et al. 2009; Parr and Fyfe 2013; Rossmo 2000, 2003, 2014).

When individuals go missing, one of the factors to consider is their spatial behavior, that is, how they move around the area surrounding the disappearance zone. This information can be inferred from resolved cases, where missing persons were found, both alive and deceased, in specific locations. Identifying and classifying such information would have significant value in optimizing search team operations in terms of both the quantity and quality of resources employed. The primary goal is to quickly find the missing persons, increasing the chances that they are still alive (Henderson and Henderson 1998; Shalev et al. 2009).

When a person disappears, it is essential to carefully consider several factors to accurately assess the risks and plan an appropriate investigation. Law enforcement operators should always base their decisions on these assessments. Upon the first report of a disappearance, it is crucial to gather as many details as possible. Every missing person case could potentially lead to dangerous situations, so the principle of the "golden hours" mentioned earlier should be applied to every case. This concept underscores the importance of speed in investigations, as the early stages are considered crucial and can make a difference in solving the case. Missing persons may be at risk of physical harm due to various factors. These include their ability to cope with weather conditions, the risk of becoming victims of violent crimes, or other dangers related to the people they were last seen with, the places they are located, or the circumstances they were found in. They may unknowingly be involved in criminal activities such as human trafficking or exploitation. Carefully assessing these aspects is essential to determine the appropriate level of risk (Goodwill et al. 2014).

In many countries, lists of missing persons are regularly compiled, divided by gender, age, and specific categories such as the disabled, drug addicts, and people with neurodegenerative diseases. However, studies on the movement patterns of these people are rarely found. One study, for example, analyzed police reports from major cities in the United States, comparing the disappearances of adults and minors. This work revealed that most people were found or returned home within a week of their disappearance. Adults were tracked down after longer periods than young people. On average, the disappearance lasted about 10 days, and about a third of the people were found in public places or at friends' homes. This fundamental information is valuable for understanding the movement patterns of missing persons (Perry 2013).

In resolved disappearance cases, a report should be drawn up that includes the geographic coordinates of the discovery, to compare with those of the home or last sighting. This process aims to create statistical behavioral models to apply to similar cases and provide search operators with a scientific tool. Although as early as 2005, the Association of Chief Police Officers of England, Wales and Northern Ireland (ACPO) emphasized the importance of considering missing persons'behavioral patterns, many countries, like Italy, currently lack an interview model to gather detailed information from those who have been found. This model should include places visited, times spent during the absence, and exact coordinates of the discovery to understand the movements, paths, and distances traveled (Fyfe et al. 2015).

English research dating back to 2003 showed that 45% of missing persons had moved to another region and 22% abroad. Further studies have highlighted that most cases involve people missing from home, public places, or institutions. Accurate collection of information, including disappearance and discovery addresses, is crucial for identifying patterns and optimizing search resources. Identifying spatial behavior patterns is of great relevance, allowing the police to identify the most likely areas for the search (Biehal et al. 2003). This approach enables the recovery of missing persons before they come to harm, saving time, resources, and money. For this reason, starting in 2020, the author and colleagues have devised a variation of Rossmo's approach uniquely dedicated to searching for missing persons and have called it locus operandi (Barone et al. 2022a, b).

To better understand the potential of locus operandi as an "intelligent agent" in searching for missing persons, one must first understand its origin and what it entails. Geographic profiling is a criminological method used to approximate the area where a serial criminal resides. While it is a useful organizational tool and an increasingly popular field, this method is constantly updated as the mathematical bases are continuously refined. Among other advanced mathematical calculations, the basic calculations involve applying the distance formula and finding the centroid (central point) from which to start a series of regions of interest (defined hot zones) depending on some criteria of attendance. Today, this technique is often used in criminology, and most research funding is dedicated to developing more powerful computational software to delineate increasingly precise areas in ways similar to the film Minority Report with Tom Cruise.

The principle of locus operandi is similar to traditional geographic profiling, but instead of focusing on the criminal and their area of interest, it focuses on analyzing the areas frequented by the missing person before the disappearance. The information obtained from law enforcement must be very accurate, and for this reason, it would be advisable to ask specific (so-called "geographical") questions at the time of the missing person report. Consequently, for effective geographic profiling, it is necessary to process geographic data using computational geometry. The GIS, then, duly queried, will create a predictive spatial analysis model, focusing, with good approximation, the search area at times to a few square kilometers, whereas normally many hectares are covered, often with negative results. As seen, locus operandi proves to be a very useful tool for law enforcement to predict areas where the missing person may be found, whether alive or not. The importance of this method, created and tested by the author during the Covid-19 pandemic crisis, has achieved a series of very positive results with a discovery rate within the predictive model of about 90% (33 out of 37), combining cases of missing persons in Italy and abroad.

The geographic data that can be extracted from missing person reports are a desirable source of Big Data used to perform an "intelligent" and automated spatial analysis. The feasibility of executing such artificial intelligence is enhanced within GIS and leads to automating the process with the construction and implementation of an artifact that produces visualizations and statistical results to develop "intelligent" geographic profiles that support the predictive analysis of the area where the missing person might be found. A prototype of a search information system guides the investigation and uses the disappearance as the dependent variable and a body of geographic information on frequented places accompanied by geolocation and remote-sensing data (such as satellite or camera images) as the independent variable. This inevitable processing of spatial information as a predictive variable of the disappearance is key to making such analysis increasingly solid and secure (Barone et al. 2020, 2021; Chainey and Ratcliffe 2013; Isaaks 1990; McKinley 2017) (Fig. 1.1).

Due to the complex and multifaceted nature of forensic investigations, which often require operating in different countries, police forces and emergency services face the enormous responsibility of effectively coordinating search and rescue (SAR) efforts while ensuring accurate and up-to-date information is disseminated to stakeholders promptly, minimizing the potential for errors, delays, or miscommunications that could hinder their ability to respond quickly and efficiently to emergency and other critical situations.

In cases where the implications of the investigations lead to the search for missing persons who are still alive or to the confirmation of their death, remote-sensing (RS) methods provide a territorial analysis using satellite images, not only to remotely enable an analysis of the disappearance territory but also to highlight, through time-lapse images (i.e., before and after the disappearance), any changes in the territory through a series of multispectral filters, such as infrared, NDVI (Normalized Difference Vegetation Index, a vegetation growth index), NDWI (Normalized Difference Water Index, a water change index), VARI (Visible Atmospherically Resistant Index, an index that simulates an NDVI only in the visible spectrum using RGB bands), or LiDAR (Light Detection and Ranging),

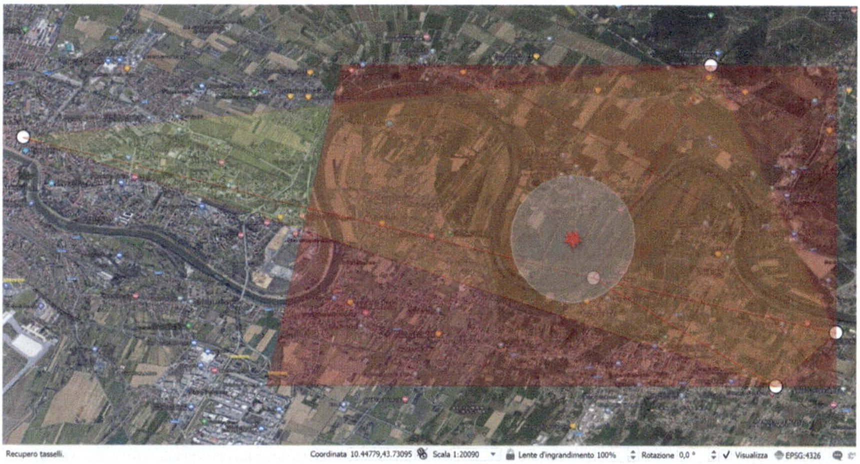

Fig. 1.1 An example of the georeferenced map obtained thanks to the locus operandi. This method narrowed down the research area significantly (the gray circle) allowing us to find the missing person

especially in wooded areas (Barone et al. 2021, 2023; Pensieri et al. 2020; Rocke and Ruffell 2022).

These preliminary computerized analyses are necessary during the field intervention preparation phase and significantly reduce the search field, favoring a more precise and focused autopsy investigation of the locations. Therefore, using techniques ranging from macroscale to microscale, identifying all peculiarities and useful information for the search, reducing the use of human resources, possibly limiting intervention times, and allowing operations in difficult and/or dangerous conditions for rescue teams are all financially sustainable solutions.

Combining such remote-sensing results with other geoarchaeological methods within a simple GIS platform represents a secure method for collecting all this information and developing predictive models to find missing persons. Identifying spatial behavior patterns is extremely important, as the information can be used by police forces to locate probable search areas.

Given the importance of effective search and rescue operations in missing persons' cases, it is imperative to explore all available methods and techniques that can contribute to locating and recovering these individuals.

Consequently, a variable to consider in disappearances is the possibility of using remote sensors to "see the invisible." Thousands of satellites orbiting the Earth serve different purposes, both civil and military. Some of these satellites continuously take pictures of the Earth's surface for various purposes (environmental monitoring, weather forecasting, urban expansion, security, etc.). Satellite images are acquired by sensors that capture images at non-visible frequencies. In fact, the electromagnetic spectrum, the range of all possible frequencies of electromagnetic radiation, has lower frequencies (radio waves, microwaves, and infrared waves) and higher frequencies (ultraviolet rays, X-rays, and gamma rays) than the visible spectrum. These frequencies are not detectable by the human eye but only by specific sensors (Barone and Groen 2018).

Infrared (IR) radiation is a particularly useful spectrum in remote sensing. IR has a lower frequency band than the visible range but higher than radio waves. The wavelength of this band ranges from 700 nm to 1 mm. IR is used, for example, in night vision devices when there is insufficient visible light. Infrared sensors convert incoming radiation into an image. This image can be monochromatic (e.g., hotter objects will appear brighter) or a false color system can be used to represent different temperatures. However, IR is also used in infrared spectroscopy to characterize materials. This latter use is crucial in the forensic field and, in particular, in the search for missing persons.

As a remote-sensing index designed to assess water content in vegetation and water bodies, the NDWI (Normalized Difference Water Index) has become a widely adopted tool for identifying and mapping water bodies using remotely sensed data from various satellite platforms. Integrating other search methods, particularly non-invasive and remote-sensed ones, the NDWI can contribute to the overall goal of locating and recovering missing persons, ideally alive but also sometimes deceased. The NDWI index's ability to detect water surface changes has proven to be a crucial element that can be used in searching for missing persons in water bodies such as lakes or rivers, although it has not traditionally been used for this purpose. Leveraging the NDWI index's ability to detect water surface changes, SAR operations can integrate it as an additional tool to help locate missing persons in water bodies. While this may not be its primary application goal, the NDWI index's potential in assisting missing persons search efforts underscores its versatility and potential in various contexts (Barone et al. 2023) (Fig. 1.2).

Therefore, using techniques ranging from macroscale to microscale, identifying all peculiarities and useful information for the search, reducing the use of human resources, possibly limiting intervention times, and allowing operations in difficult and/or dangerous conditions for rescue teams are economically sustainable. Combining such remote-sensed results with other geoarchaeological methods within a simple GIS platform is a secure method for collecting all this information and developing spatial predictive models to find missing persons. Identifying spatial behavior patterns is extremely important, as the information can be used by police forces to locate probable search areas (Di Maggio and Barone 2017).

These preliminary analyses performed on a GIS platform are necessary to prepare to go on-site and allow a significant narrowing of the search field, favoring a more precise and focused autopsy investigation of the places (the so-called fieldwalking, or systematic reconnaissance of the territory by walking on the surface following specific patterns). Such reconnaissance can help create a further map that helps narrow the field search even more. This map is the so-called RAG (Red Amber Green) map or traffic light map, highlighting the sectors where the presence of a possible cadaver is highly, moderately, and unlikely (Donnelly et al. 2021).

In recent decades, there has been an extraordinary technological evolution that has made enormous progress. Among the most recent innovations is the remarkable improvement in drone performance and their miniaturization. Although the first prototype was developed during World War I, over the years, drone sizes have been

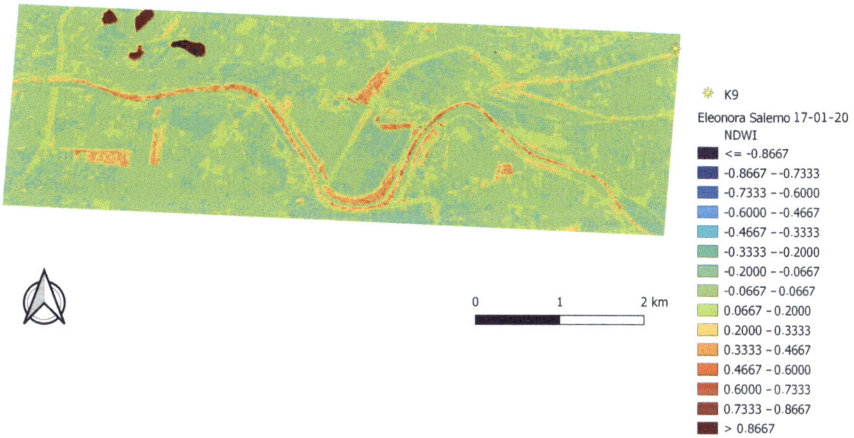

Fig. 1.2 The figure shows the result following the application of NDWI. Negative values are noted, which are important for determining the presence of anomalies in water bodies

significantly reduced, becoming as small as a mosquito. These drones, capable of operating both in flight and underwater, are now adaptable for a wide range of purposes.

One of the sectors where drones have shown exceptional value is in supporting the search for missing persons. In this field, drones offer undeniable advantages. Their compact size, maneuverability, and good autonomy allow them to fly over vast areas at low altitudes, reducing the need to deploy human search teams that require significant resources. Additionally, the use of drones allows safe operations in hard-to-reach areas, avoiding risks for operators.

A significant advantage is the ability to equip drones with cameras for video recording. This allows immediate investigations and later careful analysis of the images. If equipped with thermal cameras, drones can even detect the presence of living beings by measuring body temperatures, enabling search operations to continue even at night. Speed is a crucial factor in increasing the chances of success, especially in finding people alive.

Worldwide, missing persons' search systems are becoming increasingly refined, also with the use of technologies such as aerial drones, marine drones, and robotic drones, thanks to the new era of artificial intelligence. Already in 2016, the Riverside County Police Department in California, United States, began using drones equipped with high-definition cameras to record and transmit real-time images to a ground crew trained for search and rescue missions. The department has a fleet of helicopters, but these cannot always be used due to weather conditions, while the use of Remotely Piloted Aircraft (RPA) has proven to be much more effective and versatile. Moreover, they can be designed to face adverse weather conditions (such as wind, rain, etc.). They can respond immediately to intervention requests, and rescue operations can be carried out by a team reaching the target via ground after detection.

Between 2018 and 2019, some prefectures in Italy signed "coordinated intervention plans for the search and rescue of people affected by neurodegenerative diseases," which include the use of geolocation devices, training for healthcare operators, and useful recommendations and information for citizens and operators in critical situations (Pensieri et al. 2020).

The versatility of the drone allows it to be employed in different areas and for different uses, representing practical support for human activities. Thanks to their small size and maneuverability, drones can fly at low altitudes (about 5/10 meters) and cover vast areas. They offer the opportunity to coordinate a team through remotely transmitted images and information, and if equipped with thermal tracking equipment and software, they can detect human presence even in the dark, without interrupting night search operations. Other implementations include SAR (synthetic aperture radar, an active and coherent remote-sensing system), thermal cameras, multispectral sensors (a multispectral sensor is a tool capable of recording the amount of energy reflected by objects on the Earth's surface in different wavelengths of the electromagnetic spectrum), ALS, and LiDAR (two types of aerial or remote laser scanners) (Barone and Groen 2018).

In the restricted areas deduced from the above analyses, further control can be carried out through geophysical surveys (usually using GPR), which, when used by experienced personnel, in a completely non-invasive and repeatable manner, allows for very accurate subsurface mapping, highlighting anomalies potentially related to the case in question.

The search with GPR is commonly used in crime scene investigations (CSI) worldwide thanks to its fast, precise, and non-destructive technique (NDT). These advantageous characteristics make GPR an efficient and widely used method for locating missing persons in various environments. Due to the challenge of finding missing persons, especially in Italy, the use of non-destructive methods, such as GPR, can greatly assist investigations and forensic research. In many cases, bodies are buried in the ground, and the geomorphological components of the soil combined with the relevant elements of body decomposition indicate anomalies perfectly detectable by ground-penetrating radar. This method, employed after a large-scale territorial analysis as seen earlier, can narrow the search areas, identifying potential burial sites. This non-destructive and rapid approach provides information on subsurface characteristics, locating the missing person‘s body and other forensic evidence (Barone 2016; Barone and Di Maggio 2019a, b; Barone et al. 2022a, b; Di Maggio and Barone 2017; Donnelly et al. 2021; Pringle et al. 2021) (Fig. 1.3).

Subsequently, if necessary, all the methodologies employed and illustrated so far, in an absolutely non-destructive manner, can produce a very narrow search area with a high probability of identifying the investigative target. At this point, only an accurate, scientific, stratigraphic archaeological excavation (following geoarchaeological procedures) and not arbitrary (with bulldozers or improper means) allows collecting all the evidence necessary to properly reconstruct the crime scene and possibly have a relative chronology, drawing the necessary investigative considerations (Barone and Groen 2018).

The forensic excavation must be conducted meticulously and not arbitrarily (e.g., arriving directly at the buried target using bulldozers or similar equipment) with the appropriate tools. The archaeologist must document and preserve everything found (e.g., paint fragments, hair, clothing, receipts, etc.) at every stage and depth of the excavation, using the proper precautions and storing them in appropriate containers.

Stratigraphy and examination of every piece of evidence found in the removed soil testify to relative chronology, where, for example, an element buried with a date (e.g., a milk bottle or a receipt) above or below the forensic target can provide information on the burial time. Moreover, taphonomic evidence (how materials degrade or decompose over time and under specific conditions) can be important because it can help determine, for example, how long a body has been buried by the state of clothing or surrounding soil or nearby finds. Unfortunately, forensic archaeology practice is poorly applied in Italy, and the excavation and recovery of human remains in forensic contexts are mostly conducted by police officers without archaeological or forensic anthropological training (Fig. 1.4).

SAR activities involve intense and constant teamwork, seeing forensic geoarchaeology as a first collaboration and a first step toward a correct approach to searching for missing persons. However, two indispensable elements that combine

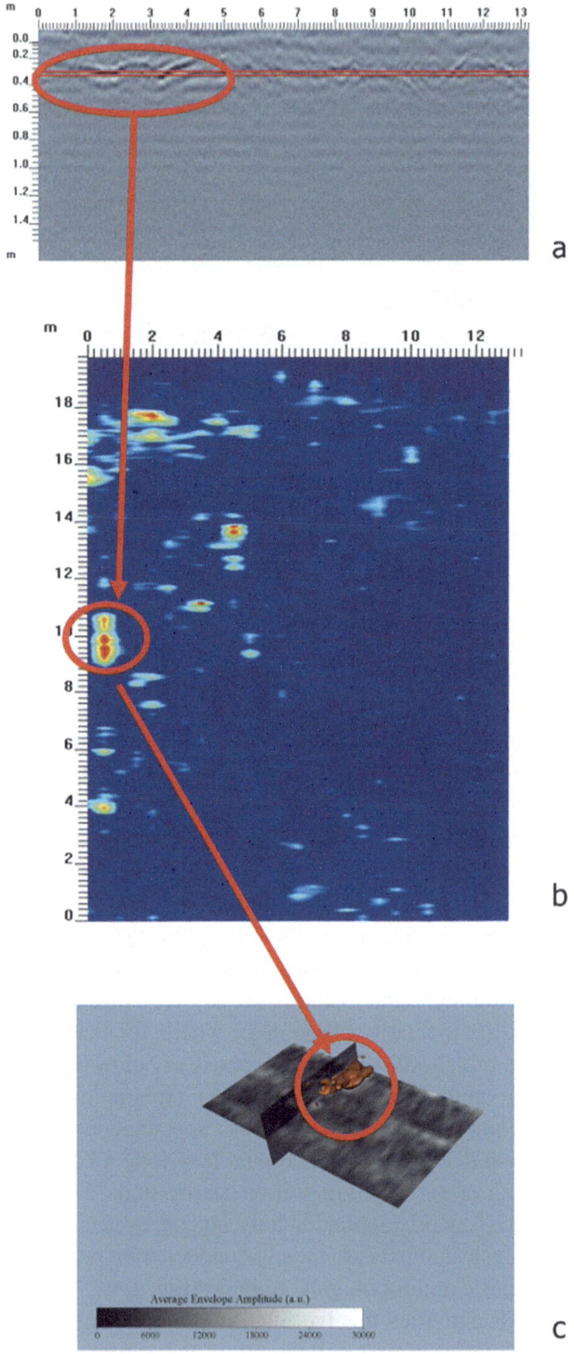

Fig. 1.3 The three typical representations of GPR of the same forensic target (red circle): radargram (**a**), depth slice (**b**), pseudo-3D (**c**)

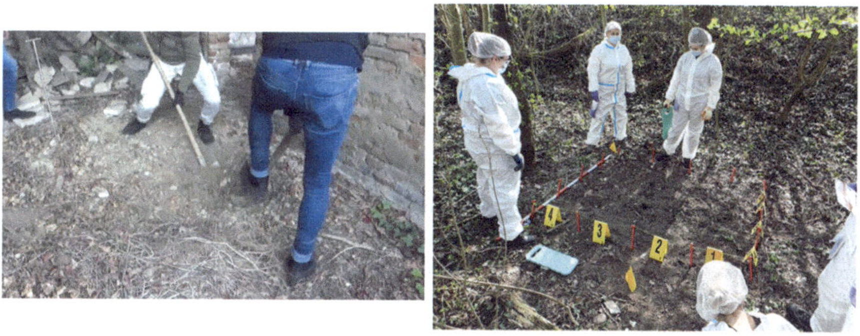

Fig. 1.4 Two examples of excavating concealed bodies: on the left, an incorrect example of forensic archaeological excavation done arbitrarily and without any technical-scientific consideration; on the right, an example of a proper forensic archaeological-stratigraphic approach

well with the previously mentioned geoarchaeological methods in the search for missing persons are forensic geology and canine units.

Forensic geology is a broad field that applies the fundamental principles of geological sciences to identify and/or evaluate geological materials related to forensic issues. Forensic geology also applies these principles to define the appropriate geological context of a crime scene. Specifically, forensic pedology is a branch of forensic geology that involves the research, study, and analysis of soil traces connected to a crime to assist a judicial investigation. Since soil can be transferred from one place to another on mobile surfaces (shoes, tires, clothing, etc.), it can provide important information to link a missing person to a place, or it can shed light on the dynamics of a crime. However, soil is a complex system composed of different microscopic components formed and developed during its long genesis and evolution. This process depends on a multitude of factors, such as climate, geomorphology, topography, environment, human activity, and the type of organic and inorganic substances in the soil. Due to this complexity, it is easy to find significant differences between soil samples even when the soil is considered "homogeneous," to the point that the soil components and their mutual relationship report variations in small areas. For these reasons, a pedological analysis is an excellent tool to support SAR activities. This type of approach is sometimes referred to as "environmental profiling" and is analogous to geographic profiling and psychological profiling (Di Maggio and Barone 2017; Donnelly et al. 2021).

Dogs, on their part, commonly known as K9 by law enforcement due to the anglicized homophony with the word "canine," have played an important role in forensic investigations for decades thanks to their acute sense of smell. The use of canine units aims to find the person as quickly as possible. The search with dogs is more effective the timelier and closer to the time of disappearance their deployment is.

Dogs trained for search and rescue operations are employed in emergency situations such as earthquakes or avalanches. On the other hand, there are dogs specialized in searching for missing persons, known as "molecular dogs" or in the field of mantrailing. These dogs are trained to locate a specific person, equipped with the ability to distinguish between different human scents and follow a particular trail. The handler activates the dogs using a "scent witness," an object belonging to the person being sought, and the dogs then begin the search following that specific trail.

In the SAR field, sometimes it is also necessary to use so-called cadaver dogs trained specifically to follow the scent of decomposing flesh to locate the bodies of deceased humans. Whether the body is on the surface, buried underground, or underwater, a dog's nose is powerful enough to detect the smell. Cadaver dogs can not only locate human remains but also identify locations where a cadaver or body parts may have been previously stored, tracing residual odors. Depending on the use of the cadaver dog, the dog may be trained to detect specific decomposition odors (Ricci et al. 2021; Ruffell and Powell 2021).

1.2 Conclusion and Future Directions

In light of the above, in searching for missing persons, it is desirable to make efforts to collect and record this type of information with maximum accuracy and speed possible: never move from the operational centers without having implemented the steps previously illustrated. Therefore, the use of techniques ranging from macroscale to microscale, identifying all peculiarities and useful information for the search, reducing the use of human resources, the possibility of limiting intervention times, and the ability to operate in difficult and/or dangerous conditions for rescue teams are economically feasible for everyone today.

The integration of cutting-edge technologies like geographic profiling, GIS, drones, GPR, and RS represents a significant advancement in the search for missing persons. These technologies enhance the efficiency and effectiveness of search operations, providing critical data and insights that guide search efforts.

Future efforts should focus on further refining these technologies and integrating them into standard search and rescue protocols. Continued innovation and interdisciplinary collaboration will be key to advancing search methodologies and improving outcomes in missing person cases. Additionally, it is essential to address the ethical and practical considerations associated with these technologies to ensure their responsible and effective use. It is important to emphasize, however, that specific training and experience are required in both fields (geoarchaeological sciences and legal sciences). Venturing into this field without proper qualifications or falsely claiming credentials causes harm primarily to oneself and to the community. Moreover, the field of missing person searches necessitates an ethically and professionally proper and correct approach to avoid not only actions that harm the integrity and emotions of the involved parties but also potential legal sanctions.

In this regard, the regulatory activity in the field of unregulated professions has, over the years, produced a substantial body of regulations that has recently extended to the figure of the Criminalist. Indeed, the standard UNI 11822:2021 "Unregulated professional activities – Criminalist – Knowledge, skills, autonomy, and responsibility requirements" has been published on the website of UNI—Italian Organization for Standardization. This UNI standard defines the requirements related to the professional activity of the Criminalist, an expert who uses scientific and technological methods to identify the perpetrator of a crime through the analysis of the crime scene. The standard specifically outlines 10 specialist profiles for the professional figure, including Forensic Geoarchaeology (No. 8) (Barone and Di Maggio 2023).

In conclusion, the journey from traditional search methods to technology-enhanced search operations has been transformative, offering new possibilities and solutions in the search for missing persons. By embracing technological synergy and continuing to innovate, we can further revolutionize search efforts and bring hope to families and communities affected by missing person cases.

References

Barone PM (2016) Understanding buried anomalies: a practical guide to GPR. LAP Lambert Academic Publishers, Saarbrücken. ISBN: 978-3-659-93579-4

Barone PM, Di Maggio RM (2019a) Forensic geophysics: ground penetrating radar (GPR) techniques and missing persons investigations. Forensic Sci Res 4(4):337–340

Barone PM, Di Maggio RM (2019b) Low-cost CSI using forensic GPR, 3D reconstruction, and GIS. J Geogr Inf Syst 11:493–499

Barone PM, Di Maggio RM (2023) Exploring the growing importance of forensic geoarchaeology in Italy. Forensic Sci 3:533–543

Barone PM, Groen WJM (2018) Multidisciplinary approaches to forensic archaeology: topics discussed during the European Meetings on Forensic Archaeology (EMFA). Springer, New York

Barone PM, Mesturini S, Pensieri MG, Volpini L (2020) L'AI nella ricerca di persone scomparse. In: Uricchio AF, Riccio G, Ruffolo U (eds) Intelligenza Artificiale tra Etica e Diritti. Prime Riflessioni a Seguito del Libro Bianco dell'Unione Europea. Cacucci Editore, Bari

Barone PM, Di Maggio RM, Mesturini S (2021) Forensic geoarchaeology in the search for missing persons. Forensic Sci 1:8–15

Barone PM, Di Maggio RM, Mesturini S (2022a) Materials for the study of the locus operandi in the search for missing persons in Italy. Forensic Sci Res 7(3):371–377

Barone PM, Matsentidi D, Mollard A, Kulengowska N, Mistry M (2022b) Mapping decomposition: a preliminary study of non-destructive detection of simulated body fluids in the shallow subsurface. Forensic Sci 2:620–634

Barone PM, Di Maggio RM, Mesturini S (2023) A complementary remote-sensing method to find persons missing in water: two case studies. Forensic Sci 3:284–292

Biehal N, Mitchell F, Wade J (2003) Lost from view. Missing persons in the UK. Policy Press, Bristol

Chainey S, Ratcliffe J (2013) GIS and crime mapping. Wiley, New York

Commissario straordinario del Governo per le persone scomparse (2024) Relazione semestrale. Ministero dell'Interno https://www.interno.gov.it/it/contatti/commissario-straordinario-governo-persone-scomparse

Congram D (2016) Missing persons. Multidisciplinary perspectives on the disappeared. Canadian Scholars' Press, CSPI, Toronto

Di Maggio RM, Barone PM (2017) Geoscientists at crime scenes: a companion to forensic geoscience. Soil forensics. Springer International Publishing, New York

Donnelly LJ, Pirrie D, Harrison M, Ruffell A, Dawson LA (2021) The geological society of london—a guide to forensic geology; GSL Miscellaneous Titles. GSL, London

Fyfe NR, Stevenson O, Woolnough P (2015) Missing persons: the processes and challenges of police investigation. Policing Soc 25(4):409–425

Gibb G, Woolnough P (2007) Missing persons: understanding, planning, responding – a guide for police officers. Grampian Police, Aberdeen
Goodwill AM, van der Kemp JJ, Winter JM (2014) Applied geographical profiling. In: Bruinsma G, Weisburd D (eds) Encyclopedia of criminology and criminal justice. Springer, New York, NY
Henderson M, Henderson P (1998) Missing people: issues for the Australian Community. National Missing Persons Unit, Canberra
Isaaks EH (1990) An introduction to applied geostatistics. Oxford University Press
McKinley J (2017) The application of geographic information system (GIS) in forensics geoscience. Episodes 40(2):166–171
McKinley J, Ruffell A, Harrison M, Meier-Augenstein W, Kemp H, Graham C, Barry L (2009) Spatial thinking in search methodology: a case study of the 'No Body Murder Enquiry', West of Ireland. In: Ritz K, Dawson L, Miller D (eds) Criminal and environmental soil forensics. Springer, Dordrecht, pp 285–302
Morewitz S, Sturdy Colls C (2016) Handbook of missing persons. Springer International Publishing, Cham
Parr H, Fyfe N (2013) Missing geographies. Prog Hum Geogr 37(5):615–638
Pensieri MG, Garau M, Barone PM (2020) Drones as an integral part of remote sensing technologies to help missing people. Drones 4(2):15
Perry WL (2013) Predictive policing: the role of crime forecasting in law enforcement operations. Rand Corporation
Pringle JK, Stimpson IG, Wisniewski KD, Heaton V, Davenward B, Mirosch N, Spencer F (2021) Geophysical monitoring of simulated clandestine burials of murder victims to aid forensic investigators. Geol Today 37:63–65
Ricci G, Nittari G, Campanozzi LL, Feola A, Mazzalupi G, Ceglie L, Sirignano A (2021) Use of detection dogs in forensic investigations: the Italian scenario. Rom J Legal Med 29(1):69–73
Rocke B, Ruffell A (2022) Detection of single burials using multispectral drone data: three case studies. Forensic Sci 2:72–87
Rossmo DK (2000) Geographic profiling. CRC Press, Boca Raton
Rossmo DK (2003) Geographic profiling. In: Encyclopedia of murder and violent crime. SAGE Publications, Inc, pp 206–209
Rossmo DK (2014) Geographic profiling. In: Bruinsma G, Weisburd D (eds) Encyclopedia of criminology and criminal justice. Springer, pp 1934–1942
Ruffell A, Powell N (2021) Search strategy for buried objects in water: geophysics, probes and dogs. Forensic Sci 1:130–137
Shalev M, Schaefer M, Morgan A (2009) Investigating missing person cases: how can we learn where they go or how far they travel? Int J Police Sci Manag 11:123
Stevenson O, Parr H, Woolnough P, Fyfe N (2013) Geographies of missing people: processes, experiences, responses. The University of Glasgow, Scotland

Chapter 2
Homicide Reconstruction from Metal Paint Particles in Urban Soil

Alastair Ruffell

Abstract The body of a strangled woman, found in a duvet cover, stained with a light gray and black soil prompted an investigation of what the stains were. Through comparison to the rear stairs, flat roof and footwear of a suspect, and exclusion from the body deposition site and local samples, an association between the duvet cover and the suspect was made. Millimeter-sized gray curls of metalliferous paint in dark stains from the duvet and exterior of the suspect's home were noted. A seizure of a re-painted satellite dish from outside the suspect's flat suggested a source for the paint curls. Some conjecture is made on how these items may have connected is made.

Keywords Forensic science · Forensic geology · Trace evidence · Unique particles · Fe-Ox/CO3

2.1 Unique Particles and Their Transfer in Forensic Geology

In their introductory paragraph, Sugita and Marumo (2004) provide a summary of the usefulness of distinct or unique particles ("identifiers" in some terminology) in forensic geology and forensic science in general. They summarize how, if such trace evidence is present, the need for exhaustive analyses is diminished. Murray (2011) argues that the diversity of soil makes all soils unique: a challenge is finding and characterizing the individual components. Sugita and Marumo's (2004) counterpoint is that while correct, the presence of unusual particles not present in any other samples can help the process of exclusion. With the issues of transfer and persistence considered (French et al. 2012; Proctor et al. 2019), such individualization may allow exclusion of samples and a possible link between suspect and crime

A. Ruffell (✉)
School of the Natural, Built Environment, Queen's University, Belfast, UK
e-mail: a.ruffell@qub.ac.uk

P. M. Barone, WJ M. Groen (eds.), *Forensic Archaeology and New Multidisciplinary Approaches*, Soil Forensics, https://doi.org/10.1007/978-3-031-86308-0_2

scene. Here, the presence and spatial distribution of unusual sub-millimeter metal paint fragments recovered during an urban homicide investigation is described.

Terminology is clarified here at the outset of this article. "Soil" is used non-pejoratively for the fabric stains, surface residues, and urban debris considered: the collected samples are indeed soils, in being mixes of organic/inorganic material capable of supporting life, albeit in mineral/metal dust, asphalt, moss/algae. "Control" samples (syn.: "known" or "reference") have a recorded collection location, be it a crime scene, suspect location(s) or from the surrounding area (Pirrie et al. 2021, p. 100). The original location of "Questioned" samples is unknown, being present on evidential items associated with the suspect or victim (commonly clothing, footwear, vehicles, weapons)—in this case, a duvet cover found covering the victim. Unusual particles (syn. "unique particles" or "unique identifiers") are referred to in the context of being different to the common additions to urban soils (Ruffell et al. 2013), such as glass, paint, plastic, and combustion residues. Body deposition site (BDS) and injured party (IP) are standard terms in UK (and other) jurisdictions for body deposition site (the location where the victim was found) and injured party (the victim). Soil sampling methods depend on the location (on a hard substrate or not, thickness, moisture content) and so described for each location.

2.2 Case Description

On September 26, 2006, a street cleaner noticed a black plastic bag partly covering blue fabric in an alleyway (Fig. 2.1) leading from a church hall fire escape door. Noticing what appeared to be a human limb exposed at one end, he called the police, who revealed the body of a young woman.

The IP was identified as someone of similar appearance who had been reported missing the night before, with the identity confirmed by relatives. The body had been partly wrapped in black plastic "bin" bags and then placed in a knotted duvet cover. A postmortem suggested death by strangulation. Examination of the duvet cover by officers from the regional forensic laboratory revealed two colors and areas of staining on the outer side. At the end of the duvet where the injured party's (IP's) head had been, extensive (approximately 30 cm × 60 cm) gray staining was observed; where the middle of the IP's body had been was a smaller (approximately 10 cm × 10 cm) darker gray to black area of staining. Each area was brushed to remove the material. A visit to the body deposition site (BDS) established a visual similarity between the light gray staining and loose sediment in the church carpark and in the alleyway where the body was found. No visually comparable material could be found in the surrounding area, but this did not preclude the light gray staining originating from locations as yet unidentified. At this point, the origin of the dark gray material was not determined. In early December 2006, police intelligence led to the questioning of a known offender who lived in a flat on an adjacent street to the BDS. This person had a previous conviction for the attempted strangulation of his former wife and was associated with witness reports as both soliciting young women in the days before the body being discovered, as well as being the last

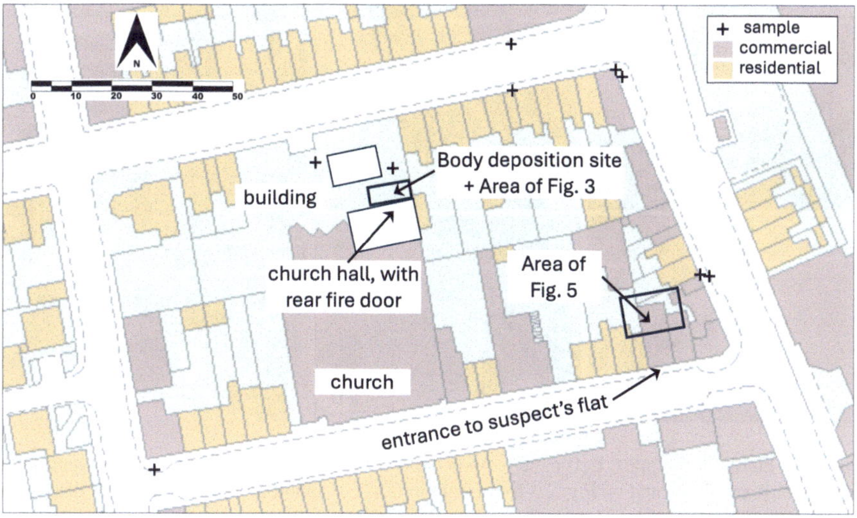

Fig. 2.1 Location of body deposition site in relation to suspect's residence, surrounding samples (not in Fig. 2.3 [BDS] or Fig. 5 [suspect's residence]) and detailed maps. (Basemap (modified) from © Crown Copyright & Database Right 2024—SpatialNI—A service provided by Ordnance Survey of Northern Ireland®)

person to be seen in the company of the IP. His home was searched and sampled, and loose materials were collected from the suspects: flat interior; front door; rear door; rear (fire escape) steps; adjacent flat roof; alleyway to public street; workplace (an abattoir) exterior and interior. The suspect's boots were also seized—he had no other footwear present in the flat.

Visual examination of the above samples initially excluded samples from the flat interior, front doorsteps, rear alleyway, and workplace, comprising building products, asphalt, fibers, foodstuffs, insect remains, and leaf and plant particles. Samples from the rear door, rear fire escape stairs, flat roof, and suspect's boots comprised a black, algae-rich material that was slimy when wet and dried to a black crumbly material that was considered possibly comparable to the dark staining on the BDS duvet: this material formed the focus of our work.

2.3 Methods

2.3.1 Field

Outdoor samples were collected by a variety of means, depending on location. All sample sites had less than 5 mm thickness of material above a hard surface, so were photographed, loose materials lifted by either: disposable plastic spatula/stainless steel spatula (acetone-cleaned between sampling) from damp locations or by

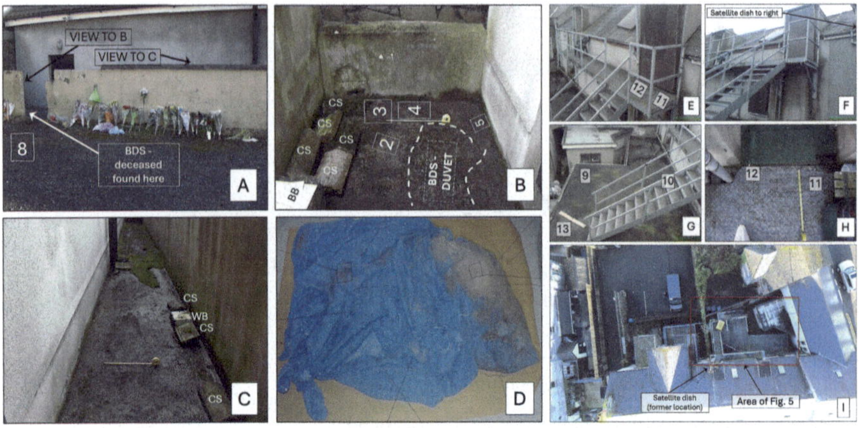

Fig. 2.2 Field photographs. Left panel—body deposition site and rear of suspect's residence. All field photos are all located on Fig. 2.3 for orientation, A, B, C photographed 5 days after discovery and removal of remains. (**a**) The car park comprises surface comprises a mixed gray aggregate with gray clay. (**b** and **c**)—tape measure extended to 50 cm. (**d**) knotted duvet in which the deceased was found, with extensive pale staining (right) and isolated patches of dark staining (throughout), original laboratory photography, supplied courtesy of Forensic Services Northern Ireland

brushing with new, disposable toothbrushes onto pristine paper at dry locations. The area sampled was then re-photographed, with each sample position and area of sample mapped using Zeiss laser distance meter and tape measures (Fig. 2.2).

2.3.2 *Laboratory Screening*

The presence of sub-millimeter scale curled particles within dark-stained areas of the duvet was noted by staff at the local government forensic science laboratory. Between the seizure of the duvet by police officers at the postmortem, through transport and laboratory examination, this dark staining was dry. Samples from the duvet, BDS, suspect's flat, and surrounding areas were variably moisture-saturated to damp/dry, so all samples were covered by pristine filter paper and air-dried for a minimum of 1 week in separate, cleaned fume cupboards. The process of visual examination followed the procedures developed by Skip Palenik, as described in Murray (2004). Bulk residues were examined using Ruper 10x objective handlens, with which a variety of metalliferous and sometimes oxidized fragments could be observed if not adequately imaged. Oxidation indicated the presence of iron, so the dried residues were divided in half using a thin steel blade, with one half gently disaggregated by a dental pick. A magnet was then placed in a new Ziploc bag for each sample and passed over each disaggregated sample; the magnet was then removed from the Ziploc bag over filter paper, causing magnetized particles to dislodge, these were gathered onto standard microfossil examination slides, with cell graticules of 2 mm. Static charge from the Ziploc bag caused some particles to remain, these were dislodged to the same slides using a single-hair brush.

2.3.3 *Microscopy*

An Olympus SZX12 binocular microscope, fitted with DF Plapo objectives and Diagnostic Instruments camera linked by Yenway Microscopes digital transmitter, was used to examine all materials and particles within, concentrating on the unusual metal paint curls seen by handlens.

2.4 Sampling Locations

2.4.1 *Non-specific Controls*

To assess the makeup of urban soil and surface debris around the area of interest, eight samples were collected (Fig. 2.1). While not statistically representative, these serve as controls to the focus BDS and the suspect's residence. Prior to the work described here, it was already known from the local forensic laboratory, that metal paint fragments might show significance: therefore, one possibility was that some manufacturing process occurred in the area that generated such particles and spread them more widely, diminishing their forensic significance for this case.

2.4.2 *Body Deposition Site*

The site is an alleyway, leading from a church hall fire escape door to aggregate car park and street. The specific location of the BDS comprised a sheltered, north-facing, and recently cleaned area of wet concrete, with patches of algae growth and residues of moss from clearing before the murder (Fig. 2.3). The location has many of the features typical of urban body disposal sites (Berezowski et al. 2021), with access from an under-used carpark, no direct street or building lighting, no CCTV, behind a low wall, and besides a fire escape (as opposed to commonly used entry/exit). Loose building materials such as concrete slabs, weathered concrete walls, and a rough concrete base were noted: all provide decayed building products in a damp, organic residue. Sampling occurred 5 days after the removal of the IP, but in the presence of police Major Crime Forensic Advisers equipped with photographs of the wrapped body resting on moss-cleared concrete, in situ. Areas around where the IP's body had lain and ingress/egress points with a sufficient layer (~0.5 cm depth) of soft material were sampled (see Methods). Temporary steps of concrete breeze blocks had been placed (previous to the murder) by church authorities: it was noted that these were unstable to walk on and the alleyway around the BDS was slippery. Given the five-day passage of time between discovery and sampling, commemorative flowers had been placed against the exterior wall, presumably to be visible, but likewise as the specific BDS location was not publicized and not inviting

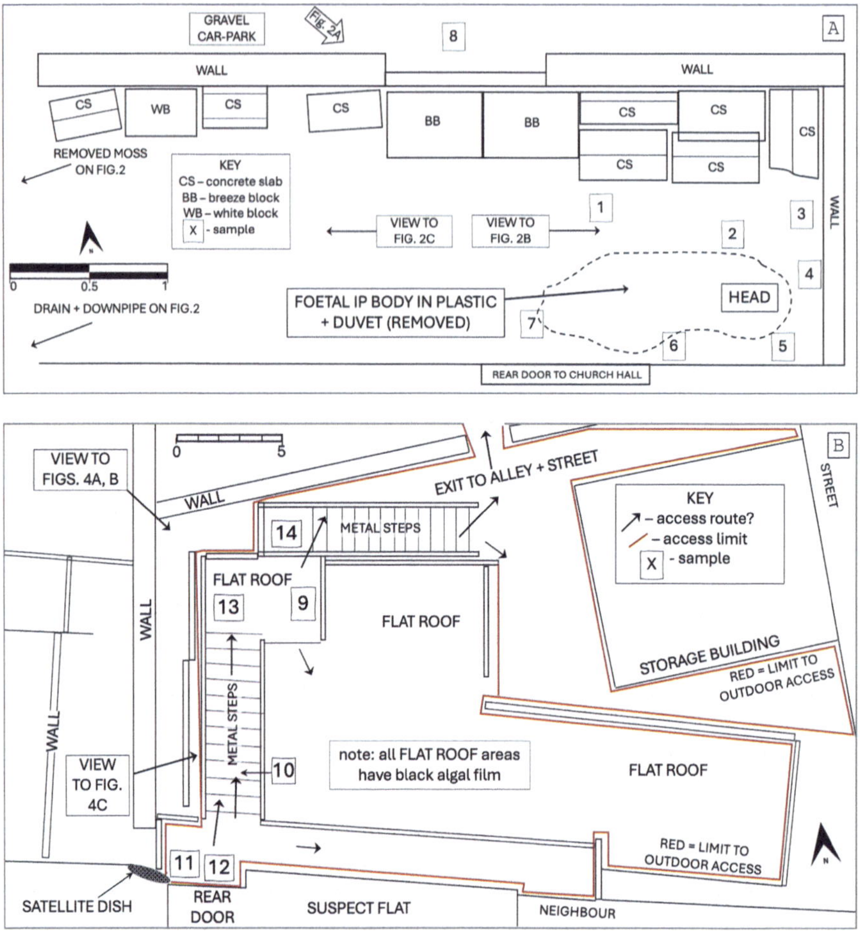

Fig. 2.3 Sketch maps of body deposition site and rear of suspect's flat, locations on Fig. 2.1 insets, with orientation of photographs in Fig. 2.2 and location of samples gathered (see text for sampling procedure). Sample box outlines are indicative of the surface area from which soil was gathered; Sample 8 forms part of the wider set, also shown on. (**a**) mapped 5 days after discovery and body removal, map is author's own work. (**b**) mapped 1 month after the suspect was charged, maps are author's own work

to walk onto. Some compromise of the BDS sampling area was thus possible, but unlikely.

Right panel—rear of suspect's flat in December 2006. E: flat exit door with security screen, photograph taken from adjacent wall; F: flat exit door, showing proximity to metal fire escape steps; G: rear exit steps to flat roof and rear exit; H: rear door with security screen removed for sampling. Locations of photographs A–D shown in Fig. 5. I: drone aerial image (taken November 2023 using a DJI MiniPro-3), showing fire escape steps, flat roof, exit to alleyway and street and location of Fig. 2.3b.

2.4.3 Rear of Suspect's Flat

This area of the suspect's residence was sampled 2 months after the murder, following work by the police and forensic scientists, who had not located anything that could explain the dark staining on the duvet: this could indicate another source and throw into question suspicion of the occupant. To exclude this possibility, the rear exit to the flat required soil sampling by the authors. The location had been secured, with a barrier door installed: this led onto a galvanized (zinc-coated steel) fire escape walkway and steps to felt-covered flat roof, further steps and backyard-alleyway to the street (Figs. 2.2 and 2.3). The area has no lighting and cannot be observed from surrounding residential properties: in checking for lighting, specifically outdoor automated security/safety lights, a re-painted satellite dish was noted, attached to the north-west corner of the suspect's residence. A green astroturf style doormat was observed (Fig. 2.2h) and seized by forensic science staff: our sampling (see Methods) concentrated on areas of loose, possibly transferable material on the steps and flat roof (Fig. 2.2g). Likely ingress/egress and likely barriers to movement were considered and mapped on the ground by tape measure and laser distance device. The authors are not trained crime scene mappers, so to check accuracy, online town plans were consulted—with no major change evident. This was verified by returning in November 2023 and flying a Mavic MiniPro drone vertically from an adjacent (disused) car park then over the former suspect's residence. Light conditions were not ideal (Fig. 2.2i), but sufficient to allow verification and some minor modifications to the ground-based mapping of 2006.

While analysis was ongoing, it was thought the metal paint may prove of diagnostic value, so some conjecture as to a source was considered. Observations while sampling at the suspect's flat included the presence of the re-painted satellite dish, which is perforated by 4-mm-diameter holes, about the same diameter of one of the metal paint curls, if reconstructed from fragments. The satellite dish was seized by police and sampled by brushing at the regional forensic laboratory, then subjected to the same preparation procedures of drying, disaggregation and magnetic separation as the soil samples.

2.5 Sample Summary

Loose soil and sediment/dust on hard substrates were collected from twenty-three locations, with sixteen reported on here. These included nine samples from surrounding streets. One sample from footwear seized from the suspect (a pair of work boots) and seven samples from the BDS; six from the rear of the suspect's flat and one from the satellite dish. The geostatistics of sampling (Diggle 2010) suggests equivalency in numbers by location. Reality is determined by availability, herein, we sampled all areas with sufficient quantity of surface layer for microscopy.

A further set of samples were gathered that are not reported on here, as none had the presence of the unusual particles forming the focus of this work. These included eight in the alleyway at the rear of the suspect's house and two at the suspect's front door. Samples that could compare to the dark staining on the duvet were those from the suspect's rear steps/flat roof and footwear (boots). Nonetheless, like the light gray staining on the duvet that was visually comparable to the BDS, the dark staining on the duvet and black material from the steps and roof could have come from locations unknown. This dark material on the duvet had been excluded (by visual analysis) from the BDS and surrounding control locations, but not shown to have any definitive comparison to the steps and flat roof except visual comparison, so required further analysis (below). A single sample of oxidized, partly-painted metal paint fragments came from the satellite dish.

2.6 Results: Handlens and Binocular Microscope

Visual examination confirmed the black, crumbly samples had a residue of anthropogenic materials (glass, glass spherules, plastics) as well as metal fragments, some of which were curled in nature (Fig. 2.4), in both the dark duvet cover material and the stairs/flat roof of the suspect.

This preliminary analysis suggested the black material comprises organic matter, mixed with largely anthropogenic materials. Similar residue appeared to occur in the dark stain on the duvet, on the stairs and flat roof of the suspect, and on the suspect's boots. Nonetheless, a location (as yet unidentified, but excluded from the rear alleyway to the suspect's flat, his front door, the BDS, or surrounding area) could still have existed. No black "slime" (when wet) or black crumbly material (when dry) could be found on visits to the suspect's workplace (an abattoir) or known, visited locations (local pub, local shop). Nonetheless, the duvet cover could have contacted an unidentified location with such material, where transfer could have occurred. Metal pain curls were most abundant in samples from the satellite dish (n—over 100); the rear door and steps from the suspect's flat ($n = 132$) and finally the duvet cover ($n = 17$), from which a selection are shown in Fig. 2.4. Notable are the numbers of paint curls from the rear of the suspect' flat, summarized in Table 2.1.

The question remained as to what may exclude the questioned items (the duvet cover) from controls on the suspect's rear stairs/adjacent flat roof?

2.7 Discussion

The presence of dark, crumbly material containing gray painted and/or oxidized fragments of curled metal in both the dark stain on the duvet cover and in the dried residue collected from the rear stairs and flatroof of the suspect's flat is of interest. The lack of any similar material in the control samples taken from the vicinity of the suspect's flat, surrounding streets, or observed at his workplace or frequently-visited

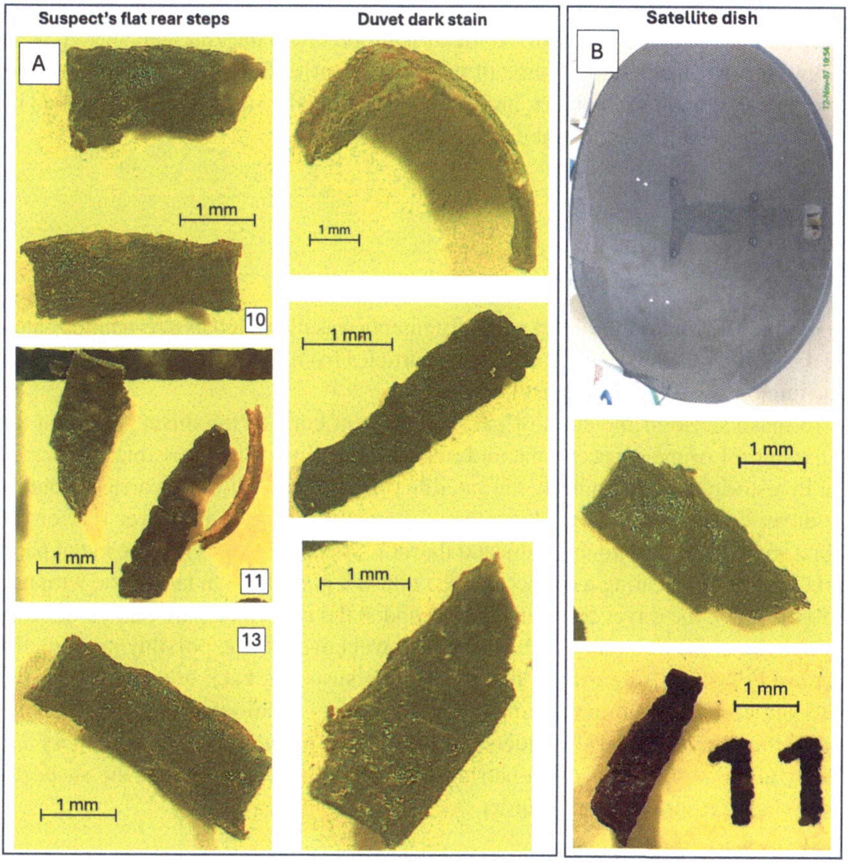

Fig. 2.4 Binocular microscope image comparison of magnetic particles recovered from: A: the black residue sampled from the rear steps of the suspect's residence and the duvet cover found wrapping the IP (box numbers refer to original location, see Figs. 2.2 and 2.3); B: the satellite dish (top, being sampled by brushing onto paper at the regional forensic laboratory), seized by police officers from the exterior of the suspect's flat, the size and shape of the perforations can be seen. Note the visual similarity between metal paint curls

Table 2.1 Location (see Fig. 2.3b), sample number (also Fig. 2.3b), and counts (n) of magnetic particles with gray paint and/or Fe oxide, from the rear of the suspect's flat

Location	Sample number	n = magnetic particles
Rear doorstep	11, 12	42
Upper stairwell, 3rd step	10	16
Flat roof	13	31
Flat roof	9	24
Lower stairwell, 1st step	24	19

locations is part of the exclusionary process we followed. The consistent shape, size, and presence of gray/oxidized metal paint preclude the zinc-galvanized metal walkway/steps as being the source of metal paint curls. The light stain on the duvet cover, the gray mud of the BDS, and the brushings of the suspect's footwear had no easily-recognizable metal paint curls.

2.8 Conjecture

A possible source for the curled metal fragments was identified as a re-painted satellite dish seized from the suspect's house: particles from this object were obtained by brushing the surface with a pristine brush.

To make sense of the curls of gray metal paint curls in the duvet cover, on the stairs/flatroof of the suspect's flat and in/on the satellite dish, a possible scenario is that in restoring and re-painting the satellite dish, whoever did this, carried it out on the duvet cover (and maybe other items), then either shook this cover out, or the debris somehow fell onto the stairs and flatroof. These two items had the metal paint curls on them, indicating a connection via unusual particles. On taking the wrapped IP to the BDS, the duvet contacted the ground at the church carpark and yard, causing transfer of the light gray staining on the duvet cover. While possibly random, the decreasing number of particles found from the suspect's back doorstep to the flat roof, and absence from the flat interior, surrounding locations and BDS, lend support to this connection. This evidence together with other information (witness testimony and data from fiber and hair analysis found on the IP and in the suspect's house) led to a conviction of murder.

Acknowledgments John Logan (Forensic Science, Northern Ireland) first noted the stains on the duvet cover and is thanked for contacting the authors. Major Crime Forensic Adviser Trevor Cooke (Police Service of Northern Ireland) and Drs. Antoinette Keaney and Jennifer McKinley assisted in the field.

References

Berezowski V, MacGregor D, Ellis J, Moffat I, Mallett X (2021) More than an offender location tool: geographic profiling and body deposition sites. J Police Crim Psychol 38:3–19. https://doi.org/10.1007/s11896-021-09475-6

Diggle PJ (2010) Geostatistical inference under preferential sampling. J R Stat Soc: Ser C: Appl Stat 59:191–232. ISBN: 0035–9254/10/59191

French JC, Morgan RM, Baxendell P, Bull PA (2012) Multiple transfers of particulates and the dissemination within contact networks. Sci Justice 52:33–41. https://doi.org/10.1016/j.scijus.2011.05.001

Murray RC (2004) Evidence from the Earth: forensic geology and criminal investigation. Mountain Press, Missoula, 226pp. ISBN: 0878424980

Murray, R.C. (2011) Evidence from the Earth. Mountain Press, Missoula, 200pp. ISBN: 9780878425778

Proctor FA, Swindles GT, Barlow NLM (2019) Examining the transfer of soils to clothing materials: implications for forensic investigations. Forensic Sci Int 305:110030. https://doi.org/10.1016/j.forsciint.2019.110030

Ruffell A, Pirrie D, Power M (2013) Issues and opportunities in urban forensic geology. In: Pirrie D et al (eds) *Environmental and criminal geoforensics*, vol 384. Geological Society Special Publication, pp 147–161. https://doi.org/10.1144/SP384.1

Sugita R, Marumo Y (2004) 'Unique' particles in soil evidence. In: Pye K, Croft DJ (eds) Forensic geoscience: principles, techniques and applications, vol 232. Geological Society, London, Special Publications, pp 97–102. https://doi.org/10.1144/GSL.SP.2004.232.01.10

Chapter 3
Prospects for the Development of Forensic Archaeology in the Countries of Central and Eastern Europe

Maciej Trzciński

Abstract The activity of forensic archaeology in the countries of Central and Eastern Europe is focused primarily on researching crimes related to the activity of Nazi and communist totalitarianism, which is a consequence of historical conditions. In this part of Europe, law enforcement authorities still have limited awareness of the extent and to what effect the methods and techniques used by modern archaeology can support activities carried out in connection with a criminal investigation. The presented text is an attempt to determine the actual state and prospects for the development of this discipline in the countries in question.

Keywords Forensic archaeology · Central and Eastern Europe · Practical use · Development prospects

3.1 Introduction

The activity of forensic archaeology, its possibilities, and prospects for application have already been recognized and described many times (Morse et al. 1983; Hunter and Cox 2005; Barone and Groen 2018). A laconic but very accurate definition of the discipline, which states that forensic archaeology essentially means *the presence of an archaeologist at a crime scene*, seems to fully reflect the essence of what forensic archaeology deals with. We already know that forensic archaeologists can be involved in cases concerning war crimes and genocide, as well as in cases of common crimes committed recently; not only murders but also crimes against cultural heritage.

M. Trzciński (✉)
Faculty of Law, Administration and Economics, Department of Forensic Sciences, University of Wrocław, Wrocław, Poland
e-mail: maciej.trzcinski@uwr.edu.pl

P. M. Barone, WJ M. Groen (eds.), *Forensic Archaeology and New Multidisciplinary Approaches*, Soil Forensics, https://doi.org/10.1007/978-3-031-86308-0_3

There is no doubt that this discipline already has an established position in the broadly understood Anglo-Saxon countries and a significant part of Western European countries. However, forensic archaeology is perceived and applied much differently in the countries of Central and Eastern Europe. Successful attempts have already been made to present globally how forensic archaeology as a scientific discipline is represented in the world (Groen et al. 2015). While in Western European countries, the connotation of forensic archaeology seems clearly perceptible, and in some countries of Central and Eastern Europe, this discipline is poorly represented and quite often confused with traditional archaeology. A separate issue is how forensic archaeology is perceived by law enforcement agencies (police, prosecutors) in these countries. In many cases, archaeology is perceived through the prism of a persistent romantic stereotype that is associated with archaeological research in Egypt or, worse still, the adventures of the otherwise nice Indiana Jones. How can an average policeman or prosecutor be helped by an archaeologist if they associate archaeology only with a pith helmet, Egyptian pyramids, and a shovel? Of course, this question contains some simplification, but the fact is that in many cases law enforcement agencies do not have fundamental knowledge of what archaeology deals with today and what its research possibilities are. So, what is the current situation in the countries of Central and Eastern Europe? The author attempted to diagnose this situation based on the available literature on the subject and several fundamental questions asked at the beginning of the research. These questions concern the following issues:

1. Is forensic archaeology as a subject taught during university studies or training for prosecutor and police officers at police academies?
2. What are the relations between a forensic archaeologist and law enforcement agencies?
3. Do forensic archaeologists work within the police structures?
4. In what types of cases does a forensic archaeologist cooperate with law enforcement agencies (inspection at disaster sites, searching for murder victims, searching for hidden items from crimes, searching victims from communist times or war graves, participation in the crime scene inspection)?
5. What archaeological institutions does the police cooperate with?
6. Are there archaeologists in the police who can use their knowledge during the investigation?
7. Do archaeologists (forensic archaeologists) support the police during inspections of archaeological sites damaged by looters?
8. In your opinion, what are the prospects for the development of forensic archaeology in your country (your region), and what needs to be done to improve cooperation between law enforcement agencies and forensic archaeologists?
9. How do you see the prospects for the development of forensic archaeology as a scientific discipline (globally)?

The above questions were asked to both archaeologists and representatives of law enforcement agencies in the following countries: Germany (Saxony), Poland, Czech Republic, Slovakia, Hungary, Romania, and Lithuania. It is difficult to assume that the answers provided to the author precisely and unambiguously determine the situation in individual countries, but they undoubtedly allow for an up-to-date diagnosis of the issues in question.

3.2 Research Results

3.2.1 Germany (Saxony)

Germany, as a federal country, has diverse situations both in the context of applicable legal provisions and the functioning of administration. The differences between the individual states, of which there are 16, have their historical determinants. The result, among others, is from the centuries-old traditions of the separateness of individual states as well as from the division of the territory of Germany in 1949 into two separate states, that is, the Federal Republic of Germany and the German Democratic Republic. This division commonly established the concepts of West Germany and East Germany that still function today. In 1990, Germany was reunited, but certain cultural and customary consequences of its long-lasting independence are still visible today. While the western part of Germany was associated with the traditions of Western European culture, its eastern part, due to remaining under Soviet occupation until 1990, was saturated with communist traditions imposed by the Soviet Union not only on the German Democratic Republic but also on the then Czechoslovakia, Romania, Hungary, Poland, and Lithuania, which are also described in this article. This situation, as we know, was a consequence of the new geopolitical division of Europe at the end of World War II in 1945. The Eastern Bloc countries operating until 1989 behind the so-called Iron Curtain were more or less separated from the way Western Europe functioned and developed. This problem also concerned scientific research, as foreign contacts, trips, research internships, conferences, and access to literature were strictly rationed or completely limited. This situation had an impact on most post-communist countries, including the German Democratic Republic.

The issue of implementation of forensic archaeology in the work of German law enforcement agencies has already been discussed in the literature (Neumann et al. 2015) The functioning of a special unit (*Arbeitsgruppe Forensische Archäologie*) within the German Bundeskriminalamt (Federal Criminal Police Office), operating as part of the broader Crime Scene Unit (Tatortgruppe), confirms that the German federal criminal police fully appreciated the possibilities of using forensic archaeology in their everyday work. The activities of this unit, based in Wiesbaden, concern the entire territory of Germany, but when the investigation is conducted under the competence of the federal police. However, what does forensic archaeology in the eastern federal states look like when the case being investigated is not of such importance that it could be handled by the BKA?

The attempt to determine this situation was based on one of the eastern states (Saxony).[1]

In Saxony, once a year Patricia van der Burgt and Stäuble (2019) conducts theoretical lectures at the police academy for 3–4 h. The lectures are conducted as part of a two-week course (securing traces at crime scenes) intended for investigators. In some years, practical 2-day workshops, also only for investigators, on detecting a mock grave and excavating it were conducted. The same person also conducts lectures for crime scene documentation teams once a year at the police academy in Brandenburg.

The cooperation between law enforcement agencies and forensic archaeologists in Saxony is informal. The police is not convinced of the formal necessity of appointing an archaeologist as an expert witness or an expert so that one can function officially in the investigation (Hemker et al. 2023). These are rather courtesy consultations on matters related to, for example, World War II (war graves, military items). The police do not want to involve anyone from outside their structures and are convinced that they will be able to cope on their own. Archaeologists do not work in the structures of the Saxon police but are sometimes included in cases involving the search for contemporary murders' victims. Law enforcement agencies sometimes ask for help in providing and interpreting aerial photos, LiDAR maps or access to historical maps. Throughout Germany, including Saxony, law enforcement agencies cooperate with heritage protection offices when necessary: The State Archaeological Heritage Office (*Landesamt für Archäologie*) (Wanke and Linck 2024). They also cooperated with scientific institutions and museums, for example, *Die Römisch—Germanische Komission*, Reiss—Engelhorn-Musseen Manheim.

In Saxony, archaeologists from the heritage protection office are engaged by the police in cases involving illegal searches for artifacts. This applies to their participation in inspections at damaged archaeological sites and participation in searches in apartments where stolen items as well as old ammunition or explosives may be found. In Saxony, to search for artifacts, one needs to obtain a permission from the heritage protection office. It is illegal to conduct searches without such a permission.

It is noteworthy that the police and the prosecutor offices generally do not see the need or benefits of cooperation with an archaeologist, which results from a lack of understanding of how an archaeologist could help law enforcement agencies. When talking about the prospects for changing this situation, the need to make prosecutors aware of the practical benefits that may result from the presence of an archaeologist at the crime scene is emphasized. The development of forensic archaeology is not perceived solely through the prism of the new technologies and the possibility of efficient use of such equipment. It is rightly emphasized that the strength of archaeology is the knowledge and understanding of human behavior. It is accentuated that greater attention is paid to criminological issues and the possibilities of using forensics and criminology in traditional archaeological research.

---

[1] I wish to offer my thanks to thank Patricia van der Burgt, an archaeologist employed at the Landesamt für Archäologie Sachsen, for help in obtaining information.

In Germany, there is no academic center where separate classes in forensic archaeology would be conducted. As part of the cooperation between the *Bundeskriminalamt* and the *Landesamt für Archäologie in Saxony*, the international conference the *tenth European Meeting on Forensic Archaeology* was held in Dresden on August 25–26, 2022.

3.2.2 Poland

In Poland, in recent years, there has been a continuous development of forensic archaeology, although it is not dynamic. Archaeologists cooperate with law enforcement agencies in cases of searching for hidden bodies as expert witnesses, but these are still individual cases. By far the greatest activity of forensic archaeology still concerns the search for victims of war crimes and communist regime crimes, which is a consequence of historical conditions. During World War II, Poland experienced the terror of both totalitarianisms, that is, Nazi and communist ones. Communist regime crimes were committed in Poland still in the 1950s. In 2016, the Office for Search and Identification was established within the Institute of National Remembrance. It is a state institution whose task is to research crimes committed against persons of Polish nationality or Polish citizens of other nationalities in the period from November 8, 1917, to July 31, 1990: Nazi crimes, communist crimes, crimes of Ukrainian nationalists, and members of Ukrainian formations collaborating with the German Third Reich, other crimes constituting crimes against peace, humanity, or war crimes. In the first half of 2024, this institution employed 11 full-time archaeologists who constantly cooperate with the special investigative department of the prosecutor office, conducting investigations into war crimes and communist regime crimes, which are not subject to a statute of limitations under Polish law. Search and exhumation works are carried out mainly in Poland, but the Institute of National Remembrance also sent archaeologists abroad: to Lithuania, Belarus, Georgia, and Germany. The vast majority of search work carried out by the Institute of National Remembrance concerns the search for victims of communist regime crimes. It is estimated that approximately 50,000 people who fought against the communist government are still being searched for. These are both people who were executed as well as soldiers of the Polish underground who died fighting the communists. Currently, there are two genetic databases in Poland that help in the process of identifying people: Polish Genetic Database of victims of totalitarianism (Pomeranian Medical University in Szczecin) and IPN genetic material database (based on CODIS-FBI system). The Office for Search and Identification has also started cooperation with the American government organization DPAA (Defense POW/MIA Accounting Agency), which searches for American soldiers killed during armed conflicts. Since 2019, several archaeological missions have been carried out in Poland, the aim of which was to find the remains of American airmen who died during World War II. In addition to American archaeologists and anthropologists, Polish archaeologists also participated in this work. Due to its competences, the Institute of National Remembrance coordinates or conducts exhumations of war graves itself.

The state of research on forensic archaeology in Poland has already been presented in the literature (Borkowski et al. 2023; Trzciński 2021; Trzciński and Borkowski 2015; Borkowski and Trzciński 2018). This discipline is the subject of classes at the University of Wrocław, where a lecture on forensic archaeology is conducted for archaeology students. The University of Wrocław has also been offering specialized postgraduate studies in forensic archaeology since 2011. The course program includes, in addition to the methodology of archaeological research, legal foundations, classes in anthropology and forensic medicine, classes with forensics experts (examination of firearms and ammunition), inspection at the crime scene and conservation of artifacts. Unfortunately, no police academy in Poland considers issues related to the possibility of applying archaeology in the work of law enforcement agencies during training and courses. When necessary, the police employ ad hoc archaeologists as expert witnesses, especially in cases of searching for hidden bodies.[2] The situation is different in the Military Police, which conduct training at their Center in the field of non-invasive methods used to search for objects hidden in the ground, including buried corpses. Soldiers of the Military Police participated in 2023 in training in the use of geophysical methods, including the use of a magnetometer and the ERT method, as well as verification of revealed anomalies using invasive methods (geological drilling), and training was also conducted in the interpretation of stratigraphy and conducting open area excavations in the place of activities. Training on the practical use of GPR when searching for buried objects and corpses was also conducted at the military training ground. The Military Police also participated in the examination of war graves, developing documentation using laser scanning and photogrammetry. The standard equipment of a Military Police forensic technician is a metal detector, which is used during inspections. Unmanned aerial vehicles equipped with a thermal imaging camera or LiDAR system are commonly used during search operations. Thus, it can be clearly stated that the Polish Military Police are more aware of the possibilities of methods used in forensic archaeology than the Polish police and are better technically equipped to conduct inspections at crime scenes.

As part of the cooperation, the next edition of the workshop entitled *Forensic Search and Recovery of Clandestine Graves* was held on September 20–21, 2021, in Wrocław, Poland. The main organizer was the Department of Forensic Sciences of the University of Wrocław and the Office for Search and Identification of the Institute of National Remembrance in cooperation with the Provincial Police Headquarters in Wrocław. However, activities of this type are organized sporadically. When talking about the activity of forensic archaeology in Poland, we also need to mention crime against archaeological heritage. Illegal searches for artifacts combined with the destruction of archaeological sites have been a big problem for years. The destruction of a monument and illegal searches are treated as crimes in

[2] In 2024, six forensic archaeologists were registered on the lists of District Courts.

Poland. In criminal proceedings conducted by the prosecutor's office or the police, the need for cooperation between law enforcement agencies and archaeologists is quite common. The archaeologist's task is, among others, an indication of what was destroyed, whether the artifacts seized by the police are original, what their material value is, etc. This cooperation is formalized. In accordance with criminal procedure, law enforcement authorities appoint a specific archaeologist as an expert witness or commission the preparation of an opinion by a scientific institution or museum. In some regions of Poland, the police structures employ police officers who are archaeology graduates, but this is not the result of a planned policy to strengthen the police formation with people with archaeological experience. The police still do not use archaeology and archaeologists in the process of broadly understood crime scene inspections.

3.2.3 The Czech Republic

Forensic archaeology as a scientific discipline has the correct connotation in the Czech Republic (forenzni archaeologie) and is recognized as a scientific discipline, but it is not taught as a subject in academic centers or police academies.[3] Archaeology of the recent past is an increasingly and dynamically developing discipline in the Czech Republic, which very often deals with the issue of armed conflicts as the subject of research. This trend of research, although not directly related to forensic archaeology, may indirectly concern it in situations when, for example, during research on battlefields, burials of fallen soldiers or civilian victims are revealed. Such situations may also arise when examining extermination camps, prisoner-of-war camps, or forced labor camps. In recent years, Czech archaeologists have intensified archaeological research on the traces of both totalitarianisms, Nazi, and communist ones (Vařeka 2023; Hasil et al. 2020). The subject of research includes, among others: battlefields of World War II, branches of the Nazi Gross Rosen concentration camp, places of forced labor, and searching for burial places of victims of totalitarianism. The main goal of this type of research is to identify and document the remaining material remains, for example, related to the infrastructure of such places, but researchers must consider that during their research, they will discover burials of prisoners who died or were murdered. A separate issue, as in Poland, is the subject of discussion, which is the problem of commemorating such places and providing them with appropriate legal protection. To date, these places have not been the subject of archaeological research or heritage protection. In the Czech Republic, there is a state institution (*Institut Paméti Národa*-Institute of Memory of the Nation), which, similarly to Poland, deals with research and commemoration of the victims of German and communist totalitarianisms. However, this institution

[3] I would like to thank Tomasz Cymbalak from the National Heritage Institute *(Národní památkový ústav)* for help in identifying the issues discussed and Jan Hasil from the Institute of Archaeology of the Czech Academy of Sciences, Prague *(Archeologicky* Ustav).

does not directly employ archaeologists. If it is necessary to conduct search and exhumation work, such research is performed by archaeologists from state institutions, primarily from the National Heritage Institute. Such research was recently carried out together with his colleagues by Jan Havrda, who found the burial of priest Jan Toufar, murdered by the communists and buried in an unmarked grave at the Prague-Dáblice cemetery. The priest's remains were identified and solemnly buried (Pexa et al. 2018). This cemetery contains the burials of other victims of communist and Nazi regimes, who will probably be the subject of searches and exhumations in the future.

Archaeologists have also recently been involved in searching for the burial place of the remains of victims of the communist regime, which was carried out on the premises of the Prague-Pankrác detention center, where cremated remains of about 80 victims were buried in the years 1948–1965, as reported by the local press.[4] Similar to the Prague-Dáblice cemetery, these burials were hidden and all traces of graves were erased. Archaeologists used geophysical methods and geological drilling to partially confirm the burial places in search of previously cremated human remains hidden in unmarked places. This work was carried out by archaeologists from the Institute of Archaeology of the Czech Academy of Sciences, Prague (*Archaeologicky Ustav*) under the supervision of Jan Mařík.[5] However, the Czechs themselves identify these activities more with the archaeology of totalitarianism than with forensic archaeology.

Also, in the Czech Republic, there is a problem of illegal excavations, which destroy archaeological sites and theft of artifacts. Archaeologists from state institutions (scientists, museum workers) support police activities during field inspections and when determining the provenance of artifacts and their material value. The police do not employ archaeologists who would support police activities during crime scene inspections or when searching for hidden bodies. If necessary, the police commission such activities to archaeologists from state institutions. The issue of forensic archaeology has become increasingly popular in recent years, but generally in the context of searching for victims of totalitarianism. The University of Plzeň plans to open a specialization in forensic archaeology.

3.2.4 Slovakia

The issues of forensic archaeology in Slovakia have already been presented in the literature (Masnicová et al. 2015).

Similarly to the Czech Republic, in Slovakia, when necessary, law enforcement authorities primarily cooperate with archaeologists employed in state institutions,

[4] https://www.denik.cz/z_domova/pamatnik-pankracka-sekyrarna-vazebni-veznice-pankrac-praha-archeologicky-ustav.html

[5] https://www.idnes.cz/zpravy/domaci/archeologove-veznice-pankrac-ostatky.A230612_120048_domaci_nema

for example, Archaeological Institute of the Slovak Academy of Sciences (*Archaeologický Ústav Slovenskej Akademié Vied*). This cooperation mainly concerns crimes against archaeological heritage. In Slovakia, as in other Central European countries, archaeological sites are being damaged, mainly during illegal searches by treasure hunters, and in addition to stolen artifacts, fake archaeological items are also traded. Those responsible for destroying archaeological sites are detained by the police and accused of committing crimes. In criminal cases, archaeologists are needed in this type of cases as experts who would help secure evidence at the crime scene, cooperating with the local criminal police or being the authors of evidence such as a court opinion issued by an expert (archaeologist). These opinions concern, for example, determining the scale of damage to the archaeological site (cultural context), determination of the material value of the finds, and whether they are authentic. The activity of forensic archaeology also concerns the search and exhumation of war graves from World War I and II. However, archaeological work in this area is not carried out systematically and war graves are generally discovered accidentally.

Archaeologists also cooperate with the police when searching for hidden bodies of contemporary murders' victims. The Slovak police searches for missing persons, with particular emphasis on criminal disappearances when it can be assumed that the missing person was a victim of a crime. These searches are carried out by the criminal police using, among other things, geophysical methods (GPR), thermal imaging, chemical probing for the detection of decomposition products, and cadaver dogs. Since the Slovak police structures lack specialized equipment in the field of geophysics and personnel who can operate such equipment, civilian experts, that is, archaeologists, are appointed. In cases of searching for human remains, archaeologists are appointed as expert witnesses. When exhuming discovered bodies, the Slovak police apply methods other than archaeological methodology, quite often using the help of a forensic anthropologist. The Police Academy conducts classes for forensic technicians in the field of forensic anthropology (2 h of classes), which cover aspects of forensic archaeology.[6] In Slovakia, similarly to the Czech Republic, there is the *Ústav Pamäti Národa* (Institute of the Memory of the Nation), but this institution does not conduct planned searches and exhumations in which archaeologists would be involved.

3.2.5 Hungary

In Hungary, forensic archaeology is recognized as a scientific discipline.

As in other countries of the former Eastern Bloc of socialist countries, the problem of searching for victims of both totalitarianisms is present. Apart from the

[6] I would like to thank Dr. Jozef Metenko from Academy of Police Forces in Bratislava for help in obtaining information.

victims of the Holocaust, victims of the communist regime are also searched for and exhumed. In Hungary, searches of this type are part of the concept of humanitarian exhumation and are carried out by a special organization, The Network of Forensic Science Institute (*Igazságügyi Szakértői és Kutató Intézetek -ISZKI*), managed by the Ministry of Justice. Searches and exhumations concern the location of unmarked graves, which are located, for example, in existing cemeteries (e.g., The Budapest New Public Cemetery), former prison cemeteries (The Vac Prison Cemetery), mass graves of Holocaust victims (Kőszeg, Lovagló Ridge). Such works are carried out based on archaeological methods with the participation of archaeologists and forensic anthropologists (Susa et al. 2015).

There are no separate lectures or workshops devoted to forensic archaeology in police academies and academic centers. However, the police are aware of the possibility of applying some methods used in archaeology, primarily during activities involving the search, exhumation, and examination of bodies that were buried or were the result of death in the open space. This situation is confirmed by practice, which indicates the use of archaeological methods in forensics. There are methodological similarities between archaeology and forensics perceived. It seems that the Hungarian police, more than local archaeologists, are aware of the interdisciplinary nature of modern archaeology, which, like forensics, commonly uses remote sensing methods during inspections, several geophysical methods, and 3D scanning during documentation activities (Angyal and Petretei 2020). It is recognized that in addition to the use of new technologies when examining the crime scene, forensic archaeology may prove helpful in reconstructing the course of the event based on the analysis of the discovered traces. Police practitioners also see the possibility of directly linking forensic archaeology with forensic taphonomy, primarily in the context of the search and exhumation of hidden bodies. Even though forensic archaeology is not the subject of lectures (workshops) in academic centers or police schools, it is well recognized, and it seems that in the near future it will be used more often in Hungary in the activities of law enforcement agencies. Currently, theoretical awareness of the possibilities associated with the use of archaeological methods in forensics has not yet been translated into practice. The Hungarian police's central crime scene investigation unit has GPR, and many forensic doctors at the Hungarian Institute of Forensic Medicine have basic knowledge of searching for hidden bodies. The Hungarian Institutes for Forensic Sciences also employs a forensic anthropologist dedicated to the examination of skeletal remains, and four forensic pathology institutes of medical schools also have expertise in skeletal remains. Some members of the Hungarian CSI have basic knowledge of hidden grave exploration—but this is based on experience rather than formal training. One member of the CSI Central Unit will join the ENFSI Forensic Archaeology Working Group in October 2024.[7] It seems that currently Hungarian law enforcement agencies cooperate more often with forensic anthropologists than with archaeologists.

[7] I would like to thank David Petretei from the Hungarian Institutes for Forensic Sciences for help in obtaining information.

The greater interest in forensic archaeology is undoubtedly evidenced by the fact that in 2024 the Hungarian Institutes for Forensic Sciences is the organizer of the next edition of the 12th European Meeting on Forensic Archaeology, organized jointly with the Expert Working Group (EWG) "Scene of Crime" of the European Network of Forensic Science Institutes (ENFSI).

3.2.6 Romania

Another country where searches and exhumations of victims of both totalitarian regimes are carried out is Romania. In the case of this country, the work is focused primarily on searching for victims of communist crimes. Similarly to Poland, the new geopolitical division after the end of World War II was unacceptable to some Romanians. Remaining under Soviet influence, with all its consequences, resulted in underground resistance units taking up the fight. The current searches and exhumations concern both the search for the graves of partisans who died in combat[8] and those who were murdered by the communist regime in prisons. In Romania, as in Poland, the Czech Republic and Slovakia, a special institution was established to conduct investigations related to communist crimes, that is: Institute for the Investigation of the Crimes of Communism and the Memory of Romanian Exiles—*Institutul de Investigare a Crimelor Comunismului și Memoria Exilului Românesc (IICCMER).* This institution founded in 2005 cooperates with the Unit of Military Prosecutor's Office at the High Court of Cassation and Justice, conducting numerous archaeological excavations to identify the graves of political prisoners. The activities carried out by this institution are based on the program: *archaeology of the crimes of communism.* This research is carried out by archaeologists hired by the military prosecutor's office. However, these are not specialized forensic archaeologists, but the ones working in museums on a daily basis. This permanent team of archaeologists is: Horatiu Groza from the Museum in Turda, Paul Scrobota from the Aivd Museum, Gabriele Ristoiu—director of the Museum in Alba Iulia. The search and identification works were conducted by this team both in open areas where Romanian guerrillas fought, for example, in Muntele Mare,[9] as well as in prisons where political prisoners were murdered, for example, in the prison in Sighet, Aiud, Targu Oca. The dead were buried in unmarked graves, without coffins, in single graves, or in mass graves either in the prison cemetery, municipal cemeteries, or in open areas. Such research was also carried out in connection with the search for victims of the forced labor camp in Periprava (Diana 2015).

Forensic archaeology is not the subject of lectures or workshops either in academic centers or in police schools. Its activity mainly concerns research on

---

[8] https://www.descopera.ro/istorie/16703675-ramasitele-a-trei-partizani-anticomunisti-omorati-de-fortele-de-securitate-au-fost-descoperite-intr-o-groapa-comuna

[9] https://ziarulunirea.ro/drumul-oaselor-partizanii-ucisi-de-securitate-pe-muntele-mare-bistra-vor-fi-reinhumati-la-alba-iulia-385568/#google_vignette

communist crimes, but it is conducted by archaeologists who practice traditional archaeology daily. There is no separate specialization in this area and the police occasionally use the help of archaeologists when searching for hidden bodies.[10]

However, it should be noted that there is a serious problem with illegal excavations in Romania. Despite restrictive legal regulations, archaeological sites are being destroyed and looted, while valuable artifacts are exported abroad. An archaeologist (M. Ciută) worked in the Romanian police until 2022, dealing with combating crimes against cultural heritage. Archaeologists cooperate with law enforcement agencies as expert witnesses, helping to determine the scale of damage to monuments and artifacts, to establish their authenticity, and to make valuations. International scientific conferences devoted to combating this type of crime have been organized several times in Romania (Lazăr et al. 2009).

3.2.7 Lithuania

In Lithuania, forensic archaeology is recognized as a scientific discipline, but its activity is represented primarily from the perspective of the forensic anthropology.[11] Also in Lithuania, there is a state institution dealing with the research and commemoration of the victims of both totalitarianisms—*Lietuvos gyventojų genocido ir rezistencijos tyrimo centras (Genocide and Resistance Research Centre of Lithuania).* The search for victims covers both the times of World War I and II and the period of communist terror after 1945. Similarly to Poland and Romania, also in Lithuania, after the end of World War II, the local resistance movement started fighting against the Soviets. One of the places better recognized by archaeologists, anthropologists, and forensic medicine experts is the area of the former Tuskulenai estate, where in the period 1944–1947 the Soviets buried executed people in unmarked mass graves. A team of anthropologists and archaeologists from the University of Vilnius also successfully searched for historical personalities, including members of the magnate Radziwiłł family.

Since the homicide rate is relatively high in Lithuania, the problem of searching for hidden bodies of crime victims is known to the police. In such activities, the police cooperate primarily with experts in medicine and forensic anthropology, generally without the participation of archaeologists and without the implementation of archaeological methods and techniques. Police schools do not offer lectures or workshops on the possibility of applying archaeological methods and techniques in police activities, and these issues are not discussed. There are no police officers within the police structures who would use archaeological methodology during police operations. Academic centers also do not offer separate classes in the field of

[10] For help in obtaining information, I would like to thank the former Prosecutor General of Romania, Mr. Augustin Lazăr and Prof. Sorin Alamoreanu from the University of Cluj.

[11] For help in obtaining information, I would like to thank Prof. R. Jankauskas from the University of Vilnius and G. Petrauskas from the Klaipeda University.

forensic archaeology, but these issues appear in ongoing research projects. It should be noted that more and more attention is being paid in Lithuania to the issues of archaeology of armed conflicts, with which forensic archaeology is sometimes closely related (Čepulytė and Petrauskas 2012; Ivanovaite and Petrauskas 2019). The only effective and practical examples of cooperation between archaeologists and law enforcement agencies are cases involving the destruction and looting of archaeological sites, illegal trade in artifacts, and their export abroad.

3.3 Conclusions

In most of the countries in question, the activity of forensic archaeology focuses primarily on investigating the crimes of totalitarian regimes (Nazi and communist ones). These crimes constitute war crimes or crimes against humanity and, according to the standards of international law, these are not subject to statute of limitations. In some countries, such as Poland, the legislator has introduced a separate category of communist crimes, the prosecution of which is also not subject to a statute of limitations. Matters related to the search for victims of this type of crime are carried out as criminal investigations by local entities and institutions specially appointed for this purpose. When searching for burial and exhumation sites, archaeologists act as expert witnesses appointed by judicial bodies (usually prosecutor offices). Historical conditions related to the course of World War II and its dramatic consequences in many countries of Central and Eastern Europe made it necessary to search, identify, and commemorate hundreds of thousands of victims. This process will certainly continue for many years. The presence of archaeologists in this type of work seems necessary and justified, as evidenced by several studies related to the search for victims of war crimes or genocide (e.g., Katyn, Srebrenica). The nature of this type of work has shaped concepts in literature such as the archaeology of totalitarianism and even martyrological archaeology. This type of activity fits into a much broader concept of the archaeology of armed conflicts, with which the archaeology of battlefields may sometimes correspond. These disciplines indicate an increasing interest in the most recent times in archaeology. Keeping in mind the laconic but very true definition of forensic archaeology, which states that it essentially means *the presence of an archaeologist at a crime scene*, one can easily find a point of contact between this discipline and the archaeology of armed conflicts, the archaeology of totalitarianism or the archaeology of battlefields. This point of contact is a crime. War crimes and crimes of genocide have always accompanied conflicts around the world, as evidenced by the tragic events related to Russia's aggression against Ukraine, which began in February 2022.

When it comes to contemporary crimes (especially murders), there is a certain regularity that in countries where law enforcement agencies have started cooperation with archaeologists, it concerns primarily the search for burial places or hidden (usually underground) objects related to the crime. Therefore, this type of work involves primarily ground detection methods, with the very often used GPR and a few other methods related to remote sensing. In this type of activity, laser scanning of the area and analysis of aerial photos are quite often used. This specific modus operandi is repetitive and quite commonly associated with forensic archaeology. Meanwhile, these methods were effectively introduced into modern archaeology, expanding the catalog of so-called non-invasive methods. As a rule, however, these are not strictly archaeological methods, but only those that archaeology has adapted, like many others, for its research purposes. Many non-invasive ground detection methods are related to forensic geophysics, which, however, has not yet developed as a specialized discipline in most countries of Central and Eastern Europe. Geophysical methods are quite commonly used in traditional archaeological research, although generally not to locate burials but rather traces of settlements, underground structures, etc. The media popularity of most geophysical methods, especially GPR, magnetometer, and metal detector, has resulted in these methods being quite commonly, but incorrectly, associated primarily with archaeology. It is stereotypical and somewhat misleading. This association means that the average prosecutor or policeman in the countries of Central and Eastern Europe links forensic archaeology primarily with the use of geophysical methods. Although there are also those for whom archaeology still means the study of Egyptian pyramids. This phenomenon fits into the already recognized so-called CSI effect, which generally distorts or even falsifies the essence of the research capabilities of many disciplines represented by forensic sciences, including forensic archaeology.

It is symptomatic that in most of the countries in question, the police do not receive training in the use of selected archaeological methods and techniques. This issue is not the subject of lectures or workshops in police schools, and no need is perceived to introduce such topics into the training program.

The police structures also do not employ archaeologists who could join forensic crime scene teams. Only in the eastern German states (Saxony and Brandenburg) are conducted police training courses or lectures on the possibilities of using archaeological methods. The police structures of the countries described do not employ forensic archaeologists. The exception here is Romania and Poland, where archaeologists are employed to investigate crimes against archaeological heritage. In Poland, practical workshops on the use of certain archaeological methods to search for hidden corpses or objects are conducted by the Military Police. Forensic archaeology as a subject of lectures or workshops is conducted at one of the Polish universities (University of Wrocław), which also offers specialized postgraduate studies in the field of forensic archaeology. In the other countries in question, forensic archaeology is not the subject of teaching in academic centers.

In all these countries, there is a problem of illegal excavations, to varying degrees of intensity, which destroys archaeological sites, theft, smuggling, and counterfeiting of artifacts. In cases of this type, law enforcement agencies cooperate with archaeologists, usually employed in state institutions: (research centers, heritage protection offices, museums).

To sum up, it must be said that there is a clear difference between the way forensic archaeology functions in Western European countries and most of the countries of Central and Eastern Europe. Forensic archaeology has been and probably always will be a niche discipline. Nevertheless, it is significant that in Western European countries, law enforcement agencies more often use archaeological methods and techniques not only during the process of searching for hidden bodies but also during routine inspections at the crime scene. It was noticed that archaeology is not only the ability to use specialized ground detection equipment or make measurements but above all, the ability to recognize, secure, and analyze forensic traces, which may result in the reconstruction of a past event, in this case resulting in the construction of a hypothesis or investigative version of a criminal event. The practical use of forensic archaeology may therefore have measurable, positive discovery and evidentiary effects in connection with the investigation. It may be disturbing that in the countries of Central and Eastern Europe, law enforcement agencies do not seem to notice these possibilities, and forensic archaeology is perceived through the prism of the ability to use specialized equipment, which sooner or later forensic technicians will master. It seems that the introduction to forensic and police standards, Best Practice Manuals (BPMs), and Forensic Guidelines, as part of the implementation of selected archaeological methods and techniques during crime scene inspections, would increase the efficiency and quality of activities performed by the police at crime scenes, while consolidating the position of forensic archaeology in the Member States of the European Union. Actions in this area were undertaken several years ago by the Forensic Archaeology subgroup of the ENFSI EWG "Scene of Crime" but have not yet been completed.

References

Angyal M, Petretei D (2020) Forenzikus archeológia – Bűnügyek felderítése a háromdimenziós képalkotás és a kiterjesztett észlelés felhasználásával. Rendőrségi Tanulmányok 3:4–57

Barone PM, Groen WJ (eds) (2018) Multidisciplinary approaches to forensic archaeology. Topics discussed during the European Meetings on Forensic Archaeology (EMFA). Springer

Borkowski T, Trzciński M (2018) Interrogating the ground: an archaeologist at a crime scene. In: Barone PM, Groen WJ (eds) Multidisciplinary approaches to forensic archaeology. Topics discussed during the European Meetings on Forensic Archaeology (EMFA). Springer, pp 155–164

Borkowski T, Kawecki J, Szleszkowski Ł, Szwagrzyk K, Trzciński M (2023) Archeologia sądowa w teorii i praktyce, wydanie 2. Wolters Kluwer

Čepulytė A, Petrauskas G (2012) Archeologiniai partizanų bunkerių tyrimai: naujo lūžio pradžia? In: *Sibiro alma mater. Ave, vita! Būk sveikas, gyvenime!* Šiauliai, pp 182–191

Diana A (2015) Forenscic archaeology in Romania: present and future of a new discipline. In: Groen WJ, Marquez-Grant N, Janaway R (eds) Forensic archaeology. A global perspective. Wiley Blackwell, Hoboken, pp 133–134

Groen WJ, Marquez-Grant N, Janaway R (eds) (2015) Forensic archaeology. A global perspective. Wiley Blackwell, Hoboken

Hasil J, Hasil P et al (2020) The materiality of forced labour: settlement waste of communities at WWII mining plant and PoW camp in Rolava (North-West Bohemia). J Confl Archaeol 15(2):91–117

Hemker C, Hönig H, Van der Burgt P (2023) Der Mann im Berg – ein Kriminalfall aus dem Erzgebirge. Der Anschnitt. Zeitschrift für Montangeschichte 5:167–175

Hunter J, Cox M (2005) Forensic archaeology. Advances in theory and practice. Routledge, London

Ivanovaite L, Petrauskas G (2019) Investigating bunkers: Lithuanian partisans, archaeology and excavation in Pagrenda Forest. Europa Orientalis. Studia z Dziejów Europy Wschodniej i Państw Bałtyckich 10:179–206

Lazăr A et al (eds) (2009) Combating the criminality against the European cultural heritage. Patrimonium II, Cluj-Napoca

Masnicová S, Beňuš R, Obertová Z (2015) Forensic archaeology in the Slovak Republik. In: Groen WJ, Marquez-Grant N, Janaway R (eds) Forensic archaeology. A global perspective. Wiley Blackwell, Hoboken, pp 159–164

Morse D, Duncan J, Stoutamire J (eds) (1983) Handbook of forensic archaeology and anthropology. Tallahassee, Florida

Neumann R, Klenke K, Fischer A (2015) The working group 'forensic archaeology' at the German Bundeskriminalamt. In: Groen WJ, Marquez-Grant N, Janaway R (eds) Forensic archaeology. A global perspective. Wiley Blackwell, Hoboken, pp 67–75

Pexa T, Krajsa J et al (2018) Identification of the skeletal remains of the Czech communist regime crime victim, priest Josef Toufar. Forensic Sci Int 291:13–17

Susa É, Éry K et al (2015) Forensic archaeology and anthropology in Hungary: current trends and future perspectives. In: Groen WJ, Marquez-Grant N, Janaway R (eds) Forensic archaeology. A global perspective. Wiley Blackwell, Hoboken, pp 83–90

Trzciński M (2021) Kryminalistyka i archeologia sądowa w procesie poszukiwania ukrytych zwłok. Wolters Kluwer, Warszawa

Trzciński M, Borkowski T (2015) Forensic archaeology in Poland: theory and practice. In: Groen WJ, Marquez-Grant N, Janaway R (eds) Forensic archaeology. A global perspective. Wiley Blackwell, Hoboken, pp 121–127

Van der Burgt P, Stäuble H (2019) Kriminalistische Methoden in der Archäologie – ein Anwendungsbeispiel aus Sachsen. In: Meller H et al (eds) Rituelle Gewalt – Rituale der Gewalt: 12. Mitteldeutscher Archäologentag, Halle, pp 731–740

Vařeka P (ed) (2023) Pozůstatky taboru nacistickė a komunistické totality v západnich Čechách, Plzeň

Wanke T, Linck R (2024) Auf Spurensuche mit der Kriminalpolizei. Der Fund des Scheunen – Skeletts von Bad Kissingen. Denkmal Information Bayern 182:26–29

Chapter 4
Forensic Archaeology and Anthropology Within Swedish Law Enforcement Agencies

Clara Alfsdotter, Jesper Olsson, Christoffer Hagberg, and Anja Petaros

Abstract This chapter examines the development and current state of forensic archaeology and anthropology within Swedish law enforcement, specifically the Swedish Police Authority (SPA) and the National Board of Forensic Medicine (NBFM). It traces the history of regional initiatives and identifies past challenges, including a lack of standardization and formal recognition. The chapter details recent formalization efforts, including the establishment of dedicated forensic archaeology positions at the SPA's National Forensic Centre and steps toward formalizing forensic anthropology at the NBFM. Key aspects of the ongoing process are discussed, such as the development of standard operating procedures, quality assurance measures, and proficiency testing. This chapter highlights the benefits of developing these disciplines within law enforcement, including improved collaboration, access to case information, and the ability to influence investigative strategies. However, challenges remain, particularly in terms of resources and nationwide implementation. The authors argue for the continued development and formalization of forensic archaeology and anthropology in Sweden in order to enhance the quality and consistency of investigations pertaining to forensic archaeology and anthropology. This chapter provides insights into the process of establishing new forensic specialties within the existing law enforcement structures.

Keywords Forensic archaeology · Forensic anthropology · Swedish Police Authority (SPA) · National Board of Forensic Medicine (NBFM) · Standardization and protocols

---

C. Alfsdotter (✉)
National Forensic Centre, Swedish Police Authority, Malmö, Sweden

National Board of Forensic Medicine, Lund, Sweden
e-mail: clara.alfsdotter@polisen.se

J. Olsson · C. Hagberg
National Forensic Centre, Swedish Police Authority, Malmö, Sweden

A. Petaros
National Board of Forensic Medicine, Linköping, Sweden

P. M. Barone, WJ M. Groen (eds.), *Forensic Archaeology and New Multidisciplinary Approaches*, Soil Forensics, https://doi.org/10.1007/978-3-031-86308-0_4

4.1 Introduction

The disciplines of forensic archaeology and anthropology are currently being formalized within Swedish law enforcement. This formalization work takes place at the National Forensic Centre (NFC, Sw. Nationellt forensiskt centrum), the forensic science institute within the Swedish Police Authority (SPA, Sw. Polismyndigeten), and at the National Board of Forensic Medicine (NBFM, Sw. Rättsmedicinalverket), respectively. To the best of our knowledge, the concept of providing in-house forensic archaeological services within the national police authority is unique. Operating within the SPA comes with unique challenges and possibilities. Similarly, the NBFM, where forensic examination of human remains takes place, is a national state agency. Both entities operate under the Ministry of Justice. This chapter addresses the organizational structure, past developments, the ongoing formalization processes, the type of work that is conducted within the trajectory of forensic archaeology and forensic anthropology, and the demands that need to be met to successfully develop the disciplines when operating within these forensic institutions. For a brief overview of Swedish forensic archaeological and anthropological initiatives outside of law enforcement, see Alfsdotter (2021a) and Alfsdotter et al. (2022), as this is outside the scope of the current chapter.

While it is recognized that forensic archaeology and forensic anthropology are two distinct disciplines with their own demands regarding standards and professional proficiency, this chapter will, in part, address the disciplines in tandem, as the development of forensic archaeology and anthropology are intertwined in several regards in Sweden, owning in part to the Swedish academic structure. In Sweden, historical osteology (bioarchaeology and zooarchaeology) is a sub-discipline of archaeology, and the two have been closely linked since the 1960s (Ahlström et al. 2011; Stjernquist 1992). Nils-Gustaf Gejvall, a Swedish mid-twentieth century zoologist and osteologist, was influential in this disciplinary development, as were several of his students after him (Iregren 2003). Due to this educational structure, osteologists educated in Sweden are generally also archaeologists. Those who work in contract-led osteology and archaeology generally utilize and expand their dual competencies, while those continuing in academia generally specialize in osteology (bio-archaeology or zoo-archaeology, respectively).

4.2 The Organization of the Swedish Police Authority (SPA) and the National Board of Forensic Medicine (NBFM)

In Sweden, death investigations are primarily managed by two main entities: the SPA, the largest governmental agency in the country, and the NBFM, a government agency that provides forensic expertise in multiple fields to judicial authorities and law enforcement. The NBFM gathers specialists in forensic pathology, odontology, psychiatry, toxicology/chemistry, and genetics. These specialists are distributed across departments and divisions located strategically nationwide, ensuring that high-quality forensic services are available throughout Sweden. Established in its current form in 1991 to unify previously scattered forensic services for improved efficiency and equal quality across the country (Eriksson and Wayne 2017), the organization underwent a subsequent internal reorganization in 2017. The Department of Forensic Medicine, specifically tasked with postmortem and clinical forensic examinations (including age estimation in the living), operates today out of six regional divisions. This distribution is based on population density which varies greatly in Sweden, resulting in some divisions covering larger geographic areas than others (National Board of Forensic Medicine n.d.; Eriksson and Wayne 2017). For example, the NBFM division in Umeå covers an extensive area of 225,000 km^2, representing over half of Sweden's land area but serving a sparse population of only 0.9 million people (Statistikmyndigheten SCB 2022).

Similarly, the SPA underwent significant restructuring in 2015, merging 21 county police government agencies and the National Police Board into a single organization (Fig. 4.1). This reorganization included the incorporation of the Swedish National Laboratory of Forensic Science (Sw. Statens kriminaltekniska laboratorium, SKL) into a department under the SPA under the new name of the National Forensic Center (Riksdagen 2013). These changes aimed to improve nationwide service standardization, operational efficiency, and communication among departments. Today, the Swedish Police Authority covers seven regional departments (Fig. 4.2), encompassing 95 local police districts distributed across the country (Swedish Police Authority n.d.). The NFC is a national department that consists of national divisions, one of which contains regional laboratory sections. The NFC is responsible for the development, standardization, and maintenance of forensic processes within the SPA and the execution of forensic investigations. This

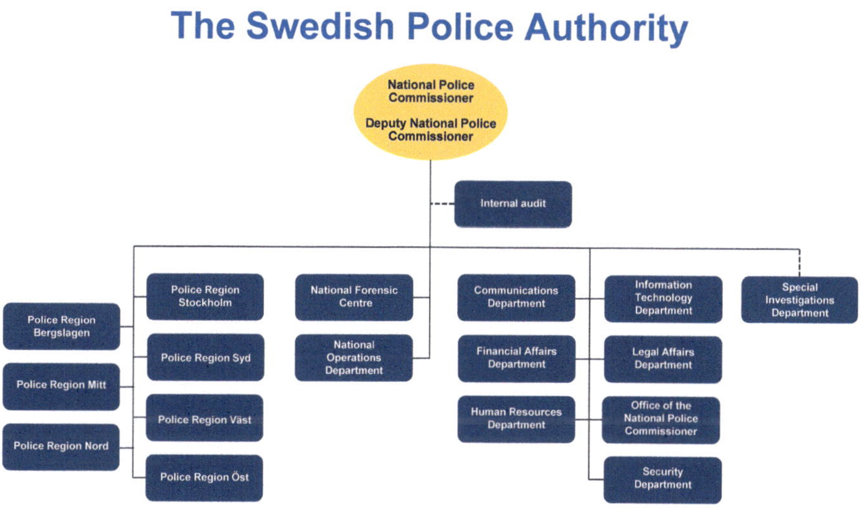

Fig. 4.1 Organizational chart of the Swedish Police Authority

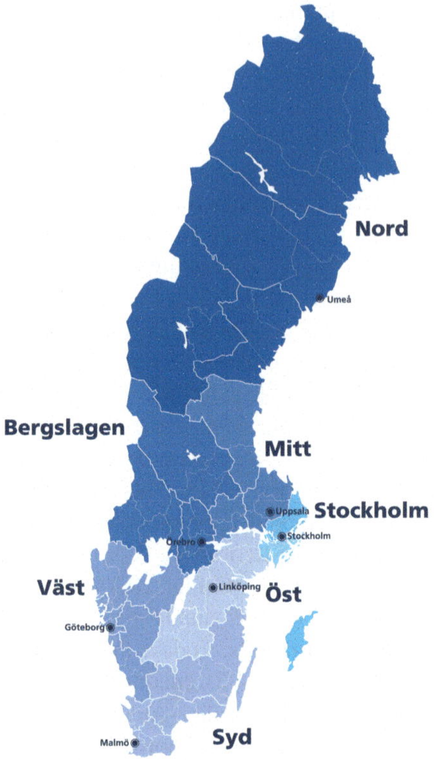

Fig. 4.2 The seven police regions of Sweden

entails expert consultancy, forensic education, and strategic R&D to ensure forensic competence within the SPA. While the NFC is still heavily laboratory-based, given the organizational history, some forensic specialists at the NFC are increasingly involved in scene investigations, including fire specialists, sensor and photo documentation specialists, and forensic archaeologists.

4.3 Past Forensic Archaeological and Anthropological Structure Within Law Enforcement

As the current national SPA consisted of 21 independent county police agencies until 2015, a background based on regional forensic archaeological initiatives within the police follows.

At the Stockholm county police, a working group in forensic archaeology "AFFA" (Sw. Arbetsgruppen för forensisk arkeologi) was created in 1991 on the initiative of CSIs that engaged with external partners, including archaeologists at Stockholm University, an osteologist at the National History Museum, and a medicolegal doctor at the National Board of Forensic Medicine (RPS 1996). The AFFA initiative followed the visit of one of the CSIs to an archaeological excavation, where he found that archaeological techniques were of interest to outdoor and fire scene investigations. AFFA was influential in increasing awareness of forensic archaeology within the police through lectures and workshops. The AFFA members attended two archaeological excavations, worked at scene investigations with a forensic archaeological "profile," and wrote a report on forensic archaeological practice (Alfsdotter 2021b; RPS 1996). The project amounted to a handbook for crime scene investigators covering applicable methods from archaeology (RPS 1996).

As the work with AFFA was not sanctioned by the police as a primary work task but rather as an interest group, the AFFA initiative depended on the engagement of a few key individuals, and the work was largely conducted outside of ordinary work time (RPS 1996). Due to these challenges, AFFA work came to a standstill in 2010. This led AFFA CSI members to push for a forensic archaeological excavation course taught to crime scene investigators. The course was organized in 2013 by a bioarchaeologist at the Osteological Research Laboratory at the Department of Archaeology and Classical Studies, Stockholm University, on assignment by the Police through AFFA. A similar course was planned for 2020 but was canceled due to the pandemic. The CSIs that founded AFFA have since left the Police Authority. While the organization has dissolved, the Stockholm region is a Swedish police region with multiple police employees with educational backgrounds in archaeology and osteology, while being employed in other capacities such as CSI. This is largely because the region has opened up to employ non-police CSIs with an academic background in addition to those with a police background, creating the opportunity for individuals with a university degree in other fields (among those archaeology, likely owned to the awareness in the Stockholm region created by AFFA) to be employed and educated as civilian CSIs. In the majority of police regions, it is still necessary to be a police officer before you get trained to become a CSI.

Another informal regional forensic archaeological initiative took place in the southernmost Swedish Police county in 2008. One of the authors (JO), who at the time was employed in computer forensics, was tasked with allocating 20% of his working hours to forensic archaeology, given his professional background in archaeology, including geophysics. This role aimed to support CSI work, primarily at outdoor scenes by using existing archaeological techniques in forensic contexts. This work involved collaboration with various archaeological institutions, including museums and universities, as well as with individual researchers from different disciplines related to forensic archaeology. The majority of cases during this interval, from 2008 to 2018, primarily involved the use of metal detectors, although others focused on understanding and interpreting outdoor crime scene site formation processes and conducting excavations. Competence in Ground Penetrating Radar (GPR) and geophysics proved essential. The casework frequently resulted in the recovery of bullet casings, bullets, weapons, contraband, explosives, and human remains. Another common request within the SPA involved identifying bones encountered by the general public or the Police, to determine whether they were human or non-human. An informal protocol for bone assessment was initiated in collaboration with osteologists and anthropologists.

Since its establishment, the NBFM has not had a formally recognized position for forensic anthropologists. Skeletal investigations have traditionally been conducted by forensic pathologists, and in some cases, the NBFM has relied on the assistance of external consultants, such as osteoarchaeologists or employees at local museums or skeletal collections. The quality of the issued reports has varied significantly depending on the professionals' acquaintance with forensic anthropology methods and standards, which depended mainly on their training, interest, and professional exposure. In addition, the high workload of pathologists could have negatively impacted the quality of some analyses, as basic and cursory examinations of bones under time pressure could lead to important details being overlooked that could be avoided with the in-depth analysis provided by a forensic anthropologist. Eventually, individuals with formal training in forensic anthropology have been employed on staff at the NBFM, though assigned to other duties, or existing staff members have pursued formal training in the discipline. Currently, three individuals, two forensic pathologists, and one autopsy assistant hold an international certification and/or formal degree in forensic anthropology. Although they are still not formally employed in this role, they have been increasingly engaged as consultants in forensic anthropology cases over the past few years.

4.4 Identified Challenges and Development Areas

Despite multiple successful cases within the SPA, both regional forensic archaeology/anthropology initiatives suffered from a lack of official mandates, sufficient working hours, manpower, national infrastructure, and standard operating procedures. Furthermore, only two regions utilized employees with archaeological and osteological competence, leading to heterogeneous access to forensic archaeological and anthropological competence benefitting police investigations.

Focusing on the overlapping skill sets from forensic archaeology and anthropology, a study from 2021 concluded that Swedish investigations of outdoor crime scenes involving fragmentary, skeletal, or concealed human remains were not standardized in terms of investigation and analysis (Alfsdotter 2021b). Regional variations were evident despite the nationalization of the SPA. This led to significant responsibility placed on individual investigators to select appropriate methods and consultants for addressing cases that pertain to clandestine burials and hidden objects, as well as analyses of skeletal remains, resulting in inconsistent investigation quality. When forensic archaeological or anthropological competences were utilized in Swedish police work, it occurred ad hoc, with practitioners consulted from within and without the SPA, and without demands on specific educational backgrounds, proficiency testing, or training in forensics. The study suggested the following key steps for advancing forensic archaeology and anthropology (FAA) within the SPA and NBFM:

- Identifying the types and quantities of cases that would benefit from FAA
- Establishing FAA as an independent subject within the SPA and the NBFM
- Developing a national infrastructure to ensure uniform competencies, with minimum requirements, experience, and accreditation for FAA practitioners
- Offering professional education in FAA
- Developing national standards and best practices for outdoor CSI and FAA to improve evidence collection and legal security

For post-mortem analysis, it has been suggested that the creation of a forensic anthropological position within the NBFM would complement the work of forensic pathologists and odontologists. Forensic anthropological and archaeological expertise was suggested to be involved in crime scene investigations relating to fragmentary, skeletal, or concealed human remains to gather comprehensive evidence, enhancing site formation interpretation and expediting feedback for police investigations and laboratory analyses (Alfsdotter 2021b). While the examination of skeletal remains generally falls under the auspices of the NBFM, there are specific instances where human skeletal remains are handled or transferred for analysis to other actors. Despite the NBFM responsibility, there has been a lack of continuity in the development, planning, and maintenance of forensic anthropology expertise within the NBFM over the years. Most often, adherence to contemporary forensic anthropology practices and staying up-to-date with the latest developments in the field relied on individual interests and efforts rather than on a comprehensive system providing consistent and uniform professional development. This resulted in specialized forensic anthropology expertise being unevenly distributed across the country and completely lacking in multiple forensic medicine divisions.

The reasons for the lack of a structured approach to the development of forensic anthropology and archaeology likely stem from two prevailing misconceptions. First, there is no need for FAA expertise in Sweden, as the number of cases does not justify the existence of a distinct professional profile. The second misconception is that these two disciplines do not require highly specialized training. Historically, forensic anthropology was often practiced by pathologists who possessed some knowledge of human osteology and skeletal anatomy, which was sufficient to address specific forensic cases; the same cannot be said today. Over the years, forensic anthropology has developed into a highly specialized field and independent discipline, requiring specific knowledge, long-term practical experience, and specific technical skills. Furthermore, forensic cases today, beyond those involving skeletal remains, require a multidisciplinary approach and the involvement of different highly specialized disciplines, including forensic anthropology. A targeted specialization in forensic anthropology is thus required to ensure expertise when analyzing and interpreting skeletal remains and other related questions in forensic practice.

The same can be said for forensic archaeology, which is often misidentified as a "set of methods" that can be applied by anyone (Connor and Scott 2001, Márquez-Grant et al. 2012; Sigler-Eisenberg 1985). The AFFA report attests to this, as the group was tasked with presenting forensic archaeological methods that could be utilized by the police (RPS 1996). However, the authors of the AFFA report highlight that it is beneficial and sometimes crucial to have archaeologists and osteologists involved in search and excavation scenes from an early stage of police investigation. The material record does not speak for itself; instead, it is gathered and interpreted through a framework that depends on the investigators' background knowledge. Such a framework is essential for reconstructing both natural and man-made material manifestations at a stratified scene, thereby providing information about events before, during, and after the event under investigation (Boyd and Boyd 2011; Groen 2018). Likewise, "general" archaeology does not include skills pertinent to forensic work. Archaeologists working in forensics must have substantial field experience in traditional archaeology and education in forensic procedures, including knowledge of chain of evidence, evidence and result evaluation, confidentiality, court systems, forensic responsibilities, ethics, and basic criminalistics and criminology (Dirkmaat et al. 2008; Cheetham and Hanson 2009; Skinner and Sterenberg 2005; Groen 2018).

4.5 The Formalization Process

4.5.1 The National Board of Forensic Medicine

There has been a growing interest in the competencies offered by forensic anthropology, both within and outside the NBFM, and an expanding recognition of the importance of the presence of forensic anthropology skill sets for enhancing the quality of a spectrum of medico-legal investigations. In line with this trend, the NBFM has taken important steps in evaluating some of the issues and misconceptions addressed above.

One of the first concrete steps undertaken was to elucidate how the handling of skeletal remains at the NBFM is conducted and to clarify the procedures for processing, registering, and management of such cases. In 2022, a retrospective analysis was conducted to identify the number and type of cases that could benefit from forensic anthropology expertise. The analysis covered 4 years (between January 2018 and December 2021) and showed that approximately 60 cases that could be handled or assisted by forensic anthropologists were overseen by NBFM on a yearly basis. Almost half of these cases were related to human-non-human bone identification (33%) and cases in which the forensic significance of a finding needed to be assessed (15%). The remaining cases were related to the analysis of single skeletal elements (6%), complete or almost complete skeletons (10%), fragmented burned remains (9%), or heavily burned human corpses (7%). In the statistical analysis, corpses that had undergone substantial decomposition and showed elements of skeletonization (19%) were included because forensic anthropology expertise can still be of great importance in their analysis.

Besides showing that forensic anthropological cases account for 1% of all cases managed yearly by the NBFMs forensic pathology divisions, the analysis identified other important aspects that had not been previously addressed: (i) the registration system used at the time did not allow for an appropriate statistical analysis due to the use of different categorization systems for the registration of skeletal remains, which could have caused some cases to fall out of the count. It was also noted that registration of forensic anthropology consultations done by phone or mail (both internally and externally) needs to be optimized and standardized to allow the inclusion of these cases in statistics and guarantee the possibility of a second opinion; (ii) there were no operational guidelines dedicated specifically to the registration, management, and examination of skeletal cases; (iii) there was no formal position in forensic anthropology, despite the presence of trained forensic anthropologists and the number of cases that could benefit from their specialized competence.

After the statistical analysis was disclosed, several concrete measures to address the observed issues were undertaken, acknowledging the specific nature of these cases and marking the initial steps toward formalizing the role of the forensic anthropologist at the NBFM. By 2024, new operational guidelines on skeletal case registration and handling were compiled and implemented in the existing NFBM quality system. In 2024, the drafting of guidelines on how skeletal remains should be analyzed, derived from existing recommendations from international professional organizations but adapted to fit the Swedish forensic system, commenced. Proposals to involve personnel with formal forensic anthropology training and expertise in all cases involving skeletal remains, either as responsible executors of the analysis or consultants and/or reviewers, have been made, well received, and widely supported by board members. Simultaneously, lectures and courses in forensic anthropology for forensic pathologists, as well as other forensic practitioners, are starting to be organized on a regular basis and are supported by NBFM and in collaboration with the NFC (see Sect. 4.5.4). All the measures undertaken and proposed to date were carefully considered to meet the NBFM's long-term goals, as well as existing operational procedures and the accreditation system under which NBFM is operating (e.g., report quality peer-review and control are essential parts of forensic pathology practice at NBFM).

Standardization and formalization of forensic anthropology expertise within NBFM is thought, by those actively working with the issue, to be an indispensable step to ensure that the work conducted at the NBFM remains at the forefront of scientific advancements and maintains high working standards, enabling more robust analyses in an interdisciplinary and collaborative working environment. Given the growing demand for this proficiency, even in other types of forensic cases, and because a forensic anthropologist is already part of the Board's DVI organization, it seems fitting that the role of forensic anthropologist becomes formally recognized in all aspects of its operations, as has already been done for forensic odontology (NBFM has a full-time forensic odontologist who is involved in identification and age estimation cases). Even if this formalization has still not been concretized, important steps, including risk assessment and consequence analysis, have been undertaken, and options are currently being evaluated to enable its implementation in the near future.

4.5.2 The Swedish Police Authority

One step toward the formalization of forensic archaeology occurred within the SPA in 2018. Because of the increased recognition of forensic archaeology by the division head, one of the authors (JO) was transitioned to a full-time position as a forensic archaeologist at the NFC, with the task of establishing the forensic archaeological process within the SPA. Between 2018 and 2022, an average of approximately 50 cases were processed annually, with the following task distributions: 10% allocated to GIS analysis and documentation, 10% to bone identification, 10% to excavations, 20% to metal detection surveys, and 50% to consultations, with a natural decline during the COVID-19 pandemic. The responsibilities encompassed visual searches, drone searches, collaboration with search dog handlers, metal detection, ground-penetrating radar (GPR) search, coordinating efforts linked to searching for human remains, and other evidence with maritime archaeologists, non-profit organizations, and government agencies. To establish an international network, contact with the Forensic Archaeology subgroup of the Expert Working Group (EWG) "Scene of Crime" of the European Network of Forensic Science Institutes (ENFSI) was made in 2018, leading to representation initially for the southern regional division and subsequently nationally as a representative of the NFC in the Forensic Archaeology subgroup.

Another aspect of the formalization process pertains to a former AFFA member, and CSI with a Ph.D. in osteology is now formally a representative of Interpol's Disaster Victim Identification (DVI) sub-working group in forensic pathology/anthropology. In Sweden, DVI is primarily executed by Swedish CSIs and follows Interpol directives, with NBFM executing for post-mortem identification.

In 2022, two more positions in forensic archaeology were developed within the SPA, making the total of forensic archaeology positions within the SPA three (the authors JO, CA, CH), of which one is also a forensic anthropologist. As employees at the NFC, forensic archaeologists are tasked with keeping up to date with the international development of the field, research and development, forensic process management, education, advisory roles, and casework.

The NFC's SPA forensic archaeology resource, located in the south (Malmö), serves a national mandate. The forensic archaeology subject is currently organized under the Sensor Technology group, formerly "Crime Scene Documentation," of the Information Technology Division, owing to its use of sensors such as laser scanners, cameras, ground-penetrating radar, and metal detectors. However, forensic archaeology is not equivalent to sensor technology, as it is inherently multifaceted, with an emphasis on investigations relating to site formation processes and hidden or concealed remains (artifacts or human). Consequently, the subject is developed accordingly, in collaboration with other relevant fields within the NFC and the SPA at large.

Development of a Forensic Archaeology

At the end of 2022, with increased resources dedicated to forensic archaeology at the NFC, a project was launched to formalize and establish forensic archaeology as a structured discipline. Standard operational procedures, quality assurance documents, and proficiency testing regulations are being developed to regulate forensic archaeological casework and processes at the SPA. This initiative aims to enhance the visibility, reliability, and application of forensic archaeology across Sweden, ensuring that it can contribute fully to the nation's criminal justice system. The project incorporates methods, techniques, and theoretical frameworks from archaeology and anthropology and is currently structured into four concepts that are integral to forensic archaeology: Locate, Investigate, Document, and Analyze. These principles serve as the framework for categorizing various types of tasks and aligning them with the corresponding deliverables, methodologies, and standard operating procedures, as is required for every type of forensic investigation conducted by the NFC. The first SOPs pertain to excavation, species identification of bones, and location using a metal detector.

At the NFC, different types of forensic assignments are categorized as follows:

- *Descriptive assignment*: This involves simply describing findings, such as documenting the location and details of items found using a metal detector. The report is a purely technical or factual description of the findings without a conclusion.
- *Classification assignment*: Assignment of an object to a particular category. This may be criteria-based or evaluative, focusing on categorizing items based on predefined standards or assessments. The report provides a categorical (criteria-based) or evaluative conclusion.
- *Source determination assignment*: An evaluative task that identifies the origin of a specific item or material. The report considers propositions regarding the source of some physical matter and provides an evaluative conclusion.
- *Activity determination assignment*: Another evaluative task that aims to determine the activities that took place at a site based on the evidence collected. The report considers the propositions of human activity or an incident and provides an evaluative conclusion.
- *Investigative assignment*: The forensic specialist conducts a part of the investigation on delegation from the main investigator. This involves deeper analysis and synthesis of findings to address specific forensic questions. The report may contain several conclusions and an overall assessment of what has occurred.

The assessments resulting in conclusions are evaluated in line with the Bayesian theorem. Forensic archaeology encompasses several types of assignments. For example, metal detection might typically be viewed as a descriptive task, simply yielding the location and identification of an item. However, it can also be part of a broader investigative effort, contributing to a larger case inquiry, such as locating a buried cache of weapons and interpreting site formation processes. Moreover, metal detection may sometimes be evaluative, especially when assessing the likelihood of discovering sought-after evidence. This multifaceted approach underscores the complexity and versatility of tasks on forensic archaeology, highlighting the need for procedural rigor in handling different types of forensic assignments.

One benefit of the formalization project will be the implementation of a standardized request procedure for forensic archaeology within SPA, which will streamline the process for requesting forensic archaeological expertise. As statistics on forensic archaeological investigations are currently lacking, given the previous ad hoc procedures within the SPA, it is uncertain how many investigations are actually conducted or needed. The potential caseload for forensic archaeology is unknown, as to request this specialism, the investigator needs to know when it can be beneficial. Formalizing forensic archaeology means that investigative methodologies can be clearly communicated, which in effect can lead to a higher frequency and specificity of forensic archaeological cases. A formalized system is expected to offset greater legal security, traceability, and homogenous potential to request competence across the country.

Proficiency documents developed for forensic archaeology serves as a foundation for proficiency testing undertaken during general forensic scientist education at the NFC. In addition to documents used to examine forensic archaeologists, examination documents will also be developed for those methods that are not forensic archaeological per se, but that are used in archaeology and thus can be taught to other SPA employees. Methods that the NFC teaches but is not the primary executor of go under a so-called forensic process mandate, where the NFC regulates the guidelines and education for the methods that are primarily used by CSIs. To be able to focus on cases that can benefit most from forensic archaeological competence, such as cases that target buried objects or remains or other scenarios involving site formation processes, it is ideal that frequent routine cases, such as metal detection for bullet casings, which is becoming volume cases in Sweden, be conducted solely by CSIs under the forensic process mandate (this is a request that is today often posed to forensic archaeologists).

Forensic archaeological/anthropological casework is currently conducted by the NFC, while on a limited basis, given the need to formalize the subject, includes the following:

- Search for/excavation of concealed objects or human remains
- Environmental crimes where deposits of illegal material in the ground are expected
- Fire scene investigation where fragmentary human remains are expected
- For osteological remains: species identification and initial assessment of forensic significance in situ as well as forensic anthropological analysis in collaboration with the NBFM

4.5.3 Formalization Process on Forensic Anthropology Division of Responsibility

As part of the formalization process, forensic anthropologists at the NFC and the NBFM are developing a proposal as grounds for a decision on which state agency will be responsible for different overlapping aspects of forensic anthropological assessments and consultations within the SPA and the NBFM. It is expected that the division of responsibilities in broad strokes will result in the forensic anthropological process relating to scene processing at stratified scenes (such as certain outdoor scenes and fire scenes) being developed by the forensic anthropology/archaeology function at the NFC, while the postmortem analysis of the remains will be overseen by the NBFM. However, this division of duties has not been formally decided. At present, collaborative work is conducted across the board, as competence in forensic anthropology within the two state agencies consists of a small number of individuals. Ideally, close collaboration would still be the norm, following a more structured division of primary responsibilities. However, a formal decision over the division of tasks is needed to make it easier for the police to submit their requests as well as to develop SOPs and proficiency descriptions that align with the types of inquiries received.

4.5.4 Forensic Archaeology and Anthropology Education and Information Within Law Enforcement

As of 2020, a one-day forensic archaeology and anthropology information session is included in the routine CSI education in Sweden. In addition, regular lectures are provided upon request for senior CSIs and police investigators.

By 2024, two new courses with elements of forensic archaeology were developed. One was an advanced fire scene course given to a few CSIs per region that specializes in fire investigation. The course included a half-day theoretical session on fire and bodies from a forensic anthropological and forensic medicine perspective as it pertains to fire scene, as well as an upcoming practical scene processing exercise. The other course was given to forensic pathology (legal medicine) residents, which included one-and-a-half days of basic forensic anthropology sessions, with both theoretical and practical components. It is clear that short-term courses, even if longer than a few days, cannot meet the demands needed to address all necessary skills for working with complex cases. However, they can raise awareness of the complexity of skeletal investigations and promote a system that enables effective collaboration between forensic anthropologists and other forensic professionals, guiding the latter in determining when and where to seek forensic anthropology consultation.

Increased promotion of the diverse tasks that forensic anthropologists and archaeologists can be involved in is needed, and cannot be achieved just through courses. Sensibilization of this growing discipline and its benefits is essential. This effort should reach a broad range of stakeholders, including law enforcement and forensic pathologists as well as other legal professionals, policymakers, and the general public. By understanding the specific contributions of forensic anthropologists and archaeologists in various cases, more effective collaboration and forensic outcomes in certain Police investigations can be achieved.

4.6 Looking Ahead

4.6.1 Forensic Archaeology at the SPA

While it is a significant step in establishing three full-time positions in forensic archaeology within the SPA, work remains before forensic archaeology is fully established within the agency. As the resources are slim, it will take time and effort before the standardization process is complete and the forensic archaeology infrastructure is available and known throughout the country. Despite these challenges, significant opportunities have come with forensic archaeology as a discipline established within the SPA. It opens up many collaborations that feed into both the research and development within the SPA at large, but also to forensic archaeological development as it pertains to Sweden. For example, it is easier to gain information about *the modus operandi* of past cases of hidden objects and deceased individuals, which can be fed back into coming police investigations as well as the development of forensic archaeology.

Although a previous paper (Alfsdotter 2021b) emphasized CSIs as the main collaborator for forensic archaeologists, it has become increasingly clear that work from within the SPA allows for collaboration with various police capacities, such as police investigators. Collaboration in the early stages of police investigation has become significantly easier. This entails collaboration throughout the case, allowing forensic archaeological competence to influence the investigation strategy. Such cases allow for a more thorough and well-planned forensic archaeological execution, in contrast to cases where the scene is already encountered and under imminent investigation. This sort of cooperation would be more difficult if forensic archeologists and anthropologists were not working in the same organization and were not subject to the same confidentiality agreements as the police investigators. Another benefit is organic learning from colleagues within the SPA, who have different skills and knowledge regarding the forensic and legislative fields. Being part of the SPA also opens doors in terms of collaboration with other institutions and organizations, both nationally and internationally, such as the ENFSI.

4.6.2 Forensic Anthropology at the SPA and the NBFM

Implementation and formalization of the role of forensic anthropologists within the NBFM would help alleviate the workload of forensic pathologists, allowing more time and specialized personnel to be dedicated to skeletal examinations requiring thorough analysis and streamlining the handling of other forensic casework. In this way, the quality of forensic investigations can be improved through a specialized, focused approach. Given that the caseload is limited, redirecting specific skeletal cases from forensic pathologists to a smaller group of forensic anthropologists would allow these specialists to consolidate and deepen their expertise, retain their competence, and gain relevant experience. Their expertise should however not be limited solely to skeletonized remains but should also be emphasized in other related areas, such as taphonomy and decomposition, PMI assessment, trauma analysis, and bone histology, to name a few. In addition, forensic anthropologists could readily engage in scientific research projects or other developmental projects within the NBFM, allowing them to contribute to advancements in the field while enhancing their own expertise. Formalizing this role would also establish a stronger communication channel with the police authority through networking and collaboration with the SPAs forensic anthropologists and archaeologists, building up an interdisciplinary network for handling this type of specialized cases.

Achieving this vision requires strategic planning for the development, implementation, and acceptance of the role. A clear plan defining which cases fall under the responsibility of forensic anthropologists, along with guidelines for when forensic pathologists should seek specialized expertise, will be important to ensure that the role is effectively utilized and not underexploited.

To build this system effectively, quality control and regular assessments of professional capabilities must be carefully planned in advance and conducted consistently. Oversight of those handling forensic anthropological casework, including the accuracy and consistency of report writing and methodologies used during skeletal examinations, should be applied to forensic anthropological analyses. To facilitate this and the cross-verification of findings, as already practiced at the NBFM, the system will require more than one expert in place, which would also reduce vulnerability to individual limitations or absences and promote a stringent quality control process.

To further strengthen the system, considering the different backgrounds that forensic anthropologists may have across European countries and, thus, in Sweden, it would be highly beneficial to engage in international certification examinations as an additional means of formally assessing the competencies of those involved in forensic casework. Another essential aspect to consider once implementation is in place is to establish a structured program for the continuous professional development of these individuals to build and maintain long-term expertise. Subspecializations within forensic anthropology (e.g., taphonomy and bone histology) could further expand the skill sets of these professionals.

References

Ahlström T, Iregren E, Jennbert K, Strid L (2011) Sweden. In: Márquez-Grant N, Fibiger L (eds) The Routledge handbook of archaeological human remains and legislation. Routledge, London

Alfsdotter C (2021a) The corporeality of death: bioarchaeological, Taphonomic, and forensic anthropological studies of human remains [PhD dissertation]. Linnaeus University, Kalmar

Alfsdotter C (2021b) Forensic archaeology and forensic anthropology within Swedish law enforcement: current state and suggestions for future developments. Forensic Sci Int Rep 3:203–225

Alfsdotter C, Petaros A, Güvencel A, Molnar P, Teglind R, Alkass K (2022) Development and implementation of forensic anthropology in Swedish forensic practice. Scandinavian J Forensic Sci 28:10–19. https://doi.org/10.2478/sjfs-2022-0015

Boyd C, Boyd D (2011) Theory and the scientific basis for forensic anthropology. J Forensic Sci 56:1407–1415. https://doi.org/10.1111/j.1556-4029.2011.01852.x

Cheetham P, Hanson I (2009) Excavation and recovery in forensic archaeological investigations. In: Blau S, Ubelaker D (eds) Handbook of forensic anthropology and archaeology. West Coast Press, Walnut Creek

Connor M, Scott DD (2001) Paradigms and perpetrators. Hist Archaeol 35:1–6

Dirkmaat DC, Cabo LL, Ousley SD, Symes SA (2008) New perspectives in forensic anthropology. Am J Phys Anthropol 137:33–52. https://doi.org/10.1002/ajpa.20948

Eriksson A, Wayne JA (2017) History of forensic medical sciences in Sweden. In: Madea B (ed) History of forensic medicine. Lehmanns Media, Berlin

Groen M (2018) Forensic archaeology: integrating archaeology with criminalistics and criminology. In: Barone PM, Groen M (eds) Multidisciplinary approaches to forensic archaeology, 1st edn. Springer International Publishing

Iregren E (2003). Vad är osteologi, hur kan vi osteologer samverka och hur bör universitetens utbildning fungera? Unpublished paper. Lund University, Lund. Available at: http://www.arkeologiskasamfundet.se/document/arc

Márquez-Grant N, Litherland S, Roberts J (2012) European perspectives and the role of the forensic archaeologist in the UK. In: Dirkmaat D (ed) A companion to forensic anthropology. Wiley, Chichester. https://doi.org/10.1002/9781118255377

National Board of Forensic Medicine (n.d.) The medical link in the judicial chain. https://www.rmv.se/wp-content/uploads/Ny-rmv-broschyrengelska-pdf.pdf. Accessed 3 July 2024

Riksdagen (2013) A new organization for the police. https://www.riksdagen.se/sv/dokument-och-lagar/dokument/betankande/en-ny-organisation-for-polisen_h101juu23/. Accessed 3 July 2024

RPS (1996) Arbetsgruppen för forensisk arkeologi. Forensisk arkeologi. RPS-FK Stockholm

Sigler-Eisenberg B (1985) Forensic research: expanding the concept of applied archaeology. Am Antiq 50:650–655. https://doi.org/10.2307/280329

Skinner M, Sterenberg J (2005) Turf wars: authority and responsibility for the investigation of mass graves. Forensic Sci Int 151:221–232. https://doi.org/10.1016/j.forsciint.2004.12.034

Statistikmyndigheten SCB (2022) Statistikdatabasen. https://www.statistikdatabasen.scb.se/pxweb/sv/ssd/. Accessed 3 July 2024

Stjernquist B (1992) Nils-Gustaf Gejvall och hans forskning. Fornvännen 87:115–120

Swedish Police Authority (n.d.) The Swedish Police Authority. https://polisen.se/en/the-swedish-police/the-swedish-police-authority. Accessed 3 July 2024

Chapter 5
Hands-on Workshops on Forensic Archaeology in Europe: Benefits and Requirements

Patricia van der Burgt

Abstract Forensic archaeology workshops in Europe offer vital training for police, forensic specialists, and archaeologists, focusing on excavation and documentation techniques critical to crime scene investigations. These workshops simulate scenarios involving illegal graves, incorporating human behavior, taphonomic processes, and archaeological methodologies. However, challenges such as limited access to human taphonomy facilities and reliance on non-human analogs reduce realism. Interdisciplinary workshops benefit all forensic team members, enhancing understanding and collaboration, while specialized workshops tailored for forensic archaeologists address advanced skills and professional accreditation. Standardizing training and increasing access to taphonomy facilities are essential for improving forensic archaeological practices in Europe.

Keywords Forensic Archaeology · Excavation Workshops · Illegal Graves · Taphonomic Processes · Interdisciplinary Training

5.1 Introduction to Forensic Archaeology Workshops

In several countries around the world, the benefits of involving a forensic archaeologist in forensic excavations have long been recognized. Although in most European countries it still is not standard practice to have an archaeologist present at such crime scenes, the number of European forensic archaeologists is slowly growing. At the same time, there is a growing need for adequate advanced training opportunities for these archaeologists.

Several institutions and facilities throughout Europe organize yearly forensic excavation workshops, among them the Forensic Archaeology Subgroup of the

P. van der Burgt (✉)
State Archaeological Heritage Office of Saxony, Dresden, Germany
e-mail: Patricia.vanderBurgt@lfa.sachsen.de

P. M. Barone, WJ M. Groen (eds.), *Forensic Archaeology and New Multidisciplinary Approaches*, Soil Forensics, https://doi.org/10.1007/978-3-031-86308-0_5

Scene-of-Crime Working Group of the European Network of Forensic Science Institutes (ENFSI). Usually, participation is open to police and forensic specialists, in which case the participating forensic archaeologists often are asked to supervise a small team. Although the interdisciplinary team management experience gathered in this way is invaluable, forensic archaeologists also need special training opportunities tailored to their exact needs.

One factor has a limiting effect on the practical training potential in these exercises. In the European training, life-sized dolls or plastic human skeletons, and sometimes pig cadavers, have to be used. Experience in excavating and decomposing human remains is duly necessary, but if this is desired or needed, almost always a workshop has to be found outside of Europe. Presently, eleven human taphonomy research institutes are in operation worldwide, and several if not all facilities offer short courses or have visiting scientist programs. The only opportunity to gain experience in the excavation and recovery of decomposing human remains in Europe would be at the currently only research facility in the Netherlands (ARISTA). More human taphonomy research facilities are urgently needed for the specific research involved as well as to offer training in dealing with decomposed human remains to police and forensic specialists. Until this becomes a reality, excavating dolls or maybe pig cadavers will be the default training experience.

As mentioned above, it is still not standard procedure to call in an archaeologist for any forensic search, excavation, or recovery of an outdoor surface scatter of human remains. For this reason, basic archaeological methods should be taught to police and non-archaeologist specialists, so they have experience in excavation and documentation techniques if they need to excavate without guidance.

After having organized and supervised several excavation workshops for police and having presented on the topic at the Annual Meeting of Forensic Archaeologists (EMFA) in Denmark 2019 (van der Burgt 2019), in this article I will elaborate on the organization and orientation of hands-on workshops.

5.2 Parameters Influencing an Illegal Grave

To allow direct control over the learning outcome, the exact content and execution of the workshop needs to be planned in detail and in consideration of the type of workshop that is intended before the mock grave is made accordingly. This requires the assessment of the degree of impact of several parameters on the illegal grave, such as human behavior, depositional history, and taphonomic processes. These also apply to clandestine single graves as well as to surface scatters of human skeletal material, mass fatality incidents, and mass graves (Moran and Gold 2019); and partially also to pits in which material evidence like weapons or drugs are hidden.

Broadly speaking, three categories of parameters can be defined that have a direct influence on an illegal grave: in the first place human behavior, available options and circumstances, followed by taphonomic processes, and finally the quality of excavation and documentation, and the resulting reconstruction of events.

Determining factors concerning human behavior are quite difficult to model, as they depend not only on the existing circumstances in any given situation but also on the character and abilities of the perpetrator, whose behavior, strength, and state of mind have a direct impact on the choice of location and manner in which the grave is made. Furthermore, practical issues like available transportation, access to tools, soil type, and the weather at the time of concealment have to be considered. While preparing mock graves, these factors will be different and thus have a very different impact, the most obvious being that the location of the graves will be chosen to accommodate teaching purposes.

Taphonomic processes cause changes that are quite problematic to reconstruct in a workshop in which dolls or plastic skeletons have to be used. In the absence of a corpse, there is no decay and putrefaction, there is no smell, and there are no thriving bacteria, insects, mammals, or birds that may actively change the crime scene. Other biological processes, like animal burrowing and plant root disturbances, will also be different from a normal grave situation. By default, the burial of a doll or plastic skeleton will always be more similar to a cache used for hiding objects than to an authentic illegal grave. Some possible traces will be the same, like recently cut tree roots in, or tool negatives on the pit walls. Because of the disturbance of the soil, differences in vegetation may be apparent if the mock grave was prepared shortly before the workshop. Also, general soil formation processes will continue to take place. Depending on soil type, type of refill, weather, and time, the lack of a decaying corpse will cause the refill to sooner regain the same consistency as the undisturbed soil, and after a relatively short period, signs of changes in vegetation and soil disturbance will no longer be perceptible.

The deposition history or reconstruction of events, as well as the contextual association and classification of the material evidence, can be simulated quite easily. Data from a real case could be used, or a detailed scenario could be drafted, according to which the grave and its contents may then be realized. Together with the skeleton or doll, a range of objects and traces fitting the scenario can be buried. During the excavation, the focus should be on detailed excavation and documentation. If the excavation is executed following archaeological standards, the reconstruction of the deposition history, by creating a Harris matrix, helps toward "solving" the case. A full documentation of each layer and object, including a photo, the exact location, and a description, ensures that a correct association, contextualization, and interpretation is possible. This is necessary to generate an accurate reconstruction of the sequence of events—a regular procedure on archaeological excavations. The reconstruction can then be compared with the original scenario. The more similar these are, the better the excavation and documentation have served their intended purpose.

It is important to keep in mind that not all of the parameters can be simulated, as their absence plays a role in the reconstruction of events after the excavation exercise. However, some of the parameters can be easily modeled in a mock setting to achieve a realistic learning environment. An interesting and challenging learning environment can be created by several different measures like an unexpected shape of the grave pit, a specific layout of the doll or skeleton, and the amount and location of evidence.

5.3 General Remarks on the Development of Excavation Workshops

Forensic archaeology is not just about a list of standard gear and choice of methods needed for an excavation. It includes a set of theoretical approaches to human behavior, site formation, and site transformation, which offer a framework for search, recovery, and interpretation, as well as considerations concerning the practical execution of an excavation. This background should be explained to non-archaeologists, or else the taught excavation and documentation methods will not be understood as paramount to the full excavation process and may be incorrectly modified or skipped altogether.

Typically, a range of specialized knowledge and skills from neighboring sciences are incorporated within a forensic archaeological investigation. This includes entomological, palynological, and pedological analyses and their interpretation, physical anthropological assessments, and facial reconstruction. It also encompasses searches by remote sensing, cadaver dogs, and the use of special equipment like Total Station, Global Positioning System (GPS), and 3D-scanner, including the analysis and interpretation of the results. It is advantageous for all participants to practice certain skills during a workshop, such as assessing the local geomorphology, determining the undisturbed soil structure, and conducting an extensive search. However, in a forensic setting, most specialisms and skills will have to be executed and reported on by experienced specialists.

As excavation workshops are usually planned for only two days, there is almost no time to include even a small selection of the analyses and techniques mentioned above. Especially extensive assessments like remote sensing techniques demand a lot of time. For this reason, these should ideally be conducted in advance of excavation workshops, during which it then also would be possible to practice not just one but several non-invasive techniques, and their results could then be analyzed and compared.

The above shows that the workshop needs to be scheduled exactly with enough time reserved for a full excavation experience. If a search is to be included in the training, it should be as short as possible. The localization and first documentation of the grave pit also will take time, before the actual excavation may start. Simple concepts, like the setting up of special work areas, where to put the spoil heap and the choice of excavation method suiting the actual circumstances, need to be addressed. The chosen method should have a verifiable degree of standardization to ensure that the results achieved using it in a real case will hold up in court (Evis 2016). The archaeological excavation process will allow a detailed reconstruction and interpretation of the sequence of events, which can be used for profiling. Therefore, it is important to reserve enough time after the excavation itself is finished, to generate a reconstruction and discuss the details about the victim and perpetrator that were noticed, as well as to generate a sequence of deposition of contexts and objects and check if all interpretative statements derived from the results are justified.

Depending on the general direction and goal of the workshop, a homemade life-size doll made of stuffed old clothes makes the situation very lifelike, and the recovery can be very quick. A plastic, unassembled, life-sized human skeleton has a somewhat higher learning potential. If the skeleton is put in the grave without clothing, the participants learn to differentiate human skeletal elements, they get some practice in exposing the "bones," and they learn to assess the position of the skeleton from only a few exposed bones (e.g., direction, supine or prone, position of extremities). Also, this enables participants to recognize the importance of documenting the exact position of the skeleton as a whole.

A large variety of trace evidence can be simulated, like shoe and tool traces, fingerprints, DNA, and hairs. Their exact locations need to be documented during the preparation of the grave, so it can be established during the workshop which items were recovered—and which were missed. Even though for financial or other reasons it may not always be possible to analyze all recovered material, it might be interesting to create certain special conditions, to see how materials will react to the environment and which trace evidence can be recovered after a certain amount of time: Is the letter that was put in the pocket of the jacket still readable after one year? Are the fingerprints on the credit card in the wallet still there? From each of such try-outs, one can learn, even if they are conducted in a non-scientific manner. The result of any analysis that can be carried out because the trace was recovered in the first place emphasizes the advantages of using archaeological methods in forensic settings.

It is interesting to note that more trace evidence is preserved as generally expected. One example is the recovery of personifiable DNA from an unexpected location during a workshop that took place 1.5 years after the preparation of the grave.

In another workshop, while preparing the mock grave, a pistol was fired several times into the "body" in the pit, and subsequently, the gun was thrown into the pit as well. The excavation took place about eight months later. It was established that the bullet channels were still visible in the undisturbed soil at the bottom of the pit, and their exact directions could be documented (the bullets were recovered too). This allowed a reconstruction of the position of the marksman (Losert 2023).

5.4 Interdisciplinary Trainings

All specialists who usually present at an exhumation or excavation of an illegal grave take profit from participating in an interdisciplinary workshop, which allows for intensive cooperation, exchange of expertise, and implementation of new techniques. The main goal of a training workshop for non-archaeologists is to teach a better understanding of the archaeological methodology and process. Ideally, this should lead to the realization that forensic archaeologists are very well equipped to execute a forensic excavation, as well as to the practical idea of calling in a forensic archaeologist the next time an excavation is necessary. If possible, the generally present notion "anyone can dig, so let's just do it" should be modified into "an archaeologist could be helpful here, so let's call them." This principle is important to convey. The presence of an archaeologist on site is also helpful if the recovered human skeletal remains are archaeologically relevant. The correct action that needs to be undertaken in such cases (cease all work and call an archaeologist) is sometimes disregarded, although conducting an unauthorized excavation is a breach of law in all European countries (van der Burgt 2023; Hemker et al. 2023).

As mentioned in the introduction, the benefits of involving an archaeologist and the use of archaeological methods in forensic investigations have been recognized for several decades; however, in most countries in Europe and in the majority of cases, the calling in of a forensic archaeologist is still not standard procedure. Moreover, public prosecution often has no idea of the existence of specialists in forensic archaeology and their relevance in an investigation.

Due to the fact that an archaeologist will not always be present during forensic excavations, police should have the opportunity to learn how to excavate with minimum standards, while getting a brief overview of theoretical and other topics to get some idea of this archaeological framework. Forensic specialists and police generally have an approximate idea about how to excavate, as the process is similar to crime scene documentation. However, some of the necessary steps, like preparation, systematic excavation, and the generation of full documentation, are ignored or overseen because their relevance is underestimated or unknown. This means that workshops designed for police, covering not only basic excavation and documentation techniques but also general archaeological theory and background, become all the more important. *A Best Practice Manual of Forensic Archaeology*, in which also minimum standards are specified, would be helpful for police in conducting excavations without the presence of an archaeologist.

A forensic excavation workshop is a very good opportunity to demonstrate that full archaeological documentation and working within a local or a national grid—something that is not a standard on police excavations—have many advantages. The use of reference points with exact coordinates of the grid system that is used is very helpful, as photos with such points can be optically rectified and allow the exact localization of a Structure for Motion model or drone photos.

During the workshop, it should be conveyed that documentation is more than taking just a photo and participants should obtain a better understanding of how and when to exactly document which situations. In situations where all modern technology is available on site, they need to know when to tell the GPS specialist to take coordinates of certain points, how to put in reference points for drone photos, when the next 3D scan is necessary, when a full description is necessary, and much more.

5.5 Training for Archaeologists

The urgent need for special workshops solely for forensic archaeologists has become apparent over the last ten years. Continuing training opportunities need to be prepared in such a way that the learning outcome and the intended assessment of the degree of professionalism are controlled and can be documented. Non-archaeologists should not be allowed to participate in these workshops, as this would blur the learning experience or examination of the forensic archaeologists, who need to be able to focus solely on executing the excavation and evaluation correctly and should not carry any responsibility for potential mistakes made by others during such workshops.

To allow quality control of forensic archaeology practice, an accreditation option for forensic archaeologists offered by an independently accredited institution would be helpful. Part of a basic accreditation program could be excavation workshops, combined with a theoretical examination (Evis 2016). To guarantee that workshop results are generally comparable and a straightforward assessment of candidates can be achieved, it would be necessary to prepare mock graves that are consistently similar and of consistent quality.

The currently only forensic archaeology accreditation in Europe (not related to a specific institute) is offered by the British Chartered Institute for Archaeologists (CIfA) and is based on British excavation methods and legal framework, which makes it less suitable for other European countries.

5.6 Conclusions

Forensic excavation workshops as continuing training opportunities should be planned meticulously beforehand, to ensure a certain control over the desired learning outcome. Parameters that have a direct influence on the burying of a victim are addressed, which partially also influence the making of a mock grave. Participants need to understand archaeological methodology, as well as the possible consequences of not following general excavation protocol.

Ideally, excavation workshops could be organized by human taphonomy research facilities using human body donations, which is only one of the reasons why the foundation of further facilities across Europe would be welcomed.

Excavation workshops should be divided into (at least) two types: an interdisciplinary, basic exercise open to all forensic specialists and one developed solely for forensic archaeologists. Until standard operating procedures include always having an (accredited) forensic archaeologist on site during searches, excavations, and the recovery of surface scatters, police must have at least a general idea of archaeological methods and theory, to recover as much court-admissible evidence as possible. This means that as continuing learning opportunities hands-on excavation exercises are urgently needed for police and other forensic specialists.

Apart from such basic exercises, forensic archaeologists need specially developed, advanced workshops, which could also be part of an accreditation program.

Bibliography

Evis L (2016) Forensic Archaeology. The application of comparative excavation methods and recording systems. Archaeopress, Oxford

Hemker C, Hönig H, van der Burgt P (2023) Der Mann im Berg—ein Kriminalfall aus dem Erzgebirge. Anschnitt 75:167–175

Losert A (2023) Forensische Archäologie. Workshop des K7 Würzburg. Antenne PP Ufr 3:52–54

Moran KS, Gold CL (2019) Forensic archaeology. Multidisciplinary perspectives. Springer Nature Switzerland, Cham

van der Burgt P (2019) Some thoughts on exercises in forensic archaeology in Germany. Paper presented at the 8th European Meeting of Forensic Archaeologists, Moesgaard Museum, Aarhus, Denmark, 22–23 August 2019

van der Burgt P (2023) The man in the mountain—documentation and forensic excavation. Paper presented at the 11th European Meeting of Forensic Archaeologists, Institute of Legal Medicine and Forensic Sciences, Madrid, 27–29 September 2023

Chapter 6
Forensic Archaeology, Forensic Taphonomy, and Outdoor Crime Scene Reconstruction in America: Personal Perspectives, 40 Years in the Making

Dennis C. Dirkmaat, Luis L. Cabo, and Joe Adserias-Garriga

Abstract This chapter presents a personal perspective on the evolution of forensic archaeology and forensic taphonomy in the United States over the last 40 years. Initially a niche application within forensic anthropology, forensic archaeology and taphonomy have transformed into essential components for reconstructing outdoor crime scenes. The authors highlight key historical developments, including the paradigm shift from a laboratory-focused discipline to one incorporating field-based outdoor scene processing. They discuss the integration of archaeological principles, taphonomic interpretations, and crime scene reconstruction methods to improve evidence recovery and analysis. Three case studies illustrate the growth and applications of forensic archaeology and taphonomy in diverse outdoor contexts.

Keywords Forensic Archaeology · Forensic Taphonomy · Outdoor Crime Scene Reconstruction · Forensic Anthropology Evolution · Postmortem Interval Analysis

6.1 Introduction

Most of us are familiar with the traditional "March of Progress" figure, which represents human evolution as a set of profile figures marching in line, with a modern human leading the way. This modern human is followed by a series of hominins that become increasingly dissimilar to him (the leader of the pack is almost invariably a male) as the sequence moves rearward until the series is closed by a quadrupedal primate. The original figure appeared as "The Road to *Homo sapiens*" in the classic book *Early Man* by Francis Clark Howell (1965), although it was inspired by a long

D. C. Dirkmaat (✉) · L. L. Cabo · J. Adserias-Garriga
Department of Applied Forensic Sciences, Mercyhurst University, Erie, PA, USA
e-mail: ddirkmaat@mercyhurst.edu; lcabo@mercyhurst.edu; jadseriasgarriga@mercyhurst.edu

P. M. Barone, WJ M. Groen (eds.), *Forensic Archaeology and New Multidisciplinary Approaches*, Soil Forensics, https://doi.org/10.1007/978-3-031-86308-0_6

line of similar "Ladder of Progress" representations (Dawson 2024; Gould 1989). The book was extremely popular, and variations of the illustration have become ubiquitous across all forms of popular culture, from ads and dorm wall posters to t-shirts and bumper stickers.

As this is a volume mainly aimed at students and professionals with archaeology and biological anthropology backgrounds, most readers will also identify the depiction as a gross and fundamentally misguiding oversimplification that not only fails to appropriately describe the historical process leading to the emergence of modern humans but also contradicts key evolutionary principles.

Outlining just the main misrepresentations of evolutionary biology that the "March of Progress" contains would require its own chapter, if not a whole volume (we warmly recommend the first chapter in Gould 1989 as a superb introduction to the subject), but all of them ultimately derive from the presentation of human evolution as a linear, deterministic process—a sort of road to perfection that misses all the nuance, variability, and related but diverse species trajectories that constituted human evolution.

Similar to how evolutionary theory and evolutionary history go hand-in-hand, the proper understanding and discussion of any scientific field is incomplete without a critical understanding of its history and evolution, including landmark findings and conceptual changes that led to its current form, the problems and questions it sought to answer at each step, and the methodological or conceptual obstacles it had to overcome to do so. Also, as in evolutionary history, historical context, circumstance, and environmental conditions are key to understanding that sequence of landmark changes, problems, and obstacles. The evolution of a scientific discipline is not a deterministic progression through any Platonic scale of perfection, deriving solely from academic introspection, but an accumulation of gradual adaptations to maximize fitness in changing conditions. It is sometimes born from pure intellectual disquisition, but more often from accident, and always from necessity, through a wide variety of tentative views, steps, missteps, and individual circumstances. Scientific fields do not progress in a single direction as monolithic structures, and personal perspectives, experiences, and circumstances are important both to configure and to understand the end results.

However, when tasked with describing the historical development of a discipline, it is rather difficult to avoid falling into "March of Progress" oversimplifications, particularly when having to synthesize the story for introductory courses or brief communications, such as book chapters or journal articles. The problem is that the linear march narrative can also be highly misleading in this context and induce potential misconceptions that can affect the debate on alternative visions of the field, how its practitioners should be formed and trained, or in what directions the field should seek to advance in the future.

We have tried our hand at presenting general outlines of the historic development of forensic archaeology and forensic anthropology in past publications, mainly from a U.S. perspective but also trying to pay attention to broader conceptions and developments in other countries (Cabo and Dirkmaat 2015; Dirkmaat and Cabo 2012; Dirkmaat et al. 2008). Although we have always tried to avoid falling into simplified timelines and to present reasonably nuanced discussions of external factors and influences, technical and conceptual innovations, historical contexts, and alternative views, we feel that those necessarily streamlined narratives were still missing some important points and perspectives, and perhaps left the door open to some potential "March of Progress" misinterpretations.

One such misinterpretation is a view of the debate about alternative views of forensic archaeology (namely, either as a component of forensic anthropology, or as a completely independent field), as rooted in either ethereal academic disquisitions or, even worse, maybe in some sort of guild interests or mindsets, as opposed to in actual forensic and scientific needs. One of the central elements of the view of the field that we tried to share in past publications is that the discussion should not revolve around the title in the degree that forensic archaeology practitioners should hold, but rather on how they should be trained, and what skill sets they should possess and cultivate. This view also stresses the need to think not in terms of individual profiles, but relative to team processing efforts, to be carried out by a variety of professionals with broad, complementary backgrounds. In terms of training and education for the next generation of forensic archaeology practitioners, this also means that one can not only arrive at the same spot from different degrees and general backgrounds, but also that such diversity of training paths and perspectives is actually a necessity for the investigation of outdoor scenes, such as burials, mass graves, fire scenes, and searches. In other words, the practical and conceptual frameworks of forensic archaeology should be founded on the needs of the forensic scene and forensic investigation, rather than on the academic placement of the discipline.

We believe that this needs-based, scene-centered view has played a much more central role in the development of modern forensic anthropology/archaeology than purely academic debates. A key element that is hard to convey and easily missed in traditional linear narratives of the evolution of the field is the dependence of forensic anthropology/archaeology on the awareness, understanding, and perceptions of law officials regarding what the field can contribute to their forensic investigations. Unlike other scientific fields, the development of our discipline required not only research, as well as conceptual and methodological innovation, but a sustained effort to convince law enforcement and legal system officials of its utility and reliability, almost agency by agency, from the local to the federal and international levels. In this evangelizing mission, the converts were not brought into the fold through academic arguments and research articles, but through practical demonstrations of how forensic investigations were dramatically improved through the inclusion of forensic anthropology and forensic archaeology.

Here is where personal perspectives can add some relevant nuance, fill some of the voids in traditional historical overviews, and help prevent "March of Progress" misinterpretations. In our case, the three authors possess more than 80 combined years of experience processing forensic cases. One of us (DCD) started practicing forensic archaeology more than three decades ago, his career covering roughly three-quarters of the development of modern American forensic anthropology, and the key period during which forensic archaeology was developed and became broadly accepted as a valuable component of forensic scene investigation. He started applying forensic archaeology during a time when forensic anthropology was understood as a discipline exclusively focused on decedent identification through osteological analysis at the laboratory, and forensic archaeology was alien not only to law enforcement but also to most forensic anthropologists. During the following decades, he was intimately involved and can be considered one of the driving forces in the gradual acceptance of the discipline by both of those groups of professionals. He also was a firsthand witness and participant in the evolution and improvement of the field through the growing influence of forensic taphonomy as the guiding element in forensic archaeology.

In this chapter, we present a more personal perspective of the development of forensic archeology in the United States, as seen "from the trenches" during the last three and a half decades, and discuss its impact throughout this time period through case examples.

6.2 A Brief Overview of the History of Forensic Anthropology/Archaeology in the United States

Before getting into the personal perspective, we feel we must offer at least a quick, simplified outline of the history of our field(s), as practiced in the United States. For a deeper review of the subject, we direct the reader to previous publications (Dirkmaat et al. 2008; Dirkmaat and Cabo 2012; and, especially, Cabo and Dirkmaat 2015; and references therein).

The story begins in the early 1970s when a group of biological anthropologists who were more or less frequently consulted by law enforcement founded the *Physical Anthropology* section of the American Academy of Forensic Sciences (AAFS). At that point, forensic anthropology was defined as an applied laboratory field that borrowed physical anthropology techniques to estimate some biological characteristics of the decedent, later termed the *biological profile* (sex, age, population affinity, and stature), with the sole stated goal of aiding in decedent identification. Although some archaeologists are documented to have been very episodically involved in some forensic cases as early as the late 60 s, the term *forensic archaeology* was not in use yet, and the name of the AAFS section had indeed been carefully selected precisely to prevent archaeologists or cultural anthropologists from joining the section (Cabo and Dirkmaat 2015; and references therein).

Although a few journal articles started proposing the concept of forensic archaeology by the mid to late 70 s (Bass and Birkby 1978; Morse et al. 1976), the field did not start gaining real visibility until the early 80 s. Snow (1982) provided the first reference describing the utility of archaeology in forensic cases (interestingly, also providing a surprisingly early and lucid understanding of the importance of taphonomy for the future development of the field), but what first brought the field to the forefront was the publication of not one, but two forensic archaeology manuals the following year (Morse et al. 1983; Skinner and Lazenby 1983).

However, by the early 90 s forensic archaeology was still an oddity, practiced regularly only by an extremely small number of American forensic anthropologists. The number of practitioners started increasing during the second half of the decade, stirred by two developments.

One of these was the development of modern forensic bone trauma analysis, primarily by forensic anthropologists Hugh E. Berryman and Steven A. Symes, who were both employed at the Memphis, Tennessee Medical Examiner's Office (with credit to the Chief ME at the time for his foresight). They pointed out that bone trauma analysis requires the examination of even the smallest of bone fragments associated with the trauma. It also requires detailed scene information to detect and remove taphonomic biases (separating blunt force trauma damage due to carnivore activity vs. a baseball bat, for example). These interdigitated requirements therefore relied on efficient scene recoveries that maximized the recovery of all related evidence, even tiny pieces of bone, and included much more extensive documentation of the scene context than was typically or previously acquired. Their suggestion that skeletal trauma analysis did not start in the lab, but at the scene, provided a great argument for the standard employment of forensic archaeology on all forensic scenes.

This perspective also served to expand the focus of forensic anthropology from just decedent identification to the reconstruction of events surrounding death and deposition, including manner of death and postmortem alteration, thus introducing an important new and unique component to the theory and practice of forensic anthropology.

The second and closely related element that came to favor a more widespread acceptance and recognition of forensic archaeology during that decade was the emergence and rapid embrace of the field of forensic taphonomy by American forensic anthropologists. One of the main impulses for this development was the publication of the first forensic taphonomy volume by Haglund and Sorg (1997). Bone trauma analysis fell directly under the purview of forensic taphonomy, and both those fields benefitted directly from the detailed documentation of the scene's context through forensic archaeology.

These three novel components (forensic archaeology, forensic taphonomy, and skeletal trauma analysis) combined to allow new and unique scientific inferences not only on potential trauma but also on other events surrounding the death and deposition of the remains, including hypotheses on the original position and location of the remains, the post-mortem interval, and specific actions and tools utilized to attempt to hide the body or destroy evidence, etc. The confluence of these three closely interrelated disciplines decisively changed the very definition, focus, and scope of forensic anthropology (Dirkmaat et al. 2008; Cabo and Dirkmaat 2015).

By 2012, in a survey carried out by two of the authors (DCD and LLC) among the members of the, at the time, *Physical Anthropology Section* of the American Academy of Forensic Sciences (AAFS), a majority (78%) of American forensic anthropologists declared considering forensic taphonomy as the most important component of forensic anthropology. Forensic archaeology came third, just after osteology, and a similar majority declared preferring to process their forensic scenes themselves, pointing toward forensic archaeological techniques as the appropriate toolset to do so (Cabo and Dirkmaat 2015).

The results of that survey led the following year to a referendum and overwhelming positive vote to change the name of the AAFS section from *Physical Anthropology* to just *Anthropology*, with the explicit goal of recognizing the contributions of forensic archaeology and allowing practitioners with a strict archaeological background to join as members.

Still, for more than three decades, from the early 70s to the early 2000s, and almost half of the first author's career, an overwhelming majority of forensic anthropologists still viewed their field as basically just an application of osteology, in which the anthropologist expected to receive a box of skeletal remains in their lab, for the nearly sole purpose of providing an estimate of the biological profile (population affinity, sex, age, and stature). The results of these analyses were used to reduce the number of missing persons with the express purpose of reaching a positive identification. Law enforcement understood that rather limited role as the primary, if not exclusive, role of forensic anthropology, and for the better part of that period was extremely wary to allow forensic anthropologists (civilians) onto their forensic scenes, and even more reticent to let them take charge of the recovery through forensic archaeological techniques.

Changing that mindset demanded more than research publications, meeting presentations, and academic debates. It required a sustained effort, through the years, to show officers of the law and medicolegal authorities the benefits of forensic archaeology for their investigations of outdoor and other types of forensic scenes. During that process, each scene served to reveal new applications, expected outputs, and inferences, not only to the involved law enforcement but also to the forensic anthropologist/archeologist. In the remainder of this chapter, we present three forensic anthropology cases in a chronological order, starting from the time in which forensic archaeology was still a foreign concept both to law enforcement (who performed almost all scene recoveries) and to most American forensic anthropologists, and ending with a case example in which the fully developed field of forensic archaeology/forensic taphonomy is presented. Even when this is an extremely small number of examples, we think that they illustrate the progressive increase in the number of scenarios and applications of forensic archaeology that have characterized the development of the field and served to define it. These scenarios, applications, and outputs surely have not only exceeded the expectations of law officials at the time but also upended the narrow original conceptions of forensic archaeology as only an auxiliary field focusing primarily on excavation and mapping, rather than a discipline focused on scene event reconstructions.

6.3 Being an American Forensic Anthropologist in the Late 1980s

The primary author (DCD) started out in the field of forensic anthropology in the 1980s, armed with a Ph.D. in Anthropology, and co-concentrations in physical anthropology (specifically, human skeletal biology, bioarchaeology, and paleoanthropology) and archaeology (North American archaeology and zooarchaeology).

Dirkmaat's original focus was on human skeletal biology, which he applied to the analysis of prehistoric Native Americans and paleoanthropological remains (Neanderthals and other Middle Pleistocene hominins). He was also trained in zooarchaeology, having analyzed many large assemblages of animal remains (fragmented and significantly altered) from archaeological sites throughout the United States. These skill sets would prove not only applicable but extremely useful for dealing with outdoor forensic scenes throughout the northeastern United States.

The earliest forensic cases in which Dirkmaat was involved at that time focused on the analysis of bones discovered in outdoor contexts and brought to the attention of medicolegal authorities. Most of these cases simply involved the evaluation of the bones as to whether they represented animal or human remains. These forensic significance evaluations continue being the most common cases conducted throughout the year nowadays.

Law enforcement and medicolegal professionals (including forensic pathologists) face these assessments every day, during forensic searches and when citizens come across suspicious bones in the woods. Law enforcement can either dismiss them immediately as animal bones, and thus deemed to be not forensically significant and unworthy of further investigation, or they may conduct "just-in-case-they-are-human" recoveries, which involve significant use of resources (manpower and time) to secure and process the scene. Thus, by quickly deferring these evaluations to an outside expert before proceeding directly into scene processing, law enforcement can prevent wasting efforts and resources. The forensic anthropologist trained in biological anthropology can differentiate human from animal bones in situ, and at a variety of levels, including relative to complete skeletons, isolated bones, bone fragments, and even highly altered (e.g., burned) bones. This is a key skill not only for initial evaluations, but also when processing the scene, as the remains in a burial can be those of a pet, or the bones found scattered on the surface may represent an unrelated (non-forensically significant) set of animal remains.

Thus, the forensic anthropologist's specialized training in human skeletal biology and animal osteology provides unique opportunities for inclusion in the medicolegal investigation, as no other forensic specialists possess similar training and expertise. This was particularly important during the infancy of forensic archaeology in the early 90s, as the ability to apply forensic archaeology first required being called to the scene. The rapport with law enforcement officers or medico-legal professionals, gained from previous successful consultations or collaborations, especially for assessing forensic significance at the scene, exponentially increased the possibility of proposing a forensic archaeological intervention during scene investigations.

Still, most of the early cases in which Dirkmaat was involved at that time followed the old conception of forensic anthropology: law enforcement collected the bones and dropped them off at the laboratory for osteological analysis (usually only if identification by other means had proven difficult). These drop-offs often happened long after the recovery, and after other specialists had examined and manipulated the bones. Typically, the bones had been cleaned of soft tissue at the morgue (after all, forensic anthropologists do not deal with soft tissue, do they?) and sometimes somebody had introduced alterations such as putting molding clay on the cranial elements. The specialists to which the bones were submitted before resorting to the forensic anthropologist, almost as a "Hail Mary," ranged from criminalists and forensic pathologists to odontologists or orthopedic doctors. Many of these professionals were inexperienced and either undertrained or completely untrained to deal with human remains and (unsurprisingly) often provided inaccurate guesses. Providing the right assessments and correcting these previous mistakes served both to increase rapport with the investigating agency and to increase their awareness of the convenience of involving the forensic anthropologist earlier in the investigation.

In addition to arriving late in the process, the box-of-bones usually came with little or no contextual information at all (i.e., "they were found outside, exposed to the elements." Why would it matter if "outside" meant the deep woods, a backyard, inside a burial, on a steep slope, or floating in the river?). There were neither requests nor attempts to reconstruct what happened at the scene (e.g., is this a homicide or a suicide?), or to provide hypotheses regarding elements such as the time that had elapsed since death and deposition. One of the main guiding principles of that conception of the field was that forensic anthropologists could not/should not provide opinions on the cause or manner of death, as it fell historically outside of their purview.

One could ask questions and make observations, though, both to the investigators and to oneself: Were these remains buried or on the surface? What does the staining of the bones mean? Why are some bones fractured, missing, or exhibiting gnaw marks? Why were they scattered? Could these remains have been originally deposited in the river somewhere upstream? How long they were at the scene? And even, does this suggest a homicide? One could also ponder and discuss with the investigators how some properly documented contextual information (even just a bit) might have helped to answer these and many other questions. For someone trained in archaeology, it was crystal clear that the recovery and, especially, the interpretation of outdoor forensic scenes would benefit dramatically from the introduction of archaeological principles, methods, and practices—especially and most particularly, the consideration of the *context* of the evidence, as understood in archaeology.

A comparison between how law enforcement processed indoor scenes with how outdoor scenes were processed also revealed sharp differences in standards, goals, and expectations. In contrast with the paucity of contextual information gathered during outdoor scene recoveries (where the main goal appeared to be quickly plucking the body from the scene to get it to the forensic pathologist ASAP), during the processing of the indoor scene, the location, position, and orientation of everything that could be potentially relevant were carefully noted in situ. All elements of the scene, and not only the human remains, were evaluated for forensic significance (i.e., whether they could be directly related to the death or deposition event), and all potential evidence was carefully documented through a variety of means and methods. In brief, at indoor scenes, the context was meticulously assessed and documented and provided the fodder for the construction of precise hypotheses on what had transpired at the scene before, during, and after its formation.

The main problem for law enforcement was that precise crime scene recovery techniques developed for indoor scenes did not translate well to outdoor scenes. Some of the key differences between indoor and outdoor scenes have to do with time and the degree of alteration of the bodies and the associated evidence. The indoor scene has usually been relatively pristine since the time it was created. Additionally, the timeframe between the deposition event and the discovery at the indoor scene is often relatively short (days and weeks). Outdoor scenes, on the other hand, may not be discovered for weeks, months, or years, during which they were exposed to the elements and a wide array of ecological factors and conditions. Outdoor scenes typically are also much larger and contextually more complex than indoor or urban scenes. Without walls, floors, and ceilings, outdoor scene boundaries appear largely undefined and lack the straightforward structural references for the creation of precise maps through simple techniques and instrumentation. Substrate surfaces at outdoor scenes exhibit complex topographies and likely multiple and varied levels of stratification. These additionally include not only the classic soil stratigraphies of classic archaeology but also those created by living soil elements (e.g., leaf litter). A wide variety of plants, vertebrates, arthropods, and many other natural environmental agents likely have significantly altered the evidence. This means that defining, documenting, and interpreting the contextual elements and relevant relationships at the outdoor scene required different and more sophisticated techniques than those being applied at indoor scenes. These were different principles, methods, and techniques for which law enforcement was not trained.

Paradoxically, in the early 90s law enforcement's answer to this added complexity was simplifying and lowering both standards and expectations when processing outdoor scenes. The assumption was that outdoor scenes had been altered by such a variety of natural factors and conditions, and often for such a long time, that it wasn't worth investing too much time or effort to process them, as most evidence would have been destroyed anyway. We could describe their standard approach to outdoor scenes at the time as "photograph-and-pluck."

If the "all-evidence-is-lost" (*lasciate ogni speranza*) argument was harder to defend when it came to burials, the main excuse in that case became that it would surely take far too long to excavate them using archaeological techniques ("archeological excavations take weeks, or months!"). Instead, just unearthing the remains with pickaxe and shovel (or better yet, the backhoe) to bring them as fast as humanely possible to the pathologist became the preferred "recovery" approach.

The result of these misconceptions was that the same critical questions and hypotheses routinely addressed at indoor scenes through law enforcement efforts could not be addressed scientifically at outdoor scenes. However, anybody with some training in anthropology and archaeology could see that archaeologists and paleontologists had solved most of the complications associated with the outdoor scene long ago and had been addressing and successfully answering the same kind of questions raised at these outdoor scenes for more than a century. Their main tool to do so was called archaeology. If forensic scenes displayed some differences in timing and composition as compared to typical archaeological sites, adapting to those novel contexts might only require a bit of retooling and tweaking of standard archaeological methods, principles, and practices, rather than the creation of a totally new discipline.

6.4 Early Influential Cases

Dirkmaat was allowed to put action behind his words ("archaeology has a place in medicolegal contexts") in two early cases, which were very influential in his early understanding of forensic archaeology and the configuration of outdoor crime scene processing protocols. The first case provided a clear example to illustrate the utility and benefits of archaeology, both to forensic anthropologists and law enforcement. The second one showed that taphonomic principles and interpretations provided an optimal backbone around to articulate forensic archaeology and to allow outputs and reconstructions of past events similar to those obtained at indoor scenes. Of course, those realizations were neither instantaneous nor completely (or particularly elegantly) articulated at the time, but significantly influenced his eventual conception of the fields of forensic anthropology, forensic archaeology, and forensic taphonomy.

6.5 Burned-out House Recovery, 20 Years After Body Deposition, Pennsylvania (1986)

After presenting a talk to a medicolegal group, one upper-level law enforcement official asked if Dirkmaat might be interested in attending a proposed search/recovery/excavation of a burned structure (an old wooden clapboard house) that recent investigations suggested contained the remains of a 17-year-old female, suspected to have been murdered 20 years earlier.

The site has been abandoned and overgrown since then (Fig. 6.1). The police were bringing heavy equipment to dig up the burned debris and assumed that they would be able to recognize significantly burned human bones and solve the mystery,

Fig. 6.1 The first forensic anthropology case of Dirkmaat was in 1986. Law enforcement suspected that the remains of a juvenile female individual were interred in the basement of a burned structure covered in dirt by a bulldozer 20 years earlier. The first steps of the recovery required the location of the structure in the deep woods and then the determination of the depth of the debris to the basement floor (**a**). Four feet of debris was removed by a backhoe while archaeologists monitored (**b**). Following excavation by hand of the lowest 2 feet of debris on the bottom of the basement (**c**), animal and human bones were located, as well as soil and artifacts such as pottery sherds (**d**). Following the recovery of the feature *en masse*, careful excavation and sifting (with geological sieves) in the laboratory resulted in the identification of hundreds of fragmented human teeth (**e**) and skeletal elements (**f**), leading to the creation of a biological profile of the decedent (late teenage, likely female individual)

even if in fact they were not sure of whether it could be reasonable to expect that anything could still be left of the decedent after 20 years.

Dirkmaat and three other graduate students in North American Archaeology from the University of Pittsburgh conducted the archaeological recovery. This included top-down excavation techniques to expose artifacts/evidence, consideration of complex stratigraphic profiles, context documentation and construction and interpretation of hypotheses of association based on evidence provenience (location, position, and orientation). That archaeological effort, and the presence of a forensic anthropologist with expertise in human and animal bones, allowed for the recognition of very small, highly fragmented, and badly burned human bones, differentiating them from similarly altered animal bones also found in the basement of the burned house.

The first step in the process involved determining the location of the original structure within the overgrown locality, which was eventually indicated by partially buried foundation stones. Following vegetation removal and test pit excavations, it was determined that the structure had a basement that extended nearly eight feet (around 250 cm) below the surface. It was also learned that a bulldozer had been used to fill in the cavity left by the house foundation after the fire.

A backhoe was brought in to remove the first 5–6 feet (~150–180 cm) of disturbed fill over the basement floor, where it was expected that the remains could be found. The controlled excavation (horizontal removal of 3–6 inches of disturbed fill at a time) by the backhoe and the dumping of the bucket scoops were carefully monitored by the archaeologists. The remaining 1–2 feet of fill were excavated by hand with archaeological trowels, brushes, and dental picks. After two days of excavation and exposure of the dirt floor of the basement, several small, scattered bone fragments were discovered. They were determined to be animal bones. However, numerous small fragments of calcined human bone and teeth, including a small fragment of a human mandibular condyle, were identified in an area of approximately 1 m × 1 m in dimension (Fig. 6.1d).

Given adverse weather conditions and lighting issues in the deep woods, it was decided to recover *en masse* the feature and take it to Dirkmaat's laboratory for detailed excavation under better lighting, with dental tools, and screening through fine-mesh geological sieves. This operation revealed hundreds of tiny fragments of bone and teeth, consistent with a single individual, and representing areas of the entire body, head to toe, torso to appendages, indicating that the body was likely brought to the scene shortly after the murder (and not secondarily moved from a suspected off-site burial location).

The primary lesson learned from this case was that the successful recovery of human remains from this type of forensic scene (an outdoor forensic scene involving highly altered human remains) required specialized skills and instruction beyond those provided by law enforcement training. It required methods, approaches, and techniques not derived from criminalistic indoor scene processing methods. The law enforcement classic method of location and recovery of the buried, burned human remains, using heavy equipment, would not have yielded a single human element, since the remains were so small, fragmented, and altered. They would have disturbed the scene greatly and, even if they had come across a human bone fragment by chance, they would not have been able to identify it as remains, much less animal or human. The use of archaeological methods to locate the miniscule human remains coupled with the ability to evaluate the forensic significance of those small bones in real time saved the day. In addition, the remains were found and documented in situ, in the location where they were placed at the time of original deposition. This information, in fact, provided important details of the history of the deposition event.

Cases like this demonstrated that archaeological methods, practices, principles, and goals (the archaeological skill set) are *uniquely* applicable to the recovery and interpretation of the outdoor forensic scene, which is vastly different from indoor scenes. They also made clear that the goal went beyond locating the evidence, but included understanding and interpreting its spatial distribution, as well as whether and/or how it had been altered. Further, it was possible to reconstruct elements such as the original position, location, and orientation of the evidence at the time of deposition.

A short list of skill required to complete a proper recovery at this type of forensic scene, meeting the standards and outputs expected from the processing of indoor crime scenes, includes (i) a detailed knowledge of human and animal osteology, at a level proficient in recognizing not only complete bones, but also highly fragmented and altered ones; (ii) understanding and properly documenting the environmental components of outdoor contexts (plants, animals, soils, ecological factors and conditions, etc.) that are relevant for the reconstruction of scene formation and depositional history of the remains; (iii) the theoretical and practical knowledge and understanding of archaeological methods, practices, and principles necessary to conduct effective and efficient searches, excavations, stratigraphic recognition, and interpretations, guided by the concepts of *context* (understanding the scene) and *association* (relating evidence to other evidence, to the scene, and to the event); and (iv) understanding the relevance and application of cartographic (mapping) documentation methods (creating small and large scale maps) to the interpretation not only of the spatial and stratigraphic distribution of the evidence and other materials, but of those taphonomic alterations observed on the human remains.

And thus, stricken on the road to Damascus, Dirkmaat decided to openly add forensic archaeology to the advertised repertoire of services to be provided as a forensic anthropologist and spent the rest of his career in the pursuit of developing and testing concepts, principles, and protocols for the application of forensic archaeology in searches, recoveries, and interpretations of a growing variety of forensic contexts. These range from surface scatters to buried bodies, through fatal fire scenes, and mass disaster scenes.

This unique configuration of archaeology applicable to forensic scenes suggests a discipline different from classic archaeology. Besides the need for skills in human and animal osteology, the evidence also required interaction with actively decomposing soft tissues, and therefore an understanding of the decomposition process. The information relevant for the estimation of elements such as postmortem interval (PMI) or taphonomic alteration under currently acting conditions is very different than that required for the interpretation of classic archaeological materials and requires documentation methods more related to those of the environmental sciences than of geology or archaeology. The medium and substrate to be excavated in forensic contexts can also differ sharply from those traditionally encountered in classic archaeology. For example, the loose ashes in fatal fire scenes, debris in mass-disaster scenes, leaf litter and other loose organic materials at surface scatters, or fresh, uncompacted layers of organic silts deposited inside a car submerged in a river do not lend themselves to classic archaeological techniques. Event reconstruction is much more finely grained, at a much finer time scale, typically in the range from hours to months, rather than decades to hundreds of years. To top it off, medicolegal considerations (chain of custody, handling of evidence, etc.) also had to be incorporated into forensic archaeological practice.

At that time, although a few references, such as the aforementioned Morse et al. (1983) and Skinner and Lazenby (1983), provided some good guidance on how to excavate classic forensic burial scenes, there was no guidebook on how to confront all those new materials, goals, constraints, and expanded contexts. Early practitioners in the 1980s and 1990s, like DCD, were essentially required to start from scratch and develop new protocols, approaches, and applications to cover that variety of forensic scenes, tasks, and contexts, from searches to recoveries in the woods, and to fatal fire scenes. All major concepts, including those of *context* and *association*, provenience, stratigraphy, Steno's Laws, etc., obviously had roots in traditional archaeology but, again, classic archaeological training was far from providing all answers.

Another major differentiating element demanding the development of new protocols was that most outdoor scenes do not involve burials but remains and evidence laid on the ground surface. The next case example illustrates how those scenes (to which we refer as *surface scatters*) were confronted in the early-mid 90s, and how forensic archaeology is also useful in those scenes, despite being very different from the classic excavation of archaeological sites.

6.6 A Second Case: Three Individuals in the Deep Woods on the Hillside, Pennsylvania (1994)

In late November of 1994, in the deciduous forests of southcentral Pennsylvania, a hunter stumbled upon a gruesome sight (Fig. 6.2). Human remains were peeking out from a thick layer of deciduous leaf litter. To the coroner's credit, who responded to the scene initially, he did not immediately start plucking bones from the pile but instead sent a picture to Dirkmaat for an opinion on how to proceed. Dirkmaat responded the next day to conduct a forensic archaeological recovery, which involved the search of the area for any displaced remains; detailed notation of context via written, photographic, and cartographic means; exposure (excavation) of the remains from beneath the leaf litter; and the creation of a detailed plan-view map of the distribution of the remains, combining hand-mapping techniques with electronic total station data. It was observed before the recovery that the fresh leaf litter, corresponding to the previous fall season, appeared only over the remains. This meant that the bodies had been deposited on the scene prior to the leaf fall (before October).

Fig. 6.2 An early forensic anthropology (forensic archaeology and forensic taphonomy) case conducted by Dirkmaat involved the discovery of three individuals in a dense deciduous forest in Pennsylvania (**a**). The remains were covered in recent leaf litter providing a postmortem interval (PMI) estimate of at least 3 months. The ensuing recovery (**b**, **c**) and scene mapping protocols (**d**) provided detailed evidence of the location, position, and orientation of the individuals, and further PMI details (e.g., remaining soft tissue) (**e**) provided more evidence to estimate time since death and deposition. The simple hand-drawn map provided the basis for the detailed past events reconstruction of a murder-suicide event by gunshot (**f**)

The plan view map showed that the individuals were sitting together in close proximity, on a bit of a slope. An adult individual was situated between two juveniles. Each of the individuals exhibited a single gunshot defect to the cranium (which provided important clues relative to the cause and manner of death). A gun was found lying at the knees of the adult.

It was noted that almost all the skeletal elements were still situated in anatomical position, suggesting that the remains were disturbed neither by animals nor humans after emplacement. The cranium of the adult individual in the middle, however, was displaced downward, but this could be more parsimoniously explained by displacement downslope simply by gravity.

Limited amounts of desiccated soft tissue still remained, which suggested a rough PMI estimate of at least a month or two, but no longer than a year. The clothing worn by the individuals did not indicate cold weather conditions (Pennsylvania winters and late falls are bitter).

The analysis of the position and orientation of the remains, relative to the topography and details of the scene, permitted the construction of a hypothesis on the sequence of events (and hence, the manner of death). The individuals were sitting closely together on a slight slope, in the middle of the woods. The adult pulled out a gun (with his right hand) and shot the older juvenile (his daughter) first, catching her by surprise, as she showed no signs of struggle (arms to the side and legs splayed as clearly illustrated in the plan-view map). The younger juvenile (his youngest daughter) was then shot in the head. However, her body position and orientation showed evidence of a struggle in which she was apparently trying to pull away from the adult. As a further indication of a struggle, the adult's leg was situated directly over her legs, suggesting a restraining effort. A third shot was a self-inflicted wound to the head of the adult, who was holding the gun in his right hand. The arm dropped, and the gun was released at the knees of the adult.

This case reaffirmed the critical importance of processing the outdoor scene via forensic archaeological methods. It did not involve the classic excavation of a body interred in the ground, but the concepts of context, superposition, and association were applied to other materials, and all associated evidence was documented in situ following detailed and systematic searches of the surrounding areas to determine scene boundaries, contents, and context. At a small scale, the remains were situated on a slope at a clearing, good spot to suggest sitting down and resting during a walk in the woods. On a large scale, this location was in a thickly wooded context, far from roads and potential encounters with inopportune witnesses. The position and orientation of the individuals relative to one another, to the scene, and to the remaining evidence were carefully documented via written, photographic, and cartographic means and told a sad but parsimonious and cohesive story.

Importantly, in addition to the comprehensive forensic archaeological recovery, it was realized that many more questions—most related to the history of the body on the scene—could be addressed by expanding the consideration of the contextual setting beyond just the body. There was now a concerted effort to document the natural components of the scene (plants, geology, environment) to better understand: (a) how the body and associated evidence has been impacted (i.e., moved, removed, and altered) by natural environmental factors, as well as (b) how the scene itself (i.e., the local environment) has been impacted and changed over time by the addition of a decomposing human body. This strongly suggested that the focus of the recoveries could not be solely on the body in isolation but required more of an ecological approach in which attributes of the surrounding scene are carefully considered. More precise methods to record and document the local environmental factors and conditions (e.g., temperature measurements, canopy coverage, local hydric regime, soil characteristics, insect and vertebrate presence) could further improve PMI estimation and, in other more complex cases, answer other types of questions regarding the events having transpired at the scene.

Therefore, the goal is not just plucking the body from the outdoor scene, but reconstructing the history of the body and associated evidence at the specific scene, from the time of original deposition until recovery. There must be attempts to explain why things are out of place or missing (i.e., what criminal or taphonomic agents are likely responsible). Could alterations at the scene be attributed to humans? Might it be possible to reconstruct what the scene looked like at the time of creation, paralleling the processing goals sought at the indoor scene? This also requires incorporating documentation, and perhaps analysis techniques and principles from disciplines beyond archaeology and anthropology, such as edaphology and field ecology.

It is also notable how, in addition to a PMI range (time since death and deposition), the forensic archaeological effort described in this example allowed the determination of a sequence of events not only for the criminal action but for the alterations suffered by the scene and the remains after deposition. The bodies were covered by leaf litter during the fall. The head of the adult individual fell from the body as it decomposed and rolled down the slope. This kind of timeline becomes more complex and also more relevant in cases with more postmortem alterations, particularly when distinguishing between human and natural modification of the remains or the scene. Initial PMI estimates can also incorporate more elements, adding to the body decomposition patterns exhibited by the clothing apparel and other biological tissues associated with the remains, taking into account their stratigraphic position, as we did with the leaf litter in this case example. This new focus on creating a historic rendering of body and scene through a consideration of the natural context and biological elements is, again, a perfect fit with taphonomy that, in short, is the study of what happens to a biological entity from the time of death and deposition to recovery and analysis (Beary and Lyman 2012; Dirkmaat and Cabo 2016a, b; Cabo et al. 2023; Ost et al. 2019). When applied to forensic contexts and situations, it is called forensic taphonomy (Haglund and Sorg 1997).

Law enforcement and medicolegal authorities could now look to the forensic anthropologist (uniquely) when dealing with scenes other than shallow graves and other burials, and to provide answers to their questions regarding the time and sequence of events transpiring at the scene. Besides assessing the forensic significance of skeletal elements (human vs. animal bone), the forensic anthropologist could now do the same for suspected trauma, and even for other alterations of the scene. The new contextual information recovered through the forensic archaeological effort could contribute to assessments of the manner of death (homicide vs.

suicide; natural vs. accidental) and even cause of death through skeletal trauma analysis. This depth and breadth of information and data interpretation should be recognized as similar to what is expected of the processing of indoor scenes. However, the skill set required for these contributions is found neither in the law enforcement or medicolegal fields nor in the classic training of biological anthropologists or archaeologists.

Based on these advancements, the late 1990s and early 2000s saw a marked increase in both the number of cases in which the forensic anthropologist (at least among these authors) was requested to participate, and in the diversity of these cases, that now ranged from the traditional burials or bone evaluations for forensic significance (now often from photographs sent by email, and later by text messaging), to surface scatters and fatal fire scenes (Ost et al. 2019). In addition, by the mid-90s, Dirkmaat had started organizing and offering week-long forensic anthropology short courses to national and international audiences, which helped outline and further popularize the new and effective forensic archaeology protocols as applicable to a wide variety of contexts. Forensic archaeology and forensic taphonomy started becoming part of the vocabulary not only of their practitioners but also of law enforcement and medicolegal professionals. The next challenge was making those professionals see them not as external tools for which to reach occasionally, maybe in particularly hard cases, but as a key element of crime investigation, to be applied whenever they encountered outdoor scenes, including those of mass disasters, fatal fire scenes, or suspected burials. The definition of Outdoor Crime Scene Reconstruction is intended to help in this purpose by framing the practice of forensic anthropology and forensic archaeology in the same context as other areas of forensic investigation.

6.7 Defining Outdoor Crime Scene Reconstruction (OCSR)

With the standard implementation of forensic archaeology and forensic taphonomy principles, practices, and interpretations in a wide variety of outdoor contexts, the focus shifted from getting the body off of the scene as quickly as possible to the forensic pathologist with little or no contextual information (or hypotheses of association) to recovering all of the evidence in situ and constructing the history of the remains at the scene since deposition during the postmortem interval.

From law enforcement perspectives, the critical outcome/product of recoveries conducted at both indoor and outdoor scenes is the reconstruction of events surrounding the specific time of the body deposition (and often death) at the scene. The timing, details, and sequence of events related to the specific activities of *humans* are the critical piece of the puzzle. When applied to the understanding of indoor scenes, these approaches are called *Crime Scene Reconstructions*. When applied to outdoor forensic scenes, we have given this the name *Outdoor Crime Scene Reconstruction (OCSR)*.

We can use our reconstruction of the forensic taphonomic interval—in which we identify and account for all the forensic taphonomic agents that have impacted the evidence during that interval—to roll back the clock and try to understand what the scene looked like at the time of deposition and at the beginning of the postmortem timeframe (the forensic taphonomic interval). By weeding out the effects (and degree of impact) of the natural environmental factors and, specifically, the natural forensic taphonomic agents, what we are left with is a decent snapshot of what the scene looked like at the time of the deposition of the body. By figuring out where the body was located at the time of deposition, it is also possible to acquire clues as to how the body was positioned and oriented at the time of deposition on the scene, and whether other artifacts were directly associated with the evidence (e.g., branches or metal placed over the body to hide it).

Essentially and ultimately, what we are attempting is do, and what is of most interest to law enforcement, is to metaphorically create a picture of the scene five minutes after the deposition of the body on that scene. Perhaps the best way to present this approach is through our third case example.

6.8 Case Number Three: A Decomposing Body in the Woods

Law enforcement and a county coroner's office approached Dirkmaat about assisting with the processing of an outdoor scene containing human remains. Following an investigation into a missing person, law enforcement interviewed an individual who claimed to have been involved in (or at least present for) the murder. The informant led police to a scene in the woods in which a decomposing body was indeed found. Police did not disturb the remains at all but conducted a general search of the area for evidence that was located away from the body. They did not disturb the remains because they were familiar with the value of forensic archaeological scene processing procedures when processing an outdoor crime scene.

The informant provided details of the events surrounding the death of this individual. These details can then be considered as *hypotheses* of the events surrounding the death and deposition of the body at this scene. Even though the informant led police to the scene, it was not clear whether all of the details (including sequence and timing) of his account of the activities of that death and body deposition were accurate. Law enforcement was now familiar with how forensic archaeological recovery would be able to test aspects of their working hypotheses. They had specific questions that needed to be addressed which were out of their range of expertise, including estimates of PMI, original location of the body, and position and orientation of the body at the time of deposition.

The details of the account that was presented (now the working hypotheses of past events at this scene of law enforcement) were as follows: a drug deal meeting occurred in a flat grassy pull-off area of a country road three weeks prior to the individual's disappearance. Three individuals in one group met with the now-missing individual. Things did not go well, and the single individual took off running into the woods. He was tackled by one member of the group. That individual had a knife and proceeded to stab the decedent, who was in the prone position, in the back, head, and neck, and held him down until he died.

The body of the newly deceased individual was dragged into the woods by his legs down a descending path and deposited face-up into the weeds along the path. It was decided that they would dispose of the body through burning; however, they did not have the resources, nor any idea of the timeframe or what would be required to thoroughly burn the body (typically this would require at least 10–12 hours). Instead, lighter fluid was poured over the body of the supine individual and lit with a match, which resulted in a brief episode (i.e., minutes) of flames, after which the fire extinguished itself to little ultimate effect. The perpetrators then removed the wallet and other personal materials and attempted to burn them in another location along the path approximately 15 feet away. They then left the area and did not return.

The forensic archaeological recovery (Fig. 6.3) began with a review of the meeting location near the road, and then progressed down the path into the woods (on a slight downslope). The body was, in fact, located in the weeds on the side of the path. About 15–20 feet up the path was a burned grassy area which either represented an area where an attempt to burn the body took place or the location where the personal effects were burned separately from the body.

A detailed shoulder-to-shoulder pedestrian search of the area surrounding the body and up the path was conducted in the area surrounding the remains to locate evidence not directly associated with the body. Only a right slipper was found (which matched the left slipper still on the foot of the decedent).

The initial general examination and documentation of the remains (without disturbing anything) revealed significant information of interest to assess the hypotheses of past events. The individual was face up (supine position), with the arms above the head. The shirt and the pants were bunched superiorly, all consistent with dragging a body down a path by the legs. Directly beneath the body was darkly stained soil, grass, and tall weeds, interpreted as a "decomposition stain." This stain indicated that the body had not been moved since deposition. All the body parts were still present, suggesting that animal activity was minimal or non-existent (which would later be confirmed in laboratory analyses). The body presented moderate amounts of desiccated soft tissue throughout, with some exposed skeletal elements. An initial estimate of less than 3 months PMI was established. This estimate was also based on the lack of leaf litter covering the body, the warm weather clothing, and the death of the plants under the body due to decomposition purge.

There was evidence of burning of some of the clothing (melting of artificial polyester clothing) on the anterior surface of the remains. The burning did not impact the soft tissue, further indicating that the burning was minimal and not long-lived. Once examined in the morgue, there were no signs of burning on any other parts of the body, including the posterior surface of the remains.

The first steps of the forensic archaeological recovery involved the removal (denuding) of vegetation around the remains to more clearly define the boundary of the *immediate scene* (the main concentration and furthest dispersed evidence), note

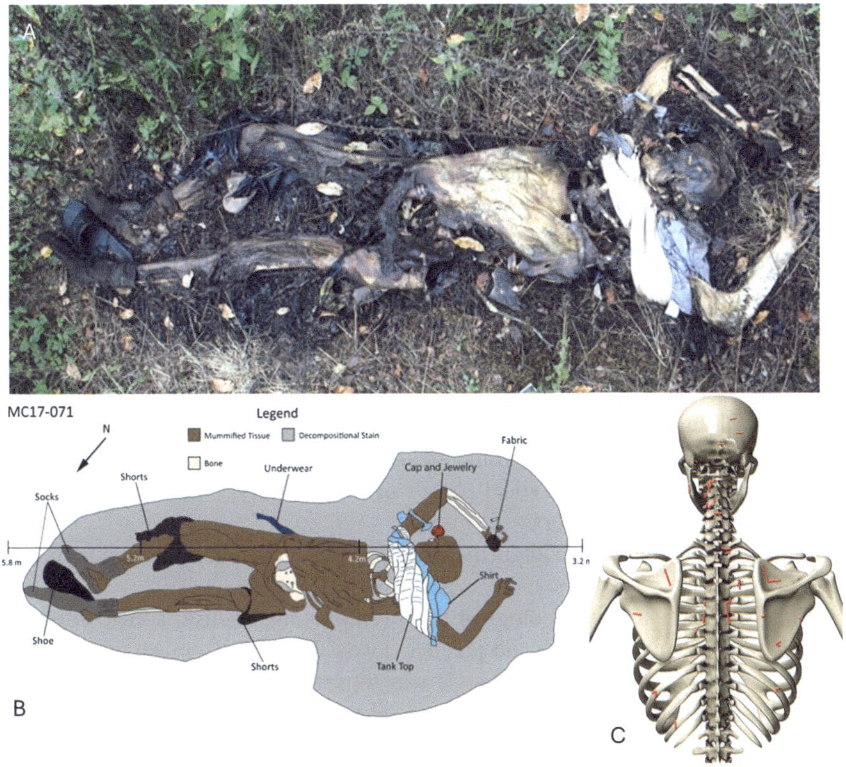

Fig. 6.3 A surface-deposited forensic anthropology (forensic archaeology and forensic taphonomy) case involving one individual in a dense deciduous forest context in Pennsylvania. The analysis of the location, position, and orientation of the decedent relative to features of the scene and associated evidence prior to recovery (**a**), in conjunction with subsequent forensic archaeological recovery and the hand-drawn map (**b**), provided significant and well documented evidence that helped corroborate law enforcement hypotheses of past events (generated from the account of an informant), including the dragging of a deceased body down a dirt path based on the position of the arms, bunching of clothing (Aa), placement of the body in weeds along the path, burning attempts (Ab), lack of animal modification of the remains, location and extent of decomposition stain (Ac), and even removal of one sandal (Ad). The subsequent forensic osteological analysis of the skeletal remains provided details regarding traumatic sharp force trauma events (C), relevant to cause of death (COD) evaluations, and corroboration of hypotheses related to past events (stabbing of the individual while face down) of relevance to manner of death (MOD) evaluations.

the extent and location of the decomposition stain relative to the body, and locate any evidence in the vicinity hidden by vegetation.

Next was the creation of the hand-drawn map of the body on the ground surface, which was created to highlight the location, position, and orientation of the body relative to other forensically significant features/evidence on the scene, and to individualize all of the evidence (i.e., to provide them with a unique designator that is noted on the map, in the photographs, on the evidence bags, and in the lab).

The burned area on the path a short distance from the body was excavated. There were no human remains associated with it as evaluated by the forensic anthropologist. It was confirmed that the burning episode of the body did not occur in that location but instead occurred after the body was subsequently deposited in the weeds.

While these other actions were taking place at the forensic recovery, an electronic total station was employed to map the location of the body at the scene, as well as to note the outline of the body, course of the path, location of meeting field, the location and outline of the decomposition stain, location of the isolated slipper, trees in the immediate area, and, importantly, the topographic contour of the scene. A GPS unit was used to obtain precise global positioning of the scene and to provide provenience for later incorporation into Geographic Information Systems (GIS). GIS allowed for the extraction of information such as road courses near and beyond the local area, tree cover, and even historical information of the site (including aerial photographs of the area through time), and provided further contextual data (specifics of tree cover, common soils in the area, distances to important locations in the area), during subsequent analytical phases of the recovery, and eventually during the production of the site history.

Following mapping procedures, the body was placed in a body bag and removed from the scene.

What the forensic anthropological team (employing forensic archaeology and forensic taphonomy principles and practices) was able to accomplish with a forensic archaeological recovery of this style was to test law enforcement's hypotheses relative to details of the informant account. The location, position, and orientation of the body were documented. It was noted that the body had not been moved, and that it had not been impacted by animals (nor humans coming back to hide evidence). Information was collected at the scene during the recovery that was relevant to the estimation of PMI, which proved consistent with the decedent's disappearance.

In the forensic anthropology laboratory, the biological profile was consistent with the characteristics of the missing person in question. The analysis of the skeletal trauma indicated knife stab wounds to the posterior head, neck, and upper torso, consistent with the story provided by the informant.

All in all, the forensic anthropological recovery was able to construct and test hypotheses of the details of the timeline and timeframe of the body at this scene, and importantly corroborated the informant's account of past events.

6.9 Summary and Final Considerations

The field of forensic anthropology in the United States has witnessed a significant (r)evolution since the 1970s and its early construction and configuration. Originally focused only on the laboratory analysis of human skeletal remains to create a biological profile in the hopes of providing clues for resolving personal identification issues, the addition of forensic archaeology and forensic taphonomy in the 1990s resulted in a dramatic reframing of the role of forensic anthropology within medicolegal pursuits, especially in those cases of significantly decomposing remains found in a variety of outdoor contexts. Rather than just taking a few pictures and collecting the remains into body bags, as was the prior common law enforcement protocol, the focus on the recovery was now on the location and documentation of all of the evidence, thorough and comprehensive documentation of context, creation of hypotheses of association of the evidence to other evidence, to the scene, and to the events, and ultimately the creation of a detailed history of the postmortem interval, as well as (re)creating a snapshot of the scene minutes and hours after the body emplacement event itself. These altered perspectives of what forensic anthropology could provide for the recovery of the outdoor scene have permitted us to suggest that the field of forensic anthropology has witnessed a paradigm shift in the last 20 years (Dirkmaat et al. 2008; Dirkmaat and Cabo 2012) from a bones-only discipline to one that now includes forensic archaeology and forensic taphonomy, leading to medicolegal and law enforcement-oriented outdoor crime scene reconstructions.

The forensic anthropologist, trained in forensic archaeological methods, practices, and perspectives, and with a forensic taphonomic interpretative orientation, is now called/requested, on a regular basis, to direct outdoor crime scene recoveries. This suggests that it is now clearly recognized by the medicolegal and law enforcement communities that the skill sets possessed by the forensic anthropologist provide the best fit for properly extracting information and interpretations from outdoor crime scenes.

The proper and effective recovery of the outdoor scene requires much different skill sets than are required for the indoor scene recovery. It requires the following (incomplete) list of specific skills and training in: (i) basic osteology in terms of differentiating animal from human fragmented and altered skeletal remains, (ii) constructing the human skeletal biological profile, and (iii) analyzing human skeletal trauma. Additionally, forensic anthropologists must have specialized training in: (iv) forensic archaeological methods, practices, and principles; (v) possess abilities and training to note the spatial distribution of the evidence through efficient cartographic means; (vi) possess abilities to comprehensively document context at a wide variety of outdoor scenes from surface scatters, to burials, to fatal fire scenes; (vii) possess abilities to document potential forensic taphonomic agents that may affect the evidence; and finally, (viii) possess an understanding of field ecology to reconstruct a history of the scene from the emplacement of the human body to the discovery of that body.

These skill sets are unique to the discipline of forensic anthropology and specifically to the approach labeled as Outdoor Crime Scene Reconstruction. OCSR embraces/encompasses the subfields of forensic anthropology (osteology), forensic archaeology, and forensic taphonomy as integrated and integral components.

This package of unique skills resides in an extensive training regimen in forensic anthropology in which human osteology, forensic archaeology, and forensic taphonomy form the analytical triumvirate that is applied to the effective location, recovery, and interpretation (processing) of the outdoor forensic scene. No other discipline comes close to having the depth and breadth of this toolbox.

Finally, we argue (emphatically) here that the most comprehensive, illustrative, and informative recoveries of outdoor scenes can only be done through the forensic anthropological lens in which forensic archaeological methods and practices are systematically employed, and the interpretations of past events require forensic taphonomic perspectives for understanding, and ultimately, reconstructing the postmortem history of the remains on the natural landscape.

In conclusion, the main point of this article is to point out that forensic anthropology (with the components of forensic osteology, forensic archaeology, and forensic taphonomy) is a unique (and standalone) scientific discipline. It encompasses and requires a great diversity of unique skill sets uniquely applicable to the outdoor forensic scene via the Outdoor Crime Scene Reconstruction approach. These components are not found individually, much less within an integrated package of unique skills within the law enforcement, medicolegal, or forensic pathology fields.

References

Bass WM, Birkby WH (1978) Exhumation: the method could make the difference. FBI Law Enforcement Bulletin 47(7):6–11

Beary MO, Lyman RL (2012) The use of taphonomy in forensic anthropology: past trends and future prospects. In: Dirkmaat DC (ed) A companion to forensic anthropology. John Wiley & Sons, pp 499–527

Cabo LL, Dirkmaat DC (2015) Forensic archaeology in the United States. In: Groen WM, Marquez-Grant N, Janaway R (eds) Forensic archaeology: a global perspective. John Wiley & Sons, pp 255–270

Cabo LL, Dirkmaat DC, Zurek-Ost AM (2023) Taphonomy and biological anthropology. In: Larsen CS (ed) A companion to biological anthropology. Wiley Blackwell, pp 347–364

Dawson G (2024) Monkey to man: the evolution of the march of Progress image. Yale University Press

Dirkmaat DC, Cabo LL (2012) Forensic anthropology: embracing the new paradigm. In: Dirkmaat DC (ed) A companion to forensic anthropology. John Wiley & Sons, pp 1–40

Dirkmaat DC, Cabo LL (2016a) Forensic archaeology and forensic taphonomy: basic considerations on how to properly process and interpret the outdoor forensic scene. Acad Forensic Pathol 6(3):439–454. https://doi.org/10.23907/2016.045. Epub 2016 Sep 1. PMID: 31239919; PMCID: PMC6474560

Dirkmaat DC, Cabo LL (2016b) Forensic archaeology and forensic taphonomy: basic considerations on how to properly process and interpret the outdoor forensic scene. Academic Forensic Pathology 6(3):439–454

Dirkmaat DC, Cabo LL, Ousley SD, Symes SA (2008) New perspectives in forensic anthropology. Am J Phys Anthropol 137(S47):33–52

Gould SJ (1989) Wonderful life: the burgess shale and the nature of history. WW Norton & Company

Haglund WD, Sorg MH (eds) (1997) Forensic Taphonomy: the postmortem fate of human remains. CRC Press

Morse D, Crusoe D, Smith HG (1976) Forensic archaeology. J Forensic Sci 21(2):323–332

Morse D, Duncan J, Stoutamire J (1983) Handbook of forensic archaeology and anthropology. Rose Printing

Ost AM, Dunn RR, Dirkmaat DC (2019) What forensic taphonomy can do for you: a case study in rural Pennsylvania. In: Garvin HM, Langley NR (eds) Case studies in forensic anthropology: Bonified skeletons. CRC Press, CRC Press, pp 69–80
Skinner M, Lazenby R (1983) Found! Human remains: a field manual for the recovery of the recent human skeleton. Archaeology Press - Simon Fraser University
Snow CC (1982) Forensic anthropology. Annu Rev Anthropol 11:97–131. https://doi.org/10.1146/annurev.an.11.100182.000525

Chapter 7
When Forensic Entomology Becomes Essential to Document Forensic Archaeology: Enlightening Burials with Insects

Jiri Hodecek and **Vincent Varlet**

Abstract This article highlights the integration of forensic entomology into forensic archaeology, emphasizing its role in understanding taphonomic processes and burial contexts. Forensic entomology, which analyzes insect activity to estimate the minimum post-mortem interval (PMI_{min}), offers valuable insights into decomposition, burial environments, and the presence of xenobiotics. The Swiss Human Institute of Forensic Taphonomy (SHIFT) has developed protocols to enhance forensic archaeology investigations through entomological evidence, including sampling methodologies, temperature measurements, and soil analysis. The article explores how entomological analyses can contribute to reconstructing forensic and historical burial scenarios, providing a multidisciplinary approach to both contemporary and ancient cases.

Keywords Forensic Entomology · Post-Mortem Interval (PMI) · Forensic Archaeology · Taphonomy · Entomotoxicology

7.1 Introduction

Forensic archaeology is the application of archaeological principles and methodologies to locate and recover evidence within the boundaries of the criminal justice system or for use in civil lawsuits (Obledo 2009). This discipline is organized around four operations: the search and spatio-temporal mapping, the comprehension and interpretation of the taphonomic event, the reconstruction of the events, and the informed interpretation of the events surrounding the deposition.

J. Hodecek (✉) · V. Varlet
Swiss Human Institute of Forensic Taphonomy, University Centre of Legal Medicine, Lausanne University Hospital, Lausanne, Switzerland
e-mail: jiri.hodecek@chuv.ch

P. M. Barone, WJ M. Groen (eds.), *Forensic Archaeology and New Multidisciplinary Approaches*, Soil Forensics, https://doi.org/10.1007/978-3-031-86308-0_7

Consequently, forensic archaeology involves the utilization and adaptation of traditional archaeological methods for locating, documenting, and recovering human remains and associated evidence from a full range of medicolegal scene contexts (Schultz 2015). Historically, forensic archaeology developed within the field of forensic anthropology and traditional archaeology, giving human remains the full attention. Therefore, the application of field methods to contextualize and document the scene was very focused on human remains. However, various non-human remains (cigarettes, tools, artifacts, textile fibers, etc.) buried simultaneously can deliver precious information. Proper field methods targeted at the recovery of non-human indices are now routinely used for various contexts involving recoveries of human remains.

However, among the non-human indices, it is mandatory to subdivide the category and distinguish the biological from the non-biological material. Indeed, it has become very important to consider the biological material to document and understand human body taphonomy. Until now, biological material and especially entomological remains did not receive a lot of attention whereas they constitute reliable indices to enlighten the taphonomic circumstances and sometimes, to strengthen a cause of death hypothesis.

7.2 The Swiss Human Institute of Forensic Taphonomy

Since January 1, 2019, forensic investigations at the University Centre of Legal Medicine Lausanne—Geneva (Switzerland) can count on the support of a new operational unit: the Swiss Human Institute of Forensic Taphonomy (SHIFT) (https://www.curml.ch/en/swiss-human-institute-forensic-taphonomy-shift-EN).

Among its missions, SHIFT is responsible for:

- Providing an offer of advice and expertise to various public and private structures;
- Providing academic courses and professional training in the field of forensic taphonomy and associated sciences: funeral cares and Master of Science (MSc) of Human Taphonomy at Lausanne University;
- Developing research projects in the field of forensic taphonomy and associated sciences;
- Managing innovative projects: cemetery expertise, alternative funerals, and body donation to forensic sciences.

SHIFT operates in four areas of expertise:

1. Forensic anthropo-archaeology
2. Non-human genetics, that is, animal, plant, and environmental genetics
3. Human taphonomy
4. Forensic entomology

As a result, SHIFT's forensic entomology laboratory, operational since 2020, is listed as a reference laboratory for the Swiss police. The collaboration between forensic laboratories of entomology, non-human genetics, and anthropo-archaeology within SHIFT is a real added value for the documentation and resolution of investigations.

7.3 Forensic Entomology

Necrophagous insects can be used as evidence during real-case investigations. The discipline, which studies insects in the medico-legal environment, is called forensic entomology (FE). The most important aim of FE is to estimate the minimum post-mortem interval (PMI_{min}), which is possible due to two main reasons: (i) certain necrophagous flies (usually the flies of the family Calliphoridae) can arrive within minutes/hours after the death of a person and (ii) the length of the developmental cycle of necrophagous insects is predictable if the temperature profile is known (Amendt et al. 2011). The predictability of the necrophagous insect's development is mainly possible thanks to its almost "linear" dependence on the temperature. Based on this dependence, we can calculate the time of oviposition of the oldest insect found at the death scene with relatively high precision (Byrd and Tomberlin 2020). Insects as poikilothermic organisms cannot control their body temperature, and their growth is influenced by temperature. They need a certain physiological energy budget to finish their developmental cycle. This budget can be calculated by thermal summation models and the thermal units are called degree days (°D) or degree hours (°H). Every species has a lower and higher developmental threshold, that is, temperatures, which define the interval under which the species is active (Gennard 2012). For example, *Calliphora vicina* is active in the range 2–39 °C (Marchenko 2001). If the temperature gets lower than 2 °C, the development of *C. vicina* stops and in case of longer exposition to temperature above 39 °C the fly dies. Thanks to experimental data we have a good idea about the lengths of developmental cycles of the most common species under different temperature profiles as well as their lower and higher developmental thresholds and heat constants. However, due to local adaptations, the populations within the same species can differ in their developmental thresholds, which can bring a substantial bias in the calculations. It is thus of a great importance to use data of populations from the same geographical area to avoid this error (Byrd and Tomberlin 2020).

Necrophagous insects colonize dead bodies gradually and arrive in waves that overlap each other. Different species belonging to different families have different requirements and preferences and this is a reason why we can estimate PMI_{min} even in cases where the first colonizers already finished their developmental cycle and are missing (Amendt et al. 2007). In these cases, we no longer use the thermal summation model described above, and we use a complex analysis of the insect life histories instead. Certain species are active in summer, certain species are not able to live in high altitudes and certain species prefer shady places (Hodecek and Jakubec 2022). To correctly estimate the PMI_{min} of a body in an advanced state of decomposition, we need to carefully consider the spatio-temporal distribution and habitat preferences of all insects present. The resulting estimate gives a time interval with the most probable date of death.

7.4 Investigation Based on Entomological Remains

Insects have an exoskeleton made of durable materials as chitin, which makes them last for centuries under certain conditions. This is the reason why we can still find insect bodies or their fragments on an archaeological site. The methods we use in the FE can thus often be used in palaeoentomology and/or archaeoentomology as well. Palaeoentomology studies insect and insect fossils with an aim toward understanding environmental, climatic, and cultural conditions in the past, while archaeoentomology strives to reconstruct past environments (e.g., contribution to the history of stored grain pests and to the archaeology of funerary practices—often also called "funerary archaeoentomology") (Moret 1998). Unlike the FE, the aims of these disciplines are rarely the PMI_{min} estimation as the questions the archaeologists ask are rather "what" and "why." Insects can uncover many important messages, which would be otherwise hidden from the archaeologist. For instance, the current research in archaeoentomology focuses on funerary practices (mummies/skeletal remains from ancient Egypt to the Middle Ages; Huchet et al. 2013a; Morrow et al. 2015; Loni et al. 2019), bone alterations caused by dermestid beetles (Huchet et al. 2013b; Thompson et al. 2018), places of burial and burial objects (graves, chambers, embalming jars, etc.…; Morrow et al. 2016; Panagiotakopulu et al. 2018), and food supply storages with their pests (Henríquez-Valido et al. 2020). The situation can be slightly different in forensic archaeology (or forensic archaeoentomology) as the reconstruction of past environment is then within the boundaries of the investigation and the aims differ based on the questions the investigators need to find the answers to. The presence (or even the absence) of insects or the traces of insect activities can shed light on what happened in the past, suggest certain scenarios, and/or increase the probability of a certain scenario (Amendt et al. 2011). From the above, it follows that the methods used in modern forensic entomology can be useful also in forensic archaeology, although the PMI_{min} estimation might no longer be the main focus.

7.5 Forensic Entomotoxicology

There are cases of investigation where we can use the bodies of necrophagous insects to detect xenobiotics previously accumulated in the dead human body. These cases typically arise when there are no longer tissues and/or fluids available for toxicological analysis. Insects feeding on the dead body accumulate the xenobiotics, which are present in the body of the deceased and can therefore serve as evidence of their presence in the body of the deceased.

The term "forensic entomotoxicology" was first presented by Pounder (1991), who defined it as the detection of drugs present in a decomposing corpse via analysis of fly larvae feeding of it. Later, only the term entomotoxicology was used, although the usage was solely in studies of medico-legal purposes. Hodecek (2020) then proposed a new definition for entomotoxicology and divided it into forensic entomotoxicology and environmental entomotoxicology based on the outcomes. Today, entomotoxicology is thus defined as a science, which analyses the effects of xenobiotics on insects and uses xenobiotics present in insect bodies as evidence of environmental pollution. The environment can be pictured as carrion, soil, river, landscape, or even the body of a patient (according to the clinical applications) (Hodecek 2020).

As mentioned above, forensic entomotoxicology is not only used to detect drugs. Different xenobiotics can influence the developmental cycles of the various species of necrophagous insects in different ways and the forensic entomologist needs to be aware of these effects as they can have a serious impact on the PMI_{min} estimations. While certain drugs can speed up the development of necrophagous flies, others can slow it down or affect the population lethally. The effect depends on the dosage of the xenobiotic, the resilience of the species to its effects, and the ability of the insect to digest the chemical.

Although the influence of certain xenobiotics on the developmental cycle of necrophagous insects can be substantial, this field is still considerably understudied. A number of limitations of these studies were listed by Da Silva et al. (2017): (i) A lack of methodological standardization prevents comparisons between studies; (ii) most studies have insufficient numbers of replicates, which increases the risk of statistical inference errors; (iii) successful entomotoxicological study can be expensive which means validation against broader toxicological standards is often not possible; and (iv) most studies were conducted either only by an entomologist or a toxicologist. However, both entomological and toxicological approaches are equally important and must be carefully validated so that vital information is not overlooked. The difficulties are however even broader. For instance, Campobasso et al. (2019) emphasized that it is very hard to correlate in between the xenobiotic levels in larvae with the amount detected in the cadaver; the knowledge of the insect metabolism of certain xenobiotics is poor; the impacts of environmental factors on xenobiotic detection are unknown; the drug concentrations in different tissues vary and the sampling efforts are often uneven. Another limitation then can be that laboratory animals can produce different metabolites than humans, which may lead to some incorrect assumptions (George et al. 2009).

Indeed, despite or because of all these limitations, it is essential to broaden our knowledge in forensic entomotoxicology and bring this field to routine usage in practical work. Although we might not yet be able to enumerate the dosage of cocaine in the deceased based on its finding in the insect bodies, it can still be essential information for the investigation, which can later link the victim to the suspect. With the growing usage of various drugs for suicides and other xenobiotics as painkillers or antidepressants in our daily lives, this field becomes more and more important (Snowdon 2022). For the same reasons, we can use the methods of forensic entomotoxicology also for the purposes of forensic archaeology in in our attempts to reconstruct scenarios from the past.

7.6 Sampling Methodology

The sampling methodology to be deployed to document forensic archaeology cases is derived from surface forensic entomology. In 2020, the Swiss Human Institute of Forensic Taphonomy opened the first intercantonal forensic entomology reference laboratory available to Swiss police forces. As it is important to expand the forensic entomological knowledge among the other taphonomic experts, a sampling protocol has been optimized for forensic archaeology cases (Box 7.1, Figs. 7.1 and 7.2).

Box 7.1 Sampling Protocol for Biological Samples

1. *What to do first*
   (a) Take photos of the surrounding habitat (fauna and flora).
   (b) Take photos of the insect infestations on the body.
2. *Measuring the temperature*
   (a) Measure the temperature: external temperature above the grave, on the ground surface (1 m away from the grave), 10 cm in the soil (1 m away from the grave).
   (b) Leave the active data logger on the scene for the next five days.
   (c) Measure the temperature of the human remains (according to the taphonomy)
   (d) Measure the temperature in the lateral sides of the grave right away after exhumation

1. *Where to sample insect evidence*
   (a) Collecting from around the body (up to 10 m).
   (b) Collecting from the body.
2. *Soil samplings*
   (a) Take a small sample of soil (3 shovelfuls) from the grave, then radially away (1 m, 2 m, 5 m, and 10 m) from the corpse (head, feet, flanks).
   (b) Pool in the same sterile plastic bag minigrip all the soil samples collected at the same distance away from the corpse (5 plastic bags/body: grave, 1 m, 2 m, 5 m, and 10 m).
   (c) Label and identify the samples in the sampling form.

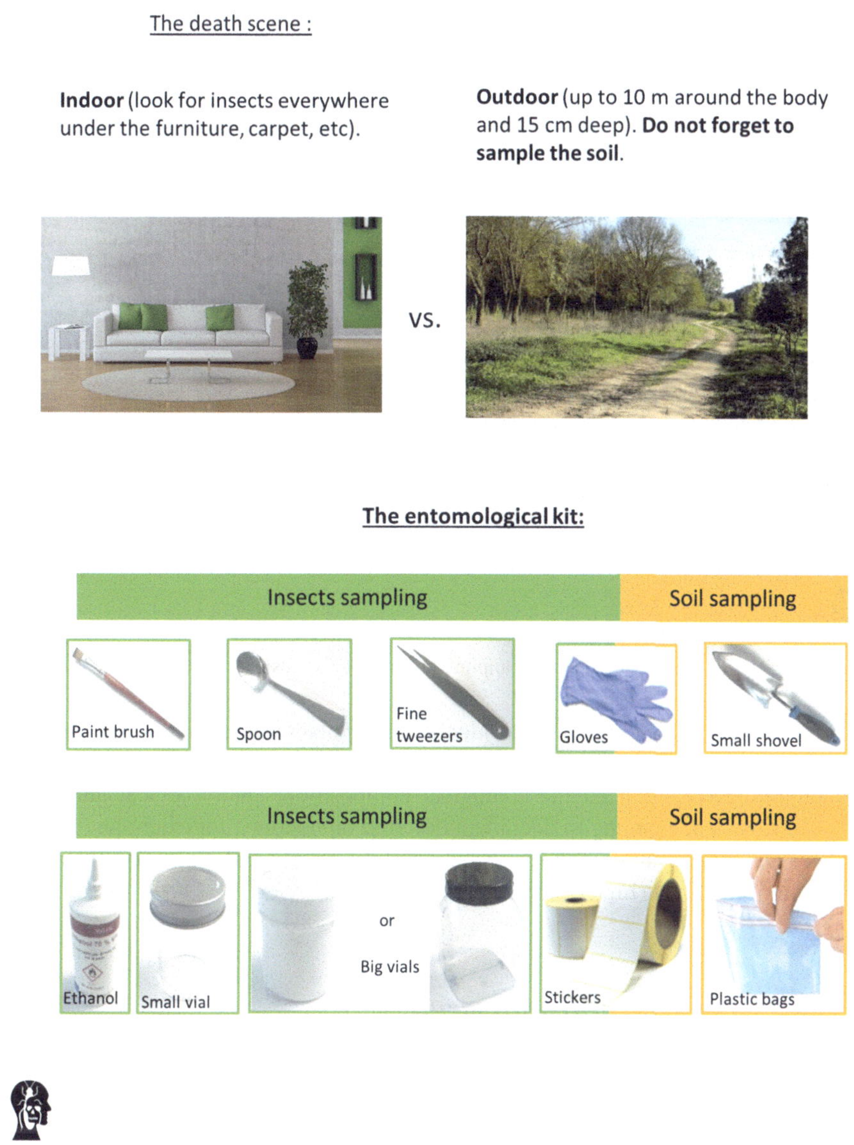

Fig. 7.1 SHIFT forensic entomology sampling protocol for forensic archaeology cases (1/2)

7.6.1 Photography/Scene Documentation

When an area suspected of containing a clandestine grave is identified, the first step is to document the area from a distance and then focus increasingly on the suspected grave. It is important to have photographs and graphic elements of the area. It is

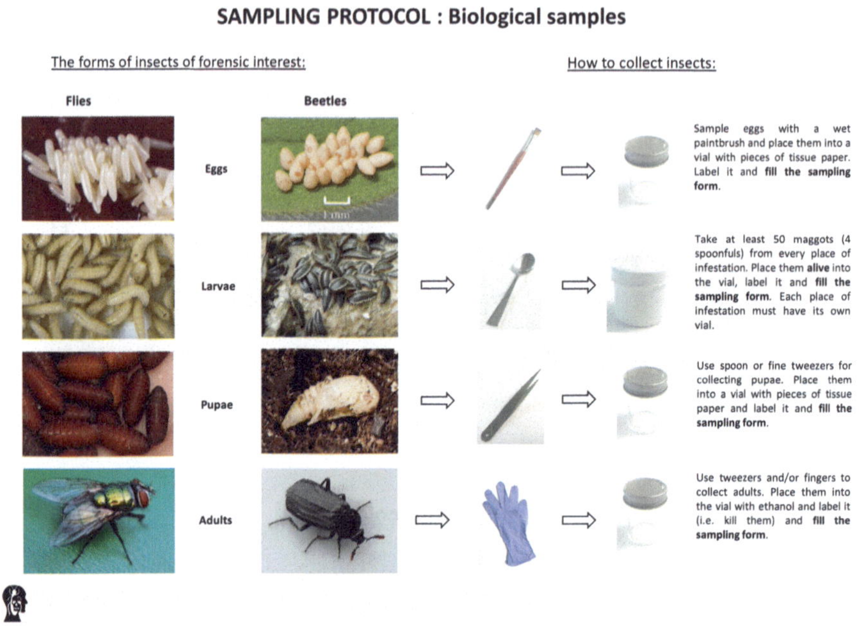

Fig. 7.2 SHIFT forensic entomology sampling protocol for forensic archaeology cases (2/2)

necessary to compile clues as to the identity of the plant and animal species present. The canopy can have an impact on sunshine and direct light in the area, as well as on rainfall. Depending on the ecological composition, entomological anomalies may be revealed, enabling to document deferred taphonomy, for example.

It is also important to mention the slope of the terrain and the geographical orientation of the body (Fig. 7.3).

7.6.2 *Temperature Measurements*

As insects are poikilotherm organisms, they need to accumulate heat to evolve from maggot to adult stage. Their development cycle is directly proportional to temperature hence the necessity to obtain a precise local temperature. So, for each case of forensic archaeology/excavation, it will be necessary to leave a data logger to measure the temperature on site. By comparing local data with data from the nearest weather stations, and calculating post-burial temperature differences, it will be possible to reconstruct the thermal evolution before the discovery of the remains, by consulting the recorded archives.

Then, before excavation, it is important to measure the external temperature above the grave, on the ground surface 1 m away from the grave, and the soil temperature at 10 cm deep. After excavation, it is important to measure the temperature

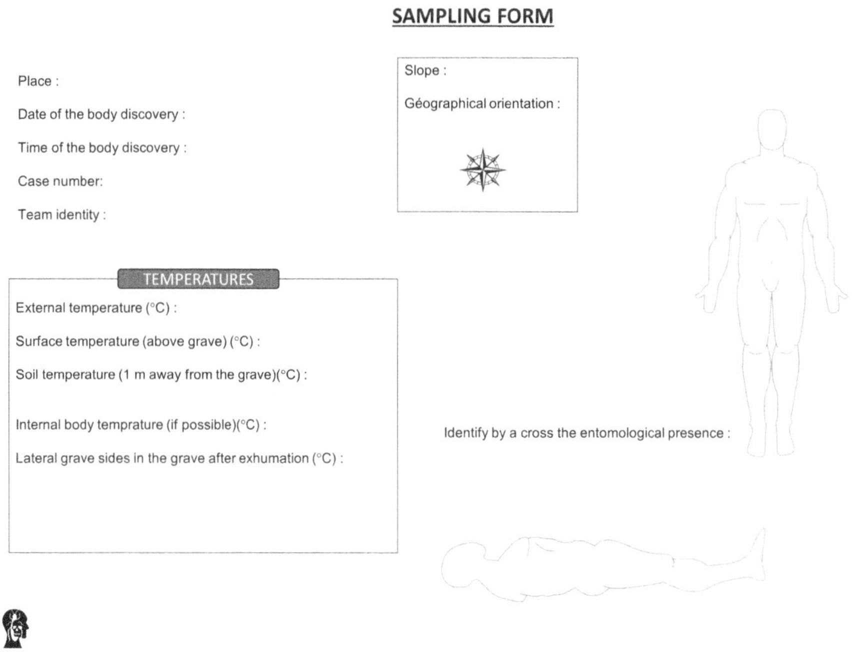

SAMPLING FORM

Place :

Date of the body discovery :

Time of the body discovery :

Case number:

Team identity :

Slope :

Géographical orientation :

TEMPERATURES

External temperature (°C) :

Surface temperature (above grave) (°C) :

Soil temperature (1 m away from the grave)(°C) :

Internal body temprature (if possible)(°C) :

Lateral grave sides in the grave after exhumation (°C) :

Identify by a cross the entomological presence :

Fig. 7.3 SHIFT forensic entomology sampling form for forensic archaeology cases

in the lateral sides of the grave right away after excavation and if possible, according to the taphonomy, the internal temperature of the body.

7.6.3 *Soil Samplings*

Before excavating, it is essential to be able to take soil samples, as any entomological clues are present in the soil. When a body is colonized by necrophagous entomofauna, the photophobic larvae look for a hiding place before pupating and tend to move away from the body. So, if the body has decomposed locally on the surface before burial, it will be very interesting to collect any pupae on the spot.

To this end, soil samples must be taken in the four cardinal directions, that is, at the center of the supposed grave pit, then radially at a distance of 1 m, 2 m, 5 m, and up to 10 m. These samples will be taken from the surface (down to around 15 cm) and will be pooled by distance from the body, to end up with just five soil samples (Fig. 7.4).

Most of the larvae can bury themselves up to 2–3 cm in the soil to evolve. It is therefore important to collect several samples and not to hesitate to dig up to 15–20 cm.

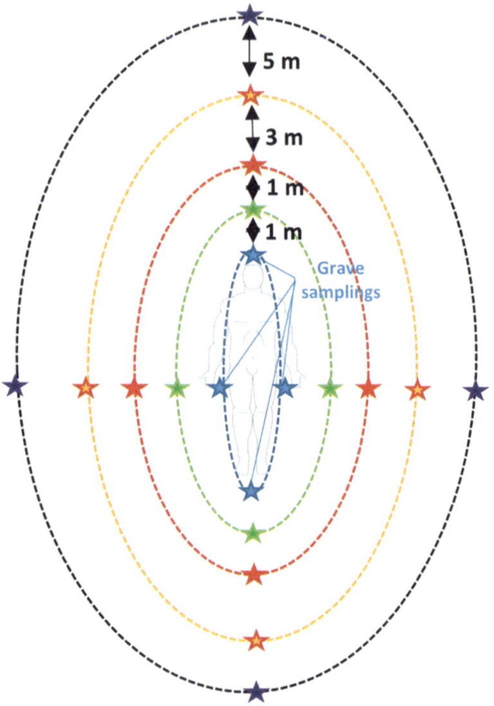

Fig. 7.4 Surface soil sampling for forensic entomological material purpose

Depending on the necrophagous entomofauna and the time required for decomposition before burial, the entomological material expected consists essentially of pupae containing living material (in the case of recent burials) or empty material (in the case of longer burials), and more rarely adult remains. In the case of living material, rearing until emergence will be necessary to subsequently identify the species present. In the case of empty material, the forensic entomologist can rely on molecular biology to identify the species more precisely from the DNA in the sample, although a morphological identification of certain species is also possible if the sample is not too degraded. In any case, empty pupae should be collected in vials containing ethanol. It is always preferable to individualize pupae on the grave scene if they have different morphologies. Indeed, grouping all the individuals in the same container increases the risk of contamination during subsequent genetic analyses.

Thus, the mere presence or succession of certain species can be very informative about the taphonomy of the case. Even before exhumation begins, it may be possible to confirm that the body has decomposed on site, prior to burial.

7.6.4 Insect Evidence Samplings

Once the body has been excavated, it is important to examine the profiles and statigraphy of the grave for any tunnels left by the larvae. If the body has decomposed on the surface, the larvae have tended to bury themselves in the first few centimeters. If the body was subsequently buried, but not deeply enough (less than 50 cm) and the soil was sufficiently loose, the larvae may have attempted to escape by moving radially away from the body, until the adults find a place to pupate. The path created by the larva and then the insect is therefore highly informative. In the case of very compact soil, or if the body has been buried at depths greater than 50 cm, it is very likely that the larval material has not entered pupation or has not been able to move away from the body, in which case the material will be found on the exhumed body.

In this case, care should be taken to collect the oldest material first, that is, pupae, whether empty or containing a living insect, in which case rearing should be organized until the emergence and morphological identification. The absence of pupae points to recent entomological colonization after death. Care should therefore be taken when collecting larval material, which may also be alive or dead. Live larvae should be placed in rearing tanks, and dead larvae in flasks containing ethanol. It is always preferable to individualize larvae on the scene if they have different morphologies. Indeed, grouping all the individuals in the same container increases the risk of contamination during subsequent genetic analyses plus there are some species of larvae, which can kill other larvae, for example, *Chrysomya albiceps*.

Thus, the mere presence or succession of certain species can be very informative about the taphonomy of the case.

After excavation, examination of the entomological material can help us circumstantiate the taphonomy. The presence of live/dead larvae or pupae allows us to conclude that a more or less decomposed body has been buried, either on site if the necrophagous ecology is consistent with the ecology of the area, or in another location if a necrophagous ecology is abnormally present on the body. These indications must be weighed against the depth of burial and the body's individual status.

In fact, all these initial conclusions need to be qualified by other local indices. The possible combustion of the body by accelerants or voluntary or involuntary antemortem impregnation by xenobiotics (drugs, narcotics, etc.) can obviously influence surface and subsurface colonization.

7.7 Conclusion

In conclusion, entomological sampling before and after excavation is crucial for documenting the taphonomy of the body and can sometimes even corroborate expert reports from other disciplines (forensics, toxicology, etc.). The forensic archaeologist must always keep in mind the need to collect these biological clues, although his or her interest will preferentially focus on available human remains or non-human material clues, if he or she is not aware of the potential biological traces offer to reconstruction. Entomological evidence, with its potential to provide insights into the post-mortem interval, the environment of the burial, and the presence of xenobiotics, can offer a multifaceted approach to forensic archaeology. The methods and principles of forensic entomology not only enhance the understanding of the circumstances surrounding death but can also contribute to the reconstruction of historical burial practices and environmental conditions. As forensic archaeology continues to evolve, integrating entomological analyses will undoubtedly provide a more comprehensive picture of past human activities and the various factors that influenced them. Moving forward, continuous collaboration between forensic entomologists, (forensic) archaeologists, and other forensic scientists will be essential in refining methodologies, improving accuracy, and broadening the applications of these interdisciplinary investigations.

Bibliography

Amendt J, Campobasso CP, Gaudry E, Reiter C, LeBlanc HN, Hall JR (2007) Best practice in forensic entomology - standards and guidelines. Int J Legal Med 121(2):90–104. https://doi.org/10.1007/s00414-006-0086-x

Amendt J, Richards CS, Campobasso CP, Zehner R, Hall MJR (2011) Forensic entomology: applications and limitations. Forensic Sci Med Pathol 7(4):379–392. https://doi.org/10.1007/s12024-010-9209-2

Byrd JH, Tomberlin JK (2020) Insect of forensic importance. In: Byrd JH, Tomberlin JK (eds) Forensic entomology: the utility of arthropods in legal investigations. CRC Press, Boca Raton, pp 15–62

Campobasso CP, Bugelli V, Carfora A, Borriello R, Villet MH (2019) Advances in entomotoxicology. Weaknesses and strengths. In: Byrd J, Tomberlin JK (eds) Forensic entomology: the utility of Arthropods in legal investigations. CRC Press, Boca Raton, pp 305–330

Da Silva EIT, Wilhelmi B, Villet MH (2017) Forensic entomotoxicology revisited - towards professional standardisation of study designs. Int J Legal Med 131(5):1399–1412. https://doi.org/10.1007/s00414-017-1603-9

Gennard D (2012) Forensic entomology: an introduction, 2nd edn. John Wiley & Sons, Chichester

George KA, Archer MS, Green LM, Conlan XA, Toop T (2009) Effect of morphine on the growth rate of Calliphora stygia (Fabricius) (Diptera: Calliphoridae) and possible implications for forensic entomology. Forensic Sci Int 193(1–3):21–25. https://doi.org/10.1016/j.forsciint.2009.08.013

Henríquez-Valido P, Morales J, Vidal-Matutano P, Moreno-Benítez M, Marchante-Ortega Á, Rodríguez-Rodríguez A, Huchet J-B (2020) Archaeoentomological indicators of long-term food plant storage at the Prehispanic granary of La Fortaleza (Gran Canaria, Spain). J Archaeol Sci 120:105–179

Hodecek J (2020) Revisiting the concept of entomotoxicology. Forensic Sci Int Synerg 2:282–286. https://doi.org/10.1016/j.fsisyn.2020.09.003

Hodecek J, Jakubec P (2022) Spatio-temporal distribution and habitat preference of necrophagous Calliphoridae based on 160 real cases from Switzerland. Int J Legal Med 136(3):923–934. https://doi.org/10.1007/s00414-021-02769-8

Huchet JB, Callou C, Lichtenberg R, Dunand F (2013a) The dog mummy, the ticks and the louse fly: archaeological report of severe ectoparasitosis in ancient Egypt. Int J Paleopathol 3(3):165–175. https://doi.org/10.1016/j.ijpp.2013.07.001

Huchet J-B, Le Mort F, Rabinovich R, Blau S, Coqueugniot H, Arensburg B (2013b) Identification of dermestid pupal chambers on southern Levant human bones: inference for reconstruction of Middle Bronze Age mortuary practices. J Archaeol Sci 40(10):3793–3803. https://doi.org/10.1016/j.jas.2013.04.025

Loni A, Fornaciari A, Canale A, Giuffra V, Vanin S, Benelli G (2019) Insights on funeral practices and insects associated with the tombs of King Ferrante II d'Aragona and other Renaissance nobles. J Med Entomol 56(6):1582–1591. https://doi.org/10.1093/jme/tjz102

Marchenko MI (2001) Medicolegal relevance of cadaver entomofauna for the determination of the time of death. Forensic Sci Int 120(1–2):89–109. https://doi.org/10.1016/s0379-0738(01)00416-9

Moret P (1998) L'archéo-entomologie, ou les insectes au service de l'histoire. Rev Med Vet 149(11):995–998

Morrow JJ, Baldwin DA, Higley LG, Piombino-Mascali D, Reinhard KJ (2015) Curatorial implications of Ophyra capensis (Order Diptera, Family Muscidae) puparia recovered from the body of the Blessed Antonio Patrizi, Monticiano, Italy (Middle Ages). J Forensic Leg Med 36:81–83. https://doi.org/10.1016/j.jflm.2015.09.005

Morrow JJ, Myhra A, Piombino-Mascali D, Lippi D, Roe A, Higley L, Reinhard KJ (2016) Archaeoentomological and archaeoacarological investigations of embalming jar contents from the San Lorenzo Basilica in Florence, Italy. J Archaeol Sci Rep 10:166–171. https://doi.org/10.1016/j.jasrep.2016.09.021

Obledo MN (2009) Forensic archeology in criminal and civil cases. Forensic Mag 6(4):31–34

Panagiotakopulu E, Buckland PC, Wickler S (2018) Is there anybody in there? Entomological evidence from a boat burial at Øksnes in Vesterålen, northern Norway. PLoS One 13(7). https://doi.org/10.1371/journal.pone.0200545

Pounder DJ (1991) Forensic entomo-toxicology. J Forensic Sci Soc 31(4):469–472. https://doi.org/10.1016/s0015-7368(91)73189-7

Schultz JJ (2015) Forensic archaeology. In: Wright JD (ed) International encyclopedia of the social & behavioral sciences, 2nd edn. Elsevier, pp 333–338

Snowdon J (2022) Drug overdose death rates in different countries: who should be alarmed? Australas Psychiatry 30(1):26–30. https://doi.org/10.1177/10398562221075192

Thompson JE, Martín-Vega D, Buck LT, Power RK, Stoddart S, Malone C (2018) Identification of dermestid beetle modification on Neolithic Maltese human bone: implications for funerary practices at the Xemxija tombs. J Archaeol Sci Rep 22:123–131. https://doi.org/10.1016/j.jasrep.2018.09.016

Part II
Forensic Anthropology and Humanitarian Investigations

Chapter 8
The Mass Grave Project

Advancing Mass Grave Investigation Through an Interdisciplinary Program of Actualistic Taphonomic Research

Hayley L. Mickleburgh, Noemi Procopio, Andrea Bonicelli, Nengi Ogbanga, Giulia Sguazzi, Sarah Gino, Rogier van der Hulst, Kennedy Doro, Timothy P. Gocha, Daniel J. Wescott, Lisette M. Kootker, and Saskia T. M. Ammer

Abstract The "Mass Grave Project" is an interdisciplinary program of taphonomic experiments simulating clandestine mass and single graves with human body donors at the Forensic Anthropology Center, Texas State University (FACTS). It aims to contribute to the development, testing, and validation of scientific methods for mass grave investigation, by increasing current knowledge and understanding of mass grave taphonomy. Specific objectives include, among others: refining remote and

H. L. Mickleburgh (✉)
University of Amsterdam, Amsterdam, NL & Forensic Anthropology Center, Texas State University, San Marcos, TX, USA
e-mail: h.l.mickleburgh@uva.nl

N. Procopio · A. Bonicelli
University of Central Lancashire, Preston, Lancashire, UK

N. Ogbanga
Northumbria University, Newcastle upon Tyne, UK

G. Sguazzi · S. Gino
University of Eastern Piedmont, Vercelli, Piedmont, Italy

R. van der Hulst
Netherlands Forensic Institute, The Hague, the Netherlands

K. Doro
Ohio State University, Columbus, OH, USA

T. P. Gocha · D. J. Wescott
Forensic Anthropology Center, Texas State University, San Marcos, TX, USA

L. M. Kootker · S. T. M. Ammer
Vrije Universiteit Amsterdam & Co van Ledden Hulsebosch Centre, Amsterdam, the Netherlands

P. M. Barone, WJ M. Groen (eds.), *Forensic Archaeology and New Multidisciplinary Approaches*, Soil Forensics, https://doi.org/10.1007/978-3-031-86308-0_8

ground-based detection methods and 3D documentation techniques, investigating the potential of biomolecular and microbial biomarkers for more precise and accurate postmortem interval and age-at-death estimation, studying DNA degradation and transfer between individuals in mass graves, and evaluating diagenesis and alteration of isotopic signatures of different human tissues. The project aims to generate recommendations for documentation, sampling, and analysis protocols, as well as develop advanced virtual reality simulation and training environments that can be used for testing scientific hypotheses as well as the training of investigators in mass grave excavation and documentation methods.

Keywords Mass Graves Investigation · Taphonomic Research · Forensic Archaeology · Geophysical Detection · DNA and Isotopic Analysis

8.1 Introduction

Modern mass graves often result from gross human rights violations, conflict, and social and political turmoil. These are not isolated incidents: every year, clandestine mass graves add to the millions of people who go missing due to human rights violations across the globe (Hamadeh et al. 2021; Human Rights Council 2020). There is an urgent humanitarian and legal need to search for and investigate these graves, identify the dead, and return their remains to their families (Klinkner and Smith 2020). Historic and prehistoric mass graves also occur in a large variety of spatiotemporal contexts, and while these generally do not require humanitarian and forensic attention, these contexts offer uniquely valuable insights into past human society and culture (Osterholtz 2015; Osterholtz et al. 2014).

Mass graves, whether of (pre)historic or forensic origin, present uniquely challenging contexts for archaeological excavation and interpretation. These sites are particularly complex because they hold the remains of multiple individuals, often exhibiting significant disarticulation and commingling of bodies and body parts (Haglund 2002; Jessee and Skinner 2005; United Nations 2016). As a result, identifying individual remains and documenting each body becomes a highly intricate task.

The arrangement of human remains and associated materials in mass graves is influenced by human actions and natural taphonomic processes occurring both during and after burial. Taphonomic processes encompass all factors that affect the preservation of an organism's remains post-mortem, such as weathering, fragmentation, human and animal activity, as well as decomposition processes like putrefaction, skeletonization, and disarticulation. These interactions between natural processes and human activities can significantly alter and bias the archaeological record.

Given the destructive nature of archaeological excavation, evidence in mass graves must be meticulously recorded to meet the standards required for various judicial mechanisms. This necessitates a high degree of expertise and specialized training among professionals involved in the investigation of these sites (Haglund & Sorg 2002; Stodder 2018).

Decomposition in mass graves is thought to be distinct from single graves, because large numbers of bodies are placed to decompose in direct contact with each other (a "body mass"), with little or no soil in between (Barker et al. 2017; Haglund 2002; Mant 1950, 1987; Troutman et al. 2014). Decay in a body mass can lead to the formation of voids and mixing of body parts (particularly when bodies skeletonize). Factors like disturbance and robbing of graves in attempts to conceal crimes can lead to high rates of commingling of the remains. The commingling of individuals poses a significant problem when investigating mass graves, as it makes the reassociation and identification of individuals extremely difficult. Displacement and dissociation also confound the reconstruction of the sequence of events surrounding death and deposition, which in forensic contexts can be critical to corroborate or negate testimony (Dirkmaat and Adovasio 1996). Mass graves have also been linked to differential decomposition patterns. This phenomenon is characterized by differences in the degree of body decomposition throughout the grave, and even within individual bodies, and can present as relatively good preservation of bodies at the center of a grave paired with skeletonization at the periphery (Barker et al. 2017; Haglund 2002; Mant 1950, 1987; Troutman et al. 2014). Differential decomposition affects the ability to identify individuals and can be demanding of field archaeologists, because digging equipment, personal protective clothing, and even packaging materials need to be adapted to the condition of the remains. Moreover, it makes it hard to identify remains, affecting the recording and interpretation of data, as well as the lifting and transportation of bodies. Differences in the condition of remains can hamper visibility and make it difficult to maintain recording standards across the grave.

The lack of knowledge of what precisely happens in mass graves during body decomposition impacts all phases of archaeological research: from the search for graves to the planning of excavations, data collection, and interpretation of results. Robust and reliable remote methods of locating graves—or monitoring them in situ until the excavation is deemed safe—are critical. Geophysical methods provide non-destructive approaches for detecting anomalies that provide investigative leads to clandestine individuals and mass graves (Keenan et al. 2018; Knaub 2019). Studies on investigating the use of geophysical techniques for locating graves and monitoring human decay have mostly relied on proxies such as pigs (Novo et al. 2011; Pringle et al. 2020). Questions remain surrounding how geophysical anomalies vary with time as bodies decay, and how changes in soil properties correlate with measured geophysical signals. Similarly, it remains unclear which methods are more suitable at the different decay stages. In addition, due to financial and logistical restrictions and security issues, ground-based techniques (e.g., walking surveys, ground penetrating radar) are not always feasible. In such cases, remote sensing using aerial and satellite images could provide viable alternatives. Remote sensing relies on contrasts between the target and its surroundings, such as soil and vegetation disturbances. Decomposition can cause a variety of alterations in spectral reflectance signatures of soil and vegetation due to microbial activity and the release of chemicals by the body (Keenan et al. 2018; Lang 2014; Usai et al. 2014). However, the relation between decomposition and spectral signatures is poorly understood, and there are currently no established criteria to detect (specific stages of) body decomposition. This means that despite the widely acknowledged potential of Remote Sensing for detecting mass graves, it remains underused (Kalacska et al. 2009; Kroker 2015; Leblanc et al. 2014; Raymond et al. 2014; Sandalinas 2015; Silván-Cárdenas et al. 2017, 2021; Son 2022; Wang et al. 2013).

The pressure of limited time and resources, combined with the need to collect and record evidence meticulously, means that documentation methods during excavation need to be efficient, reliable, and robust. Three-dimensional recording methods such as structure-from-motion photogrammetry or 3D laser scanning offer the potential to capture complex spatial data, in a rapid and increasingly low-cost manner. Nonetheless, 3D documentation is currently underutilized for deposits with human remains, both in traditional and forensic archaeological contexts (Beier and Rando 2016). For the wider adoption of such recording methods, it is important that their impact on field operations, in terms of time, costs, and required training and personnel is limited. Moreover, for their routine implementation in forensic practice and, if required, submission as evidence to a court of law, the reliability and repeatability of the data capture and post-processing of complex mass grave environments need to be demonstrated.

In practice, archaeological investigation of mass graves suffers from additional challenges. Because of limited resources, insufficiently or non-archaeologically trained personnel are often the first to respond to cases. Due to a variety of political and social pressures, they may begin to process the scenes. This can lead to inadvertent destruction of context and can hamper investigations. Affordable, realistic, and easily deployable training tools and programs are in critical shortage, and excavation and documentation practices vary considerably (Haglund 2002; Hanson 2016; Human Rights Council 2020; UNAMI/OHCHR 2018). Further challenges to mass grave investigation are posed by the need, in some cases, to quickly identify the deceased. Precise and accurate estimation of age-at-death, or the reliability of isotopic signatures obtained from buried remains, for instance, can be crucial to aid the identification of the deceased, as well as help to negate or corroborate testimonials and other evidence. Rapid developments in biomolecular and isotopic analysis methods provide potential new methods to assist identification. The reliability and accuracy of such methods must be tested and validated for use as evidence in court. Promising research on forensic omics and the development of the microbiome throughout body decomposition has found biomarkers that can potentially be used to develop age-at-death estimation techniques that are precise and accurate for all age groups and can be used on small/fragmented tissue samples, as well as shown great potential for refining postmortem interval (PMI) estimation. These methods could be particularly valuable in cases with large PMI ranges and/or fragmented or commingled remains (Mickleburgh et al. 2021; Procopio et al. 2018), but further validation research is needed to develop these methods for application in forensic and humanitarian investigations (Bonicelli et al. 2022). Similarly, while isotopic analysis to establish the geographic origin of the deceased has been widely applied in forensic investigations to aid identification, it remains unclear precisely how decomposition and diagenesis affect the antemortem isotopic compositions of different body tissues (hair, nails, bone), and the effects of laboratory cleaning procedures on isotope signatures recovered from human tissues are not fully understood (Chesson et al. 2020; Kootker et al. 2020, 2023; Toxvaerd 2020).

8.1.1 Forensic Taphonomic Experimentation

The variety of challenges facing forensic and humanitarian investigation of clandestine mass graves can impede the possibility of developing new and improving existing scientific methods of analysis. Nonetheless, there is a need for continued development and testing of the reliability of scientific methods and techniques for forensic and humanitarian purposes. Human taphonomy facilities provide unique laboratories to conduct the experiments necessary to understand the dynamic taphonomic processes of the grave to develop and test new (and existing) methods. Actualistic taphonomic experiments provide the opportunity to study and monitor changes over time and allow the controlling of conditions and collection of data in a safe and secure research environment. The replication of experiments in different environments is important to evaluate the effects of location-specific taphonomic conditions on the results and help to distinguish differences related to individual variation from environmental taphonomic variables. Moreover, replication studies support the development of environment-specific recommendations for analyses and protocols and are vital to the development of the field (Pokines and Symes 2013).

Mass grave research using human body donors was first undertaken in 2013 at the University of Tennessee's Anthropology Research Facility (ARF) and includes a grave containing 24 individuals, one with six individuals, one with three individuals, as well as single graves and empty control graves (Blau et al. 2018; Corcoran et al. 2018). More recently, a project documenting two mass graves (one with three and one with six individuals), a single grave, and empty control graves was initiated at the Australian Facility for Taphonomic Experimental Research (AFTER) at the University of Technology, Sydney (Blau et al. 2018). To date, these research programs have demonstrated the utility of remote sensing and geophysical methods to detect mass graves, as well as the impacts of multiple decomposing bodies on the microbiome and soil biogeochemistry (Blau et al. 2018; Corcoran et al. 2018; Keenan et al. 2018; Knaub 2019). These studies have also emphasized the importance of the repeatability of results, examination of temporal dynamics, and replication in different environments. The latter is fundamental for testing the validity and reliability of methods.

8.2 The Mass Grave Project

The complexity of uncovering and recording evidence in mass graves, and reconstructing the events that led to their creation, inspired the development of the Mass Grave Project (MGP). The project is designed to examine taphonomic processes in small-sized mass graves and explore and test (new) methods of investigation of these contexts. The project includes a series of taphonomic experiments using willingly donated human bodies to simulate mass and single graves at the Forensic Anthropology Research Facility (FARF), the outdoor human decomposition research facility managed by the Forensic Anthropology Center at Texas State University. FARF is located in the Texas Hill Country, near San Marcos. Body donations studied at FARF are made to FACTS under the Texas Revised Uniform Anatomical Gift Act and are exclusively acquired through the expressed and documented willingness of the donors and/or their legal next-of-kin (Gocha et al. 2022).

Donors and/or their next-of-kin are aware that donations are used for taphonomic studies. The body donation program complies with all legal and ethical standards associated with the use of human remains for scientific research.

In May 2021, a small-sized mass grave with six body donors, a control mass grave without body donors, three individual graves, and one individual control grave were placed (Fig. 8.1). The environmental and taphonomic variables in these graves were monitored over the course of 18 months, after which the graves were excavated (November 2022). Upon excavation, the human remains were collected,

Fig. 8.1 Mechanical excavation of the experimental graves, at the Forensic Anthropology Research Facility, May 2021

sampled, and placed in a secondary mass grave in a commingled fashion for phase 2 of the experiment, which is focused on complex, commingled mass graves.

8.2.1 Experiment Design

The MGP project uses an actualistic methodology to replicate clandestine human graves. Actualistic studies control for chosen observational parameters and replicate taphonomic effects by reproducing assumed causal events in a relatively controlled situation.

The FARF is located in the central Texan hill country, and its terrain consists of shallow clay-rich soil overlying deposits of limestone with grassland punctuated by woodlands of primarily oak and cedar trees (Barnes et al. 2000). The FARF has a semi-humid climate with hot summers and moderate winters. Freezing is uncommon, occurring on average 36 days per year. Vegetation consists mainly of scrub bushes, ashe juniper, and Texas live oak trees. At FARF, the soils are relatively alkaline with high carbonate content and relatively low organic matter. Because of the high clay and rock content, the soils at the FARF have relatively low permeability to air and water movement (Carson 2000; Dixon 2000; Fancher et al. 2017; Gillham et al. 2003). Groundwater is located in a deep aquifer system. The average annual precipitation is 81 cm, but the region experiences frequent droughts and flash flooding.

Prior to the excavation of the grave pits, the area was mapped and photographed. Vegetation and soil samples were collected at the surface. Weather stations at FARF record weather conditions at 30-minute intervals. Aerial and geophysical surveys were conducted of the area before excavation to document initial (subsurface) landscape and vegetation conditions. Two pits measuring 2.5 by 3 m wide and 75 cm deep and four pits measuring 2 m by 60 cm and 75 cm deep were excavated by backhoe and recorded in 3D using structure-from-motion photogrammetry. The soil in the experiment area consists of Rumple-Comfort soil (Carson 2000), which is made up of gravelly loamy clay, and extends to 75 cm deep at the location of the graves and control graves. Baseline soil samples were collected at multiple depths during excavation, and at a distance of 10 m and 200 m from the pits. Six clothed body donors were placed in the mass grave in a fresh stage of decomposition, in direct contact with each other in an "unorganized" fashion. The position of the bodies upon burial and excavation was recorded in 3D. Simultaneously, three additional body donors were buried individually in the smaller pits. Soil probes were placed in the graves containing body donors, as well as in the control graves, to measure core and periphery soil temperature, conductivity, and moisture content. Soil samples of graves and control graves were taken at monthly intervals for the first three months, and every three months thereafter, using probes at multiple depths. Probe holes were plugged and marked following sampling, to monitor changes in stable isotopic signatures and microbial communities. Monthly geophysical surveys of all graves and controls were conducted, including ground penetrating radar and electrical resistivity tomography. Unmanned Aerial Vehicles (drones) equipped with remote sensors (thermal and hyperspectral) were deployed every month, to collect data on landscape and vegetation changes.

Prior to placement, each body donor was scanned using computed tomography (CT), to obtain a record of the tissues of the body and to obtain 3D models of each body for the development of optimized 3D documentation methods and the virtual 3D training tool. Data on biological sex, height, weight, ancestry, eye color, place of residence, medical treatment, cause of death, date of death, and duration and temperature of body of storage were collected for each individual body donor. Bodies that had been autopsied or individuals who had undergone chemotherapy, radiotherapy, or prolonged antibiotics treatment within 6 months before death were excluded from the experiment as much as possible, due to the potential effects on decomposition and reduction of soft tissue (both bacterial and insect driven), and isotopic, proteome and microbiome signatures. Tissue samples (hair, nails, teeth, iliac crest bone, mid-shaft tibia bone, a fifth metatarsal, as well as swabs of the oral and rectal cavities, periocular swabs, skin swabs from different areas of the body, and muscle tissue) were collected before placement in graves, and again upon excavation of the grave.

Gross decompositional changes to the body were scored upon placement and excavation of the body donors following Megyesi et al. (2005), and indicators of gross decomposition were recorded in written descriptions and photographs during both stages of the experiment, allowing posthoc scoring according to other visual methods. Although the total body score PMI estimation method by Megyesi et al. (2005) has limitations when applied to buried bodies or in non-temperate climates, it remains widely used and understood, facilitating comparison with other studies.

8.2.2 Overview of the Project Research Pillars

The aims and objectives of the Mass Grave Project are organized within four research pillars: Detection, Documentation and 3D Visualization, Identification, and Education and Training.

Detection

Robust and reliable remote and non-destructive (i.e., without excavating) methods of locating mass graves are important as logistical restrictions and security issues can mean that land-based or destructive techniques are not always feasible or desirable options in mass grave investigations. The MGP monitors landscape/soil/vegetation changes throughout the experiments using remote sensing and ground-based geophysical techniques and evaluates the reliability of these methods to detect the presence of a mass grave with human bodies throughout different stages of decomposition.

Geophysical anomalies were measured throughout the experiment using different non-invasive geophysical techniques including electrical resistivity tomography, electromagnetic, self-potential, and ground penetrating radar for locating, to examine variation in signals with time after burial and evaluate the performance of each technique individually and in combination. Unmanned Aerial Vehicles (drones) equipped with remote sensors (thermal and multispectral) were deployed every month, to collect remote sensing data on landscape and vegetation changes.

Documentation and 3D Visualization

Due to their complexity in terms of a large "body mass," differential decomposition, disarticulation, and commingling of bodies and body parts, combined with time and resource limitations, the documentation of evidence in mass graves can pose a challenge. Digital 3D data capture and 3D visualization methods allow researchers to record complex spatial relationships to a high level of detail and provide options for posthoc analysis, as well as reconstruct events leading up to burial, or to simulate hypothesized sequences of events. The MGP uses photogrammetric 3D recording techniques to document experimental mass and single graves, both to examine alterations of human remains and evidence over time during decomposition, and to devise protocols for rapid and reliable 3D documentation of deposits with multiple commingled remains which can be efficiently and affordably implemented during investigations. This project tests the accuracy and precision of photogrammetric 3D recording techniques to rapidly, accurately, and reliably document complex mass grave deposits, and in particular, examines the impact of using these methods on the workflow of field operations. Minimal disruption of field operations is desirable for these methods to become widely adopted. The most reliable and time-efficient data collection and post-processing procedures for recording complex commingled deposits will be used to develop an open-access 3D documentation protocol.

Identification

For the continued development of forensic omics age-at-death and PMI estimation techniques, the MGP studies bone omics profiles and soil microbiome profiles before and after burial. For techniques based on the microbial communities in different parts of the body, swabs (oral, rectal, palm of the right hand, back of the neck, sole of the right foot) were collected before frozen body storage, after frozen storage, and again after excavation for DNA methylation analysis and Next Generation Sequencing. To study the effects of diagenesis and decomposition on the isotopic signatures of human tissues (hair, nails, bone), Sr-Pb isotope compositions were analyzed using thermal ionization mass spectrometry (TIMS) and multicollector-inductively coupled plasma mass spectrometry (MC-ICPMS) respectively of samples taken before burial and after excavation.

The MGP also explores the potential of using various human biological tissues (other than bone or teeth) for identification through DNA profiling in complex contexts such as mass graves or mass disasters. Traditionally, DNA extraction from human remains in advanced stages of decomposition focuses on hard tissues like bones and teeth, as these are believed to preserve DNA profiles more effectively over time. To investigate the viability of using soft tissues for DNA profiling, this study examined the degradation of DNA profiles in swab (oral, rectal, skin, periocular), nail, and muscle tissue samples from both single and mass graves. These samples were collected at three stages: fresh before freezing, fresh post-freezing, and decomposed after excavation. The study also looked for signs of cross-contamination between body donors within the mass grave.

Additionally, the impact of freezing on human DNA preservation was analyzed to evaluate the appropriateness of using frozen body donors in taphonomic experiments for genetic research. The study aimed to assess the completeness of genetic information obtained from swabs (skin, oral cavity, and rectum) taken at different stages: upon arrival at the human taphonomy facility, after freezing for periods ranging from 11 to 455 days, and after thawing before burial for 18 months. Post-burial DNA profiling was also performed on various soft tissue sampling sites, including skin, oral, periocular, and rectal swabs, nails, cartilage, muscles, and internal organs. The performance of these samples was then analyzed in relation to body decomposition, burial type (individual or mass grave), and the body's position within the mass grave.

The MGP also includes an explorative study into the effects of mass grave conditions on the preservation and recoverability of drug concentrations in different tissues. Producing an accurate drug exposure profile post-burial can assist in death investigations and the identification of unknown bodies in cases of a known history of drug use. The analyses targeted the nail of the first toe and muscle tissues, to examine tissues that are known to preserve differently during decomposition. Muscle tissue and toenail segments were analyzed to assess post-burial drug concentration profiles in the mass grave. Tissues were screened using two innovative methods: an LC-QTRAP-MS method that semi-quantitatively detects the presence of 500 substances and an LC-HRMS method that screens for over 2000 substances qualitatively. The results were compared to the medical histories of the deceased and examined for potential contamination due to mass grave conditions. The segmented analysis of the whole toenail provides a profile of antemortem drug exposure for multiple months before death, which can provide investigators with very valuable information on the deceased.

Education and Training

The complex taphonomic environment of mass graves, and the fact that the destructive process of excavation means evidence must be immediately recorded appropriately, requires a high level of training from investigators. Physical replication of mass graves for training purposes is severely limited by the amount of time and resources needed to simulate the hazardous and physically and emotionally strenuous working conditions. However, 3D visualization techniques, especially those that provide (partly) immersive and interactive experiences such as Virtual Reality (VR) environments, could provide viable alternatives and are known to improve learning, memory retention, and motivation to learn and understand (ICRC Innovation Unit 2019; Krokos et al. 2019). They offer opportunities to simulate mass grave investigation and provide training in a safe and secure manner and can be disseminated rapidly and widely among stakeholders in need of training and capacity-building. Various studies have demonstrated that 3D virtual environments play an important role in spatial learning and can help improve stress management and mitigate "sensory overload" associated with humanitarian work dealing with gross human rights violations and conflict (Ashkenazi et al. 2021; Engelbrecht et al. 2019; ICRC Innovation Unit 2019; Koutitas et al. 2021; Pollard et al. 2020).

The data generated from the various components of the project—particularly Documentation and 3D Visualization—are being utilized to create 3D virtual training tools. These tools are intended for use by international humanitarian organizations involved in mass grave investigations as well as in university teaching programs. They provide interactive 3D representations of mass grave taphonomy and excavation, serving as visual aids to illustrate the complexities of retrieving evidence from contexts with multiple commingled remains.

The tools will feature various interactive modules designed to guide users through decision-making processes in the field. These decisions include excavation strategies informed by surface features, estimated grave size, number of bodies, information from informants, field surveys, and logistical or time constraints. The tools are being developed with sustainability and accessibility in mind, avoiding reliance on commercial hosting platforms or costly, cumbersome equipment. Instead, they are optimized for use on common devices such as desktop computers, laptops, tablets, and smartphones.

Because virtual training environments are highly scalable, repeatable, and support effective learning and memory retention, these tools offer significant advantages. They can be deployed in diverse contexts with fewer logistical challenges compared to traditional training methods, enhancing accessibility and impact.

8.3 Results to Date

At the time of writing, phase 2 of the MGP is still underway, with excavation of the secondary mass grave not yet completed. Analyses of the environmental and tissue samples collected in phase 1 of the project have been completed, and the first results of the analyses are described below.

The results of the geophysical analyses (electrical resistivity tomography [ERT], electromagnetics [EM], and ground-penetrating radar [GPR]) of the first six months of the experiment showed an initial increase in resistivity across all graves, attributed to soil aeration from disturbed soil, followed by a steady decrease in resistivity, especially in the mass graves, as decaying bodies produced conductive leachates. This decline in resistivity was more pronounced in mass graves than in individual graves. EM measurements were found to be good at isolating anomalies associated with the presence of bodies in the soil in the first days after burial, while electrical resistivity was useful for longer timeframes. GPR profiles also consistently show distorted reflectors and hyperbolas indicative of ground disturbances and the presence of human remains, but were limited by the presence of rocks and site-specific geology. Quasi-3D resistivity models provided detailed imaging of these changes over time, allowing for better visualization of grave outlines and decomposition effects. Overall, the results indicate that ERT is a valuable tool for forensic investigations, particularly for locating graves and monitoring decomposition, with GPR providing supplemental data despite its limitations. The geophysical analyses were found to be effective for both individual and mass graves, with ERT proving especially reliable for tracking temporal changes linked to human decay (Doro et al. 2022a, b).

While the multispectral image data are still under analysis, preliminary thermal data (DJI Zenmuse XT2, 7.5–13.5 μm) results include a distinct heat signature of 3–4 degrees Fahrenheit difference between the mass grave and the control mass grave when measured immediately before dawn during months 3–6 of the experiment, related to greater heat retention of the grave in comparison to surrounding soils combined with warmth generated by active decomposition of the bodies during that time.

With regard to documentation, the MGP has focused on seeking affordable and efficient 3D recording procedures. We used a simple photogrammetry procedure for ground-based 3D recording of small-sized mass graves. While recording in situ evidence is the primary goal, processing the 3D models immediately and examining them in the field was found to assist excavation planning significantly. The models were processed with Agisoft Metashape, a commercially licensed software; however, future work will focus on developing protocols using common Free and Open Source Software packages to process models. Each photography round took on average 20 mins to complete, which meant coordinating the excavation team to cease all excavation work for during this time. Nonetheless, if planned well, this was found to lead to minimal disruption of field activities and did not significantly delay the scheduled time for excavation of the graves.

The results obtained by the omics analyses conducted on bones demonstrate clear differences between the pre-burial and the post-burial samples, as well as between individual and mass graves, highlighting the effectiveness of bone proteomics, metabolomics, and lipidomics in differentiating fresh and decomposed bones, as well as specimens originated from single and mass graves. First of all, proteins are less abundant in the decomposed bones in comparison with their pre-burial counterparts, especially for blood plasma proteins such as hamoglobin and hemopexin, and for muscle proteins such as actin and myoglobin, as expected due to the decomposition process and as previously found in other works (Procopio et al. 2018). On the contrary, metabolites such as amino acids and prostaglandins associated with inflammatory processes are more abundant in post-burial samples, whereas metabolite intermediates involved in nucleotide degradation and bile acids are more abundant in pre-burial samples, reflecting the activation of autolytic and microbial decomposition processes post-mortem.

Interestingly, the inter-individual variability associated with differences such as health condition, drug use, medications, and lifestyle is lower between the individuals buried in the mass grave than in the individual burials, especially for the proteomic and lipidomic profiles. When comparing bone proteins in single and mass graves, blood plasma proteins such as coagulation factor IX, pigment epithelium-derived factor, and prothrombin, as well as bone extracellular matrix proteins like chondroadherin, collagen alpha-1, and Matrix Gla protein, are significantly more abundant in mass grave samples than in the individual graves samples, suggesting overall a slower decomposition rate in the former. In a similar way, specific metabolites such as amines and selected amino acids are also more abundant in the mass grave bones, while sugars—critical sources of energy for bacterial decomposers—are instead more abundant in the single grave samples, highlighting again the differences in the decomposition processes between these two burial scenarios.

The results obtained from the analysis of the soil microbial communities in single and mass graves reinforce what was previously found with the omics analyses of the skeletal remains, in that soil microbial populations in single graves are more diverse than those found in mass graves. Additionally, machine learning algorithms applied to such samples can correctly classify soil originating from either single or mass graves collected at the end of the 18-month experiment, with an accuracy level of 95%. The main bacterial species used for the prediction are *Conexibacter* spp., known to be involved in carbon cycling in soil environments, and *Streptomyces* spp., also well-known soil decomposers. In addition to classification analyses, soil microbial data have also been used to estimate post-mortem interval in forensic contexts; however, in cases like this one, it is more precise to refer to this as time since burial estimation. Given the limited understanding of microbial dynamics in mass grave environments, it is essential to investigate the applicability of this methodology in mass graves before its implementation in real scenarios. Results from the MGP indicate that time since burial can be determined with good accuracy in single graves, with a mean absolute error of 3.2 months over the 18-month study period. In contrast, the accuracy of predictions in mass grave contexts is reduced, with an increased error of 4.9 months. Notably, the prediction accuracy is particularly low during the first 10 months of the experiment, after which subsequent samples yield more consistent estimations up to 18 months. The presence of multiple bodies in the same grave in different layers, along with the varying decomposition processes they undergo and that were well documented with the omics approaches on the skeletal remains, is likely key factors contributing to decreased accuracy in time estimations based on soil samples. These complexities in decomposition dynamics may interfere with microbial community composition and its subsequent analysis, suggesting that more research is needed to refine methodologies for estimating time since burial in mass graves.

The pre- and post-burial human scalp hair, human bone (iliac and tibia), and tooth enamel and dentine samples, as well as environmental samples of vegetation and soils, have been prepared for chromatographic separation for Sr and Pb isotope analysis. At the time of writing, the results are awaiting further analysis and interpretation. Based on previous individual grave and surface placement experiments at FARF, isotopic shifts are expected in the post-burial samples of the MGP donations compared to the pre-burial signatures. In this previous work, more densely mineralized elements (cortical tibial bone and tooth enamel samples) showed good recoverability of the pre-placement isotope signatures, while less densely mineralized samples (iliac bone) showed more susceptibility to diagenetic alteration. Hair keratin was found to be highly susceptible to diagenetic alteration, as well as sensitive to alteration during laboratory cleaning treatment (Kootker et al. 2020, 2023). A preliminary examination of the data suggests that the isotopic shifts in the bone samples within the MGP are relatively subtle. In contrast, despite employing a more optimal cleaning method, an initial assessment indicates that the biogenic Sr-Pb signatures in the keratin samples have been compromised by diagenetic processes. Further analysis of the MGP results will be used to substantiate what is known about the effects of the FARF burial environment on the preservation and recoverability of isotopic profiles. Importantly, the research will examine whether individual versus mass burial leads to differences in the recoverability of unaltered isotopic signatures.

The analysis of human DNA degradation in soft tissues revealed several key findings. The quality of DNA profiles progressively decreased from fresh to thawed and ultimately to decomposed tissue. Interestingly, the extent of DNA degradation did not correlate with the stage of gross decomposition observed during the excavation of the bodies, nor with the body's position within the grave. In fact, bodies in the mass grave exhibited higher levels of DNA preservation compared to those in individual graves, although the stage of decomposition in the mass grave was less advanced than in the individual graves overall. However, signs of DNA cross-contamination were observed in the mass grave due to the close proximity of bodies. The results also confirmed that freezing and burial led to a progressive loss of genetic information (Sguazzi et al. 2022; Gino et al. 2024). However, while freezing and burial led to DNA degradation, the research shows that personal identification can still be achieved by focusing on a variety of tissue samples. The results underscore the complexity of DNA preservation in mass graves and allow for preliminary recommendations to be made on identification procedures for mass victim contexts, including using swabs from various tissues, such as skin, oral, and rectal areas, as viable alternatives to traditional tissue and bone sampling due to their ease of collection. The research also highlights the importance of sampling as many tissue types as possible to maximize DNA yield, especially in challenging contexts like mass graves, and timely sample collection after the discovery of remains, to mitigate the effects of further decomposition on DNA quality. Additionally, training of disaster response personnel remains important to ensure procedures are followed and contamination is prevented (Sguazzi et al. 2024a, b).

The results of toxicology screening show that drugs such as amlodipine, ketamine (and its metabolite norketamine), caffeine, cotinine, lisinopril, paracetamol, morphine, desloratadine, duloxetine, and quetiapine were detected in toenail samples, indicating that these tissues effectively preserve drug profiles post-burial. In several cases, there was a correlation between the drugs found in the nails and the known medical history of the individuals. Thus far, no indications of contamination between body donors in the mass grave were found. Segmental analysis of toenails reveals a timeline of drug exposure, which provides forensic investigators with valuable insights into the deceased's drug use before death. The next step involves analyzing the toenails using Matrix-Assisted Laser Desorption/Ionization Time-of-Flight (MALDI-TOF), a mass spectrometry technique used to identify proteins, peptides, and small organic compounds, to image the spatial distribution of these substances within the nail, creating a visual map of their locations to understand drug use over time. This will also provide a more detailed understanding of how substances are preserved and distributed in nails after burial.

As described above, the MGP experimental graves were recorded in 3D before placement of body donors, and sequentially after each donor. The same process was repeated upon excavation of the graves, in reverse, that is, after lifting each body. These photogrammetry models are very helpful in showing the differences between the initial body placement and the final condition and position of remains after 18 months of burial (Fig. 8.2). However, capturing such 3D "snapshots" using photogrammetry results in a static model of only surface geometry. To develop such data further for training and education purposes, the 3D data should serve to visualize the changes in condition and spatial configuration of remains and allow a degree of interaction with objects in the grave. Virtual reconstruction and animation methods allow recreation of the graves in a dynamic, interactive way. To tackle this, the full body post-mortem CT scans of the donors, which provide a detailed three-dimensional view of the body, were processed to create 3D models of skeleton and soft tissues unique to the individual. These models were then processed using techniques used in videogame character development, including remeshing, re-topologizing, and rigging. This creates highly accurate and posable virtual representations of the donors, that can be positioned precisely as their bodies were placed in the graves (Fig. 8.3), resulting in a virtually reconstructed grave that is not merely static surface mesh, but a virtual space filled with virtual objects that can be manipulated, examined, and changed to test or visualize hypotheses. A major advantage of preparing the CT scan data in this way is that it allows visualizing the position of the skeleton when the bodies enter the graves fully fleshed. This initial data can then be compared to the final positions of the bones upon excavation (Fig. 8.4). Understanding how these transformations affect human remains and other evidence in mass graves is important to reconstructing the criminal actions involved in their creation. A better understanding of what to expect in mass graves of different ages, different numbers of individuals, and in different climates is also essential for planning of excavation of graves for legal or humanitarian purposes as well as protection of graves in situ. The virtual reconstructions from the MGP are still under development at the time of writing and will be developed further to contain additional detailed data on the physical changes of the grave over time, including information on differential human DNA degradation within the grave and how the microbiome of the grave changes over time. While these patterns can be visualized in 2D, incorporating them into a 3D virtual reconstruction helps to study, for

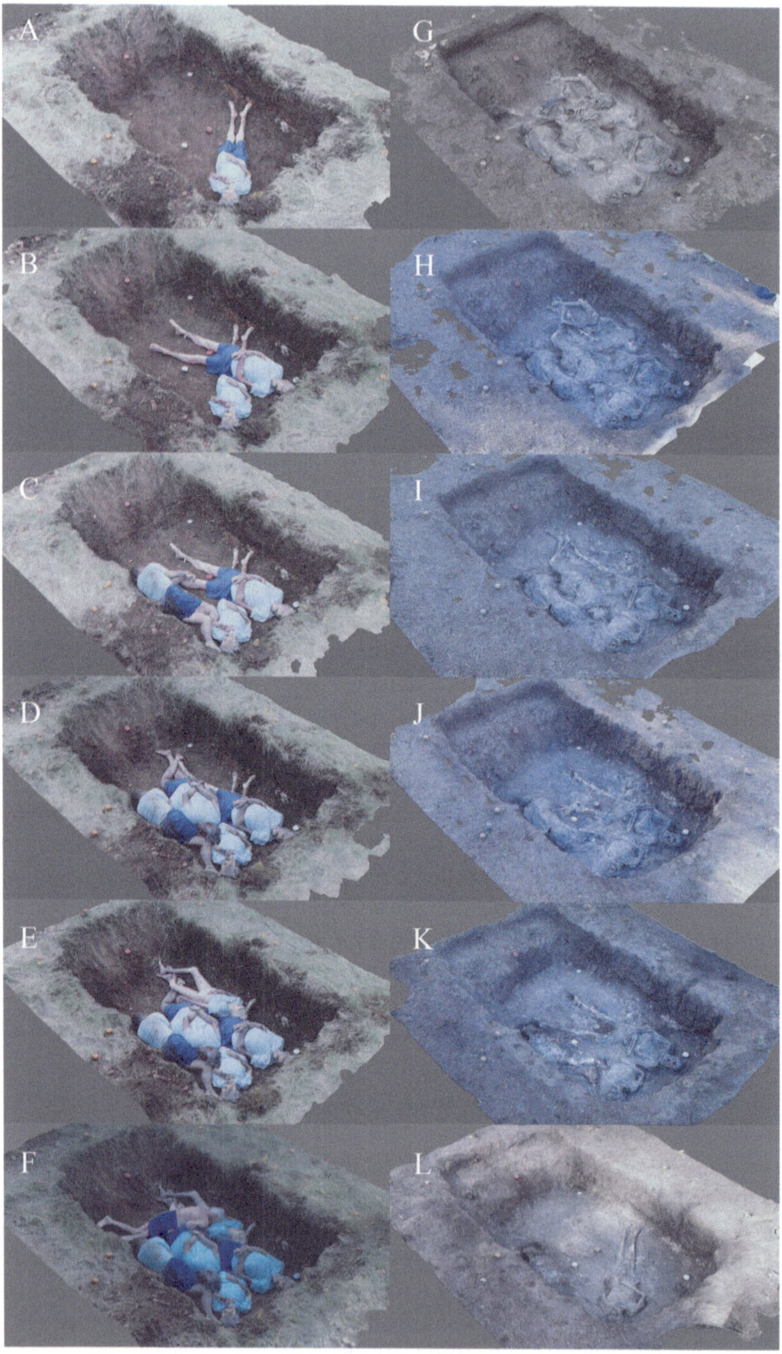

Fig. 8.2 Sequential 3D models of the experimental primary mass grave during placement (**a–f**) and during excavation and lifting (**g–l**)

Fig. 8.3 Rigged and posed virtual body donor (white) placed in original burial position during the construction of the virtual mass grave. The Left shows the fleshed body donor, right only the skeleton

Fig. 8.4 Virtually reconstructed original position of the body donor's skeleton, overlaying the final position of the remains in the primary mass grave

example, how differences in the degree of human DNA degradation throughout the grave might be related to localized microbial variation. The virtual graves with all scanned bodies, objects, and representations of the stratigraphy layers and tool marks from digging, as well as the results from other pillars of the project, will thus be processed into realistic Virtual Reality (VR) tools to enhance training for mass grave excavations, in which the user can virtually re-excavate the grave, removing individual bones and objects, and receiving step-by-step instructions on documentation and sampling procedures. The VR will incorporate animations of changes in the graves over time to help learners to understand how evidence in the grave relates to the original conditions and spatial arrangement of bodies.

8.4 Discussion

The preliminary geophysical analysis of the graves during the first six months of burial indicated that there is a need for long-term studies to monitor the progression of electrical resistivity changes beyond six months to better understand how decomposition affects geophysical signals over time. The results of the geophysical surveys in months 7–18 of the project are currently under analysis and are expected to yield further insight into the long-term effects of decomposition on soil properties, the spatial spread of leachates, and the potential for distinguishing between individual and mass graves over extended periods. Nonetheless, more research is required to refine the application of geophysical methods in diverse soil types and environmental conditions, as the current limitations in GPR due to soil composition at FARF need to be addressed. Including more advanced 3D imaging techniques and multi-method approaches (e.g., combining resistivity with magnetic or seismic methods) could enhance detection accuracy. In addition, there is an important opportunity to explore automated data processing and interpretation methods, such as machine learning, to streamline forensic investigations using geophysical data. The remote sensing data collected throughout the MGP are the topic of a PhD project, which aims to develop and validate remote sensing techniques, including spectral and thermal imaging, to detect and monitor clandestine mass graves in conflict zones. This project will use the UAV-collected data (RGB, multispectral, and thermal imaging) alongside satellite imagery and develop machine learning algorithms to analyze these images to distinguish graves from other disturbances.

The innovative application and integration of omics analyses in the context of mass graves has generated valuable knowledge into the decomposition processes unique to mass grave scenarios. This molecular-level insight has contributed to laying robust foundations for the development of improved forensic methodologies for the study of human decomposition in mass grave contexts. The limits of some methods applied here, such as the post-burial estimation via soil microbiome analyses in mass grave contexts, underline the needs for more research on experimental mass graves. Such studies are essential to improve the understanding of the biological phenomena occurring in these complex circumstances, which in turn can inform improved sampling strategies for better forensic results.

The results of previous isotopic studies on the preservation and recoverability of isotopic signatures have emphasized that further research is needed into the effects of taphonomic processes, diagenesis, and cleaning protocols on isotope compositions of different human tissues often targeted in forensic investigations. The results of the MGP isotopic study will further evaluate and substantiate previous findings, while providing unique insights into how isotopic signatures preserve in mass grave environments.

The DNA results to date provide valuable insights into how freezing, burial, and advanced decomposition can substantially impact the integrity of DNA, thereby influencing genetic identification in mass grave contexts. These findings will be further developed into recommendations for forensic practice and future research in challenging scenarios, such as mass graves and mass disasters, where cross-contamination and varying states of preservation often complicate the identification process. The research highlights the need for more refined genetic identification strategies tailored to complex contexts such as mass graves, where the risk of DNA degradation and cross-contamination is particularly high. Importantly, the results emphasize the necessity of multi-sample approaches, targeting different tissue types and sampling different locations on the body, to maximize the chances of successful identification.

The findings of the toxicology screening are encouraging, showing that significant drug profiles can be detected in nail long after burial. The detected drugs can contribute to human identification and help reconstruct the circumstances surrounding death, since exposure to certain drugs can reveal information about medical conditions, drug abuse, or poisoning. For example, the presence of cardiovascular drugs such as lisinopril may indicate high blood pressure or other heart-related diseases, while the presence of psychopharmaceuticals, such as duloxetine or quetiapine, can suggest psychiatric conditions. The toxicology results thus far do not appear to indicate that mass grave conditions hindered the detection of drug exposure from muscle or nail tissues, by comparison to individual grave conditions. However, further longitudinal studies that track drug degradation or persistence over longer post-burial periods are needed to substantiate these findings and to investigate how long drugs and their metabolites can remain detectable in various tissues under different burial conditions.

The development of 3D virtual reality training tools holds great potential for advancing both investigative and educational approaches to mass graves. Virtual graves not only aid in reconstructing taphonomic processes but also serve as dynamic archives for interdisciplinary data, supporting hypothesis testing and further analysis. They offer significant benefits for education and training, in particular, due to Virtual Reality's ability to enhance spatial memory and learning. Simulating real excavation conditions prepares trainees for the challenges of real investigations, including the impact of dealing with decomposing human remains. Moreover, their ability to be rapidly and remotely deployed is particularly advantageous in contexts with practical or financial constraints. A prototype of these tools will be tested within existing training programs used by international humanitarian organizations and among university students in Forensic Anthropology and Archaeology. Feedback from these users will be used to make modifications where needed.

8.5 Conclusion and Future Research

The Mass Grave Project, through the use of actualistic taphonomic experiments, has begun to shed light on the complex processes that occur in mass graves, contributing to advancements in both documentation and analysis techniques. A critical component of this research is the interdisciplinary approach, which recognizes mass graves as intricate archaeological and forensic contexts shaped by a variety of interconnected factors. These factors include, among other thigs, local soil conditions, weather patterns, the number of individuals interred, and the specific methods used by perpetrators to dispose of the bodies. By integrating expertise from multiple fields—including archaeology, forensic taphonomy, biomolecular sciences, geophysics, remote sensing, 3D visualization, and virtual reconstruction—the MGP examines how these variables interact to affect the evidence. This interdisciplinary perspective is essential for identifying the most effective methods for investigating mass graves and for designing training programs that address the specific challenges presented by these contexts.

Phase 2 of the project, which began in November 2022 and is scheduled for completion in 2025, builds on the work of Phase 1 by simulating the scenario of secondary deposition following the disturbance of a primary grave. In this phase, donors from the primary graves have been reinterred in a commingled secondary mass grave. The precise position of each bone and body part was recorded in 3D during placement, and additional items, such as empty shell casings, beer bottles, and cigarette butts with human DNA, were also deposited in the grave. In addition to continuing the research pillars established in Phase 1, a key goal of Phase 2 is to enhance the methods used for excavating and recording commingled deposits. This will involve analyzing the decision-making processes of archaeologists and anthropologists who are unaware of the minimum number of individuals (MNI) or their positions within the grave. Another important aim is to determine whether DNA profiles and fingerprints can be recovered from the items placed in the grave, potentially providing further insights into the forensic recovery of evidence from mass graves.

Acknowledgments Foremost, our sincerest thanks go to the body donors and their next of kin, whose extremely valuable gift make crucial research into mass graves possible. We are also very grateful to the staff and students of the Forensic Anthropology Center at Texas State, Texas State University, San Marcos, Texas, for their continuing support for the Mass Grave Project.

We also gratefully acknowledge the advice and/or assistance of: Prof. Maurice Aalders, Prof. Roelof-Jan Oostra, Samantha De Simone, Adrienne Stainton, Casey Flint, Samantha.

Sawyer, Dr. Petra Banks, Shelbey Garza, Emma Giacomello, Dr. Deborah Cunningham, Dr. Paul.

Emanovsky, Dr. Devora Gleiber, Dr. Sophia Mavroudas, Heather Nesbitt, Dr. Lauren Meckel, Ivanna Robledo, Dr. Courtney Siegert, Amar Kolapkar, Efemena Emmanuel, Jessika Bentivogli, Wendell Geigle, Lotte Wever, Samuele Voyron, Veronika Pace, Akram Alkhomaisi, Sandra Sostaric, Nicole Lambacher.

Finally, we thank the funding organizations who supported this work: the Leiden University Fund Byvanck (Grant number 5604/30-4-2015/ Byvanck), the 2017 Royal Netherlands Academy of Arts and Sciences (KNAW) "National Postdoc Prize," the VINNOVA MSCA postdoctoral research project "THANATOS" (Grant number 2019-05211), and the European Meeting on Forensic Archaeology Best Presentation Award 2021. The DNA research conducted in the Mass Grave Project is the result of a study conducted in the framework of the International PhD in Global Health, Humanitarian Aid, and Disaster Medicine organized by University of Eastern Piedmont.

References

Ashkenazi I, Rapaport C, Kelling N, Izygon M, Buras W (2021) Stress management as key factor for enhanced first responder training: virtual reality at the service of life savers. J Emerg Med Services, 9 September 2021

Baier W, Rando C (2016) Developing the use of Structure-from-Motion in mass grave documentation. Forensic Sci Int 261:19–25

Barker C, Esma A, Santana JN (2017) Post-mortem differential preservation and its utility in interpreting forensic and archaeological mass burials. In: Schotsmans EMJ, Márquez-Grant N, Forbes SL (eds) Taphonomy of human remains: Forensic analysis of the dead and the depositional environment. John Wiley & Sons Ltd, Chichester, pp 251–276

Barnes PW, Liang S-Y, Jessup KE, Ruiseco LE, Phillips PL, Reagan SJ (2000) Soils, topography, and vegetation of the Freeman Ranch. Freeman Ranch Publication Series 1. Southwest Texas State University Press

Blau S, Sterenberg J, Weeden P, Urzedo F, Wright R, Watson C (2018) Exploring non-invasive approaches to assist in the detection of clandestine human burials: developing a way forward. Forensic Sci Res 3(4):304–326

Bonicelli A, Mickleburgh HL, Wescott DJ, Procopio N (2022) The 'ForensOMICS' approach for postmortem interval estimation from human bone by integrating metabolomics, lipidomics, and proteomics. elife 11:e83658

Carson D (2000) Soils of the Freeman Ranch, Hays County, Texas. Freeman Ranch Publication Series 4. Southwest Texas State University Press

Chesson LA, Meier-Augenschein W, Berg GE, Bataille CP, Bartelink EJ, Richards MP (2020) Basic principles of stable isotope analysis in humanitarian forensic science. In: Parra RC, Zapico SC, Ubelaker DH (eds) Forensic science and humanitarian action: interacting with the dead and the living. John Wiley & Sons, pp 285–310

Corcoran KA, Mundorff AZ, White DA, Emch WL (2018) A novel application of terrestrial LIDAR to characterize elevation change at human grave surfaces in support of narrowing down possible unmarked grave locations. Forensic Sci Int 289:320–328

Dirkmaat DC, Adovasio JM (1996) The role of archaeology in the recovery and interpretation of human remains from an outdoor forensic setting. In: Sorg MH, Haglund WD (eds) Forensic taphonomy: The Postmortem Fate of Human Remains. CRC Press, Boca Raton, pp 39–64

Dixon R (2000) Climatology of the Freeman Ranch, Hays County, Texas. Freeman Ranch Publication Series 3. Southwest Texas State University Press, pp 1–9

Doro KO, Emmanuel DE, Bank C-G, Wescott DJ, Mickleburgh HL (2022a) Time-lapse electrical resistivity tomography imaging of buried human remains in simulated mass and individual graves. Front Earth Sci 10

Doro, K.O., Kolapkar, A.M., Bank, C-G., Wescott, D.J., & Mickleburgh, H.L. (2022b). Geophysical imaging of buried human remains in simulated mass and single graves: Experiment design and results from pre-burial to six months after burial. Forensic Sci Int, 335, 111289

Engelbrecht H, Lindeman RW, Hoermann S (2019) A SWOT analysis of the field of virtual reality for firefighter training. Front Robot AI 6:101

Fancher JP, Aitkenhead-Peterson JA, Farris T, Mix K, Schwab AP, Wescott DJ, Hamilton MD (2017) An evaluation of soil chemistry in human cadaver decomposition islands: Potential for estimating postmortem interval (PMI). Forensic Sci Int 279:130–139

Gillham D, Young P, Long M (2003) Atlas of Freeman Ranch. Department of Geography, Texas State University

Gino S, Sguazzi G, McCarthy-Allen M, Colombo N, Wescott DJ, Gocha TP, Procopio N, Mickleburgh HL (2024) The Mass Grave Project: the impact of freezing and burial on personal identification through human DNA analysis. In: Proceedings of the 76th AAFS Annual Scientific Meeting, Denver, February 19–24, 2024, p 878

Gocha TP, Mavroudas SR, Wescott DJ (2022) The Texas state donated skeletal collection at the forensic anthropology center at Texas state. Forensic Sci 2(1):7–19

Haglund WD (2002) Recent mass graves, an introduction. In: Haglund WD, Sorg MH (eds) Advances in forensic taphonomy: method, theory, and archaeological perspectives. CRC Press, Boca Raton, pp 243–261

Haglund WD, Sorg MH (2002) Advancing forensic taphonomy: purpose, theory, and process. In: Advances in forensic taphonomy: method, theory, and archaeological perspectives. CRC Press, Boca Raton, pp 4–29

Hamadeh N, Decker A, McDonald-Gibson C, Cruz Santiago A, Baik T-U, Klinkner M (2021) Global report on Missing Persons 2021. International Commission on Missing Persons, The Hague

Hanson I (2016) Mass grave investigation and identifying Missing Persons: challenges and innovations in archaeology and anthropology in the context of mass death environments. In: Handbook of Missing Persons pp 491–514

Human Rights Council (HRC) (2020) Report of the Special Rapporteur on extrajudicial, summary or arbitrary executions. Mass graves, highlighting the multitude of sites of mass killings and unlawful deaths across history and the world. Retrieved from https://digitallibrary.un.org/record/3888738

ICRC Innovation Unit (2019) Review article: the current state of virtual reality on behavior change. Extended Reality & Behavior Change Series

Jessee E, Skinner M (2005) A typology of mass grave and mass grave-related sites. Forensic Sci Int 152(1):55–59

Kalacska ME, Bell LS, Sanchez-Azofeifa GA, Caelli T (2009) The application of remote sensing for detecting mass graves: an experimental animal case study from Costa Rica. J Forensic Sci 54(1):159–166

Keenan SW, Emmons AL, Taylor LS, Phillips G, Mason AR, Mundorff AZ, Bernard EC, Davoren J, DeBruyn JM (2018) Spatial impacts of a multi-individual grave on microbial and microfaunal communities and soil biogeochemistry. PLoS One 13(12):e0208845

Klinkner M, Smith E (2020) The Bournemouth protocol on mass grave protection and investigation. Bournemouth University, Bournemouth

Knaub MM (2019). Mass grave detection with the use of geophysics. Chancellor's Honors Program Projects. https://trace.tennessee.edu/utk_chanhonoproj/2302

Kootker LM, von Holstein ICC, Broeders J, Wescott DJ, Davies GR, Mickleburgh HL (2020) The effects of decomposition and environment on antemortem H-Sr-Pb isotope compositions and degradation of human scalp hair: actualistic taphonomic observations. Forensic Sci Int 312:110366

Kootker LM, Ammer STM, Wescott DJ, Davies GR, Mickleburgh HL (2023) Sr–Pb isotope differences in pre- and post-burial human bone, teeth, and hair keratin: implications for isotope forensics. Int J Legal Med 138:151

Koutitas G, Smith S, Lawrence G (2021) Performance evaluation of AR/VR training technologies for EMS first responders. Virtual Reality 25(1):83–94

Kroker P (2015) Satellite imagery as evidence for international crimes. International Justice Monitor blog. Retrieved from https://www.ijmonitor.org/2015/04/satellite-imagery-as-evidence-for-international-crimes/

Krokos E, Plaisant C, Varshney A (2019) Virtual memory palaces: immersion aids recall. Virtual Reality 23(1):1–15

Lang C (2014) The hidden archive of historical human inhumations locked within burial soils. PhD Diss. University of York

Leblanc G, Kalacska M, Soffer R (2014) Detection of single graves by airborne hyperspectral imaging. Forensic Sci Int 245:17–23

Mant AK (1950) A study in exhumation data [Doctoral dissertation, University of London]

Mant AK (1987) Knowledge acquired from post-war exhumations. In: Boddington A, Garland AN, Janaway RC (eds) Death, decay and reconstruction: approaches to archaeology and forensic science. Manchester University Press, Manchester, pp 65–78

Megyesi MS, Nawrocki SP, Haskell NH (2005) Using accumulated degree-days to estimate the postmortem interval from decomposed human remains. J Forensic Sci 50(3):JFS2004017
Mickleburgh HL, Schwalbe E, Bonicelli A, Mizukami H, Sellitto F, Starace S, Wescott DJ, Carter DO, Procopio N (2021) Human bone proteomes before and after decomposition: investigating the effects of biological variation and taphonomic alteration on bone protein profiles and the implications for forensic proteomics. J Proteome Res 20(5):2533–2546. https://doi-org.vu-nl.idm.oclc.org/10.1021/acs.jproteome.0c00992
Novo A, Lorenzo H, Rial FI, Solla M (2011) 3D GPR in forensics: Finding a clandestine grave in a mountainous environment. Forensic Sci Int 204(1–3):134–138
Osterholtz AJ (ed) (2015) Theoretical approaches to analysis and interpretation of commingled human remains. Springer
Osterholtz AJ, Baustian KM, Martin DL (eds) (2014) Commingled and disarticulated human remains. Springer, New York
Pokines J, Symes SA (eds) (2013) Manual of forensic taphonomy. CRC Press
Pollard KA, Oiknine AH, Files BT, Sinatra AM, Patton D, Ericson M, Thomas J, Khooshabeh P (2020) Level of immersion affects spatial learning in virtual environments: results of a three-condition within-subjects study with long intersession intervals. Virtual Reality 24(4):783–796
Pringle JK, Stimpson IG, Wisniewski KD, Heaton V, Davenward B, Mirosch N, Spencer F, Jervis JR (2020) Geophysical monitoring of simulated homicide burials for forensic investigations. Sci Rep 10:7544
Procopio N, Williams A, Chamberlain AT, Buckley M (2018) Forensic proteomics for the evaluation of the post-mortem decay in bones. J Proteome 177:21–30
Raymond NA, Card BL, Baker IL (2014) A new forensics: Developing standard remote sensing methodologies to detect and document mass atrocities. Genocide Stud Prevent 8(3):33–48
Sandalinas J (2015) Satellite imagery and its use as evidence in the proceedings of the international criminal court. German J Air Space Law 64(4):666–675
Sguazzi G, Mickleburgh HL, Ghignone S, Voyron S, Renò F, Migliario M, Sellitto F, Lovisolo F, Camurani G, Ogbanga N, Gino S, Procopio N (2022) Microbial DNA in human DNA extracts: recoverability of the microbiome in DNA extracts stored frozen long-term and its potential and ethical implications for forensic investigation. Forensic Sci Int Genet 59:102686. https://doi--org.vu-nl.idm.oclc.org/10.1016/j.fsigen.2022.102686
Sguazzi G, McCarthy-Allen M, Colombo N, Peroni G, Hayley MH, Wescott DJ, Gocha TP, Procopio N (2024a) Forensic genetics at the service of disaster victim identification: the preliminary results of the experimental Mass Grave Project. Book of Abstracts, 26th IALM Triennial Meeting, Athens, May 21–13, 2024, p 14
Sguazzi G, Peroni G, Colombo N, Mccarthy-Allen M, Mickleburgh HL, Wescott DJ, Gocha TP, Procopio N, Gino S (2024b) Recommendations for identifying disaster victims from the "Mass Grave Project": forensic genetics issues. Abstracts Book, 30th ISFG Congress, Santiago de Compostela, September 9–13, 2024, p 175
Silván-Cárdenas JL, Corona-Romero N, Madrigal-Gómez JM, Saavedra-Guerrero A, Cortés-Villafranco T, Coronado-Juárez E (2017) On the detectability of buried remains with hyperspectral measurements. In: Mexican Conference on Pattern Recognition. Springer, Cham, pp 201–212
Silván-Cárdenas JL, Caccavari-Garza A, Quinto-Sánchez ME, Madrigal-Gómez JM, Coronado-Juárez E, Quiroz-Suarez D (2021) Assessing optical remote sensing for grave detection. Forensic Sci Int 329:111064
Son SA (2022) Watching North Korea from the sky: Remote sensing and documenting human rights in The Democratic People's Republic of Korea. Polit Geogr 92:102525
Stodder AL (2018) Taphonomy and the nature of archaeological assemblages. In: Katzenberg MA, Grauer AL (eds) Biological anthropology of the human skeleton. John Wiley, Hoboken, pp 73–115
Toxvaerd S (2020) The strontium isotope ratio 87Sr/86Sr in archaeological organic matter conserved in acidic anaerobic environments is hard to interpret. J Archaeol Sci Rep 31:102379

Troutman L, Moffatt C, Simmons T (2014) A preliminary examination of differential decomposition patterns in mass graves. J Forensic Sci 59:621–626

UNAMI/OHCHR (2018) Unearthing Atrocities: Mass Graves in territory formerly controlled by ISIL. Report of 6 November 2018. Retrieved from https://www.ohchr.org/Documents/Countries/IQ/UNAMI_Report_on_Mass_Graves4Nov2018_EN.pdf

United Nations (UN), Human Rights Office of the High Commissioner (2016) Minnesota protocol: The Revised United Nations Manual on the effective prevention and investigation of extra-legal, arbitrary and summary executions

Usai M-R, Pickering M, Wilson C, Keely BJ, Brothwell DR (2014) 'Interred with their bones': soil micromorphology and chemistry in the study of human remains. Antiquity 88:339

Wang B, Raymond N, Gould G, Baker I (2013) Problems from hell, solution in the heavens?: identifying obstacles and opportunities for employing geospatial technologies to document and mitigate mass atrocities. Stability 2(3):1–18

Chapter 9
Complex Context: Current Perspectives on Forensic Anthropology and Taphonomy in Switzerland

Negahnaz Moghaddam , Tobias Hofstetter , Jean-Loup Gassend, and Inga Siebke

Abstract Forensic anthropology and taphonomy in Switzerland offer unique challenges and opportunities due to the country"s diverse topography, climates, and socio-political structures. This study explores current practices, casework, and the evolving role of these disciplines within the Swiss forensic framework. Key challenges include the recovery and identification of remains in mountainous and forested environments, where natural agents like snow, animals, and vegetation significantly affect taphonomic processes. The case studies highlight scenarios ranging from skeletal remains scattered in alpine terrains to historical bones found in urban areas, emphasizing the interdisciplinary collaboration required for effective forensic investigations. Despite its relatively low homicide rate and specific

N. Moghaddam (✉)
Unit of Forensic Imaging and Anthropology, University Center of Legal Medicine Lausanne-Geneva, Lausanne University Hospital and University of Lausanne, Lausanne, Switzerland

Swiss Human Institute of Forensic Taphonomy, University Center of Legal Medicine Lausanne-Geneva, Lausanne University Hospital and University of Lausanne, Lausanne, Switzerland

Division of Special Services and Expertise, Forensic Anthropology and Archaeology, Netherlands Forensic Institute, The Hague, The Netherlands
e-mail: n.moghaddam@nfi.nl

T. Hofstetter
Swiss Human Institute of Forensic Taphonomy, University Center of Legal Medicine Lausanne-Geneva, Lausanne University Hospital and University of Lausanne, Lausanne, Switzerland

Institute of Humanities in Medicine, Lausanne University Hospital and University of Lausanne, Lausanne, Switzerland

J.-L. Gassend
Unit of Forensic Medicine, University Center of Legal Medicine Lausanne-Geneva, Lausanne University Hospital and University of Lausanne, Lausanne, Switzerland

I. Siebke
Zurich Forensic Science Institute, Zurich, Switzerland

P. M. Barone, WJ M. Groen (eds.), *Forensic Archaeology and New Multidisciplinary Approaches*, Soil Forensics, https://doi.org/10.1007/978-3-031-86308-0_9

forensic casework volume, Switzerland has seen advancements in forensic anthropology and taphonomy, including institutionalization, education, and innovative techniques like radiocarbon dating and 3D visualization. This study underscores the importance of contextual analysis and interdisciplinary approaches in addressing complex forensic and archaeological cases in Switzerland.

Keywords Forensic anthropology in Switzerland · Taphonomic processes · Interdisciplinary collaboration · Environmental challenges in forensics · Radiocarbon dating and identification

9.1 Introduction

Located in central western Europe, bordering Germany, Austria, Liechtenstein, Italy, and France, Switzerland is a small landlocked country that stands out as an interesting region where the implementation and practicalities of forensic anthropology and taphonomy casework can be studied. This state of fact derives from Switzerland's diverse and contrasted geographic, demographic, social, political, and criminological characteristics, all of which are concentrated within an area no bigger than 41,277 km^2 (FDFA 2023).

In geographical terms, Switzerland displays a broad topographical and environmental diversity, ranging from high Alpine peaks (culminating at over 4600 m above mean sea level [AMSL]) and rugged valleys (covering 60% of the territory), through the lower Jura Mountain chain (10% of the territory), ranging between 1000 and 1500 m AMSL, to lowland plains (30% of the territory), set between 300 and 400 m AMSL, with numerous lakes and rivers (in excess of 1500) (Barbier et al. 1975; FDFA 2023; FSO 2021a; Labhart and Decrouez 1997). This diversity in relief comes along with an analogous variety of climates and vegetation coverage, ranging from high-altitude glacial environments with close to no vegetation and extreme weather to more temperate settings in the plains, where coniferous and deciduous forests are intertwined with agricultural lands and urban centers. Hence, two-thirds of Switzerland's total population (8.96 million inhabitants in 2023 (FSO 2023)) lives, works, and spends its leisure time in the lowland plains, be it in urban or rural settings. The Jura and the Alps, although much less densely populated, still represent popular destinations for tourism and summer or winter sports (e.g., hiking, mountaineering, skiing) (FDFA 2023; FSO 2012).

In sociocultural terms, Switzerland represents a plural entity, encompassing four major linguistic communities (German, French, Italian, and Romansh) as well as a series of smaller foreign subgroups. Politically, it is made up of small, independent, sovereign administrative units (called "Cantons") (FDFA 2023; Siebke et al. 2024). The country benefits from a high standard of living, although a certain degree of urban/rural divide exists, and the country is not exempt from typical contemporary issues shaping the overall forensic landscape (interpersonal violence, illicit substance trade and abuse, armed theft, etc.) (FSO 2021b, 2024b). As such, forensic practice is managed at the cantonal level, which means that each canton tends to deal with its own specific cases, depending on the region in which it is located. Additionally, every canton is responsible and equipped with relevant institutions for the prosecution of cases that took place on its territory (Indra and Lösch 2021; Lösch et al. 2015). In practice, most fatal cases are handled in centralized institutions, such as the University Center of Legal Medicine in Lausanne and Geneva (CURML), which oversees all such cases from western Switzerland. Similar institutions are based in Bern (Institute of Legal Medicine, IRM-Bern) and Zurich (Zurich Forensic Science Institute, FOR, and the Institute of Legal Medicine Zurich, IRM-UZH). As far as the objectives of forensic anthropology and taphonomy within Swiss medicolegal practice are concerned, the main standard inputs are (1) determining whether discovered osteological material is of human or animal origin, (2) identifying which skeletal elements are present, in which state, and how many individuals they account for, (3) proposing a chronological attribution of the bones, and (4) assisting in the identification process and medicolegal inquiry for forensic case work (Lösch et al. 2015; Siebke et al. 2024).

9.2 Crime Statistics in Switzerland and Forensic Institutions

As far as fatalities of interest in the forensic field are concerned, violent deaths, accidents, and suicides account for roughly 6% of the total number of deaths within the country, with males being more impacted than females (FSO, 2024a, b; Peter and Tuch 2024). More specifically, violent deaths mainly occur because of road or work accidents, notably at construction sites and in agricultural settings. Each year, a number of people also suffer fatal accidents, go missing, or die in remote areas, often reemerging later as surface findings mainly in dense forest coverage, in or near major water bodies, or in the Alps or Jura mountains (FSO 2012; SUVA 2023). Switzerland's overall homicide rate (0.5 per 100,000 inhabitants in 2022) is among the lowest in the world (UNODC 2023). The bulk of homicide cases involve sharp and blunt force trauma or firearms. The latter primarily takes place in densely populated urban centers, while the countryside is more affected by leisure- and sports-related fatal accidents. As far as suicide is concerned, Switzerland presents with a rate of roughly 10 cases of suicide per 100,000 inhabitants, mostly through firearm or hanging, followed by poisoning, jumping from height, and rail suicide (FSO 2021b, 2024b). Thus, in overall terms, while different types of cases are investigated throughout the year, the handling of archaeological remains, accidents, disappearances, and suicide cases in remote locations remains the most frequently encountered scenario from the Swiss forensic anthropological and taphonomical perspective (Indra and Lösch 2021; Lösch et al. 2015; Siebke et al. 2024). In special cases, e.g., in the case of burnt bodies or for the reconstruction of bone fractures, anthropologists can be called in by forensic pathologists for examination (Moghaddam et al. 2023). Due to the different circumstances mentioned above, anthropologists are therefore confronted with a wide range of different scenarios and thus different taphonomic conditions of human remains. The material anthropologists' face ranges from poorly preserved dry bone to bone with adherent soft tissue and adipocere, or in rare cases also burnt bone material or even assistance during the autopsy of a complete body.

Nevertheless, the most frequent requests for anthropologists continue to be finds from mountains, forests, and archaeological material discovered in various unusual situations. To provide a tangible illustration of the various taphonomic alterations for these different scenarios, we hereafter provide three case studies, detailing the circumstances of the findings and the variability of taphonomic characteristics that can be encountered within forensic anthropological practice in Switzerland.

9.2.1 Case 1: Mountainous Area

Human remains were found during springtime in a mountainous area and brought to the CURML in Lausanne for analysis. The recovery of the remains was difficult since they were found scattered over a wide area on a steep mountain slope, as well as in a creek at the foot of a slope. The creek still contained some snow, and its general altitude was estimated to be about 1478 m AMSL, while the remains were found at an estimated altitude of up to 1600 m AMSL on the overlooking slope. The region is well known for its frequent snowdrifts, and during winter, the adjacent riverbed is covered with a layer of snow around 10 m deep.

There were no forensic archaeologists or anthropologists on site, and the remains were recovered by forensic pathologists and members of the scientific police.

Due to the interventional circumstances, including difficult access to the location and time constraints, the decision was made, in coordination with anthropologists via phone, to first subdivide the location into 2 main areas, which were approximately 300–450 m apart: one closer to the mountaintop and one at the river stream downhill. Furthermore, the letters A, B, C, D, E, F, and H were attributed to various zones, in which bones or groups of bones were found (Table 9.1). Zones A, B, H, and F were all located in or near the riverbed with snow still present (Fig. 9.1). The findings included dry bones, bones still in clothes, and a left hiking boot with foot bones still inside. Additionally, some hiking equipment and a backpack were found, containing identification (ID) documents belonging to a person who had been reported missing nearly a year before. Several days after the initial recovery, the police were able to continue the search and found a corresponding right hiking boot with foot bones still present and an additional right coxal fragment (presented here as Zone X).

Considering the nature of the discovery, with the remains mostly skeletonized, the prosecution mandated forensic anthropologists to analyze the remains. Through anthropological analyses, the skeletal elements could be assigned to corresponding zones (Fig. 9.2).

The bones were in various stages of preservation, some incomplete due to taphonomic processes (Table 9.1, Fig. 9.3). These different states can be explained by the

Table 9.1 Summary of the taphonomic aspects of the remains found in the various Zones A, B, C, D, E, F, and H. Elements found several days later were assigned as Zone X. Animal bones were found only in zone F

Zone	Description of the area	Notes on the taphonomic aspects
A	Riverbed	Trousers containing both the femurs, right tibia, and fibula, and fragments of the left proximal end of the tibia. The remains are in a good state of preservation. Some taphonomic alterations are present on the distal part of the right femur and the proximal part of the right tibia, exposing the trabecular bone Mostly dry bone with some hair residues attached to the long bones Residues of vegetation, soil, and dirt attached All elements show a similar brownish color
B	Riverbed	Bone element in bad state of preservation Dry bone with some residues of vegetation and soil attached Skull fragment presents a rather light brown color
C	Close to the mountaintop, about 300 m from the riverbed	Shirt/polar containing human bones. Remains in a very good state of preservation Mostly dry bones with residues of vegetation, soil, and dirt attached Bones show mostly a dark to light brown color. The left ulna and radius show a change of color from proximal being dark brown to distal showing white color Signs of animal scavenging are present on the distal end of the right ulna and the left radius
D	Area 100 m distance around zone C.	Remains in a bad state of preservation Completely dry bones with almost no residues of vegetation and dirt attached Bones present almost a complete white color with some dark gray color on the distal end of the left fibula Signs of animal scavenging on one skull fragment and sternal ends of rib fragments
E	Within zone D	Left hiking boot with all foot bones included. Bones in a very good state of preservation Some residues of soft tissue and adipocere are present Bone elements are present in dark-brown color
F	Riverbed	Animal bones
H	Riverbed	Bones in a good state of preservation Dry bones with no residues of vegetation or soil attached Bone elements show white and some green color
Zone X: Elements were found several days later	Riverbed	Right hiking boot with foot bones included (navicular, talus, and medial cuneiform missing) Foot bones in a very good state of preservation Very few residues of soft tissue and slightly some adipocere present. Bone elements show a light brown color An additional right coxal fragment was found separately, in a bad state of preservation with some residues of vegetation attached. Bone fragment with light brown to white color. Signs of animal scavenging are present

Fig. 9.1 View from the location of the findings closer to the mountaintop (Zones C, D, and E) and looking down toward the riverbed (Zones A, B, F, H, and X) still covered with snow (red arrow)

fact that some bones had remained wrapped in clothing or footwear, while others had been directly exposed to the environment and were weathered accordingly.

As far as the human remains found closer to the mountaintop are concerned, all bones found within the clothes (such as the shirt and the polar or the hiking shoe) were still in a very good state of preservation, showing brown to dark-brown color and some adipocere present within the hiking shoes (Fig. 9.4). Only the left ulna and radius presented varying shades, their proximal extremities being dark brown while the distal ends were white, suggesting that the latter were not covered by clothing for a prolonged period and had been exposed to direct sunlight, resulting in their whitened or bleached appearance. Furthermore, all bones around Zone C, which were not covered by clothes, presented the same white bleaching.

Regarding the remains recovered from the riverbed, similar white bleaching could be observed on the bones found in Zone H and the coxal bone found several days later in Zone X. All other bones, especially those found within trousers, presented a rather brown color.

Signs of animal scavenging were observed mainly on the bones found closer to the mountaintop, except for the coxal fragment found close to the riverbed.

The fragmented proximal extremities of the left tibia, which were found within the trousers at the riverbed, could eventually be reconstructed with the tibia fragment (physical fit) found in Zone D, closer to the mountaintop (Fig. 9.2). While the proximal tibial fragments presented a similar brown color, analogous to the other long bones and the patella in Zone A (all of which were recovered from the

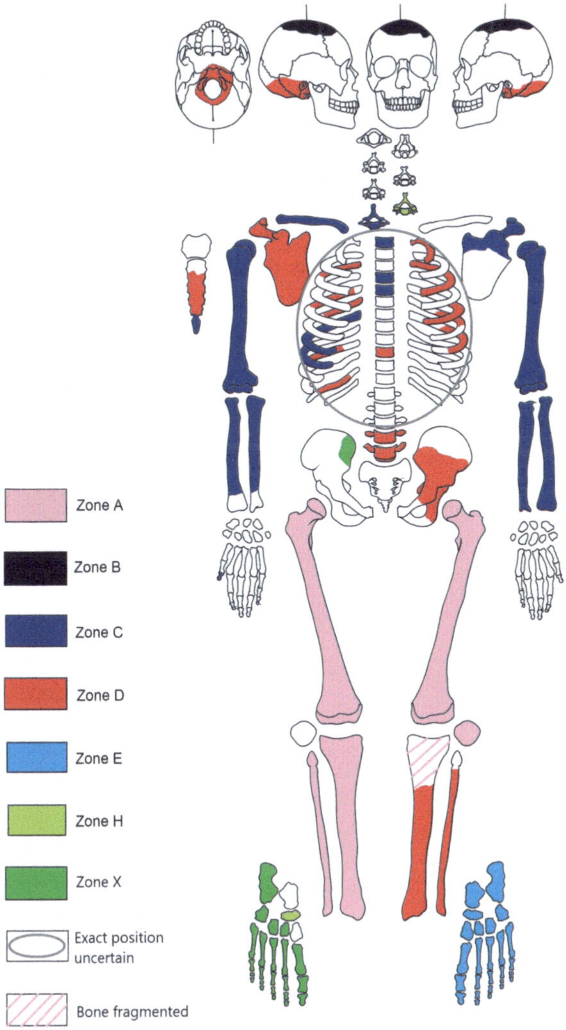

Fig. 9.2 Skeletal scheme presenting the recovered remains. The bones from the different zones are color-coded

trousers), the tibial remains showed the same white bleaching as observed in the case of all bones found in Zone D (Fig. 9.5).

The anthropological and taphonomic analyses revealed that the most likely scenario is that the body was originally located on the mountain slope, and in later stages of decomposition, parts of the remains were displaced downhill either by animal activity and/or through movements and melting of snow. The bones located on the riverbed may furthermore have been covered by snow for a longer period and were hence shielded from direct sun exposure.

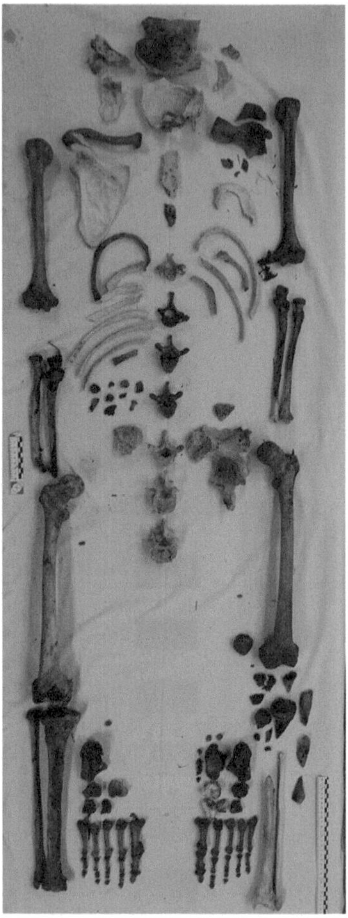

Fig. 9.3 Skeletal remains found with varying taphonomic alterations

No repeated elements or morphological inconsistencies were observed. All methods applied indicated a minimum number of individuals (MNI) of one. However, due to the significant variations in taphonomic status and the relatively large area in which the bones were found, several bone elements were chosen for DNA analyses, based on the taphonomy, location, and bone element. In combination with the taphonomic and anthropological analyses (reconstruction of the fragments from various zones, sex, age at death, and stature estimation), including the information obtained about the location of the bones, it was possible to limit the sample size. The remains were successfully identified, and the various DNA samples were assigned to the same person.

Recovering human remains in mountainous terrain can be challenging, not only because of the difficult terrain and weather conditions but also because human remains found in the mountains are often distributed over a wide area and present very different taphonomic characteristics due to the peculiar environmental conditions at higher altitudes. Corpses on the surface are particularly exposed to

Fig. 9.4 Adipocere on the left medial cuneiform

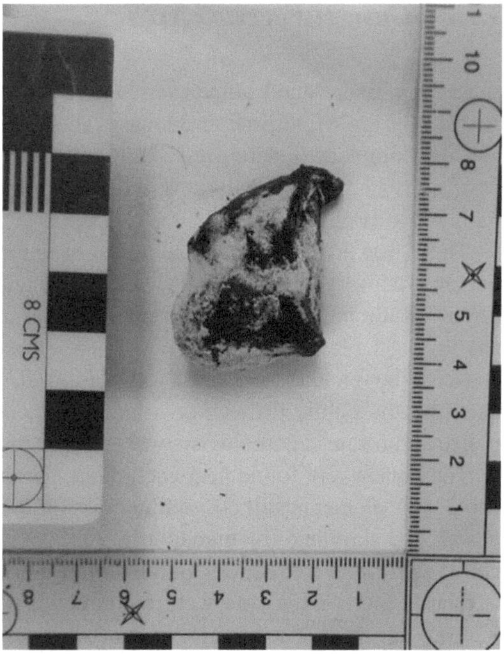

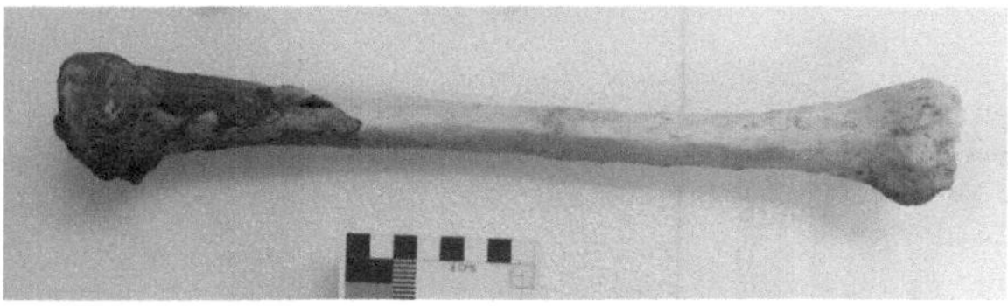

Fig. 9.5 Reconstruction of the left tibia. Fragments of the proximal end were found in Zone A, and the midshaft and distal end were found in Zone D. Varying taphonomy of the fragments can be seen, corresponding to the different finding locations

numerous environmental factors (Alfsdotter and Petaros 2021). It is rare that a skeleton can be recovered in its entirety, and in most cases, bone elements remain missing, which can complicate later investigations (e.g., when such isolated elements are recovered after the original case is closed). A thorough search for the remains is therefore crucial, and comprehensive search procedures are necessary (Keyes 2024); but this can be sometimes difficult to implement, depending on the environmental and geological circumstances at the location. This case demonstrates the importance of the interdisciplinary involvement of additional specialists when recovering human remains in an advanced stage of decomposition, especially over a large area. The subsequent involvement of forensic anthropologists with expertise in forensic taphonomy can be of significant value not only for the identification of the remains but also for analyzing the remains for possible fractures, trauma, or skeletal pathologies (Blau 2018).

9.2.2 Case 2: Forested Area

A forest worker found human remains in a forest (at an altitude of about 600 m AMSL) during wintertime, in January. There was no snow at the time of discovery, and the complete skeletonized skull was clearly visible, although the ground on which it rested was heavily covered in leaves and branches, and the soil was partially moist (Fig. 9.6).

There was no forensic archaeologist or anthropologist on site. The documentation and recovery of the remains were conducted by the police in collaboration with forensic pathologists, and the remains were brought to the CURML in Lausanne for analysis.

Since the remains were mostly skeletonized, forensic anthropologists were mandated by the public prosecutor to analyze them. All documentation made by the police and forensic pathologists was given to the forensic anthropologists.

The bones were found near each other, partially in an anatomical position, with some bone elements still covered in clothing, which was, for the most part, decomposed. The skull and the mandible were separated. Furthermore, a knife, a lighter, and eyeglasses were found with the remains.

The recovered remains were incomplete, with most parts of the lower limbs missing (Fig. 9.7). The bones were partially covered in clothing fabric, with soil and leaves attached to the bones, and presented variable taphonomic characteristics (Fig. 9.8).

Fig. 9.6 Location of the findings in the forest

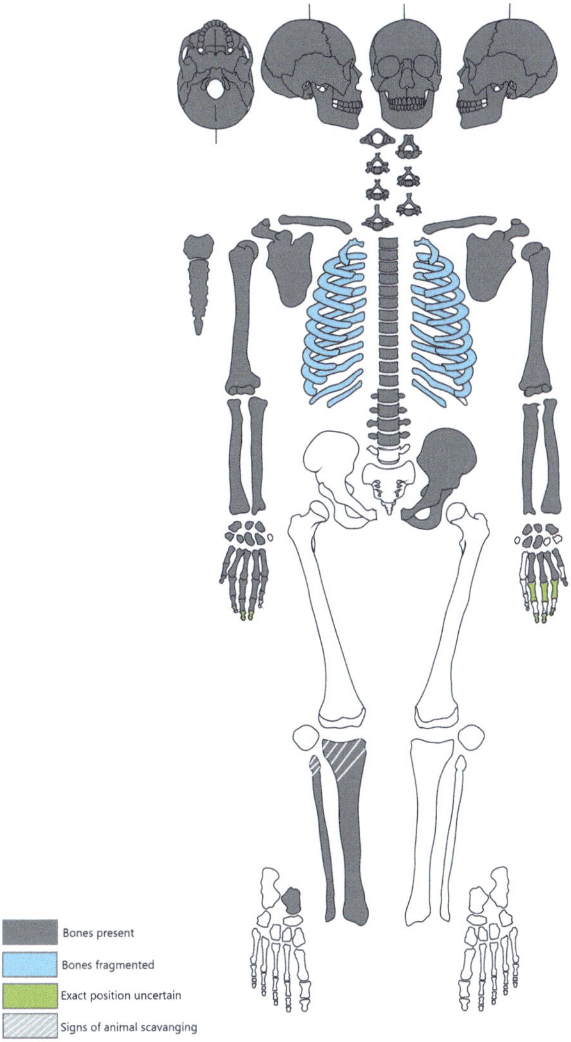

Fig. 9.7 Skeletal scheme presenting the recovered remains

For the most part, the bones were in a good state of preservation, showing brown to dark-brown color and some adipocere present, especially on both scapulas (Fig. 9.9), which were found in the clothing. The ribs—some of which were physically separated from the rest of the remains and the clothing—as well as the skull, presented white bleaching, suggesting that they had been exposed to direct sunlight for a prolonged period. The skull showed white bleaching mainly in the right and frontal areas, with some green staining due to moss adhesion (Fig. 9.10). The left side of the skull presented a light brown color. This led to the hypothesis that the skull was very likely lying on its left side for a prolonged time.

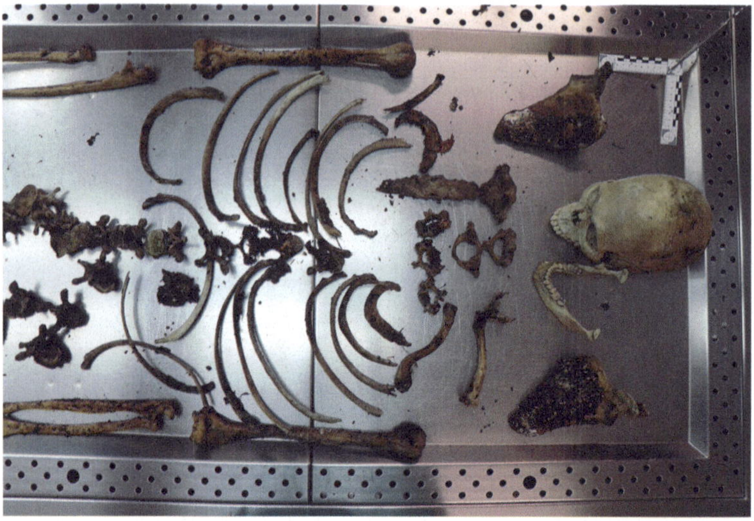

Fig. 9.8 Skeletal remains showing varying taphonomic characteristics

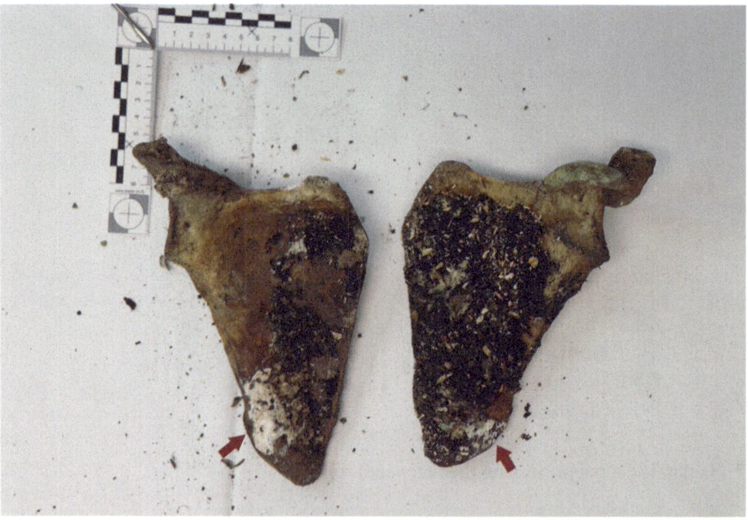

Fig. 9.9 Adipocere is present on both scapula bones (red arrows)

Furthermore, it was noticed that most of the bones of the lower limbs were missing, except for the right tibia and fibula, both of which showed signs of animal scavenging in their proximal parts. Furthermore, the rib fragments also showed signs of animal scavenging, and it is likely that the rib fragments were displaced by animal activity. The area was not on a hillside, but since it was a wide forested area, the missing bones might also have been moved by animals.

Fig. 9.10 Right side of the skull showing white bleaching and green staining from moss adhesion

No repeated elements or morphological inconsistencies were observed, indicating a minimum number of individuals (MNI) of one. After taphonomical analyses, documentation of the position of the bones on site, and anthropological examinations, two samples of different bone elements were taken for DNA analyses, leading to the successful identification of the remains. The police informed the specialists that the person had been missing for about two years prior to the recovery, which might explain the poor condition of the clothing and the missing bone elements that might have been removed by animals during this time interval.

While findings in the mountains are often difficult to locate and recover, remains in forests are more frequently discovered by walkers and their dogs during their excursions or by forest workers, as in the presented case (Keyes 2024). Due to dense forest vegetation, the remains are often better protected from direct sunlight and show less bleaching. Nevertheless, animal activity plays a very important role here. Bones can be fragmented and finally dispersed over large areas (Beck et al. 2015; DeVault and Rhodes 2002; Keyes 2024). The effects of animal scavenging, causing post-mortem alterations and disarticulation, can be manifold (Indra et al. 2022; Keyes et al. 2022) and should be considered when searching for and analyzing the remains. However, understanding species-specific scavenging patterns, as studied and explained by Young et al. (2014), could enhance the recovery rate of scattered remains in the future.

9.2.3 Case 3: Finding of Archaeological Remains in an Urban Area

It was reported to the Crime Scene Investigation (CSI) and the anthropologists that skeletal remains had been found in a well chamber. The well chamber, accessible via a gully top, was situated in a populated area in the vicinity of a church. The skeletal remains were discovered during the latest check-up of the well chamber. It was reported that the inspection should have been done a few days earlier but was not possible, as the chamber was filled with water. During the previous regular inspections, no skeletal remains had been seen. Hence, based on this information, a dump site could not be excluded. Based on the morphological appearance of the visible remains, they were confirmed to be human by the anthropologist on site. The remains were found at the back of the chamber, on a pile composed of smaller stones, while some bones were still partly embedded in the soil (Fig. 9.11). The discovery site was documented, and the skeletal elements were individually recovered by an anthropologist, forensic pathologists, and a crime scene investigator. The human remains were subsequently analyzed by anthropologists at the Zurich Forensic Science Institute.

Following the evaluation of the material, it appeared that the assemblage consisted only of human skeletal elements, mainly long bone fragments, skull fragments, and pelvic fragments. Overall, the bones appeared "dry" with no soft tissue attached and not greasy material. The visual appearance was homogeneous in surface preservation (relatively good) and color (light to medium brown), as well as the grade of completeness of the individual bones (largely fragmented) (Fig. 9.12). The bone surfaces were mostly intact, and only a few bones showed clear signs of

Fig. 9.11 Overview photograph of the skeletal remains at the back of the well chamber

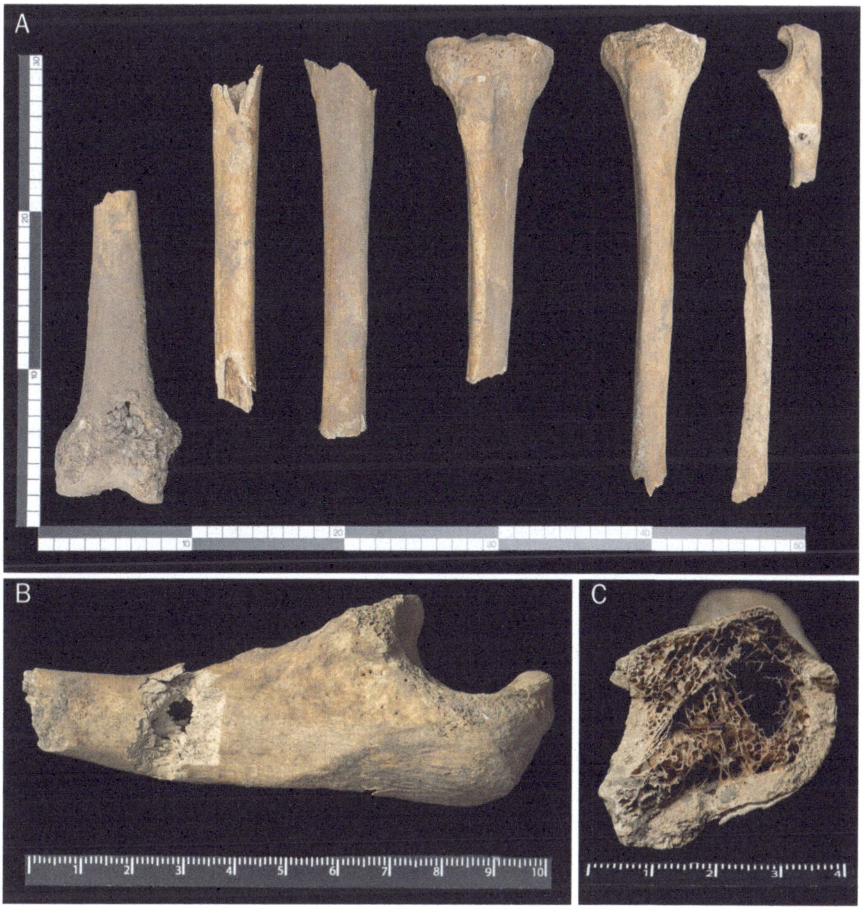

Fig. 9.12 Overview photograph of some skeletal elements (not completely cleaned) as examples of the surface preservation (**a**, **b**), fracture appearance (**b**, **c**), and grade of fragmentation (**a**, **b**)

taphonomic alterations on their outer surface. The preservation of the trabecular structure was generally good where visible. Fractured areas presented with predominantly lighter colors and were mostly with ragged but smoothed fracture edges. Indicating different stages of taphonomic post-mortem alterations. The minimum number of individuals (MNI) was estimated, and skeletal material from at least five individuals was recovered. The recovered skeletal ensemble—commingled, with no complete human skeleton, and lacking most of the small bones—was therefore handled as a secondary deposition site.

To evaluate its forensic relevance, it was decided to use radiocarbon dating (^{14}C) to estimate the post-mortem interval (PMI). This was deemed the most relevant approach, in consideration on the one hand of the discovery context and the lack of soft tissue attached to the skeletal elements, and on the other hand with regard to the overall relatively good bone preservation. The proximity to a church and prior knowledge of the construction work undertaken within the adjacent graveyard (which led to the reburial of certain affected remains) several years before yielded the assumption that the remains might have ended in the well chamber during that time. However, to clarify this hypothesis, the bones used for MNI estimation and skull fragments were sampled for ^{14}C dating ($n = 6$) and sent for analysis to an external laboratory. The analysis revealed that none of the sampled bones were younger than 1955 but were dated partly to the first half of the twentieth century. Hence, the forensic investigation was closed.

In conclusion, it seems plausible that the skeletal elements originated from the former graveyard and ended up in their discovery location during the construction work in the area. Why they went unspotted during previous inspections of the well chamber is unclear, but it is possible that a (thin) soil layer had covered them. The latter might have been (partly) washed away by the documented water.

This case presents an example of "dry" human skeletal remains found within a populated area with little or no contextual information. It is not uncommon in Switzerland, with its rich archaeological history, that prehistoric and historic skeletal remains are discovered outside their original context. In general, morphological-anthropological evaluations lead to an appropriate overview of the recovered skeletal ensembles and help to triage further analyses. In cases with such unclear finding situations, where the taphonomic alterations of the skeletal elements in general do not indicate a recent death due to "dry" bone appearance but with good preservation, radiocarbon dating should be used to evaluate the forensic relevance to overcome the limitations of estimating the PMI of skeletonized human remains. In this way, DNA analysis would only be mobilized if the radiocarbon dating indicates, in fact, forensic relevance and when meaningful comparison samples could be collected.

9.3 Perceptions of Forensic Anthropology and Taphonomy in Switzerland

Forensic anthropology in Switzerland, as in other regions throughout the globe, has been practiced for over a decade (Siebke et al. 2024). In the Swiss case, one might say that it is still in its infancy. Even though different aspects of forensic anthropology are practiced within the country (osteological analyses and facial image comparison), the distribution of knowledge about the work and "use" of forensic anthropologists varies greatly between regions (Siebke et al. 2024). Often, skeletal remains are directly transferred to forensic pathologists with no involvement of an anthropologist for various reasons. On the other hand, Switzerland, a small country, has undergone a substantial "institutionalization" effort in the discipline, as it is currently equipped with no less than three established medicolegal institutes wherein anthropologists are either employed or collaborations take place in forensic settings. Furthermore, as of 2024, the University of Lausanne also offers a newly designed master's curriculum in forensic taphonomy; all these developments show the overall increasing awareness and visibility of the discipline. This is also underlined by the great amount of interest in the discipline, as revealed in a survey conducted by Siebke et al. (2024). However, it is important to bear in mind that the overall amount of forensically significant casework regarding the typical tasks of forensic anthropologists is low. Nevertheless, the importance of being on-site and not just performing a laboratory analysis, as seen in other countries around the world, is increasingly regarded as the quality standard to aim for. This lies in accordance with the increasing number of Swiss forensic taphonomy studies (Indra et al. 2022; Indra and Lösch 2021; Szelecz et al. 2018; Varlet et al. 2020). In certain cases, forensic anthropologists can often serve as a bridge between the Swiss Archaeological Service and the police authorities. Archaeologists can thus be involved, depending on the specific question and situation, and can help expand interdisciplinary work. However, forensic archaeology has received little to no consideration over the past few decades, which possibly relates to the overall low number of "clandestine grave" cases in Switzerland.

To the best of the authors knowledge, there is only one published case in which a murdered woman was buried, and her grave was located and exhumed by the police roughly one year after her disappearance (Jokl and Loretan 2007). Compared to the "great" number of forensic anthropological "surface" discoveries presented in the studies by Schrag et al. (2014) and Indra and Lösch (2021). Even though "buried" is indicated for some cases in both studies, none of those cases were of forensic relevance, and some even turned out not to be human remains (Indra and Lösch 2021; Schrag et al. 2014). This is not surprising as Switzerland has a high density of archaeological structures, including both faunal and human remains. Overall, the preservation of such archaeological remains varies greatly depending on the taphonomic circumstances; therefore, a clear-cut distinction between "forensically relevant" and "of historic importance" based on morphological PMI evaluation of interred human remains is not always straightforward.

As pointed out above, remains with forensic relevance are often found in mountain, forest, and high alpine environments and as surface findings. However, discoveries stemming from other environments are not totally uncommon. The latter includes, e.g., findings from aquatic environments. The case of "Brienzi" (Thali et al. 2011), a torso in adipocere state that was found at the shore of a lake, precisely represents such a case and perfectly illustrates the difficulties inherent to the handling and the interpretation of discoveries from aquatic settings. As it turned out in this case, the remains were not forensically relevant but belonged to an individual who died during the seventeenth century, based on radiocarbon dating (Thali et al. 2011).

9.4 Conclusion

Forensic anthropology and taphonomy investigations into death involve a broad multidisciplinary approach to data collection and analysis, from bone recovery all the way through to its laboratory documentation. Nowadays, forensic anthropology and forensic taphonomy work closely together. The discipline of forensic taphonomy has demonstrated the need to collect contextual data for detailed taphonomic interpretation and has thus expanded the scientific field of forensic anthropology (Dirkmaat et al. 2008). While occasionally indoor body discovery sites can involve both forensic anthropologists and taphonomists, the most challenging cases tend to present in outdoor settings. This situation is mainly due to the presence of numerous natural agents, such as soil, environmental conditions, plants, and animals, that affect outdoor evidence. Forensic anthropology and taphonomy provide principles and protocols for documenting and analyzing evidence at complex outdoor scenes, including large-scale searches of remains and on-site identification of the said natural agents (Dirkmaat and Cabo 2016). Further, these principles and protocols are constantly updated, thanks to constant practical inputs from case studies of forensic or archaeological relevance, such as the ones presented in this chapter. The variety of the latter correlates directly with Switzerland's natural and geographic characteristics.

Indeed, due to the different environmental regions present in Switzerland, the state of preservation of human remains can be quite different, and taphonomic processes can vary substantially according to the place and situation of discovery. As such, the diversity of stages of preservation of recovered human remains tends to correlate well with the different topographic and climatic areas of the country. This in turn means that, with no clear contextual information, such as the presence of clothing or associated effects, an anthropological PMI estimation based solely on human remains is often challenging or even impossible without additional methods, e.g., radiocarbon dating. Indeed, the preservation of soft tissue does not necessarily mean that the remains under study are recent and of forensic relevance (e.g., Alterauge et al. 2015; Lehner and Julen 1991; Thali et al. 2011). Such cases can be somewhat tricky to handle, since the discovery of human remains in the mountain/alpine regions of Switzerland is quite common due to fatal accidents in these areas. However, the same areas were already explored by human communities in early times. Due to the environmental characteristics of the said regions, the degradation of human remains therein is slow, which can easily mislead investigators. While human skeletal remains are far less often found in populated areas, discovery situations and taphonomic alterations can vary greatly and happen to be quite challenging for subsequent analyses. Hence, an interdisciplinary approach, as well as effective collaborations between various specialists from forensic institutions, archaeological services, and law enforcement agencies during the documentation and recovery procedures of human remains, all merge to play a significant role in the efficient handling of such cases.

References

Alfsdotter C, Petaros A (2021) Outdoor human decomposition in Sweden: a retrospective quantitative study of forensic-taphonomic changes and postmortem interval in terrestrial and aquatic settings. J Forensic Sci 66:1348–1363

Alterauge A, Providoli S, Moghaddam N, Lösch S (2015) Death in the ice: re-investigations of the remains from the Theodul Glacier (Switzerland). J Glacial Archaeol 2(1):35–50

Barbier J, Piveteau J-L, Roten M (1975) Géographie de la Suisse. Presses Universitaires de France, Paris, pp 249–250

Beck J, Ostericher I, Sollish G, De Leon J (2015) Animal scavenging and scattering and the implications for documenting the deaths of undocumented border crossers in the Sonoran Desert. J Forensic Sci 60(Suppl 1):S11–S20

Blau S (2018) It's all about the context: reflections on the changing role of forensic anthropology in medico-legal death investigations. Aust J Forensic Sci 50:628–638

DeVault TL, Rhodes OE (2002) Identification of vertebrate scavengers of small mammal carcasses in a forested landscape. Acta Theriol 47:185–192

Dirkmaat DC, Cabo LL (2016) Forensic archaeology and forensic Taphonomy: basic considerations on how to properly process and interpret the outdoor forensic scene. Acad Forensic Pathol 6:439–454

Dirkmaat DC, Cabo LL, Ousley SD, Symes SA (2008) New perspectives in forensic anthropology. Am J Phys Anthropol Suppl 47:33–52

FDFA, F.D.o.F.A (2023) Geography—Facts and Figures

FSO, F.S.O (2012) Leisure. In ValueS - An information magazine of the Federal Statistical Office Vol 1

FSO, F.S.O (2021a) Arealstatistik Land Cover—Kantone und Grossregionen nach 27 Grundkategorien

FSO, F.S.O (2021b) La mortalité en Suisse et les principales causes de décès, en 2018. In: Confederation S (ed) 14 Santé. Federal Statistical Office FSO, Neuchâtel

FSO, F.S.O (2023) Current situation and change—key population figures, in thousand

FSO, F.S.O (2024a) Statistique de la Suisse: Santé. F.S.O. FSO, editor, Neuchâtel

FSO, F.S.O (2024b) Statistique policière de la criminalité (SPC): Rapport annuel 2023 des infractions enregistrées par la police. F.S.O. (FSO), editor, Neuchâtel

Indra L, Lösch S (2021) Forensic anthropology casework from Switzerland (Bern): Taphonomic implications for the future. Forensic Science International: Reports 4:100222

Indra L, Errickson D, Young A, Losch S (2022) Uncovering forensic Taphonomic agents: animal scavenging in the European context. Biology (Basel) 11

Jokl J, Loretan A (2007) Die Leiche im Wald/Tötungsdelikt am Hirzl. Kriminalistik Schweiz 12:783–790

Keyes CA (2024) Comparison of the effectiveness and efficiency of the grid and link search methods to recover scattered skeletal remains. Int J Legal Med 138:2139

Keyes CA, Myburgh J, Brits D (2022) Identifying forensically relevant urban scavengers in Johannesburg, South Africa. Sci Justice 62:399–409

Labhart T-P, Decrouez D (1997) Géologie de la Suisse. Delachaux et Niestlé, Lausanne, Paris

Lehner P, Julen A (1991) A mans bones with 16th-century weapons and coins in a glacier near Zermatt, Switzerland. Antiquity 65:269–273

Lösch S, Jackowski C, Zingg C (2015) Forensic archaeology and anthropology in Switzerland. In: Groen MWJ, Marquez-Grant N, Janaway RC (eds) Forensic archaeology. A global perspective. Wiley Blackwell, Oxford, pp 183–187

Moghaddam N, Campana L, Abegg C, Vilarino R, Voland C, Dedouit F, Genet P, Fracasso T (2023) Hidden lesions: a case of burnt remains. Forensic Sci Res 8:163–169

Peter C, Tuch A (2024) Pensées et comportements suicidaires—au sein de la population suisse en 2022 (Obsan Bulletin 08/2024). Observatoire suisse de la santé, Neuchâtel

Schrag B, Uldin T, Mangin P, Bochud F, Froidevaux P (2014) Dating human skeletal remains using 90Sr and 210Pb: case studies. Forensic Sci Int 234(190):e191–e196

Siebke I, Abegg C, Fracasso T, Moghaddam N, Obertova Z (2024) Awareness of forensic anthropology in Switzerland: a survey among forensic practitioners, police, and prosecutors. Int J Legal Med 138:1067–1077

SUVA, S.N.A.I.F (2023) UVG-Statistik 2023—Unfälle und Berufskrankheiten in der Schweiz

Szelecz I, Losch S, Seppey CVW, Lara E, Singer D, Sorge F, Tschui J, Perotti MA, Mitchell EAD (2018) Comparative analysis of bones, mites, soil chemistry, nematodes and soil micro-eukaryotes from a suspected homicide to estimate the post-mortem interval. Sci Rep 8:25

Thali MJ, Lux B, Losch S, Rosing FW, Hurlimann J, Feer P, Dirnhofer R, Konigsdorfer U, Zollinger U (2011) "Brienzi"—the blue Vivianite man of Switzerland: time since death estimation of an adipocere body. Forensic Sci Int 211:34–40

UNODC, U.N.O.o.D.a.C (2023) Intentional homice

Varlet V, Joye C, Forbes SL, Grabherr S (2020) Revolution in death sciences: body farms and taphonomics blooming. A review investigating the advantages, ethical and legal aspects in a Swiss context. Int J Legal Med 134:1875–1895

Young A, Stillman R, Smith MJ, Korstjens AH (2014) An experimental study of vertebrate scavenging behavior in a Northwest European woodland context. J Forensic Sci 59:1333–1342

Chapter 10
Investigations into the Crimes of the Soviet Totalitarian Regime in Lithuania: A Search for the Clandestine Graves of Lithuanian Freedom Fighters

Ingrida Čičiurkaitė

Abstract This article explores the atrocities committed by the Soviet totalitarian regime in Lithuania, focusing on the systematic concealment of the remains of Lithuanian Freedom Fighters and their supporters from 1944 to 1953. This highlights the partisan war, a resistance movement against the Soviet occupation, and the NKVD's (The People's Commissariat for Internal Affairs) deliberate efforts to suppress national memory through the desecration and clandestine burial of victims. Drawing from archaeological investigations in Marijampolė, Rietavas, Leipalingis, and Lazdijai, this study reveals patterns of the concealment of remains, burial practices, and the disrespectful treatment of victims. These findings contribute to the historical record, provide evidence of Soviet war crimes, and underscore the importance of interdisciplinary approaches in recovering, identifying, and commemorating victims of these atrocities.

Keywords Lithuanian freedom fighters · Soviet totalitarian regime · Clandestine graves · NKVD burial practices · Partisan resistance

10.1 Introduction

The twentieth century stands as one of humanity's greatest ages of war, not only altering the geopolitical landscape but also marked by large-scale atrocities committed against humanity in many states. It is estimated that during this century alone, deliberate acts of violence resulted in the deaths of between 170 and 230 million people (Parra and Ubelaker 2023, p. 2). Rummel distinguishes that between 1917 and 1987, approximately 61.9 million people were killed by the Soviet Union,

I. Čičiurkaitė (✉)
Department of Archaeology, Faculty of History, Vilnius University, NGO "Kultūros vertybių globos tarnyba", Vilnius, Lithuania

P. M. Barone, WJ M. Groen (eds.), *Forensic Archaeology and New Multidisciplinary Approaches*, Soil Forensics, https://doi.org/10.1007/978-3-031-86308-0_10

with 51.8 million (~84%) of these victims murdered during Stalin's rule (1923–1953) (Rummel 2008). Eastern Europe and the Baltic states were no exception. On August 23 and September 28, 1939, secret protocols were signed between the Third Reich and the Soviet Union (the Molotov-Ribbentrop Pact). As a result of this agreement, Poland, Lithuania, Latvia, and Estonia were occupied and annexed. On June 15, 1940, following France's fall, Stalin presented Lithuania with an ultimatum demanding the unlimited entry of Soviet troops and the establishment of an acceptable government of the USSR (Bater et al. 2024). Similar ultimatums were issued to Latvia and Estonia two days later. The first Soviet occupation was accompanied by rigged elections for Soviet accession and repression, the destruction of state administrative and military structures, and the deportation of civilian inhabitants.

The first crimes of the Soviet totalitarian regime began shortly after the invasion of the territory of the occupied and annexed Republic of Lithuania by the German army—June 22–27, 1941. During the retreat of the Soviet army and NKVD (The People's Commissariat for Internal Affairs) units, mass killings began. Within one week, the NKVD and the Red Army performed about 40 large-scale or mass executions of Lithuanian unarmed political prisoners (Žygelis and Čekutis 2011). Such massacres were referred to in official NKVD documents as "evacuation under the first category" (ibid). The largest killings in June were on the nights of the 24th and 25th in the Rainiai Forest, where 73 individuals held in the Telšiai prison were murdered (Šiušaitė et al. 2007; Dulkinienė 2000). On the 25th, near the Panevėžys sugar factory, 19 people were killed; that same day, three doctors from Panevėžys County and a compassionate nurse with three civilians were brutally tortured and killed (Anušauskas 1996). On the 26th, 230 prisoners (not only political) and 21 prison guards with their families were killed in the Pravieniškės prison (Balčiūnas 1942, p. 109). The Red Army, as it withdrew from each district, executed inhabitants (Anušauskas 1996). In each Lithuanian district, the Red Army carried out the looting and killing of civilian residents, characterized by brutal rampage rather than the execution of formal death penalties. People were thrown alive into pits, shot, beaten with hammers, and body parts were cut off, and other methods were used (see more: (Balčiūnas 1942)).

The experience of the first occupation highlighted the necessity of the people of the Baltic countries to unite and create structured resistance against occupiers. For these reasons, on August 13, 1943, the underground Central Board of Latvia was established to organize centralized national resistance (Neiburgs 2008) on November 25, 1943, in Lithuania, the Supreme Committee for the Liberation of Lithuania (Petraitytė-Briedienė n.d.); and on March 23, 1944, in Estonia, the underground National Committee of the Republic of Estonia (Niitsoo 2004).

The second wave of Soviet totalitarian regime crimes began at the end of World War II, after the German army withdrew from Lithuanian territory, which was occupied by the Red Army. The new occupiers began to replenish the Soviet army with local inhabitants, forcibly enlisting civilians in the occupying army. Those who refused to fight for socialist ideas were persecuted, causing residents to flee the forests, organize armed resistance groups, and fight the occupying army. It is estimated that during the occupations of 1940–1941 and 1944–1991, 135,000 people

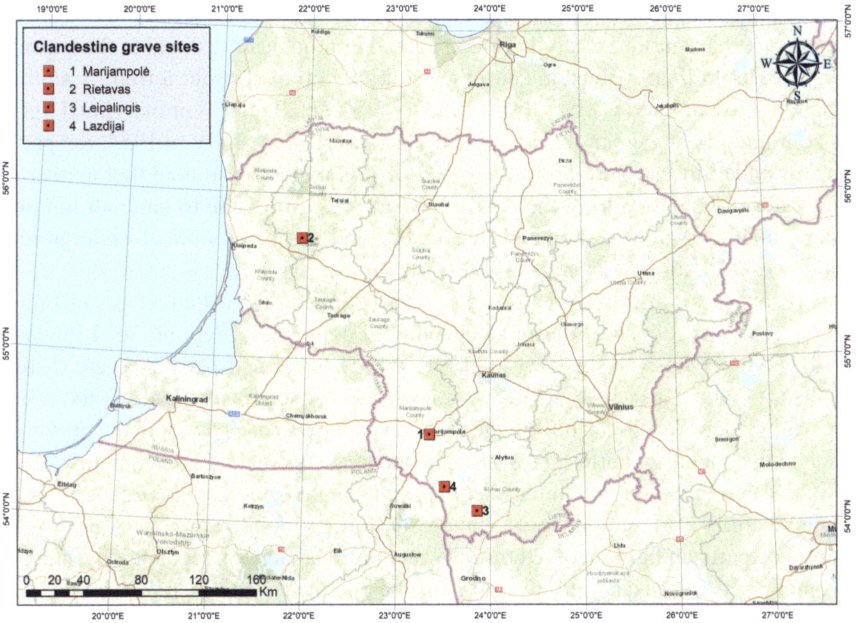

Fig. 10.1 Location of clandestine grave sites discussed in the article (Rokas Kraniauskas)

were killed or deported (repressed) in Estonia, 170,000 in Latvia, and 320,000 in Lithuania (Mežmalis 2011).

The aim of this article is to reveal how Soviet power structures organized the concealment of murdered and deceased participants in Lithuania's Freedom Fight, their supporters, and civilians in crime scenes from 1944 to 1953. The basis of this study is the analysis and synthesis of data from archaeological investigations conducted in four different locations in Lithuania—Marijampolė, Rietavas, Leipalingis, and Lazdijai—within the territories of former NKVD structures from 1999 to 2023 (Fig. 10.1).

10.2 Lithuania's Freedom Fight Against the Soviet Regime

The partisan war that took place in Lithuania from 1944 to 1953 is divided into three phases: 1944–1946—spontaneous resistance and organization formation; 1946–1948—well-organized movement—the activity of districts; and 1949–1953—the creation of centralized structures and their destruction—suppression of the partisan war. The end of the partisan war is associated with the arrest in 1953 of the Chairman of the Lithuanian Freedom Fight Movement Presidium, Jonas Žemaitis-*Vytautas,* and the mass destruction of partisan remnants and headquarters. However, resistance and its ideas continued to be represented by individual partisans until

1956 (Gaškaitė et al. 1996, p. 8). During this period, Soviet power structures carried out the secret executions of civilians considered unreliable or disloyal to the regime, using Soviet military tribunals and other courts, with or without a trial. A similar situation arose in Latvia, where from 1953 to 1956, small groups or individual fighters continued to engage in resistance (Strods 1996, p. 455–458); in 1954, the partisan war ended in Estonia (Grossmann 2024). It is important to note that neither in Latvia nor in Estonia during the post-war years was it possible to unite all fighting groups under a single responsible leadership and create a political underground leadership (Čekutis and Žygelis 2007).

Partisans were a military and social, secretly operating volunteer organization whose goal was to restore the independent and democratic Republic of Lithuania (ibid). Five reasons (Gaškaitė et al. 1996, p. 14) for armed resistance are distinguished: (1) the experience of the previous (first) Soviet occupation; (2) the resistance movement developed during the German occupation; (3) belief in the promises made in the Atlantic Charter to restore independence to countries that had lost it due to war; (4) protection of inhabitants from looting and coercion by the Red Army and Soviet security; (5) avoidance of capture or forced mobilization into the Soviet army. The partisan fight involved military and political actions regulated by statutes and bylaws (the Partisan Field Court of Justice operated), with members being only those who had sworn allegiance, obeyed the leadership, and openly carried weapons and insignia. The first article of the 1899 Hague Convention emphasizes that the laws of war, rights, and duties apply not only to the military but also to the militia and volunteer soldiers if they have a person responsible for their subordinates, a permanent identifying mark visible from a distance, openly carry weapons, and carry out their operations according to the laws and customs of war (Hague Convention, HC, (II) Annex to the convention art. 1, 1899) (this article is also in the 1907 Hague Convention). Following this article, Lithuanian freedom fighters met the criteria for combatant status, so the rules of the convention had to be followed when fighting them.

It is estimated that about 50,000 combatants could have been involved in the partisan war and about 100,000 liaisons and supporters. Approximately 20,000 Freedom Fighters and their supporters are still missing without a trace. Initially, the chaotic resistance became structured due to the involvement of officers who had served in the Lithuanian army. The declaration signed by resistance leaders on February 16, 1949, is an important document continuing state activity during the occupation. It is important to note that alongside the partisan war, there was also civil resistance—disobedience of the population to the will imposed by the occupiers, for example, abstention from elections, avoidance of service in the occupational army, or resistance to the creation of collective farms. Civilians were punished for such actions by increased taxes, exile, and confiscation of property.

The Soviet regime sought to quickly consolidate power in the occupied territory of Lithuania; hence, it was necessary to suppress the Lithuanian Freedom Fight. In Soviet propaganda, the Freedom Fighters, known as the Forest Brothers, were portrayed as Nazi collaborators, murderers, and looters (Grossmann 2024, p. 131).

Additionally, to intimidate civilian supporters of the partisans and deter people from joining the ranks of the partisans, the desecration and inhumation in remote locations of the deceased were employed. In the spring and summer of 1945, desecration and hiding of partisan remains became a widely known phenomenon (Montvydas 2022, p. 64). Existing pits or trenches were often used for hiding bodies: gravel pits, trench locations, peat bogs, lakes or rivers, thickets, Jewish cemeteries or their surroundings, and NKVD courtyard areas (Striužas 2021, p. 50–67). Lithuanian partisan bodies were desecrated and hidden not only to diminish the importance of the Lithuanian Freedom Fight, and to intimidate the population but also to erase collective memory. In other words, social death was pursued, where the social and cultural memory of individuals consciously disappeared, the deceased lost their identity and constructive social relationships with the living, and their traces of existence were destroyed (Parra et al. 2023, p. 6). We cannot speak about the graves of the deceased partisans because their bodies were not buried but were inhumed with instructions from Moscow: to bury them so that no one would ever find them. As years passed by, various construction works were carried out in these places (Gaškaitė et al. 1996, p. 373).

10.3 Advancements in the Search for the Remains of Lithuanian Freedom Fighters

The search for the remains of Lithuanian Freedom Fighters began in Lithuania in 1988–1989, amid changing political circumstances and Lithuania's movement toward independence. Prompted by calls in the press to seek out their relatives—the fallen partisans—and to honorably bury them in cemeteries, there arose a universal need to restore historical justice, to investigate crimes committed by occupying regimes, and to find and commemorate national heroes and innocently murdered civilians. This stimulated the emergence of preliminary judicial archaeological investigations in Lithuania.

The search for the remains of murdered individuals began spontaneously and altruistically, with the shared goal of marking and commemorating crimes committed against the Lithuanian population (Fig. 10.2). At that time, the search for remains was an uncontrolled and autonomous process, lacking any accounting, oversight, or documentation of events. Occasionally, specialists such as archaeologists, anthropologists, or forensic medicine representatives were called in, usually after the individual remains had already been found and moved. Due to these reasons, details such as where the searches took place, how the remains were inhumed (whether in mass graves or individually), how many sets of remains and fragments were found, and the methods used for murder and desecration remain unknown. In many cases, their identities were also undetermined, their burial places were forgotten, and the locations where the remains were laid to rest were undocumented.

Fig. 10.2 The search for remains was carried out in 1991 in Leipalingis. (Author unknown. The photo is stored in the Museum of Leipalingis Gymnasium)

State institutions of the Republic of Lithuania began to take an interest in perpetuating the historical memory of genocide victims. The State Security Department initiated pre-trial investigations and judicial processes against individuals who had worked in the structures of the occupying authorities and participated in the deportation and murder of Lithuanian citizens. Through these investigations, a mass burial site of Lithuanian citizens murdered between 1944 and 1947 was discovered. In 1994, archaeological investigations were initiated to locate the remains of individuals executed in the NKVD central building in Vilnius, and investigations were carried out in the Tuskulėnai Manor territory (1994–1996, 1998, 2003). These investigations, focused on the search for several prominent individuals' remains, marked the beginning of judicial archaeology in Lithuania (Jankauskas et al. 2005, p. 217–230).

The search for murdered individuals' remains and the initial findings in the Tuskulėnai Manor Park prompted Lithuanian archaeologists to initiate searches in other locations—in the courtyards of NKVD structures operating in various districts and their surroundings. In 1995, small-scale archaeological investigations were conducted in the courtyard of the Švenčionys NKVD (Gendrėnas 1995) and later in other former residential areas. Despite an unsuccessful attempt in 1995, between then and 2021, archaeological investigations were carried out 15 more times in the territories of former Soviet security buildings and their immediate surroundings in Lithuania, aiming to find the remains of inhumed individuals—Lithuanian partisans and their supporters. Not all of these investigations yielded positive results; successful searches included those in Marijampolė in 1999 (Dakanis 1999) and Rietavas in

2010 (Kontrimas 2011). In the courtyards and immediate surroundings of former Soviet security buildings, 12 sets of remains of Lithuanian Freedom Fighters were found, with the identities of all five remaining remains identified in the case of Rietavas.

These latter two cases revealed, and searches conducted in Leipalingis (Kvizikevičius 2022, 2023a, b; Kvizikevičius and Zagreckas 2023) and Lazdijai (Čičiurkaitė 2022, 2023, 2024; Čičiurkaitė and Kvizikevičius 2023) between 2021 and 2023 confirmed another element of crimes committed in the past by collaborators and Soviet forces—the fact of remains being concealed in the courtyards and immediate surroundings of these buildings. During archaeological investigations, it was incontrovertibly proven that the concealment of remains in such places was practiced in several different regions of Lithuania.

10.4 Research at the NKVD Headquarters

NKVD agents concealed the remains of partisans in remote locations, but they also often desecrated victims' bodies and inhumed them in the yards of their headquarters. These places were particularly suitable because the area could be guarded against local residents and partisans, preventing them from secretly reinterring their fallen comrades. This is evidenced by the recollections of contemporaries and archaeological investigations conducted in the territories of former NKVD structures. Regime-friendly individuals were settled near the former headquarters. For example, a guard lived on the territory of Tuskulėnai Manor, restricting access to the area. In Leipalingis, a person who knew the burial pits of partisans' remains was settled in a homestead adjacent to the headquarters. After some time, he would disguise the burial sites by planting a tree or burying household waste precisely over the remains. In Lazdijai, the house of a deported Lithuanian family was relocated to a neighboring plot of the headquarters, where it was inhabited by regime-friendly individuals. It is likely that more such cases will be identified through archaeological investigations in other cities.

Since 1988, relatives of the Lithuanian Freedom Fighters began searching for remains specifically in the yards and surroundings of the regional NKVD headquarters. Despite the fact that during several years of amateur searches about 2000 remains were found (exact data on the discovery sites, identities, and number of individuals are unknown, as records were not kept), until 2017, the archaeological investigations were unsystematically conducted in areas of engineering networks or specific locations indicated by witnesses. Although the practice of concealing remains in the territories of the NKVD headquarters had already been proven, not all former (regional) headquarters were included in the Register of Immovable Cultural Heritage, and targeted, detailed searches for remains were not initiated.

From 2010 to 2017, scientific research on the partisan war was conducted mostly at operational bunker sites. With the growing public need to honor the nation's heroes, the first systematic search for remains was carried out from 2017 to 2020.

These investigations involved close collaboration between historians, archaeologists, anthropologists, and DNA laboratory specialists. The searches were not conducted in the territories of the NKVD headquarters but in the Orphans (Našlaičių) Cemetery in Vilnius, where efforts were made to find the remains of the Lithuanian partisan leader Adolfas Ramanauskas-*Vanagas* (recognized as the head of the Lithuanian state by the Seimas (parliament) of the Republic of Lithuania in 2018) and other Lithuanian Freedom Fighters. Their remains had been concealed by NKVD structures in a former nineteenth and twentieth-century cemetery for beggars, orphans, prisoners, and the impoverished of Vilnius. The successful results of these investigations—the discovery of the remains of six partisans, including Adolfas Ramanauskas-*Vanagas* and the last Lithuanian partisan Antanas Kraujelis-*Siaubūnas* (Vėlius 2021)—prompted the resumption of systematic searches for remains in the territories of former NKVD headquarters as well. This article discusses four cases in which investigations were conducted according to current scientific standards.

10.4.1 Marijampolė

The investigations were carried out in 1999 (Dakanis 1999) at locations planned by the city municipality for erecting monuments. The site of the former regional NKVD headquarters at that time was in the central, sparsely populated part of the city streets. The area was bordered by a river and visually surrounded by trees. The NKVD headquarters was established in a two-story brick building built in 1932. The house was nationalized in 1940. From 1941 to 1944, it housed the German command, and from 1945 to 1953, it was taken over by the NKVD. The fact that Lithuanian partisans and their supporters were interrogated in this building is evidenced by inscriptions carved into the walls—names, surnames, dates, or initials of those imprisoned. Inscriptions on the walls date from 1946 to 1949, the years of intense partisan warfare. NKVD structures often encompass more than one plot of land. In this case, across the river, there was another building, a former property of the archdiocese (a similar situation to Lazdijai and Leipalingis). The riverbank was forbidden to be cleaned in later times, presumably out of fear that partisan remains would be uncovered. Local residents testify that plots belonging to NKVD structures were fenced with high walls, about 2 m high, until 1958–1959. Thus, NKVD structures occupied available larger brick buildings with cellars and adjacent territories.

In 1999, investigations were conducted at a distance of 5.3 m to the west from the former NKVD headquarters building (Fig. 10.3). In the archaeological trench, spaced 70–160 cm apart, three burial pits were identified. In Pit No. 1, at a depth of 90–109 cm, the remains of two individuals were uncovered. The first individual was placed centrally in the pit, with the chest supported against the sides, and a rag was found in the mouth (between the jaws). A left leg injury was observed in situ—a fracture. Fragments of chalk were also found near the remains. The second

Fig. 10.3 Marijampolė site—former NKVD headquarters and surroundings (R. Kraniauskas)

individual was placed on their side, with the chest leaning against the edge of the pit. This arrangement suggests that the pit was very small, measuring 63–87 cm in width, narrowed toward the bottom, and tapered significantly near the feet of the remains. In the second pit, the remains were uncovered at a depth of 98–128 cm. Fragmentation of the skull and distal end fracture of the left tibia were observed in situ. The remains of the second individual were found underneath the first one. A ballistic injury was identified in the right occipital bone. Chalk fragments were also discovered nearby. The burial pit for these remains, like the first, was narrow (30–70 cm wide), with the remains leaning against the pit walls. In the third pit, the remains were buried deeper—at a depth of 130–157 cm. However, once again, the remains were placed in a small pit (50 cm wide), with the remains supported against the edges of the pit and covered with chalk. Uniform material and military buttons were found nearby, confirming the affiliation of the discovered remains to Lithuanian partisans. It is important to note that the third burial pit was covered with medical ampoules up to the level of the remains. These ampoules were recorded in an area measuring 100–120 cm, and their orientation coincided with that of the remains' burial pit.

Additional remains were discovered in the second trench—the site of the former building. Here, during the investigation of one of the building's rooms, a small room, approximately 180 cm wide, was uncovered. Based on its fill, it was determined to likely be a refuse pit. Parts of the firearms were found in one of the building's rooms. According to information from a former partisan liaison, on January

27–28 and June 8, 1948, she witnessed the bodies of four partisans being dumped here, followed by the bodies of two more partisans in each case. The witness recognized the murdered individuals, but it is unknown whether investigations were conducted to confirm the identities of the desecrated remains she mentioned and the bodies found. The witness's description of skull injuries also matched those seen on one partisan. In this case, DNA testing was not conducted for identification purposes.

10.4.2 Rietavas

Investigations were carried out in 2010 (Kontrimas 2011) as part of preparations to adapt the former manor stables for tourism purposes. The location of Rietavas Manor was along the central street of the town, situated at the northern edge at that time. The area is enclosed and secluded, featuring a large manor park, ponds, and a river. During World War I and II, the German army used the manor grounds. Following World War II, an NKVD headquarters was established in the office building of the manor. The manor grounds, including the park, cover an area of more than 64 hectares, providing ample operational space for NKVD structures that are far from public view.

On September 29, 1990, and October 26, 1991, local residents initiated searches for the remains of the partisans. Specific details regarding the territory searched for Freedom Fighters' remains and the guidelines followed for checking the specific area are unknown. However, it is known that searches were conducted in the manor park situated on a hill. Light Detection and Ranging (LiDAR) data analysis revealed the presence of two hills within the mentioned territory: approximately 125 m northeast of the manor office building and about 80 m southwest of the pond. The second hill is close to the former stables where, in 1991, archaeological excavations revealed the remains of five Lithuanian Freedom Fighters. Aerial photographs from 1944 show that the areas of the stables and both hills were densely covered with trees, obstructing visibility from outsiders.

Archaeological analysis of the finds between 1990 and 1991 concluded that four burial pits were discovered. Two of these were located on the hills near the manor office, one near the pond and another by the pathway leading to the park. A total of 17 individuals were found in these localized pits, ranging from one to six individuals per pit. Details about certain pit parameters, the discovery of remains, and most importantly, whether adjacent remains were identified remain unknown. However, some conclusions can be drawn from the anthropological data and the location of the remains. For instance, near the pond, at a depth of 70 cm, a pit measuring 2 × 4 m contained six remains of individuals positioned with overlapping limbs, suggesting that multiple bodies were interred simultaneously. These remains were identified as males aged between 20 and 50 years and an unidentified pregnant woman. Of the 13 individuals identified at that time through anthropological analysis, seven were attributed to Lithuanian Freedom Fighters (Jankauskas 1990).

Yet, a collective pit near the manor park, buried at a depth of 1.5 m, separated itself from the context of the other discovered remains. This pit contained six individuals, including men aged between 18 and 40 years. Four of the men had their legs amputated, with four leg and two arm amputations observed. An autopsy of the skull vault was conducted on another individual. The amputated limbs were found buried alongside the remains. Such burial practices more closely resemble those of a field hospital during World War II, yet further verification would be needed to confirm this version by examining data on German military burial sites in the vicinity of Rietavas.

In the fourth pit found near the manor office, the burial places of four individuals were identified: three men (aged 20–40 years) and one woman (aged 25–30 years) (Jankauskas 1991). One man's skull was heavily fragmented, while another had splintered fractures in the arm bones. Similar injuries are common in other discovered remains of Lithuanian Freedom Fighters.

In 2010, three test pits were excavated around the former stable building (Kontrimas 2011). In one of them, at the site of the rainwater drainage installation, remains were laid one on another. The pit was excavated 9.3 m east of the eastern corner of the building and 20 m from the pond. In total, five bodies were found piled in a former stable refuse pit at a depth of 2.18 m. The top was covered with a layer of rubble 60–65 cm thick (such a layer was not found in other pits). Leather belts, Lithuanian Army buckles, and a ring with patriotic symbols were found near the bodies. Presumably, one of the burial pits discovered in 1990 was located 10–15 m southwest of the bodies found in 2010. Additionally, the PPSh-41 automatic weapon magazine was found near the drainage well of the farm building to the north of the office.

The remains, identified as a Lithuanian partisan, are evidenced by anthropological research data (anthropological analysis conducted by Rimantas Jankauskas in 2010). The remains of four men (aged 20–49) and one woman (aged 29–39) were laid into the pit. Gunshot wounds in the skulls of two men were identified as cases of suicide based on the direction of the bullet. Witness testimonies and partisan diaries frequently describe instances where partisans, facing hopeless situations, chose not to surrender alive to the enemy and instead detonated explosives or shot themselves. The bodies of the other three individuals exhibited multiple injuries: the woman's remains showed gunshot wounds to the skull and right femur; the man had a gunshot wound to the skull and unspecified injuries to the lower jaw, left clavicle, and both scapulae; another man's remains revealed a gunshot wound channel in the lumbar vertebrae and suspected gunshot wounds in the pelvic area. It is noteworthy that in Rietavas, as in the other sites discussed in this article, fragmented fractures in the diaphysis of the left radius were also noted.

Archaeological and anthropological research data have narrowed down the scope of identifying individuals. Historian Dalius Žygelis (Žygelis 2012) analyzed NKVD reports from Rietavas archives, where a fairly clear group of killed individuals was supposed to be sought: four men and one woman. NKVD documents only recorded one group of individuals meeting the criteria for a military-Chekist operation report. On January 26, 1952, NKVD agents conducted an operation in the Žadvainiai

Forest, located south of Rietavas. Four hundred soldiers were deployed for this task, with precise information about the location of an underground partisan bunker (provided by a tortured informant). The NKVD report also listed the surnames of the killed partisans and their ages at the time of their deaths, which coincided with the results of anthropological studies. Based on the surnames of the deceased, relatives of some of those killed were found, who provided photographs for the identification. The relatives of one partisan knew that the remains should be buried near a small dam next to the manor. Memories of individuals also coincided with archaeological findings, such as the discovery of items like a Lithuanian Riflemen (Šauliai) uniform buckle found near the remains. Additionally, Ona Juškienė's sister, *Onutė,* heard gunfire all day long on the day of the incident. This memory also aligns with the gunshot wounds documented in the remains of Lithuanian Freedom Fighters found during the research. The Rietavas case, up until the investigation began in the Orphans' Cemetery in 2017, was the only example of good interdisciplinary research practice.

10.4.3 Leipalingis

Successful investigations of the Orphans' Cemetery spurred the continuation of searches initiated by the public in 1991 for the remains of Colonel Juozas Vitkus-*Kazimieraitis*, leader of the Partisans of Southern Lithuania. Since 2019, efforts have focused on refining data from Leipalingis' independent community searches, including the re-exhumation of previously discovered remains for identification (Vėlius 2021), with systematic investigations commencing in 2021—employing archaeological methods to locate burial pits of partisans. In order to find Lithuanian Freedom Fighters, including Colonel Vitkus-*Kazimieraitis*, who were killed in the Leipalingis area, the Center for the Research of Genocide and Resistance of Residents of Lithuania (LGGRTC) conducted archival research, determining that 207 individuals perished in the vicinity. Additionally, efforts were made to locate relatives of the deceased and collect their DNA samples. In contrast to the first two cases discussed, specialists from various fields immediately joined the search for remains in Leipalingis: archaeologists, anthropologists, historians, and DNA laboratory researchers.

The former NKVD headquarters were located in the northern part of the town, near the town square, in a less densely populated area. This brick building was also used during World War II by the Germans, who surrounded the area with a 3-meter-high double-board fence. The gap between the boards was filled with sand (testimony from a local resident). Adjacent to the plot, before World War II, was the headquarters of the Lithuanian Riflemen's Union. It is likely that NKVD used a large area for its needs between the main streets of Leipalingis and to the west of one of them, up to the existing fence. Some of the searches for remains were conducted in 1991. One preliminary search plan has survived, indicating that four burial pits were found in the courtyard of the headquarters and one outside the fence. It is known that several other burial sites were found near the slope in former World War II trenches. In total, 16 burial pits were discovered in 1991, containing the remains of 33 Lithuanian Freedom Fighters, ranging from one to seven individuals per pit. In 2019, following re-exhumation, some of the remains were identified through DNA testing. Analyzing the results of public searches revealed that the remains were hidden in two locations: the courtyard of the headquarters and along the fence, and the second location, west of the headquarters on the slope where the World War II trenches were located. Upon identifying the identities of several killed individuals, it became clear that the remains inhumed in the courtyard date back to before 1949. Partisans holding exceptionally high ranks were interred outside, while ordinary partisans and operatives were buried in the courtyard. The remains found to the west of the headquarters belonged to individuals who died later, from 1950 onward. These findings indicate that efforts were primarily made to inhume the bodies of Lithuanian Freedom Fighters in visually and physically controlled NKVD territory.

In 2021, archaeological investigations (Kvizikevičius 2022) began, following the localization of search sites since 1991 (Fig. 10.4). Geophysical Ground Penetrating Radar (GPR) surveys were conducted for this purpose, identifying the locations of pits from 1991 and trenches and pits from World War II. In 1991, small human bones and fragments were found at the search sites, identified by anthropologists as belonging to exhumed remains. During the initial years of research, efforts were made to pinpoint the exact locations where remains were discovered in 1991, and new searches were conducted nearby.

Fig. 10.4 Leipalingis site—former NKVD headquarters and surroundings (R. Kraniauskas)

In the eastern part of the former NKVD headquarters, where a warehouse stood in 1991, remains were found. Additional GPR anomalies were also recorded nearby, leading to the formation of an archaeological trench. At the trench site, a mound was identified, under which an oval-shaped pit was uncovered at a depth of 80–85 cm. The deceased was placed in the pit on their right side, with an autopsy incision observed in the skull vault and a severed part placed beside the right hand. Archaeologists noted the position of the boots in situ in the pit and the absence of foot bones. The boots were likely placed in the pit before the body, as one boot was found under the right femur of the remains, and the other on the right side of the remains, 30 cm away (Fig. 10.5). Foot bones were found inside the boots after their discovery, and one of the boots showed a deformation resembling an imprint of a rope.

Upon exhumation of the remains, a rectangular deepening measuring 90 × 150 cm was observed at the bottom of the oval pit's northeast corner, which deepened approximately 10–20 cm into the natural soil. This indicates that an existing pit was used for inhuming the remains, which was deepened, but the body was not placed in the newly prepared pit. A wedding ring, a religious medallion inscribed in Lithuanian "Širdie Jėzaus pasigailėk mūsų" ("Heart of Jesus, have mercy on us"), and several personal hygiene items were found near the remains.

In 2022, investigations continued (Kvizikevičius 2023a, b), focusing on the courtyard of the former NKVD headquarters and its immediate surroundings. At a distance of 4.5 m north of the remains found in 2021, another pit was discovered along the fence. One more pit was also found in the southern part, also within the

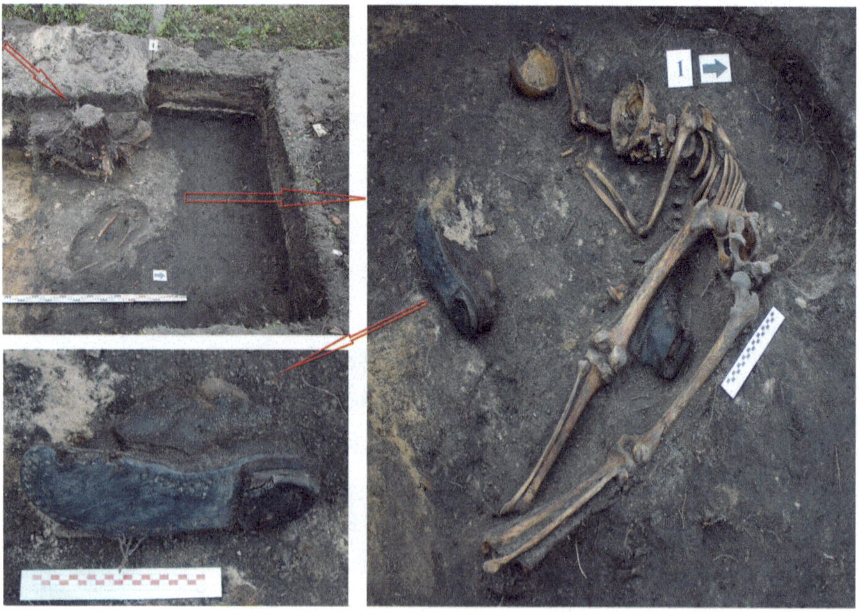

Fig. 10.5 Remains found in Leipalingis in 2021 (Eimantas Aranauskas)

Fig. 10.6 Remains found in Leipalingis in 2022 (E. Aranauskas)

perimeter (Fig. 10.6). The fill of the first pit contained remnants of grenades. The rectangular pit measured 130 × 230 cm and contained the remains of two partisans that had been hastily buried. Their identities were confirmed as the leader of the unit, Petras Bankieta-*Kanapynas*, and the liaison Kazimieras Vaikšnoras-*Laiminas*, who died in a battle with the NKVD on November 5, 1947 (genocid.lt 2023). The remains were buried at a depth of 86–106 cm. It was noted that both bodies had bent iron nails found near their shoulder blades.

In the southern part of the former NKVD headquarters, a burial pit was discovered that coincided with witnesses' accounts stating that a person was imprisoned in the basement at that exact location. Through a small window, they observed NKVD personnel excavating recently buried remains a few days earlier for identification. It was believed that the deceased was Juozas Vitkus-*Kazimieraitis*, the leader of the Southern Lithuania Partisans' Region. These accounts were corroborated by the results of archaeological investigations.

The remains of a single individual were found within the line of sight of the window, at a depth of 58–95 cm. A significant portion of the remains had been disturbed due to utility network installation works carried out several years ago (a pretrial investigation was conducted in this case). However, the pit confirmed the witnesses' statement that the remains were excavated, photographed, and reinterred in the same place, and items bearing the initials "J.V." were found nearby. A rosary and a Vytis (the Lithuanian Knight) engraved on a Bakelite plate suggested that the remains belonged to Colonel Juozas Vitkus-*Kazimieraitis*. DNA comparison confirmed the identification of the found remains as those of Colonel Vitkus-*Kazimieraitis*.

According to anthropological studies (Jankauskas et al. 2023a, b), Petras Bankieta-*Kanapynas* died from a gunshot wound to the skull above the left eyebrow arch. It is presumed that Kazimieras Vaikšnoras-*Laiminas* may have fallen into the hands of the NKVD alive. The remains showed extensive perimortem fragmentation of the skull and notably poor preservation of the chest area's bones. In Colonel Vitkus-*Kazimieraitis*' remains, there was a perimortem fracture of the upper branch of the right ilium, although a more detailed reconstruction was hindered by the lack of bone fragments.

The 2023 research (Kvizikevičius 2024—report in preparation) continued focusing on the areas west of the former NKVD headquarters, where World War II trenches and pits were located. In two of these, mass burial pits of partisans were found—five individuals in each. Remains in both pits were haphazardly thrown in, leaning against the narrow walls of the pits. In the first pit (Fig. 10.7), a large stone tied with a wire and sheets of metal were thrown over the heads of the remains. In the second pit (Fig. 10.8), a stone was thrown over the remains. Currently, more details about the burial circumstances are unknown, as the identities of the murdered individuals are still under investigation. The remains found in both pits were men aged between 20 and 45 years. Anthropological studies indicate severe body injuries (Kozakaitė et al. 2023). Remains No. 1—gunshot wounds to the skull, indirect fractures of both collarbones, fractures of two right scapulae, fractures of the second and third right metacarpals and one phalanx, damage to the right mandible, fracture of the first left rib, damage to ribs VI-IX, and likely damage to the thoracic spine. Evidence of burns on the legs. Remains No. 2—bullet or shrapnel wound to the right occiput, injury to the lower jaw, and damage to the right scapula. Remains No. 3—perimortem injuries to the skull vault, typical of blunt force trauma, include damage to the second metacarpal of the right arm. Burns were found on the skull,

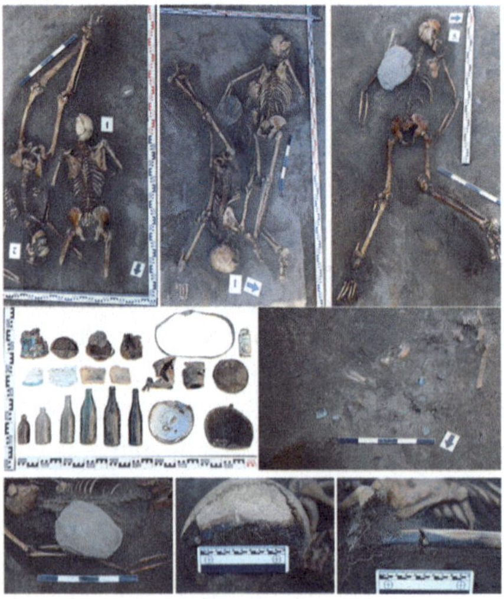

Figs. 10.7 and 10.8 Remains found in Leipalingis in 2023 (E. Aranauskas)

chin, and knee areas. Remains No. 4—gunshot wound from above. Remains No. 5—gunshot wound to the skull, fracture of the left mental crest. The injuries observed in the bodies of these Lithuanian Freedom Fighters require a detailed analysis by investigators and a reconstruction of events.

In the remains found in the second pit, injuries were also extensive and differed from the context of previously discovered remains, resembling combat injuries—predominantly multiple gunshot wounds, with some bodies showing signs of burns. It is expected that identifying the individuals will reveal the precise circumstances of their deaths. Importantly, these pits were located approximately 10 m apart and exhibit significant differences. In the second pit, where fewer injuries potentially linked to interrogation and torture were found, the remains were haphazardly thrown. In the first pit, numerous injuries that raised questions were noted. A stone tied with wire and sheets of metal were thrown into the pit, but the remains were arranged more orderly, with the heads oriented in one direction and the limbs not crossing.

To date, the area around Leipalingis NKVD headquarters has yielded the highest number of Lithuanian Freedom Fighters' remains identified. Unfortunately, many remains were found without meticulous documentation, yet each discovered partisan burial pit adds to the understanding of NKVD operational patterns.

10.4.4 Lazdijai

In 2021, excavations in the Lazdijai NKVD headquarters' courtyard began coincidentally when, during construction, human remains were discovered (Fig. 10.9) (Čičiurkaitė 2022). The former NKVD headquarters in Lazdijai occupied the territory of six current plots, with at least two buildings used for the detention and interrogation of partisans, liaisons, and their relatives. During archaeological investigations in 2021, in the central part of a former garage, at a depth of 110–115 cm, the remains of three individuals were found. In the black peaty soil, the indistinct contours of the pit were visible only around the legs of remains No. 2 and No. 3. Thus, suggesting that individuals died at different times but were buried close to each other, approximately 80 cm apart. All uncovered remains showed significant disturbances due to previous earth-moving activities.

Anthropological studies indicated that three men, approximately 25–35 years old, were buried. Gunshot wounds were identified in the skulls of two of them: two penetrating gunshot wounds were found in the skull of remains No. 2 and one in the skull of remains No. 3. Blunt trauma is suspected in the skull of remains No. 1, although the mechanism or tool responsible could not be identified due to its highly fragmented condition. Next to the remains No. 1, Lithuanian military uniform buttons were found with the Vytis emblem, columns of Gediminas, and a button with the columns of Gediminas. No artifacts were found near remains No. 2, as most of them were disturbed by the garage foundation. On the left hand of remains No. 3, a silver ring with the Vytis cross was found, and a wire loop was found around the

Fig. 10.9 Lazdijai site—former NKVD headquarters and surroundings (R. Kraniauskas)

neck area (Fig. 10.10), which presumably was used to drag the body of the deceased to the burial site.

Research on the courtyard and immediate surroundings of the former NKVD headquarters during 2022–2023 continued with a change in the search strategy, focusing on verifying verbal information regarding probable burial locations. In 2022, GPR surveys were initially conducted (Čičiurkaitė 2023). Within one of the detected anomalies, approximately 7 m northwest of the location where the remains of three Lithuanian Freedom Fighters were discovered in 2021, the remains of two additional Freedom Fighters were found. At a depth of approximately 60 cm below the current courtyard surface, a skull was uncovered. Upon excavating all the remains to a depth of about 90 cm, the outline of a pit measuring approximately 100 cm wide and 180 cm long became visible. Considering the position of the left hand of remains No. 2, it is presumed that the pit had sloping sides. The fill of the pit consisted of abundant charcoal, unburnt wood fragments, household ceramics and glass shards, corroded metal stove doors, cologne bottles, and numerous eggshell fragments (Fig. 10.11). Stones and fragments of shoe soles were found on top of the remains. The pit contained the remains of two men aged 25–35 and 17–20, showing numerous peri-mortem bone fractures caused by strong traumatic force but without signs of blast trauma. It was observed that both sets of remains lacked wrist and foot bones (the latter were not in anatomical position), and no bone damage was detected during anthropological examinations, indicating that the remains were likely buried during a later stage of mortuary practices. The crowns of the upper right mandibular canines of remains No. 2 were broken while the individual were

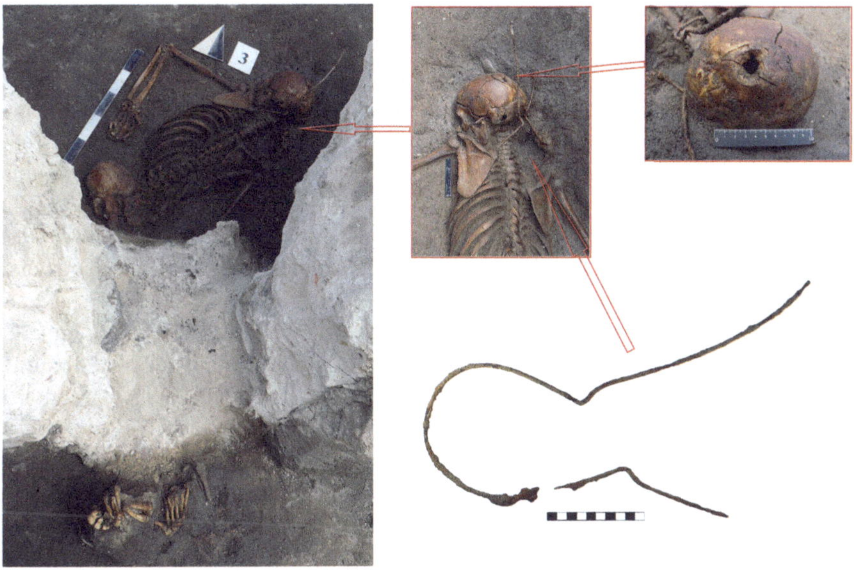

Fig. 10.10 Remains found in Lazdijai in 2021 (Ingrida Čičiurkaitė)

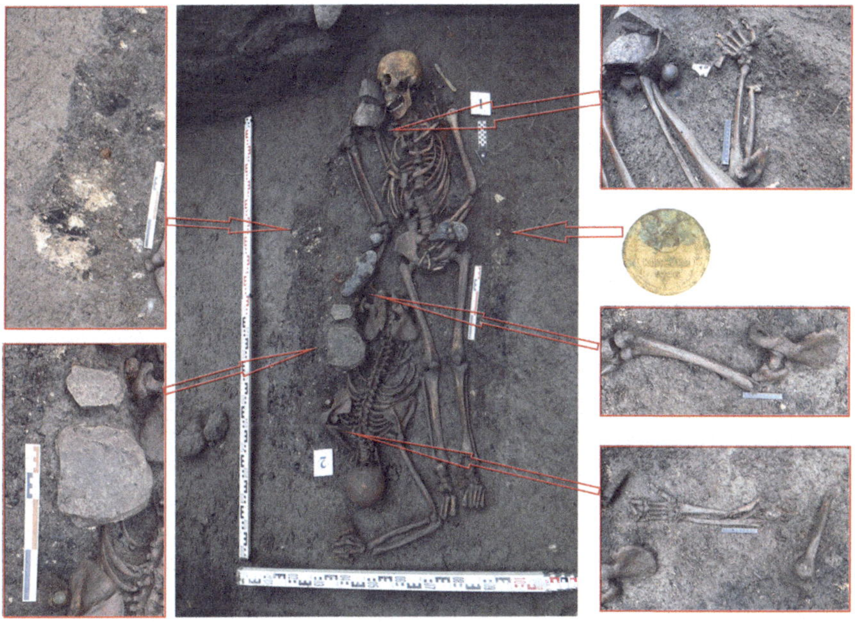

Fig. 10.11 Remains found in Lazdijai in 2022 (I. Čičiurkaitė)

likely alive, indicative of trauma effects. The bodies of the two Lithuanian partisans in the refuse pit were concealed no earlier than 1946, as confirmed by a Soviet-era 3-kopeck coin found alongside the remains in the pit fill.

During the 2023 investigations (Čičiurkaitė 2024), only isolated bone fragments from remains disturbed by previous construction work were found, confirming that the courtyard of the Lazdijai NKVD headquarters still contains concealed remains of Lithuanian Freedom Fighters. Additionally, two refuse pits related to NKVD activities were located along the boundary of plots at Vytauto St. 18 and 20, containing state vehicle and motorcycle registration plates with Cyrillic characters, household waste, and fragments of firearms: disks from a Soviet PPSh-41 submachine gun magazine, a Mosin rifle lock part, a modified Mosin rifle barrel segment, a fragment of a German P-18 pistol magazine, fragments of Soviet Tula Tokarev (TT) pistol magazines, and shells. Lithuanian partisans also used such weapons, suggesting that parts were disposed after being seized from fighters. These weapons were dismantled and rendered irreparably damaged within the former NKVD premises to prevent future use, while the bodies of the killed partisans were buried nearby. It is noteworthy that individual firearm parts were also discovered in other former NKVD headquarters areas discussed in this article.

10.5 Conclusion

Various methodologies were applied for the localization of burial pits and narrowing down the search area: assessment of soil particle density through probing and drilling, excavation and shovel tests for stratigraphic evaluation, and geophysical surveys. The courtyards and adjacent plots of the former Leipalingis and Lazdijai headquarters were systematically investigated over three years. Despite sporadic investigations in Marijampolė and Rietavas, the four cases discussed reveal the systematic actions of NKVD structures.

Primarily, hiding remains within the courtyard area, especially in secluded and adjacent plots under visual control of NKVD or assisting individuals, was observed. In all four discussed locations, burial pits were found near buildings at distances of 5–9 m or within a 30–50 m radius, often adjacent to former fence boundaries. Existing pits, such as former World War II trenches and household waste or refuse pits, were used for burials. In the absence or completion of these, small, shallow, irregularly shaped pits with narrowing bottoms were dug, unable to accommodate entire bodies. Another significant feature was their shallow depth. Partisan remains were typically buried at depths of 60–105 cm. Attention is drawn to the fact that bodies of higher-ranking partisans were often hidden near plot fences.

The burial sites of the killed Lithuanian Freedom Fighters were concealed by filling them with various debris or planting trees. It is likely these methods were used to further hide remains, confusing their comrades and relatives. Between the burial pits, confiscated weapons likely taken from fighters were also buried within courtyard spaces.

Archaeological and anthropological research data highlighted disrespectful treatment of the deceased and torture during detention and interrogations. Of particular note was the repeated discovery of splintered hand bone fractures in skeletal remains.

Today's efforts to locate remains aim not only to find deceased individuals but also to identify their identities, combat circumstances, and demise. Identifying the remains of Lithuanian Freedom Fighters not only ensures a dignified burial for Lithuania's heroes but also reveals historical truth.

The goals and actions of the Soviet regime, ranging from illegal combat methods (deception) to the murder of partisans, their supporters, differently minded individuals, and civilian populations, to the desecration of human remains, are not only classified as war crimes but also identified as crimes against humanity and genocide. Therefore, the search for murdered Lithuanian partisans primarily serves as evidence collection for previously committed crimes.

References

Anušauskas A (1996) Lietuvių tautos sovietinis naikinimas 1940–1958 metais. Vilnius

Balčiūnas J (1942) Lietuvių archyvas. Bolševizmo metai. T. I, Kaunas

Bater JH, Stranga A, Misiunas RJ, Meškauskas K (2024) Encyclopedia Britannica. Lithuania. Retrieved July 14, 2024, from https://www.britannica.com/place/Lithuania

Čekutis R, Žygelis D (2007) Laisvės kryžkelės. Laisvės kovos Latvijoje bei Estijoje. Bernardinai.lt. Retrieved July 7, 2024, from https://www.bernardinai.lt/2007-04-16-laisves-kryzkeles-laisves-kovos-latvijoje-bei-estijoje/

Čičiurkaitė I (2022) Lazdijų m., Vytauto g. 18 detaliųjų ir žvalgomųjų archeologinių tyrimų 2021 m. ataskaita, Vilnius

Čičiurkaitė I (2023) Lazdijų m., Vytauto g. 20 ir Dzūkų g. 13 sklypų palaikų užkasimo vietų paieškos (detaliųjų archeologinių tyrimų) 2022 m. ataskaita, Vilnius

Čičiurkaitė I (2024) Lazdijų m., Vytauto g. 18, 20 sklypų palaikų užkasimo vietų paieškos ir detaliųjų archeologinių tyrimų 2023 m. ataskaita, Vilnius

Čičiurkaitė I, Kvizikevičius L (2023) Genocido nusikaltimų ir įkalčių paieška buvusių NKVD/MGB būstinių Lazdijuose ir Leipalingyje teritorijose ir jų aplinkoje. Archaeologia Lituana 24:49–83. https://doi.org/10.15388/ArchLit.2023.24.4

Dakanis B (1999) Rezistentų užkasimo vietos Marijampolėje, Vytauto g. 26 žvalgomųjų archeologinių tyrimų ataskaita 1999 m, Vilnius

Dulkinienė R (2000) Rainių tragedija. 1941 m. birželio 24–25 d, Vilnius

Gaškaitė N, Kuodytė D, Kašėta A, Ulevičius B (1996) Lietuvos partizanai 1944–1953 m. Kaunas

Gendrėnas G (1995) Švenčionys. 1995 NKVD aukų kapavietės paieškos ataskaita

genocid.lt (2023) Rasti ir identifikuoti penkių Šarūno rinktinės partizanų palaikai. Retrieved July 14, 2024, from http://genocid.lt/centras/lt/3932/a/

Grossmann M (2024, February 02) The Forest Brothers in the soviet-occupied Baltic States. Baltic Yearbook of International Law Online https://doi.org/10.1163/22115897_02101_007

Hague Convention (II) Annex to the convention art. 1, Convention (II) with Respect to the Laws and Customs of War on Land and its annex: Regulations concerning the Laws and Customs of War on Land (The Hague July 29, 1899)

Jankauskas R (1990) 1990 m. rugsėjo 29 d. Rietavo m. parke iškastų palaikų apžiūros aktas. Vilnius

Jankauskas, R. (1991). Palaikų iš Rietavo parko antropologinės analizės ataskaita. 1991 m. spalio 26 d. Vilnius

Jankauskas R, Barkus A, Urbanavičius V, Garmus A (2005) Forensic archaeology in Lithuania: the Tuskulėnai mass grave. Acta Medica Lituanica 12(1):70–74
Kontrimas D (2011) Tyrimai Rietavo Oginskių dvaro sodybos teritorijoje. Archeologiniai Tyrinėjimai Lietuvoje 2010 metais
Kozakaitė J, Miliauskienė Ž, Kadikinaitė J (2023) Skeletuotų žmonių palaikų iš Leipalingio (Dzūkų g. 10), Druskininkų rajono, antropologinių tyrimų ataskaita. Vilnius
Kvizikevičius L (unpublished 2024) Archaeological fieldwork raport
Kvizikevičius L (2022) Leipalingio NKVD-MVD būstinės pastato ir Lietuvos partizanų užkasimo vietos ir kapų komplekso (43184) ir Leipalingio mstl. Druskininkų sav. detaliųjų archeologijos tyrimų 2021 m. ataskaita. Vilnius
Kvizikevičius L (2023a) Leipalingio NKVD-MVD būstinės pastato ir Lietuvos partizanų užkasimo vietos ir kapų komplekso (43184) teritorijos ir jos aplinkos Leipalingio mst., Druskininkų sav., Dzūkų g 13, Nr, 15, Sodų g. 7 detaliųjų archeologijos tyrimų 2022 m. ataskaita. Vilnius
Kvizikevičius L (2023b) Pulkininko ir kitų Lietuvos partizanų palaikų paieška Leipalingyje. In V. Vitkus, Pulkininkas Kazimieraitis
Kvizikevičius L, Zagreckas R (2023) Lietuvos partizanų užkasimo vietų paieškos Leipalingyje. Archeologiniai tyrinėjimai Lietuvoje 2022 metais, pp 545–550
Mežmalis A (2011) Historical background (1939–1991). In: Damage caused by the Soviet Union in the Baltic States. Riga, pp 9–21
Montvydas Ž (2022) Lietuvos partizanų laidotuvės 1944–1969 m. Būdas 2(203):63–74
Neiburgs U (2008) The resistance movement in Latvia during the Nazi German occupation (1941–1945): research problems and achievements. Genocidas ir rezistencija 2(24)
Niitsoo V (2004) Pasipriešinimo sąjūdis Estijoje (1955–1985). Genocidas ir rezistencija. Retrieved from http://www.genocid.lt/Leidyba/2/viktor.htm
Parra RC, Ubelaker DH (2023) The anthropology of violent death and treatment of the bodies: an introduction. In: Parra RC, Ubelaker DH (eds) Anthropology of violent death: theoretical foundations for forensic humanitarian action, p 2
Petraitytė-Briedienė A (n.d.) Vyriausiasis Lietuvos išlaisvinimo komitetas. Retrieved July 7, 2024, from Visuotinė Lietuvių enciklopedija. https://www.vle.lt/straipsnis/vyriausiasis-lietuvos-islaisvinimo-komitetas/
Rummel R (2008) Death by government, 6th edn. Transaction Publishers, New Brunswick
Šiušaitė A, Urbanavičius J, Landsbergis V (2007) Pamirštas SSRS karo nusikaltimas. Rainiai 1941 06 24–25 (Antras papildytas leidimas ed.). Baltijos kopija, Vilnius
Striužas V (2021) Lietuvos partizanų užkasimo vietos ir kapai. Būdas 5
Strods H (1996) Latvijas Nacionalo Partizanu Karš *1944–1956*. Preses Nams, Riga
Vėlius G (2021) Našlaičių kapinių (Vilniaus m.) archeologiniai tyrimai—Lietuvos partizanų palaikų paieškos. Archaeologia Lituana 22:62–96. https://doi.org/10.15388/ArchLit.2021.22.3
Žygelis D (2012, June 20) Sugrįžę iš nebūties: partizanų palaikų identifikavimas. bernardinai.lt. Retrieved July 13, 2024, from https://www.bernardinai.lt/2012-06-20-dalius-zygelis-sugrize-is-nebuties-partizanu-palaiku-identifikavimas/
Žygelis D, Čekutis R (2011, June 20) Laisvės kryžkelės. Masinės žudynės 1941 metų birželį. bernardinai.lt. Retrieved June 29, 2024, from https://www.bernardinai.lt/2011-06-20-laisves-kryzkeles-masines-zudynes-1941-metu-birzeli/

Chapter 11
Forensic Archaeological Investigations of the Former Mother and Baby Home in Tuam, Ireland

Niamh A. McCullagh, Linda G. Lynch, and Aidan Harte

Abstract This chapter examines the pivotal role of forensic archaeology in investigating the historic deposition of infant and juvenile remains at the former Mother and Baby Home in Tuam, Ireland. This study traces the history of the Mother and Baby Homes, details how the burial practices at Tuam came to light and outlines subsequent forensic archaeological investigations. Key findings include the discovery of human remains in a chambered structure initially believed to be a sewage tank, with evidence confirming that these remains were dated to the operational period of the Home (1925–1961). This work also discusses the legal and governmental responses to the findings, culminating in the enactment of the Institutional Burials Act (2022), which recognizes forensic archaeological standards for addressing such cases. This study underscores the critical role of forensic archaeology in uncovering historical injustices and facilitating transitional justice through the identification and dignified treatment of the deceased.

Keywords Forensic archaeology · Mother and baby homes · Tuam · Ireland · Institutional Burials Act · Transitional justice

Background

This chapter sets out the key role that forensic archaeology has played in an Irish context, specifically relating to the deposition of infants at the Mother and Baby Home in Tuam, Co. Galway. This chapter comprises five sections. The first sets out what Mother and Baby Homes were and how the burial practices at one such site became a public issue. The study also sets out where and how forensic archaeology

N. A. McCullagh (✉)
Consultant Forensic Archaeologist, Cork, Ireland

L. G. Lynch
Consultant Osteoarchaeologist, Dublin, Ireland

A. Harte
Consultant Forensic Archaeologist, Galway, Ireland,

Consultant Forensic Archaeologist, Cork, Ireland,

P. M. Barone, WJ M. Groen (eds.), *Forensic Archaeology and New Multidisciplinary Approaches*, Soil Forensics, https://doi.org/10.1007/978-3-031-86308-0_11

was employed. The second section outlines the test excavations that took place at the Tuam site, followed by the details of the stratigraphy encountered during the excavations. The evidence of the human remains that were recovered or identified on-site during the excavations is discussed in the fourth section, while the fifth section sets out the response of the Irish government to the findings and the role that forensic archaeology will play in future work at the Tuam site.

11.1 What Is a Mother and Baby Home?

Mother and Baby Homes were not uncommon throughout the twentieth century across countries where Catholicism was prevalent. Women who became pregnant outside the bounds of the conventions of marriage were seen as something to be secreted away in such homes. These homes were run by a variety of religious institutions that were supported by the State. They admitted single pregnant women as residents, who then had to work in the institution until their babies were born. Many of the infants were then fostered or adopted but under strict religious control, to ensure that 'Catholic children' did not go to parents of other religions (Cooney 2009). Once this had been achieved, women could, in theory at least, return to society. These institutions operated in the Irish state from 1922 to 1998.

In February 2015, an independent Commission of Investigation was established by the Irish government to examine the practices of these institutions and collect evidence for their findings. This was known as the 'Mother and Baby Homes Commission of Investigation'. Their final analysis of 17 such homes stated that the most "disquieting feature" of the homes was the high rate of infant mortality occurring within them (MBHCOI 2021, 4). The Commission also found that the institutions did not necessarily protect children, and "in some years during the 1930s and 1940s, over 40% of 'illegitimate' children were dying before their first birthday" (MBHCOI 2021: 15).

Given these levels of fatalities, it is not surprising that the women who survived the institutions do not refer to them as 'homes', as the level of care they experienced was not one that would be associated with a 'home'. The Commission concluded, "the women and children should not have been in the institutions" (MBHCOI 2021: 5).

11.1.1 Mother and Baby Home at Tuam, Co. Galway

The Tuam Mother and Baby Home occupied the buildings of a former Union Workhouse. These were established by the Irish Poor Law Act (1838) to provide aid to the destitute, particularly during times of famine, and were built from three standardised layout designs by George Wilkinson. The Tuam Workhouse was founded in 1840–41, but it did not receive admissions until 1846 (O'Connor 1995). In 1920, the British Crown Forces occupied the workhouse as a barracks, which was then transferred to the Irish National Army in 1922. When the Irish State was established, the premises were repurposed by Galway County Council and the Bon Secours Sisters to form a Mother and Baby Home in 1925 (Corless 2013). It was owned and funded by Galway County Council, with the religious order being responsible for its day-to-day operations. This institution had a high rate of infant mortality. The Commission of Investigation reported that "[B]etween 1921 and 1961 (when it closed), 978 children died in the Tuam Home, 80% [aged] under one year, 67% [aged] between one and six months. Three-quarters died in the 1930s and 1940s, with 1943 to 1947 the worst years" (MBHCOI 2021: 33).

11.1.2 'Memorial Garden'

In 2013, a local historian, Catherine Corless, brought the issue of the Mother and Baby Home at Tuam to public attention and very much into the public domain. As part of a local history project, she had traced the deaths of 796 children and infants at the home in Tuam, but she was unable to confirm where they had been buried. She suggested that although there was evidence they had been buried in a location that was unofficially known as the 'Memorial Garden'. Historic maps indicated that there was a "sewage tank" at the same location (Fig. 11.1). This provoked considerable public outrage at the treatment of women and children at the home, as well as at the inappropriate location of the burial of bodies at a potential "sewage tank".

11.1.3 Forensic Archaeology and the Mother and Baby Home Commission of Investigation

In May 2015, the authors were contacted by the Mother and Baby Home Commission of Investigation (MBHCOI) to investigate claims that had been made about the Tuam site and to see if human remains were present at the location of the former sewage tank. The MBHCOI required a forensic approach to the site investigations in order to ensure that the evidence collected complied with standards that would be acceptable in a court of law, that is, forensic standards. In 2016, the MBHCOI identified four lines of inquiry pursuant to their legal obligations:

(i) To establish if there were human remains present at this location;
(ii) To establish the date range of the deposition of these human remains, if found to be present;
(iii) To establish whether there were human remains contained within the structure of the reported "sewage tank";
(iv) To provide the demographic profiles of the human remains observed (Fig. 11.2).

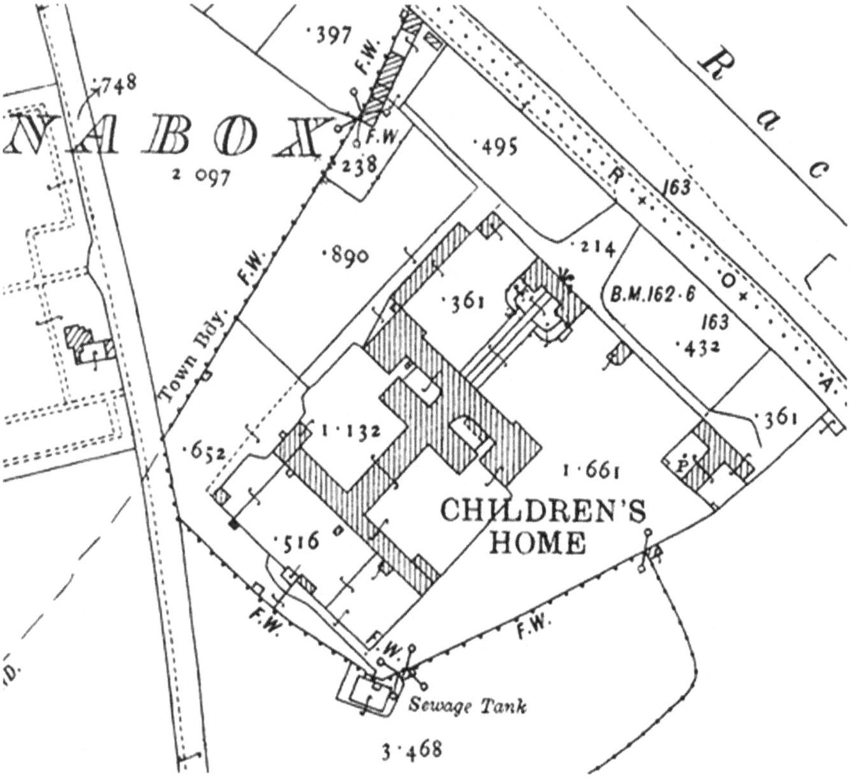

Fig. 11.1 Ordnance Survey Ireland map (1927) of the Mother and Baby Home and the associated 'Sewage Tank'. © Ordnance Survey Ireland

11.2 Initial Site Description

The investigation commenced with a desktop review of the site, looking at historical mapping, aerial photography and any archive information pertaining to the location in the local authority records.

Subsequently, a geophysical survey was carried out in an area known as the 'Memorial Garden'. This identified a number of anomalies, which warranted the undertaking of forensic test excavations. The appropriate warrant was issued by Judge Y. Murphy, and the excavation was conducted under forensic control. *An Garda Síochána* (the Irish police) were on-site throughout the works in order to preserve scene continuity throughout.

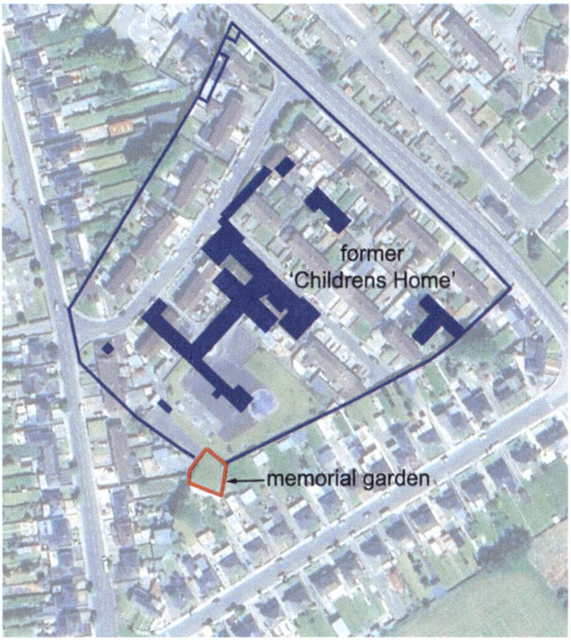

Fig. 11.2 General layout of the site. The areas marked in blue highlight the footprint of the former home over the current aerial imagery of the site (Google Maps). The memorial garden is outlined in red

11.2.1 Summary of Findings

The test excavations revealed two subsurface structures in the 'Memorial Garden' (Fig. 11.3). The first was a nineteenth-century sewage containment system that had been decommissioned and filled with debris. The second was a rectangular concrete structure divided into 20 subsurface chambers. The function of this second structure was unclear. However, it appeared to be "related to the treatment/containment of sewage and/or waste water" (Mother and Baby Home Commission of Investigation, 2017), and significant quantities of human remains were discovered in at least 18 of the 20 chambers.

The human remains were not fully accessed due to the confined nature of the chambers. Instead, analysis was conducted using photogrammetry, which was recorded on-site. Analysis of the skeletal remains indicated that the age at death of the individuals ranged from at least 35 foetal weeks to 2–3 years, with one individual being potentially 4–6 years of age. Radiocarbon dating indicated that the remains fell within the time frame of the operation of the Mother and Baby Home, that is, 1925–1961.

The sections below detail the methodology through which these findings were discovered.

Fig. 11.3 Final plan of test excavations at the 'Memorial Garden', compiled from McCullagh 2016 and McCullagh et al. 2017

11.3 Site Stratigraphy

The site was investigated using strategically placed trenches based on both documentary research and geophysical survey (Fig. 11.3). A single-context excavation method was used, and individual numbers were assigned to each context. These are described in a more simplified format here, for the purposes of clarity. Similarly, for ease of description, the northeastern part is considered as north in the text below.

The stratigraphic record from the site investigations provided a clear, if complex, sequence of events. Cartographic evidence had shown that this area, now the memorial garden, had been a 'gravel pit' in the early 1800s. The void from this earlier quarry was used to construct a large subsurface tank (Feature 3). This was altered to provide internal filtration (Feature 2) before being disused and partially backfilled. Subsequently, a long, chambered structure (Feature 1) was constructed by reusing the southern wall of the earlier Feature 3. This chambered structure was accessed through 21 small openings at the top of each of the 20 chambers. It is primarily within these chambers that human remains were discovered. Over time, these structures were covered over by topsoil, and no trace of any of these was visible prior to excavation.

11.3.1 Sewage Tank (Features 2 & 3)

The earliest structure within the site was a rectangular stone-built subsurface tank measuring c. 11.16 m × 8.02 m internally and 2.28 m in depth (Feature 3). This was found in each of the trenches investigated (Fig. 11.3). It had vertical walls of limestone, 0.46 m in thickness, squared to courses and bonded with lime mortar, with the upper edge at or very slightly above the nineteenth-century ground level. This was connected to a drainage culvert on the northern side. The stone-built culvert, 0.45 m x 0.45 m internally, was capped with large flat slabs and passed directly beneath a saddle-stone that formed an entrance at the boundary between the sewage tank and the workhouse. The culvert channelled water through the north wall of the rectangular tank (Feature 3). An alteration had been made to this end of the culvert, diverting the flow into a ceramic pipe through the north wall. A second pipe was identified to the east, suggesting that another drain was directed to this part of the north wall. These pipes opened into a rectangular space, 2.5 m × 1.22 m, defined on three sides by large iron grilles set into masonry walls (Feature 2) (Fig. 11.4a, b). This was constructed after the retaining walls of Feature 3 and provided filtration to the larger tank. The outline of Feature 3 first appeared on the map of 1892, contemporaneous to the Poor Law Union Workhouse established here in 1841. The filtration tank (Feature 2) was a later addition, and the 1927 Ordnance Survey map appears to show the outline of this (with a second probable filtration tank external to Feature 3, north of the test trench). The walls of Feature 2 were constructed of mixed limestone and brick, 0.44 m thickness, and do not 'tie' with the main Feature 1 wall. The floor of both Features 3 and 2 was of concrete, but an arrangement of bricks, which defined a concave-shaped gully, was found toward the southwest. This was truncated by the latter feature, Feature 1, but it originally served to redirect fluids to the end of the tank.

In summary, this was a large rectangular cesspit labelled as 'Sewage Tank' on both the 1920s and 1940s Ordnance Survey maps. Originally constructed to serve the earlier workhouse, the outline of Feature 1 is shown on the 1890s map. It was altered by the addition of a filtration area (Feature 2) and possibly the addition of internal gullies along the base to aid drainage.

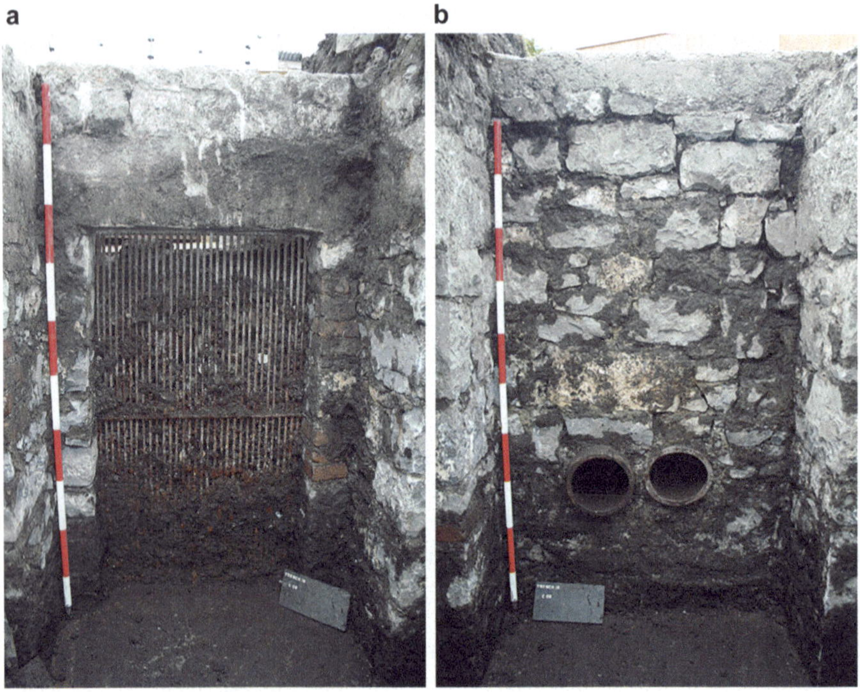

Fig. 11.4 (**a**, **b**) The south wall of the tank illustrating one of the three metal grilles; the north wall of the filtration tank with inlet pipes

11.3.2 Disuse of the Cesspit (Feature 3)

The basal fill or layer of Feature 2 was a dark brown silt 0.35 m in thickness. This also appeared to be the same basal fill further south, within the larger 'Sewage Tank', albeit greyer and sandier in composition. Where this abutted the base of Feature 1, concrete and mortar fragments were noted. This silt deposit at the base likely originates from the period of use of the tank as a cesspit. A large infill layer of rubble was then deposited from the northern side, which was up to 1.73 m in thickness. This sloped downward toward the south and stopped short of Feature 1 (Figs. 11.5 and 11.6).

11.3.3 Chambered Structure (Feature 1)

The latest structure discovered during these investigations was a long rectangular structure with 21 narrow openings at the top, leading to 20 separate narrow, deep chambers (Figs. 11.3, 11.5 & 11.7). The entire structure was 11.75 m in external length and 1.6 m in width. It consisted of stone walls shuttered with concrete,

Fig. 11.5 Entire length of the chambered structure containing the infant remains

Fig. 11.6 Southern wall of sewage tank with later shuttered concrete walls of chambered structure abutting

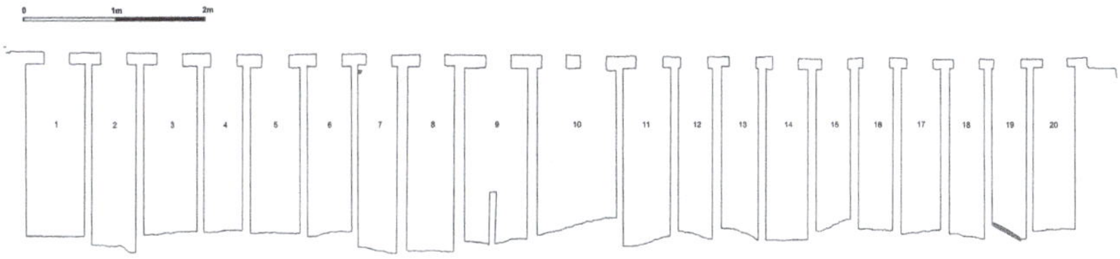

Fig. 11.7 Profile through Feature 1, facing south

utilising the southern wall and the southernmost 1.6 m of both the east and west walls of the earlier cesspit (Feature 3). This was clearly visible internally at either end and also internally along the length of the southern wall (Fig. 11.6). The north wall of Feature 1 truncated the brick-lined gully at the base of Feature 3. The sequence of construction was thus clearly indicated.

The chambers measured approximately 1.35 m in length internally and varied in width from 0.38 m to 0.86 m. The upper surfaces of the deposits within were at depths of about 1.9 m from the top opening (Fig. 11.7). The external depth of the structure was 2.2 m, and so an approximate depth of the deposits could be ascertained. No internal deposits were excavated, but these were assessed remotely. The deposits and walls showed the effects of water-level fluctuations within the chambers. The openings at the top were not evenly spaced but were generally aligned with the chambers below. The top was formed of a concrete slab, shuttered in place, with timber formwork used to create the openings (some timber was found preserved in situ). The openings were 0.82–0.85 m in length and 0.29 m in width, and these had been covered by precast concrete lids. Some of the lids were fragmented, while others were missing entirely (e.g. Chamber 13). Identifiable items in some of the chambers with broken lids provided evidence of the dates of previous access. For example, a "Castrol GTX" motor oil bottle in Chamber 16 that was released on the market on 18 April 1968 (see Fig. 11.8), meaning that particular chamber had been accessed sometime after that date.

A noteworthy aspect of the chambered feature was openings observed at the base of the northern wall. These only occur in the six eastern chambers (Nos. 1–6 in Fig. 11.3), where they comprised constructed rectangular openings, between 0.3 m and 0.4 m in estimated width and of similar height. All had been blocked from the exterior face, and they were not necessarily positioned centrally to the chambers into which they opened. This suggests that the northern wall was constructed before the internal dividing walls that separate each chamber. It seems probable that this was the original design template, which was then altered as construction progressed. Crude voids were evident at the base of this wall in many of the other chambers (except Chamber 20), which perhaps indicate openings that were filled/blocked

Fig. 11.8 Discarded "Castrol GTX" bottle found in situ in Chamber 16. (McCullagh et al. 2017)

during the construction phase. These voids were most apparent in Chambers 11, 12, 13, 16 and 17.

Outside the north wall of the chambered structure, a depression remained where the rubble-like infill material had not entirely filled the previous tank (Feature 1). This had begun to subside and wash down against the exposed north face of Feature 1. At around the same time, a very soft, dark grey clayey silt had formed up against the north wall, and although it was 0.4 m in thickness, it had poorly defined edges, clearly having been formed naturally as a result of fluctuations in the local water-table level. This layer contained ex situ human remains that were likely to have originated within the chambered structure but were later displaced through rough openings near the base of the north wall. A layer of clay was deposited over the rubble backfill in this area, although a substantial depression remained along the northern edge of Feature 1. This area was slowly filled with domestic debris such as hearth rake-out material, as well as by natural silting.

11.4 Human Remains

Human remains were identified in all of the chambers of the concrete structure (Feature 1). Remains were visible on the surface of the basal deposits of 18 of these, and later internal soil sampling identified human remains in all chambers. A small quantity of human remains was physically recovered from a number of chambers outside the northern edge of the feature. None of the chambers of Feature 1 were physically entered due to significant accessibility issues; each opening was no more than 0.8 m × 0.3 m, with deposits lying over 1.75 m beneath the opening. This presented a clear health and safety issue and was technically considered a confined space (Kelly 2017).

Soil sampling and volatile organic compound (VOC) analyses were conducted internal to Feature 1 (Dawson et al. 2017). This offered evidence that some remains had decomposed in situ (McCullagh et al. 2017). When combined with the evidence of in situ articulation, the test excavation confirmed that there was sufficient evidence that some human remains had decomposed in situ and were not transferred here from another location.

The recovered human assemblage was disarticulated (no longer in anatomical position) and commingled (the remains of two or more individuals mixed together). The primary aim of the analysis was to identify and record the remains and then undertake whatever macroscopic analysis was possible in terms of forensic osteoarchaeological analysis.

All of the recovered remains were juvenile (that is, less than 18 years old at the time of death) in origin. The ages were estimated using recognised standards (Schaefer et al. 2009), while, given the issues of estimating biological sex based on macroscopic analysis, no estimation of sex was attempted. Measurements were taken using a Powerfix® electronic digital calliper, while a Kenex® Notebook NB-2000, which weighs in 0.1 g increments, was used to weigh the individual remains. Some fragments were so light that they did not register on the scales, and so they were recorded as the minimum weight of 0.1 g.

In total, 182 human bones, fragments of bones and teeth were physically recovered. The total assemblage recovered weighed 163 g. Just seven bones, or bone fragments, were recovered from within Feature 1 itself. Most of the remaining skeletal elements were recovered in the area of the trench excavated directly to the north of Feature 1. Two bone fragments were recovered from the topsoil. In terms of the physical appearance of the human remains, those within the chambers appeared to be more complete and to have suffered less degradation than those outside the structure. This is likely due to a variety of factors, not least the process by which the remains got from inside the chambers to outside Feature 1, but also to the variations in burial environments, both within and outside Feature 1. The heaviest single human remains element (22.5 g) was that of a left temporal bone (cranium) from an infant who was aged between 6 and 12 months at the time of death, recovered from Chamber 10 of Feature 1. This single bone represented 13.8% of the total weight of the human remains recovered during the test excavation.

The seven bones recovered from Feature 1 were from two chambers, located near the centre of Feature 1. A left temporal and parietal (cranium) bone, as well as a left femur (thigh bone), were recovered from Chamber 9. These represented at least one young infant, aged between 0 and 6 months old and probably specifically between 1 and 2 months old at the time of death. All three of these bones were submitted for radiocarbon dating. A left temporal and left parietal (both cranial) bone, a left ulna (lower part of arm) and a distal first foot phalanx (toe) were recovered from Chamber 10. The latter was recovered in the soil that adhered to the parietal bone. These remains represented at least two infants, one aged between 3 and 6 months and the other between 6 and 12 months. With the exclusion of the foot phalanx, the other three bones were submitted for radiocarbon dating. Apart from those bones which were physically removed, further human remains, all of infant origin, were identified within both of these chambers, with some apparently articulated (in the correct anatomical position), possible infant ribs tentatively identified in one of the chambers.

The human remains recovered immediately to the north outside Feature 1 were all in a disarticulated state, having been redeposited there as a result of natural processes, such as fluctuations in water levels and silting. In total, the remains of at least seven juveniles were identified in the 173 fragments of bones and teeth recovered. Age estimates included a preterm and a full-term infant, two infants between 1.5 and 3 months old, a 6–9-month-old infant, a 1–2-year-old and a 2–3-year-old young juvenile. As noted, the preservation of these remains was poorer than those within the chambered structure. In addition, rodent gnawing was identified on a number of bones. Finally, fragments of an infant rib and an infant femur were recovered from the topsoil.

When all of the human remains recovered are considered together, the minimum number of individuals (MNI) represented is ten, ranging in age from 35 foetal weeks through to 2–3 years at the time of death. Further human remains were present within those two chambers, and therefore, it was not possible to estimate a more detailed MNI specifically in relation to the two central chambers. Six samples of bones from within those two central chambers were submitted for radiocarbon dating, returning dates corresponding to the years of the operation of the former Mother and Baby Home.

The remaining 18 chambers of Feature 1 were also examined to establish whether human remains were present; however, no bones or teeth were removed. The assessment of the contents was based entirely on extensive photographic and photogrammetry evidence of the interiors. Physical human remains (that is, bones or teeth) were identified in 18 of the 20 chambers, while soil testing later confirmed that the other two chambers also contained human remains. It was not possible to accurately estimate the numbers of individuals represented. However, it was evident that a number of chambers contained the remains of multiple individuals, as indicated by either duplicated skeletal elements and/or variation in bone sizes indicating individuals of differing ages at death. As with the analysis of the recovered bones and teeth, all human remains appeared juvenile in origin and specifically either infant (<1 year) or young juvenile (1–6 years). The dental remains in a cranium in Chamber 13 provided an age estimate of 1.5–2.5 years, while a vertebra and an ulna in Chamber 16 appeared to be from a 4–6-year-old individual.

There was some evidence of articulation in many of the tanks, particularly in the form of sets of ribs. In one instance, an infant was tentatively identified as lying on its side. The cranium of a 2–3-year-old individual was lying supine in Chamber 1, suggestive of an individual lying on their back. A possible edge of a coffin was identified in Chamber 6, while potential preserved wickerwork was identified in Chamber 3. Two bones appeared quite unique. In Chamber 13, the cranium of a juvenile (possibly 1.5–2.5 years) simply appeared to lie on the surface deposits. An infant humerus, lying adjacent to the cranium, was also loose on the surface and appeared to have suffered some post-mortem, natural erosion. In contrast, almost all other human remains within the chambers were at least partially embedded in the sediment material in the bases of the chambers and were well-preserved. Those bones on the surface within Chamber 13 may be a reflection of the fluctuations in water levels within the chambers over time; however, it is more likely that they represent remains that were manually disturbed or moved. It was noted earlier that two infant bones were recovered from the topsoil; on the assumption that these originated from the chambers, then it is suggestive of either deliberate or inadvertent removal of remains from the chambered structure at some unknown stage since the time of deposition.

In addition to the above evidence of some in situ remains, there were other indications that this was a primary site of deposition, rather than the human remains being redeposited here from a primary burial place. As mentioned, the bones within the chambers appeared in an excellent state of preservation. If they had been redeposited from another burial site, then more fragmentation would be expected. There was also no evidence of redeposited soil, which would likely occur if the remains had been redeposited from another burial site. The actual partial disarticulation of some of the remains appeared to be primarily due to fluctuations in water levels since deposition, as previously mentioned. In many chambers, the bones were concentrated on the south side, reflecting the natural drainage at this location. The variations in water levels were succinctly demonstrated by the identification of what appeared to be a hand phalanx of an infant or young juvenile, adhering to the coarse surface of the south-facing wall, located well above the current sediment level in Chamber 5.

11.5 Reactions to the Findings

In fulfilment of the brief, the forensic archaeological investigations, initiated by the Commission, had confirmed the presence of human remains at the site of the former Mother and Baby Home in Tuam. Although there were limitations to the investigation, there was stark evidence in relation to all four MBHCOI lines of inquiry. It also confirmed a date range for these remains, which was consistent with the period of use of the site as a Mother and Baby Home. However, it was not within the legal remit of the Commission of Investigation to recover human remains, only to establish the existence and nature of human remains at the site. Neither was it within the Commission's area of expertise to advise on how potential investigative recoveries should proceed, if deemed appropriate in the future. Therefore, the Irish government established an Expert Technical Group (ETG) to advise on appropriate actions to be undertaken at Tuam. This was a multidisciplinary team (which included the authors), which also included international expertise, that was tasked to research the international frameworks available, previous excavations and methodologies from comparable scenarios/sites. The ETG was not permitted to make recommendations but was tasked with outlining the various future options and with detailing the 'implementation of Best Practice' through which further investigation of the site could be conducted. The ETG suggested that full forensic excavation of the site complied with the requirements of transitional justice, through humanitarian forensic action, to optimal effect, both in terms of recovery and identification (Expert Technical Group 2017).

The report of the ETG provoked a response from the Irish government to support the perspective that there was a requirement for a forensic approach to the site. However, they were of the view that current legislation did not allow for the excavation of such a site. In response, the government enacted the Institutional Burials Act in 2022. This legislation allows for a 'director' to be appointed to lead the investigation of burials at given institutions, where burial practices have been deemed to have been manifestly inappropriate (Institutional Burials Act 2022). A 'director' for the Office of the Authorised Intervention at Tuam was appointed in 2023. Significantly, for the field of forensic archaeology, this act was the first time that the Irish state recognised, in law, that the standard of forensic excavation was necessary and when it must be applied.

The site at Tuam is highly complex for a number of specific technical reasons. These include, but are not limited to, the chambered structure (Feature 1) being defined as a confined space under health and safety standards; Feature 1 being within the fluctuation range of the water-table level; and the presence of commingled, at least partially disarticulated, juvenile remains, which would need to be individualized, as well as identified, if possible. As such, any future investigation requires a very specific and highly specialized response.

11.6 Conclusion

For the past decade, significant issues have surrounded the case of the historic deposition of infant and juvenile individuals at the Mother and Baby Home in Tuam. Forensic archaeology has been successfully employed to address contested narratives with regard to human remains here. Crucially, the Irish State has recognised the necessity of forensic archaeological methodologies in the further investigation and analysis of the site, and the field will play a key role in future excavation work that will be undertaken here.

References

Cooney J (2009) John Charles McQuaid: ruler of Catholic Ireland. O'Brien Press, Dublin

Corless C (2013) The home. Unpublished Local History Project

Dawson L, Shepard T, Mayes R (2017) The characterisation of samples for the mother and baby homes commission of investigation. In: McCullagh NA, Harte A, Lynch L (eds) Results of Phase IIA site investigations at the reported 'Children's Burial Ground', Dublin Road Housing Estate, Tuam, Co. Galway. Report to the Mother and Baby Homes Commission of Investigation. Included in Mother and Baby Homes Commission of Investigation Final Report (2021). Available at https://assets.gov.ie/118565/107bab7e-45aa-4124-95fd-1460893dbb43.pdf

Expert Technical Group (2017) In: McCullagh NA, Lynch L, Harte A, Tuller H, Clayton T, Farrell B (eds) Technical Report on the Tuam Site. Stage 2: Options and Appropriate Courses of Actions Available to Government at the Site of the Former Mother and Baby Home, Tuam, Co. Galway. Available at https://assets.gov.ie/47451/3314dd47812349c498b3e0fbfc06bf88.pdf

Kelly J (2017) Consultancy on health & safety in relation to working activities at tuam mother and babies home site. In Expert Technical Group, Technical Report on the Tuam Site. Available at https://assets.gov.ie/47451/3314dd47812349c498b3e0fbfc06bf88.pdf

Institutional Burials Act (2022) Number 18 of 2022, Part 2 Chapter 1. Available at https://www.irishstatutebook.ie/eli/2022/act/18/enacted/en/pdf

McCullagh NA (2016) Results of phase II site investigations at the reported 'children's burial ground', Dublin road housing estate, Tuam, Co. Galway. Report to the Mother and Baby Homes Commission of Investigation. Available at https://assets.gov.ie/37017/0fba347e42024a2b8d5cb1cb819a97d3.pdf

McCullagh NA, Harte A, Lynch L (2017) Results of phase IIA site investigations at the reported 'children's burial ground', Dublin road housing estate, Tuam, Co Galway In Mother and Baby Homes Commission of Investigation Final Report (2021). Available at https://assets.gov.ie/118565/107bab7e-45aa-4124-95fd-1460893dbb43.pdf

Mother and Baby Homes Commission of Investigation (2017) The Commission Has Completed Its Test Excavation of the Tuam Site [Press Release]. Accessed March 3, 2017. Available at https://www.tuamherald.ie/2017/03/03/statement-by-mother-and-baby-homes-commission-of-investigation/

Mother and Baby Homes Commission of Investigation (MBHCOI) (2021) Final Report. Available at https://assets.gov.ie/118565/107bab7e-45aa-4124-95fd-1460893dbb43.pdf

O'Connor J (1995) The workhouses of Ireland: the fate of Ireland's poor. Anvil Books, Dublin

Schaefer M, Black S, Scheuer L (2009) Juvenile osteology: a laboratory and field manual. Elsevier, Amsterdam

Chapter 12
Recovering Commonwealth Soldiers in France: A Forensic Archaeology Approach

Stephan Naji and Loreleï Margely-Lardeyret

Abstract The Imperial War Graves Commission, founded in 1917, organized graves registration for Commonwealth soldiers during both world conflicts. Today, the Commonwealth War Graves Commission honours 1.7 million fallen soldiers. Since 2010, discoveries have significantly increased, prompting a professionalization of the Recovery Unit and the implementation of a rapid response protocol, dedicated resources and an outreach programme to encourage reporting while minimizing site disruptions. With over 90 remains recovered every year, the Recovery Unit implements a forensic archaeology approach to assess the discovered remains, ensure meticulous documentation and preserve context. Although primarily commemorative, the RU follows a field protocol aligned with local laws, aiding identification and respecting legal processes. This approach supports rapid site assessment and jurisdiction transfer, facilitating cooperation with judicial authorities. Following excavation, detailed biological and social profiles are created to aid identification, supplemented by advanced artefact restoration techniques. Contextual research further refines identifications, with cases peer reviewed for accuracy and ethical considerations. The Recovery Unit aims to enhance its practices by adopting forensic archaeology standards, focusing on systematic desktop research and standardized site assessments. By leveraging historical data and Geographic Information System technology, the unit seeks to optimize recovery efforts, improve identification rates and ultimately honour the sacrifices of missing casualties more effectively.

Keywords Commonwealth War Graves Commission · CWGC · Recovery Unit · FWW · SWW · Forensic archaeology · Bayesian framework

---

S. Naji (✉) · L. Margely-Lardeyret
Commonwealth War Graves Commission, Beaurains, France
e-mail: stephan.naji@cwgc.org; l.margely-lardeyret@cwgc.org

P. M. Barone, WJ M. Groen (eds.), *Forensic Archaeology and New Multidisciplinary Approaches*, Soil Forensics, https://doi.org/10.1007/978-3-031-86308-0_12

12.1 Introduction

Founded by Royal Charter in 1917, the Imperial War Graves Commission (IWGC) originated amid the brutality of the Great War with its unprecedented death toll at an industrial scale. This dramatic reality spurred Sir Fabian Ware to draw up a set of detailed directives to supplement the provisions on the treatment of the dead on the battlefield contained in the 1906 Geneva Convention (International Committee of the Red Cross [ICRC] 1906) to systematize the identification, marking and recording of graves for Commonwealth casualties during the conflict. From the British Red Cross to the British Army Directorate of Graves Registration and Enquiries (DGR&E), these servicemen formed units dedicated to the management of the deceased and enquiries from living relatives (Francis 2018).

Composed of the former dominions of the British Empire that had actively participated in the First World War (FWW)—Australia, Canada, India, New Zealand, South Africa and the United Kingdom (CWGC 1917)—the IWGC signed War Graves Agreements with France, Germany, Belgium and the Netherlands, which conceded the Commission land in perpetuity for the construction and maintenance of its cemeteries and memorials. After renewing these agreements in 1951 to include the management of Second World War (SWW) casualties and cemeteries and to continue its mission of remembrance, the IWGC became the Commonwealth War Graves Commission (CWGC) in 1964 (Francis 2018). Today, the CWGC commemorates 1.7 million women and men from the Commonwealth armed forces who fell during both World Wars, and cares for war graves at 23,000 locations in more than 150 countries and territories (CWGC 2024).

In this chapter, we briefly describe the evolution and goals of the modern CWGC Recovery Unit (RU) based in Beaurains, France.

12.2 From Volunteers to Forensic Archaeologists

After the SWW and until the turn of the century, the spirit of the original Grave Registration Units endured with dedicated CWGC volunteers, sometimes directly related to some of the original unit members, regularly recovering remains of soldiers discovered incidentally on the former battlefields in France during construction sites, farming activities, or archaeological excavations. Initially, the only lead to identify these forgotten remains would have been the presence of a definite personal marker such as an identification (ID) disc, a regimental unit number, or a precise personal inscription. Without them, the remains would most likely have been buried as "unknown", with any national or regimental elements found with the remains.

More recently, several coincidental variables have played a key role in renewing interest in the Commonwealth Member States to identify the fallen and increase the number of discovery notifications. First, the global structuring of salvage archaeology in France in the 2000s allowed for greater monitoring of First and Second World War discoveries (Demoule 2002). Second, the recognition of these wars as archaeological, scientific themes, particularly the potential for identification, significantly increased the care for the investigative process in archaeology (Adam 1992, 2006; Desfossés et al. 2008). Finally, the advent of affordable DNA tests following the invention of polymerase chain reaction (PCR), rapid DNA sequencing and the completion of the Human Genome Project in 2003 (Laurent 2017), coupled with online genealogy databases, opened a whole new avenue to identify Commonwealth casualties more reliably.

Consequently, Commonwealth member nations started launching their identification programmes. In particular, the Casualty Identification Program was established in 2007 with a mandate of identifying newly discovered remains of Canadian casualties (Lockyer and Davis 2020). Similarly, the British 'MOD War Detectives' under the Joint Casualty and Compassionate Centre (JCCC) was set up in its modern form in 2015 to investigate British casualties who died on battlefields across the world from the First World War to the Korean War (Bowers 2021). Finally, the archaeological dig in 2008 that uncovered around 250 Australian and British soldiers at Pheasant Wood in Fromelles, France (Loe 2014) motivated the Australian Defence Force to search the battlefields of the Pacific and Europe as part of the new Australian Unrecovered War Casualties-Army (UWC-A) unit in 2010.

12.3 The CWGC Recovery Unit

Similarly, this trend had a significant impact on the CWGC, especially in France, where over 100,000 casualties are still missing, and prompted a "revival" of the Recovery Unit (RU) through the dedicated work of the Commission Horticultural team. In particular, the discovery in 2010 of a small mass grave with around 30 sets of British and German casualties marked the beginning of the Recovery Unit's new protocol. Synthetically, the number of discoveries in France increased rapidly from an average of 14 per year between 2000 and 2014 to an average of 50 per year since then, with the culmination of the major construction project for a new hospital in Lens, just south of Hill 70, which revealed around 120 sets of human remains between 2018 and 2020 (Fig. 12.1).

One of the main reasons explaining this increased reporting is the fact that the RU protocol was upgraded to include three main components: (i) a year-round, on-call response team; (ii) a two-hour deployment time upon notification of a discovery; and (iii) dedicated human and material resources.

Today, the RU protocol is the central piece of our outreach strategy to best support local authorities, convince any potential "discoverers" to notify the Commission systematically, and reassure them that their construction site or harvest will not be affected significantly. This "network of trust" allows us to progressively expand the number of people willing to collaborate with us once they understand our rapid deployment process and continued mission to identify and commemorate

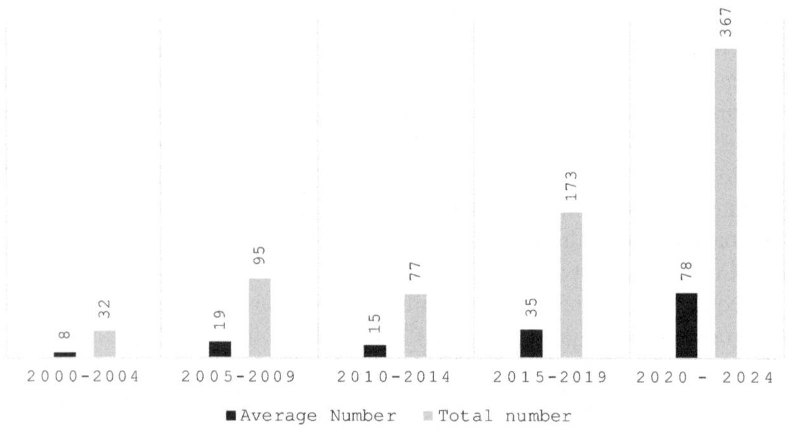

Fig. 12.1 Average number of sets of remains recovered in France since 2000

Commonwealth casualties. That process includes dealing with metal detectorists, fully illegal in France, and other battlefield "tourists" often prone to looting.

This transitional moment in the RU activity coincided with the official launch of the Canal Seine-Nord Europe project by the French government in 2019. The 107 km high-capacity canal, from Perrone to Cambrai running through the Commonwealth FWW front lines, motivated the CWGC to professionalize the Recovery Unit by creating a "Head of Recovery Unit" position in 2021 to guarantee our remit to recover Commonwealth casualties efficiently. Consequently, the RU rapidly expanded to three full-time "forensic archaeologists" and one ceremony coordinator based in France under the new Commemorations Directorate in Maidenhead (UK) in charge of Reburial and Rededication ID cases, Policy and Guidelines, Archives and Public Enquiries (CWGC 2024). This structure allowed us in the past four years (2021–2024) to recover over 300 sets of remains in France alone. During this period, we recovered an average of two sets of human remains per recovery, with several larger outlier recoveries, and each deployment took an average of about eight hours (Fig. 12.2).

12.4 Site Assessment: A Forensic Archaeology Approach?

The starting point of our investigation is the discovery of human remains. As with any archaeological endeavour, context and association are key, as they are destroyed during the investigative phase. Documenting, interpreting and analyzing field observations precisely must be our priority. To frame our protocol, we rely on archaeological methodology, which is usually question driven, and a theoretical framework to analyze and interpret our empirical observations of the material record consistently.

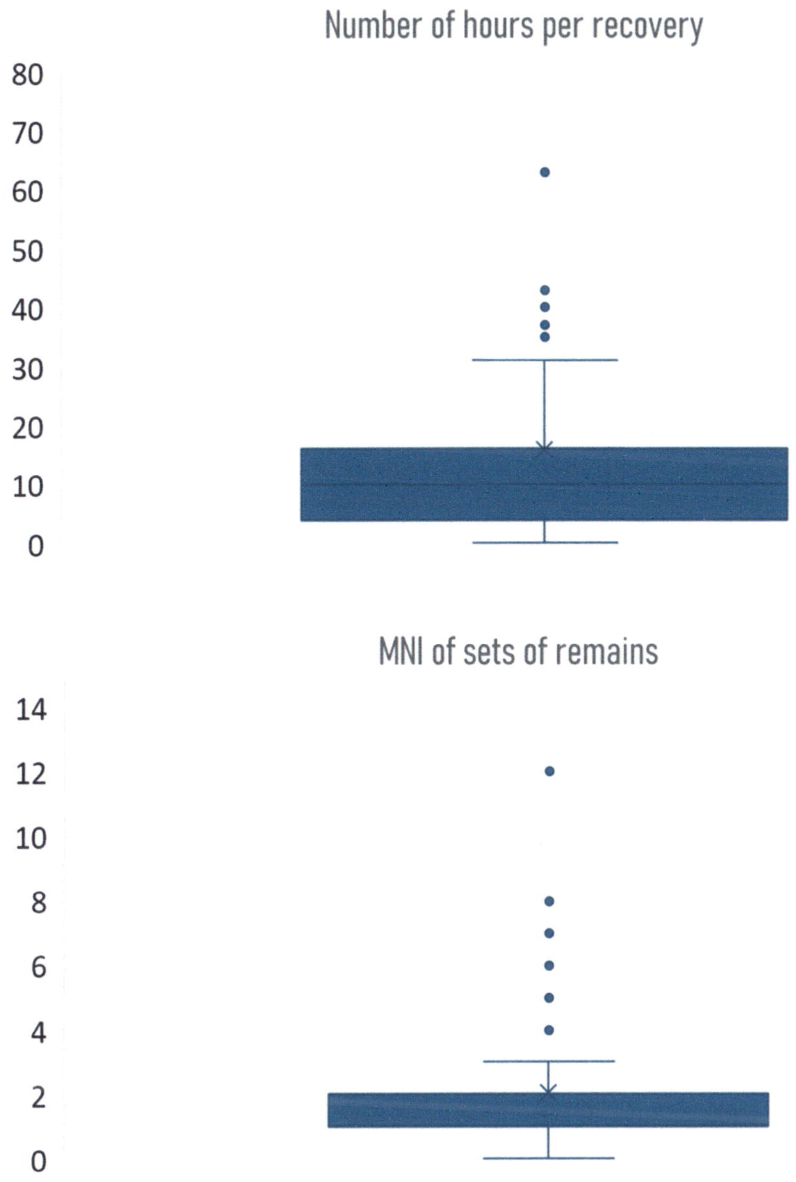

Fig. 12.2 Above: Distribution of the Minimum Number of Individuals (MNI/sets of human remains) per recovery; Below: Distribution of the number of total excavation hours per recovery

In most countries, recoveries of battlefield soldiers from historical wars are not included in the traditional forensic archaeology framework, as there are often no medical or legal outcomes to our work (for a broad review, see Groen et al. 2015; Marquèz-Grant and Errickson 2021). Nowadays, missing Commonwealth casualties from both wars are recognized as dead and have been commemorated appropriately (CWGC 2024), with the administrative consequences fulfilled (i.e., inheritance, insurance, pension), contrary to recent humanitarian crises. Therefore, the purpose of the CWGC's mission is primarily commemorative. Nevertheless, our remit in France is to recover incidental finds of all Commonwealth war casualties and support our Member Governments' efforts (MGs) to identify them. Even if we cannot name the soldier, the remains will be buried with full military honour in one of the Commonwealth cemeteries (CWGC 2024).

In this context, MGs usually replicate their local judicial process to conduct an identification board with chain of custody, and evidential value of finds and features, even though there are no formal judicial constraints such as court testimony. However, it is a clear, positive sign of ethical concern that such procedures are in place. Strategically, adopting a more constrained forensic archaeology approach to achieve our mission, as opposed to a bioarchaeology framework, serves multiple purposes. Even though these two fields greatly overlapped historically, their theoretical frameworks are distinct (for definitions and a summary of the differences, see Groen 2018).

From an operational perspective, the first benefit of a forensic archaeology framework for the CWGC RU is to conform to the local regulations pertaining to the discovery of human remains. The French Penal Code, article 74 (Code Pénal 2024), states that any discovery of human remains must be notified to local police authorities (police or gendarmerie). The public prosecutor's office is responsible for determining the context of the discovery, whether forensic, historical, or military. The first will open a formal police investigation, and the second and third cases will be closed and transferred to the Heritage agency or to the French Ministry of Defence (*Ministère des Armées*), respectively, through the "*Office National des Combattants et Victimes de Guerres*" (ONaCVG). The ONaCVG is responsible for adjudicating the national context of the remains, French or foreign (for a detailed description of the French process, see Meucci et al. 2022). If the remains are from Commonwealth troops, the ONaCVG can delegate jurisdiction to the CWGC following the CWGC International Royal Charter (1917–1963) recently restated in a joint Defence-Heritage ministerial memo (Ministère des Armées et de la Culture 2021).

The second benefit is to be able to assist legal authorities regardless of the context. The emergency contexts in which we operate, pyrotechnical clearance sites, construction sites, or preventive archaeological surveys, require that we develop excavation and field documentation methods specific to our objective, the identification of soldiers, without compromising a potential crime scene and its specific context. Therefore, the RU's initial operational step is to gather evidence to support (or falsify) the following three main research questions:

1. What is the nature of the osteological remains?
    (a) Exclude animal remains
    (b) Confirm human remains

2. What is the context of the discovery?
   (a) Exclude modern forensic, pre-war and civilian archaeological features
   (b) Confirm World Wars contexts
      (i) Exclude non-Commonwealth
      (ii) Confirm Commonwealth
3. How many individuals are present?
   (a) Define the site formation process and boundaries of feature
   (b) Exclude other adjacent areas
      (i) Expand the search area as necessary
   (c) Identify Minimum Number of Individuals (MNI)

This framework, informed by desktop historical research of conflicts at the location, past recoveries and an initial survey of the site, allows us to assess rapidly the site's context. Even though at this stage we do not calculate formal prior probabilities to predict the likelihood of the context, we still use a probabilistic framework loosely to assist local judicial police at the scene to define the context. Also, our role is to facilitate information sharing with the public prosecutor, often unfamiliar with historical military contexts, to speed up the adjudication process for site jurisdiction.

Over the last three years, we have deployed six times to contexts that were initially thought to be military but which we were unable to define precisely and thus had to transfer back to the police authorities. In these cases, the RU protocols need to be able to process the scene with minimal disturbances and maximal documentation so that a potential forensic investigation is not impacted by our initial assessment. Also, local Crime Scene Investigation (CSI) task forces might not be available immediately to process such a low-priority case. Similarly, when the CSI unit is present, they might lack the training to excavate skeletal remains. In these scenarios, we have been mandated by the public prosecutor to exhume the remains, following best practices in forensic archaeology to support them.

Finally, this approach allows us to evaluate human and material resources efficiently to achieve our goal of minimizing time on the scene. In addition to the RU anthropologists, the CWGC is structured to mobilize six additional support staff, trained in recovery protocols, as well as the use of a 3T mechanical digger if necessary.

12.5 Recovery: Documenting the Scene

Once the context is defined and the jurisdiction clear, the excavation of the human remains follows another set of research questions:

1. What is the national affiliation?
   (a) Confirm military or civilian artefacts specific to a Commonwealth member nation
   (b) Identify markings related to specific Commonwealth member nations
2. What is the regiment/unit of the soldier?
   (a) Is there a cap badge, shoulder title, or specific uniform buttons from a specific regiment?
3. Are there any unique individual identifiers?
   (a) Is there any unique identifier associated with the remains?
      (i) ID disc
      (ii) Regimental number stamped/etched on personal or military artefacts
      (iii) Are there any names or initials present on any artefacts?
4. Where are the artefacts located?
   (a) At the primary expected position
   (b) At a secondary probable location
   (c) Randomly distributed

To answer these questions, we use an archaeothanatology approach to exhume the skeletal remains (Duday 2009). This precise excavation method enables us to produce 2D and 3D maps for each skeleton and precisely associate all artefacts (Fig. 12.3).

Archaeothanatology was developed in part to precisely document site formation/taphonomy processes pertaining to human remains. The method optimises context and association and strengthens chain of custody at the scene. The associated mapping system is a dynamic assessment tool at the scale of the burial that updates our research questions directly in the field. This is a key step, since around 30% of our recoveries include more than one individual. Accurately associating skeletal elements with themselves and associating artefacts with an individual is critical if we want to respect the integrity of each individual's body and guarantee the provenience of each item.

Here, we overlap in part with criminalistics to predict the evidentiary value of each item (where was it found?) and predict its link to the deceased for identification purposes. For example, there is a greater likelihood that a shoulder title still attached to cloth, found in situ at the shoulder of a soldier, is evidence that he was wearing a jacket from a specific regiment. However, there is also a smaller probability that the badge was stolen, exchanged, or transferred to someone else entirely. Finally, there is always a possibility the badge percolated during the decomposition process or other *post-mortem* taphonomic process from another soldier deposited above, thus creating a random association. Using archaeological and criminalistics principles is central if we want to optimize our standards of collecting and sampling of evidence and ultimately increase our identification opportunities.

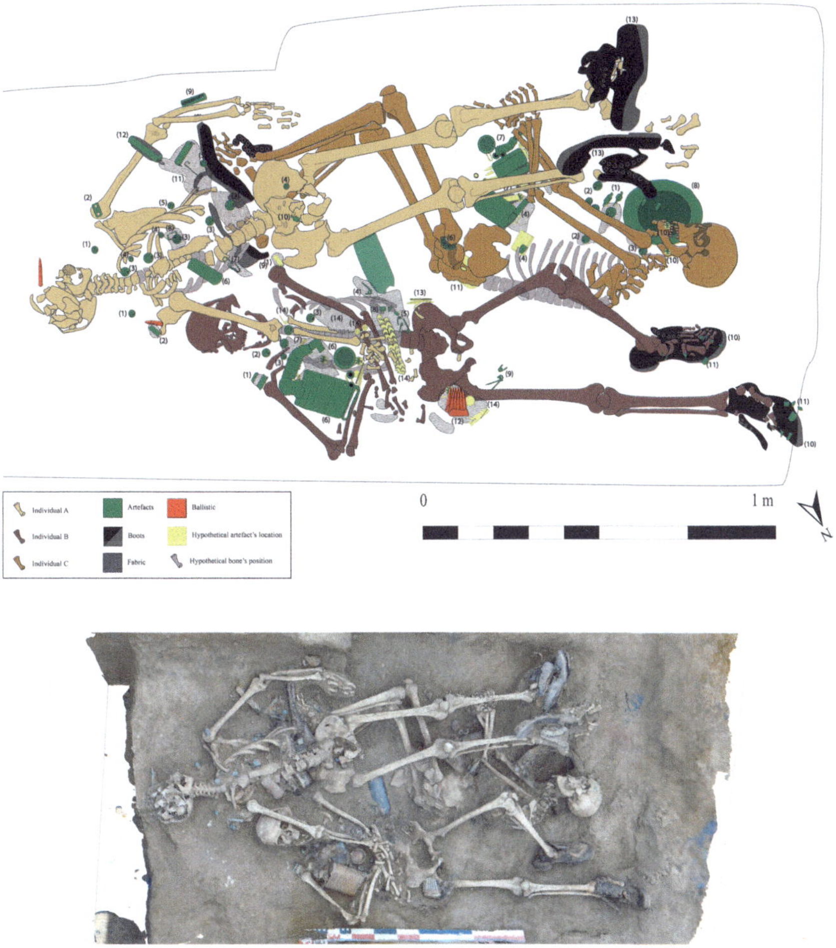

Fig. 12.3 Example of digital drawing (upper panel) and 3D (lower panel) field documentation for three soldiers buried with equipment

The reality of the wars created confusing contexts where bodies of different nations, allied or not, died together and were recovered as commingled sets of remains. We must operate under the assumption that multiple nations might be represented in a collective assemblage. The logic of site formation processes is thus instrumental to help comprehend how skeletal elements and artefacts were originally deposited and subsequently disturbed. Consequently, we must document the context accurately to transfer each set of remains to the proper country of origin and attest to the provenience of each artefact to avoid compromising the identification process (Fig. 12.4).

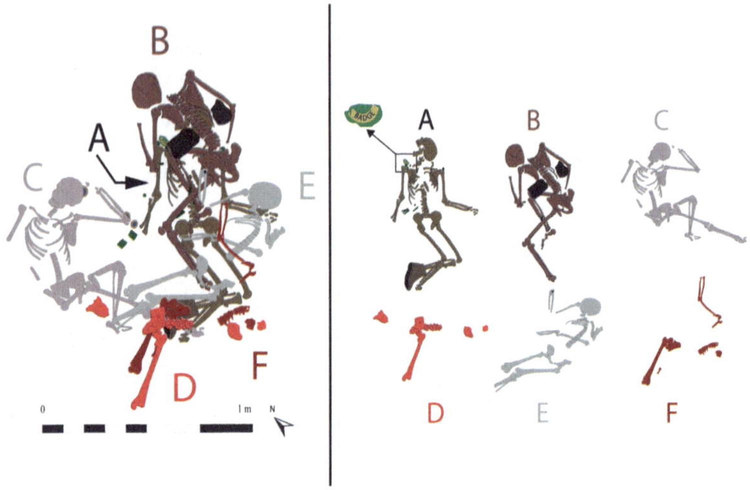

Fig. 12.4 Digital drawings of six soldiers (partially reproduced for confidentiality issues). Left panel: soldiers in situ; right panel: individualized soldiers with a close-up on individual A showing the location of the shoulder title attached to a piece of clothing (the regiment is not shown as an investigation is in progress)

With an increasing understanding of the FWW archaeological record (Desfossés et al. 2008), one additional outcome of a forensic archaeology approach is that we can simultaneously fulfil our mission more efficiently and document the archaeological contexts. We hope that we can optimize data collection to start proposing new bioarchaeological interpretations that will advance our historical understanding of the life and death of Commonwealth soldiers.

12.6 Data Analyses: Biological and Social Profiles

Once the recovery is completed, all remains are processed in our anthropology laboratory in Beaurains (France). Our official remit is to confirm the field questions (MNI, nationality, regiment, unique identifier) by cleaning and documenting the skeletal remains and the artefacts. These variables will be contextualized using Commonwealth archives and all other historical sources necessary to narrow down the list of potential casualties listed as missing at the scene. These steps have been detailed elsewhere (Bowers 2021; Margely-Lardeyret et al. in press). Once again, our goal is to conform as closely as possible to forensic standards so that we can provide clear evidence to our MGs regardless of their national standards in order to optimize the likelihood of identification.

Even though the formal identification of the soldier rests with each MG, the CWGC represents all six member nations equally and must guarantee (i) proper nationality adjudication, (ii) the chain of custody for human remains and associated artefacts and (iii) ethical standards of care for the storage of remains during the investigation.

12.6.1 Biological Profile

For the purpose of this chapter, the authors would simply like to emphasize that the use of a Bayesian framework for all biological estimates is warranted if we want to homogenize high standards of reporting, regardless of the national judicial contexts. For example, since many Commonwealth soldiers died between the ages of 17 and 22 years, the use of Bayesian posterior probability from epiphyseal fusion (Coqueugniot et al. 2010) to present an estimated age distribution is a significant improvement for court purposes from the traditional collection of overlapping inverse age prediction from phase to age (Brookstein and Morante 2021).

Likewise, even though sex estimation is normally not a problematic issue in the context of world wars where casualties are mostly represented by men, a reliable estimate is nonetheless necessary for accurate biological profiling. To this end, we always prioritize the pelvis as the most dimorphic anatomical area after hormonal changes during puberty (Costedoat 2019; Hackman et al. 2022). We use Bruzek's morphoscopic observations in the field and morphometric methods in the lab. The latter yields the highest degree of classification rate across populations worldwide (Bruzek 2002; Bruzek et al. 2017; Murail et al. 2005) and produces a posterior probability distribution. Ultimately, our goal is to upgrade all our biological analytical tools to meet the same best-practice requirements.

12.6.2 Social Profile

Most investigations usually start from the artefacts rather than from the biological profile. In fact, the biological variables account for only a limited number of formal identifications in most forensic contexts. However, after more than a century in the ground, objects are often rusty or damaged. These alterations represent an additional obstacle to the identification of the individual, as we never know which item might reveal a unique identifier and be linked to a specific casualty. For this reason, we are currently expanding the expertise of our CWGC blacksmiths in collaboration with the "*Centre de Conservation et d'Etudes*" (Conservation and Research Centre) at Ribemont-sur-Ancre (Somme, France) to document, preserve or restore metal artefacts. The use of ultrasound, chemical baths, or micro-sanding abrasion techniques are now integrated into our processes.

After the investigation is complete, a personal item may be symbolically returned to the deceased's descendant, while military items such as shoulder flash badges may be handed back to the regiment at its request. High-risk items such as ammunition are destroyed, and the rest of the clothing or personal effects are buried with the deceased. Other decontextualized artefacts are preserved for public outreach purposes.

12.6.3 Contextualization and Peer Review

Some cases are not solved initially because of a specific unique identifier or through DNA. The investigation of a King's Own Yorkshire Light Infantry (KOYLI) soldier, recovered in Héninel (Pas-de-Calais, France), was first impaired by the location of the recovery, unrelated to the known KOYLI deployment history in the region (Margely-Lardeyret et al. in press). The biological observation of a simple *peri-mortem* fracture to the forearm, associated with remains of a probable medical bandage, was instrumental in reorienting the research questions: how did the soldier die? And where was he coming from? By contextualizing these questions within a broader military context of troops' mobility, regimental deployments, and, most importantly, the care of the wounded, this new observation led to the hypothesis that the individual was transferred to the rear lines for medical assistance. By researching the local medical chain of evacuation, Private Herbert Greaves was included in the broader list of potential missing soldiers, and JCCC successfully matched his DNA sample to a living relative, confirming his identity (MoD 2022).

Finally, from an ethical, legal, and also logistical perspective, the Commission's responsibility is to make the most informed decision possible when adjudicating a case to a MG. Our head office-based Commemorations and Archive units include over a dozen professional researchers dedicated to contextualizing all recoveries, among other missions (CWGC 2024). By independently drafting a list of candidates, we provide an opportunity for a peer review framework to support our MGs in their effort to identify the soldiers in the most reliable way.

12.7 The Future of the Recovery Unit

Even though at this stage, we do not strictly apply the nine-step process recommended in forensic archaeology (Groen 2018), it is certainly our goal to build up our standards to conform to such recommendations. Operationally we must adapt our processes, in particular, the first three stages (preliminary desktop research, field survey and final desktop research), that we often combine in one step informed by internal and external priors.

Future areas of development for the RU include more systematic preliminary desktop predictions and a more standardized initial site assessment to better predict potential locations of missing soldiers. In this context, we overlap in part with criminology theory of the casuality of "crime", "crime" distribution pattern and "criminal" behaviour (Groen 2018).

For example, to optimize our resources on the Canal Seine-Nord Europe (CSNE) survey project, the largest construction site in Europe today, desktop assessment was used to generate around 50 high-density zones of missing soldiers along the 107 km canal route to focus our recovery sampling strategy. The expectation of several hundred known missing soldiers on the canal route was instrumental in estimating the resources necessary to monitor and execute the project efficiently.

Informed by historical accounts of battlefield clearance of the dead, battlefield cemetery spatial distribution and over 400 modern recoveries, we predicted specific areas of recovery in our GIS database with the highest probabilities of discovery in features such as FWW trenches and large shell holes.

This "profiling" strategy, as opposed to traditional geometric sampling methods common in large site surveys, has been successful at the time of writing, with half of our deployments revealing soldiers' remains. Furthermore, this is an opportunity to test our field survey protocols and update our hypotheses iteratively. One of the first feedback is that soldiers found today are often "forgotten" on the battlefield, as opposed to buried voluntarily. This implies that preservation and representation levels will differ greatly from a complete individual to a pair of boots.

We hope that in time, our GIS database will be used to predict the likelihood of recovery on any construction site during the project's planification stage. This active monitoring will allow us to select where to focus our effort to raise awareness prior to the start of the project, monitor high-probability construction projects and increase our recovery and identification processes in case of a discovery through a type of middle-range interpretative theory.

Our common goal is to increase the likelihood of formal identification so that the commemoration of each soldier's sacrifice can bring closure to the hundreds of thousands of descendants of the missing Fallen. We strongly believe that a holistic approach, framed within a forensic archaeology paradigm, optimizes the opportunity to identify century-old war remains. It is our hope that precise forensic archaeology exhumation methods, a Bayesian framework, and peer-reviewed identification boards will become the new global standards for Commonwealth nations.

References

Adam F (2006) Alain Fournier et ses compagnons d'arme: une archéologie de la Grande Guerre. Editions Serpenoise, Metz

Adam F, Boura F, Duday H (1992) La fouille de Saint-Rémy-la-Calonne: une opération d'archéologie funéraire expérimentale, ou l'anthropologie de terrain en quête de ses références. Les nouvelles de l'archéologie 48(49):59–61

Bookstein FL, Bravo Morante G (2021) The fallacy of forensic age estimation from morphometric quantifications of the pubic symphysis. In: Algee-Hewitt BFB, Kim J (eds) Remodelling Forensic Skeletal Age. Academic Press, London

Bowers T (2021) The Identification of British War Casualties: The Work of the Joint Casualty and Compassionate Centre. Forensic Sci Int 318:110571

Bružek J (2002) A method for visual determination of sex, using the human hip bone. Am J Phys Anthropol 117:157–168

Bružek J, Santos F, Dutailly B, Murail P, Cunha E (2017) Validation and reliability of the sex estimation of the human os coxae using freely available DSP2 software for bioarchaeology and forensic anthropology. Am J Phys Anthropol 164:440–449

Code pénal (2024) Available at Légifrance: Article 74—Code de procédure pénale—Légifrance (legifrance.gouv.fr). Accessed 30 June 2024

Coqueugniot H, Weaver TD, Houët F (2010) Brief communication: A probabilistic approach to age estimation from infracranial sequences of maturation. Am J Phys Anthropol 142:655–664

Costedoat C (2019) Quand la génétique permet de donner un nom au défunt. Revue historique des armées 294:55–66

CWGC (1917) Royal Charter of Incorporation. Royal Charter, London

CWGC (2024) Commemorating the Commonwealth Casualties of Both World Wars. Commonwealth War Graves Commission. https://www.cwgc.org/find-records/commemorations/. Accessed 30 June 2024

Demoule JP (2002) Bilan et Perspectives de l'archéologie Préventive Au Moment de La Création de l'Institut National de Recherches Archéologiques Préventives (INRAP). Bulletin de La Société Préhistorique Française 99(3):599–611

Desfossés Y, Jacques A, Prilaux G (2008) L'Archéologie de la Grande Guerre. Ouest-France, Rennes

Duday H (2009) The archaeology of the dead: lectures in archaeothanatology. Oxford University Press, Oxford

Francis P (2018) A guide to the commonwealth war graves commission, 1st edn. Third Millennium Publishing, London

Groen M (2018) Forensic archaeology: integrating archaeology with criminalistics and criminology. In: Barone P, Groen M (eds) Multidisciplinary approaches to forensic archaeology. Soil Forensics. Springer, Cham

Groen M, Marquez-Grant N, Janaway R (2015) Forensic archaeology: a global perspective. Wiley-Blackwell, New Jersey

Hackman L, Delabarde T, Roberts J, de Boerr H (2022) Forensic anthropology: a primer for courts. University of Dundee, Dundee

International Committee of the Red Cross (1906) Convention for the Amelioration of the Condition of the Wounded and Sick in Armies in the Field. Geneva, 6 July 1906. https://ihl-databases.icrc.org/assets/treaties/180-IHL-GC-1906-EN.pdf

Laurent FX, Vibrac G, Rubio A, Thévenot MT, Pène L (2017) Les nouvelles technologies d'analyses ADN au service des enquêtes judiciaires. Méd Sci 33:971–978

Lockyer S, Davis R (2020) We will remember them: The Canadian Armed Forces's Casualty Identification Program. Forensic Sci Int 316:110481

Loe L, Barker C, Wright R (2014) An Osteological Profile of Trench Warfare: Peri-mortem trauma sustained by soldiers who fought and died in the Battle of Fromelles, 1916. In: Knüsel C, Smith M (eds) The Routledge Handbook of the Bioarchaeology of Human Conflict. Routledge, London

Margely-Lardeyret L, Donnely M, Naji S (in press) The future of Commonwealth military casualties: the role of the CWGC. In: Verna E, Cabot E, Desfosses Y, Signoli M (eds) Archéologie et Anthropologie des Conflits. BAR publishing, Oxford

Márquez-Grant N, Errickson D (2021) The legislation, search, recovery, identification and repatriation of conflict casualties worldwide: introducing the WWI and WWII Special Issue. Forensic Sci Int 320:110716

Meucci M, Verna E, Costedoat C (2022) The skeletal remains of soldiers from the two World Wars: between identification, health research and memorial issues. Genes 13(10):1852

Ministère des Armées et de la Culture, France (2021 SEP 14) Joint memo #1D21018626

Ministry of Defence, and Veterans UK (2022) Sheffield Soldier of the Great War Laid to Rest 105 Years after His Death. Gov.UK. 4 November 2022. https://www.gov.uk/government/news/sheffield-soldier-of-the-great-war-laid-to-rest-105-years-after-his-death#:~:text=Private%20(%20Pte%20)%20Herbert%20Greaves%2C,on%20Thursday%20(3%20November)

Murail P, Brůžek J, Houët F, Cunha E (2005) DSP: a tool for probabilistic sex diagnosis using worldwide variability in hip-bone measurements. Bull Mém Soc Anth Paris 17(3–4):167–176

Chapter 13
The Need for Forensic Archaeology in the Investigation of Aircraft Crash Sites

Natasha J. Heap and Xenia-Paula Kyriakou

Abstract The scene of a mass fatality aircraft accident is forensically complex, involving multiple agencies, each with their own standards, protocols, and priorities. The International Civil Aviation Organization (ICAO) provides Standards and Recommended Practices (SARPs) related to Aircraft Accident Inquiry, known as Annex 13. However, despite multiple revisions since 1951, a recent ICAO audit revealed a majority of ICAO Member States had not established autonomous accident investigation authorities or developed comprehensive and detailed training programmes for aircraft accident investigators. While there are numerous political and cultural contributors to this problem, one factor is ICAO's lack of guidelines and standards for investigation training programmes, as well as for overall management of investigations, preservation of essential evidence and preparation of investigation reports. Another example is the International Criminal Police Organization's (INTERPOL) standards and protocols for victim identification, with the guidelines lacking the pre-identification step of systematic field investigative procedures. Such inadequacies in aviation accident investigation can contribute to inadequate safety recommendations and their implementation. In contrast, forensic archaeology has evidence-based investigative protocols, which could be added to existing aviation procedures. In this chapter, we describe the need for standardized, best practice, and evidence-based approaches to aircraft accident investigations and which specific aspects of forensic archaeology would be most helpful.

Keywords Forensic archaeology · Aviation accident investigation · Evidence-based protocols · DVI · Scene processing

N. J. Heap (✉)
School of Business, University of Southern Queensland, Springfield Campus, Springfield, QLD, Australia
e-mail: natasha.heap@unisq.edu.au

X.-P. Kyriakou
School of Human and Social Science (Forensic Science), University of West London, West London, UK
e-mail: xeniapaula.kyriakou@uwl.ac.uk

P. M. Barone, WJ M. Groen (eds.), *Forensic Archaeology and New Multidisciplinary Approaches*, Soil Forensics, https://doi.org/10.1007/978-3-031-86308-0_13

13.1 Introduction

A multiple-fatality aircraft accident can occur over land or water, in a densely populated city or remote farmland, in well-vegetated regions, or in other sparsely populated and inhospitable terrain. Typically, such sites are extremely complex, with fresh or actively decomposing, potentially burnt, highly fragmented human (and potentially animal) remains. These remains are commingled with personal effects, aircraft parts, and impacted structures on the ground. The debris fields can vary in size, from well-contained to extensive (Dirkmaat 2012). These scenes require the coordination of personnel from multiple agencies offering different expertise, including police, firefighters, paramedics, and aviation crash investigators. At times, these accident sites can also be attended by other multidisciplinary specialists trained in emergency response, such as pathologists, odontologists, and emergency planners/disaster recovery specialists (Easthope 2022). However, while forensic archaeologists and forensic anthropologists have demonstrated their usefulness in disaster responses (Emery 2014), these specialists are usually not included in modern aviation accident investigations. In fact, the role of the forensic archaeologist and anthropologist and the benefits they provide are nearly non-existent in the documentation provided by ICAO and INTERPOL. This is a glaring omission despite forensic anthropology's description as an established discipline in various professional and scientific institutions globally, such as the American Academy of Forensic Sciences (AAFS), the Australian and New Zealand Forensic Science Society (ANSFSS), the British Association of Forensic Anthropology (BAFA), and the Forensic Anthropology Society of Europe (FASE) (Franklin and Marks 2022).

Additionally, the numerous specialists at the scene of an accident often operate with conflicting priorities, with each specialist's agency having a different focus and requiring different information to be collected from the accident site. For example, aviation agencies, such as the International Civil Aviation Organization (ICAO 2016) and the International Society of Air Safety Investigators (ISASI 1999), offer recommendations for aviation accident scene analyses, with the aim of making aviation safer. In contrast, emergency response agencies, such as INTERPOL (2023a), provide guidelines for disaster victim identification (DVI).

However, given the diverse agencies involved, it is clear the current publications provided by ICAO, ISASI, and INTERPOL lack detailed response plans and do not provide systematic procedures for field investigations that could be used by all involved in such enquiries. Consequently, we believe there is a lack of a standardized and evidence-based best practice approach to overall aviation accident investigation, which directly affects evidence recording and collection, as well as victim recovery methods.

This lack has created operational and evidentiary gaps in parts of the process of air accident investigations. For example, *Annexure 3: Scene* of INTERPOL's DVI guide provides an explanation of the need for disaster sites to be searched and methodically processed, using a sector-by-sector approach and referring to scene gridding (INTERPOL 2023b). However, this generalized approach does not provide guidance on how to adapt the process to different scenes. Is a sector-by-sector approach appropriate on the side of a mountain? What should be done if the surface scatter of debris is non-existent due to the angle of impact of the aircraft? Furthermore, despite INTERPOL's inclusion of a scene gridding section, the emphasis of INTERPOL's documentation is on the collection of human remains for DVI and not on the evaluation of the scene and the recordation of the process of recording evidence.

Aviation accident scene processing is different from other mass disaster sites, such as a tsunami. Data from aviation accident scene analyses are a major contributor to accident investigations and are used to help determine the contributory and causal factors of each aircraft accident. Such factors are then used to prepare an accident report with safety recommendations for the aviation industry. This information is instrumental in formulating measures aimed at preventing future accidents, with resulting operational and safety-related changes being made to such concepts as aircraft engineering technology and enhancements in training protocols. The investigation of an aviation accident site cannot, therefore, be simply about victim recovery and identification. Consequently, efficient and knowledgeable cooperation, coordination, and teamwork amongst the various stakeholders are crucial for ensuring comprehensive and detailed processing of crash sites, thus facilitating thorough and effective investigations of aviation accidents.

In this chapter we suggest that incorporating established forensic archaeological protocols into currently existing aviation accident investigation and emergency response protocols can provide a standardized, uniform approach to ensure efficient crash scene processing, retention of the maximum amount of evidence and enhanced victim identification methods. We acknowledge that, because an aircraft accident can occur over land or water, marine environments dictate the use of diving and other specialized equipment and techniques (Ubelaker et al. 2014). We have chosen to focus our recommendations on terrestrial accident sites. Additionally, we approach this topic from our dual expertise in forensic archaeology and aviation, recognizing that, while this chapter is primarily written for forensic archaeologists and forensic anthropologists, there is a potential secondary audience of aviation accident investigators and other emergency response experts. For some of them, the terms and techniques used in forensic archaeology and anthropology could be previously unknown. We have therefore provided definitions of some of these terms and techniques.

13.2 Modern Aviation Accident Investigation

13.2.1 The Regulatory Framework

In 1944 the Convention on International Civil Aviation was drafted at a meeting of representatives from 54 nations to promote cooperation and 'create and preserve friendship and understanding amongst the nations and peoples of the world' (ICAO n.d.-a). At this meeting, more commonly known as the *Chicago Convention*, some of the aviation industry's core principles were established. The most notable were the Standards and Recommended Practices (SARPs), the doctrine for all activities that did and continue to affect aviation safety and harmonize international air navigation services, allowing for a coordinated international aviation industry to support growth in international transport. *The Chicago Convention* established 18 Annexes covering SARPs for areas such as pilot licensing requirements, standardized markings on airports and runways, and rules around the carriage of cargo and dangerous goods. *The Chicago Convention* also led to the creation of the specialized United Nations agency working to oversee international aviation, the International Civil Aviation Organization (ICAO). Since 1951, ICAO has provided SARPs relating to aircraft accident enquiries, known as Annex 13 (ICAO 2016). All States that are signatories to ICAO are required to abide by the practices in Annex 13. However, ICAO has no true 'power' to force signatory states to comply.

At first glance, the guidance provided in Annex 13 appears extensive and includes words such as 'requirements', 'standards', and 'guidelines'. Annex 13 contains sections referencing 'investigation management', 'investigator's equipment', 'accident site safety', and 'protection of evidence'. On further review, however, there is no mention of either required standards for best practice or methods for accident investigation (ICAO 2016). There are recommended general topics for 'advanced' investigator courses, such as 'cataloguing large wreckage', but there are no learning objectives listed to measure the type and level of competencies to be attained (ICAO 2016).

Another of ICAO's published guidance materials, *Document 9756, the Manual of Aircraft Accident and Incident Investigation* (Document 9756), includes sections entitled 'Actions at the accident site' and 'Investigation procedures', as well as one on 'wreckage investigation' on both land and in water (ICAO 2011). For example, guidance provided in Section 9.3.5, Chapter 9, Structures Investigation, Part III: Investigation of Document 9756 states that:

> As part of the initial structure examination, the investigator should look for evidence that any main part of the structure was not in its correct relative position at the time of impact. Wreckage distribution marks on the ground and telescoping of components often provide valuable clues. Evidence of missing pieces and overstressed sheet metal is also quite helpful (ICAO 2011, p. III 9 7).

However, *Document 9756* does not contain guidance or recommendations for methodologies for examining, recording, and working through the accident wreckage and debris. There is no mention of vital aspects of the material record, such as recording context and stratigraphy (the layers of the accident scene) or wreckage integrity. In fact, Part III: Investigation of *Document 9756* contains 229,640 words, while Chapter 2, Wreckage Investigation, contains only 3343, or 1.5% of this total. More words (4179) are spent on photography than on wreckage investigation (ICAO 2011).

There is no clear guidance on the removal, or excavation, packaging, and transportation of wreckage debris. The reader is left with an unresolved question about the evidentiary value of wreckage debris, that is, how each small 'bit' of wreckage can provide important evidence for the crash analysis, a point that is not addressed anywhere in the text. There is no clear guidance, standards, or protocols to be followed in this wreckage examination, nor mention or discussion of taphonomy (or related words) of the wreckage.[1] Despite the fact that maintenance of scene and wreckage integrity is of high importance, the document lacks acknowledgement that damage could occur if the wreckage were not excavated and handled appropriately. Was that fracture in the control surface caused before the crash impact, or was it the result of direct impact with terrain or actually postimpact damage during victim recovery efforts? Such questions are of immense importance in the post-recovery phase of the investigation.

In September 2024, ICAO released the first edition of *Document 10206, Manual on Aircraft Accident and Incident Investigation Training* (Doc. 10206) (ICAO 2024). This manual was described by ICAO as providing high-level guidance to States as they established evidence-based training for aviation accident and incident investigators. This statement was made despite a meeting in Montreal in 2016 where the ICAO Accident Investigation Panel concluded that, while initial investigator training provided by formal institutions was 'well-structured', it was 'not sufficiently comprehensive to prepare investigators for the field' (ICAO 2024, p. v). At this meeting it was also determined that 'training programmes would be designed to address areas of deficiency'. Competency-based training for aviation accident investigators would be the required training methodology but would include the caveat that such training would not be prescriptive. At the sixth meeting of the ICAO Accident Investigation Panel, held between 10 and 21 May 2021, although no reasoning was given, a decision was made that

> …applying a full range of competency based training and assessment methodologies would not be suitable for the function of an aircraft accident investigator, and that high-level guidance … would be more appropriate and useful for States' … which … could then determine how to apply the methodology (ICAO 2024, p. v).

The publication of ICAO *Doc. 10206*, as simply a high-level document lacking prescriptive competency-based standards, was a missed opportunity for ICAO to establish the required competencies and training standards for aviation accident investigators. Aviation accident investigation is a specialized area requiring a range of specialized skills. In general, however, 'people don't know what they don't know' (Kruger and Dunning 1999; Dunning 2011). Not providing prescriptive guidance and standards does a disservice to a State's investigative authority. Is it possible for a State to issue directives on what to teach if what is required by investigators is not known by those who author such guidance? High-level guidance is not what is needed to improve aviation accident investigations and improve compliance in ICAO's global audits of aviation accident investigation authorities. (See below for

---

[1] We define the study of the taphonomy of the wreckage as the identification, documentation, and interpretation of the variety of burial, decay and preservation changes that occur to the aircraft during the accident until recovery.

discussion of the results of the latest audit and the identified high levels of noncompliance.) As argued by Bury et al. (2020), people are poor at objectively evaluating their own competence. Prescriptive competency-based training standards would assist both States and investigators as to exactly what needs to be included in investigator training. This, in turn, would help investigators determine what they know and, importantly, what they do not know.

Another aviation industry body formed to support (but also not to regulate) aviation accident investigation is the International Society of Air Safety Investigators (ISASI). Established in 1964 to promote air safety through the exchange of ideas, experiences, and information, ISASI then published recommendations for the training of air accident investigators (ISASI 1999). These recommendations included a statement that the guidelines were evolutionary and would be updated when 'new methods and technologies become available' (ISASI 1999, p. 7). ISASI also aimed to promote the technical advancement of accident investigations (ISASI 2013), and two years later, the ISASI guidelines were updated in May 2015. This publication was the fourth and latest edition of the *Positions on Air Safety Investigation Issues*. This document stated that 'ISASI supports the development and implementation of coordinated international standards and recommended practices (such as ICAO Annex 13) to ensure the conduct of investigations using documented, uniform practices'. (ISASI 2015). However, as yet, there are none.

13.2.2 Identified Deficiencies in Modern Aviation Accident Investigations

As part of their remit, since 1999, ICAO has run a triennial Universal Safety Oversight Audit program (USOAP) to monitor the safety oversight obligations of member States (ICAO n.d.-b). The audit programme covers eight areas, one area being 'air accident and incident investigation (AIG)'. The 2019–2021 audit revealed six key areas of noncompliance in relation to Annex 13 throughout the global aviation industry (ICAO 2022): (1) Independent accident investigation authority and the investigation process; (2) Ensuring the effective investigation of serious aircraft incidents, according to Annex 13; (3) Providing sufficient training to aircraft accident investigators; (4) Ensuring proper coordination and separation between the Annex 13 investigation and the judicial investigation; (5) Establishing and implementing a State's mandatory incident reporting system; and (6) Establishing an aircraft accident and incident database and performing safety data analysis at State level. These are a significant number of areas of noncompliance.

One key area of noncompliance the 2019–2021 USOAP audit identified was that 65% of States had *not* developed a comprehensive and detailed training programme for aircraft accident investigators (ICAO 2022, p. 36). The audit further identified that existing training programmes of compliant States were often insufficient, with neither recurrent, specialized, nor advanced training addressed. The lack of published standards, acknowledged best practices, and training programmes were all identified as contributing factors to shortcomings in current aircraft accident investigations. These included the lack of preservation of essential evidence, poor management of investigations, and inadequate investigation reports potentially leading to poor safety recommendations (ICAO 2022, p. 36). Despite this, as discussed above, ICAO has not provided the required competency standards for aviation accident investigator training nor detailed a prescriptive syllabus.

As highlighted by Thallapureddy et al. (2024), much of the recent research on aviation accident investigation has focused on developing and validating incident and accident models and techniques to aid investigators in analyzing incident data. Ng et al. (2021, p. 1131) argued for the use of an expert system framework and artificial intelligence (AI) to enable investigators to 'share, access and interrogate accumulated knowledge to support the aircraft accident investigation process' but made no mention of a method of data collection. The authors also cited the 2016–2019 USOAP results and argued that their expert system framework would fill identified gaps in investigations. Bills et al. (2023) also examined the various methodology models and theories for investigation analysis but did not mention data or evidence collection. Konieczka (2017) had the promising title 'How to secure basic evidence after an aviation accident' and argued that 'the collection of basic evidence is the key procedural element related to … an aviation accident' (p. 66). However, only a short summary of the type of evidence to be collected was included. There was no explanation or guidance on how to collect it. Graser (2012) also targeted tools used in both the interpretation and the predication of incidents, focusing on data analysis. Once again there was no mention of the required step before the analysis, being the collection of evidence. While improvements in analysis methods are an important aspect of aviation accident investigation, any AI-generated outcomes or results from any database analysis will be dependent on the quality of the evidence that is within the database.

Evidence collection is the first stage of any accident investigation, and the processes around it need to be given as equal importance as the other two aspects of an investigation. These are hypothesis generation and analysis, amalgamation of findings, and generation of recommendations (ESReDA 2009). The analysis of poor-quality data can significantly undermine the outcomes of investigations and the effectiveness of safety recommendations. To enhance the results of accident investigations, any initial focus undertaken should logically be on improving evidence gathering and retention. However, there has been limited research within the aviation industry about the prioritization of processing the accident scene by aviation safety investigators.

13.3 Aviation Archaeology

13.3.1 Comparison of Historic and Modern Approaches to Aviation Archaeology and Aviation Accident Investigation

Aviation archaeology has evolved from what Ford once defined as an amateur-driven exercise in wreck salvage (Ford 2006), with an artefact-centric focus. Aviation archaeology is now a true subdiscipline of archaeology, examining 'past human interactions with flight and … the study of aircraft wreck sites, airfields, battlefields, and buildings or structures related to aviation' (Whitehead and Lickliter-Mundon 2023).

Studying aviation accidents before the jet age, i.e., 1950, was a simpler undertaking. Due to the slower impact speeds of aircraft, there was likely to be greater integrity of the artefact in situ—the aircraft and its associated material culture at the place of impact. Additionally, in those earlier years, the aircraft wreck was often left where it landed, unlike current investigation practices, which result in the removal of the wreckage (English-Heritage 2002; Lickliter-Mundon 2018). Agencies such as the Defense Prisoner of War (POW)/Missing in Action (MIA) Accounting Agency (DPAA n.d.) and Cranfield Recovery and Identification of Conflict Casualties Team (CRICC 2024) work in aviation archaeology, predominantly investigating World War II (WWII) era aircraft crash sites. Current archaeological investigation of such sites is generally divided into two categories: locating and identifying the remains of missing servicemen (and women) and studying the crash site (Ford 2006).

Recently, Eck classified historic military aircraft crash scenes into eight different crash types and how each of these crash site types was formed (Eck 2023). However, the eight 'types' of crashes are somewhat arbitrarily differentiated, illustrating a lack of application to the classification of aviation concepts, such as flight dynamics and the chain of events in accident causation. For example, Eck (2023) differentiated three of the accident scene types as a midair collision (MAC), which is different from a disintegration in flight (DIF), which in turn is different from a loss of control (LOC). However, a MAC can lead to a LOC, which in turn will lead to a DIF. If all three events occur in that order, they will create a single debris field/accident site. Eck (2023) also cited modern airliner accidents as illustrative of the accident classifications to be used in historic military crashes. However, contemporary crash scenes also differ from historic ones because the modern materials and methods used in current aircraft construction, as well as aircraft fuels and oils, are vastly different from those of the WWII era.

Modern aircraft crashes do not typically exhibit the extensive changes associated with long-term burial, as often observed in historic crash sites from several decades ago. Such sites are subject to prolonged taphonomic processes (e.g., burial, decay, and preservation affecting human, animal and plant remains and wreckage), corrosion of materials, and alterations associated with soil chemistry. Taphonomic processes significantly complicate the preservation and analysis of both biological and material evidence in comparison to more recent crash scenes. In contemporary accidents, recovery efforts are usually rapid, thereby limiting the degree and effect of environmental exposure and decomposition. Investigators of these scenes usually employ a major incident protocol (IP) associated with disaster and emergency management and response. The IP can be implemented at different levels, based on an escalation model that is dynamically assessed. Escalation frameworks provide a series of progressive stages or 'tiers' of response, ranging from local-level management to national or international interventions, based on the evolving nature of the disaster, as well as any mitigation needs. Such models are constantly evolving while the investigation is underway. Decision-making processes, personnel and resources are dynamically adjusted to ensure the level of response can be scaled up or down. They will depend on the everchanging nature of the on-ground situation associated with the disaster. Historic accident scenes will therefore most likely require a different approach to a contemporary scene in terms of standard operating procedures and protocols.

One of the most significant differences is often not well understood by those outside the aviation industry. This difference relates to what occurs *after* the process of victim identification is completed, with the outcomes of the investigation and report being vastly different for a recent aviation accident compared to a historic one. In historic settings, data analyses were rarely (if ever) used to inform current industry safety and practices. In contrast, the stated purpose of the investigations of contemporary aviation accidents *is the prevention of further accidents*. The immediate effect of a modern investigation is potentially more acute. Additionally, the aviation industry holds significant ethical responsibilities to uphold safety standards, transparently address failures, and prioritize the well-being of passengers and crew members in all investigative and preventative measures (Herkert et al. 2020; Hoppe 2020).

13.3.2 The Role of Forensic Archaeology in Modern Aviation Accident Investigations

While the ICAO and ISASI documents are recognized in aviation as being extremely helpful and appropriately having greatly contributed to aviation's ever-increasing safety, we suggest that these documents could be improved with input from investigators potentially perceived by aviation as being 'outsiders', that is, by forensic archaeologists.

Forensic archaeological aircraft accident investigation protocols could provide a framework for an evidentiary-based approach that could aid in the preservation and recovery of such accident sites and can provide a framework of best practices in accident scene investigation for the aviation industry. Such a framework could form part of a syllabus of competency-based training for all involved in air accident scene operations, at an initial and advanced level. It is of concern that ICAO's previous USOAP audit in 2016–2019 identified almost identical deficiencies (ICAO 2019) as did the most recent audit.

However, there is one conceptual difference in specific terminology used in aviation accident investigation and archaeological aviation, and that is the term '*forensic*'. From its inception in 1951, the primary focus of Annex 13 has not been to focus on finding fault and apportioning blame for an aircraft accident. In fact, the sole objective of an aviation accident investigation is the prevention of further accidents (ICAO 2016). The results of any investigation are not to be used for the prosecution of the 'guilty' but rather for the improvement of safety in the aviation industry (Michaelides-Mateou and Mateou 2010; Dekker 2011). ICAO has therefore provided a mechanism by which participants in the industry, including pilots, aircraft manufacturers and regulatory agencies, can learn from their errors.

The term '*forensic*' has its origins in Latin, referring to 'a forum or a place of assembly'. But by the 1650s, forensic meant 'pertaining to or suitable for courts of law', and by 1845, it referred to 'legal trials, as in forensic medicine' (Harper 2024). Aviation has therefore purposefully not used the term because of its legal and criminal court meanings and connotations. This is similar to the situation in healthcare, where 'medicolegal investigations' are for legal purposes, looking for 'cause' and 'who is to blame', rather than for system-oriented safety (Davies et al. 2022).

Thus, while the term '*forensic*' carries connotations of law courts, prosecution, the guilty and the innocent, punishment, and justice, in aviation and its system and safety-oriented accident investigations, there is the concept of a 'just culture'. This is 'one in which everyone knows where the line must be drawn between acceptable and unacceptable action'. However, this is not a 'no blame' culture, which 'like the excessively punitive culture it supplanted' is an approach that is 'neither desirable nor workable' (Reason 2000). Thus, investigators are not focused on *who* caused the accident but rather on what the contributing factors were. Additionally, in some countries in aviation (and in healthcare), there is not only regulatory-level protection but often an information firewall to protect information gathered from being used in '*forensic*' legal procedures (Davies et al. 2022).

In contrast, in such fields as forensic archaeology, the term '*forensic*' has evolved to mean the systematic and meticulous collection of evidence, using interdisciplinary and multidisciplinary approaches, while adhering to industry standards and best practice. This does not mean that the investigator is looking for a perpetrator. Rather, the investigation processes aim to recover and produce a record of evidence that could 'speak' on behalf of the circumstances surrounding the events that led to the accident, whether the consequence of human or nonhuman action(s). In doing so, this approach reflects the original meaning of the word 'of the forum', thus indicating that such a methodological approach to an investigation is designed to withstand the test of a legal system.

None of the policies, procedures or methodologies provided by ICAO or ISASI appear to allow for the implementation of an evidence-based/evidence-informed investigation approach, what archaeologists would term 'forensically informed'. Thus, the regulatory framework around aviation accident investigations is different from other legal forensic investigations, with aviation accident investigations theoretically operating in a somewhat liminal space within the definition of forensic science.

13.3.3 What Forensic Archaeology Could Offer Modern Aviation Accident Investigations

We suggest that aviation accident investigations would benefit from using two basic principles in forensic archaeology. First, evidence recovered from each aviation accident scene should be documented and collected as if the crash site were a so-called 'crime scene'. This would help ensure the integrity of the investigation until proven otherwise. Second, a chain of custody should be established to support the dual priorities in any aviation accident: the complete recovery and identification of all human victims and the investigation of why the aircraft(s) crashed.

To achieve these two goals, each investigation must begin with comprehensive scene processing, which includes the systematic location, documentation, and collection of all relevant information from the accident scene. This systematic approach is designed to ensure that each agency receives comprehensive and sequentially oriented information pertinent to scene processing. This would help foster transparency amongst the involved parties and facilitate a multidisciplinary approach to the investigation. Such an approach would involve implementing the use of a forensic archaeological methodological framework, which would equip investigators with the necessary knowledge and skills to effectively achieve the investigative objectives.

Yet, two questions remain. To what extent can an investigation be considered high quality in the absence of clearly defined methodologies and best practices, and how does this lack of guidance affect the overall integrity of the investigative process?

When faced with the task of processing any large-scale incident, investigators might feel overwhelmed by the sheer volume of material at the scene (Dirkmaat et al. 2012). This has contributed to the tendency of investigators to minimize the importance of proper and detailed documentation of the spatial distribution of remains. Assumptions include the information to be gleaned by the effort required to precisely document the entire scene being negligible and the expenses in terms of cost and time being too high to warrant this documentation (Dirkmaat et al. 2012). As a result, the emphasis could shift to removing evidence from the scene as quickly as possible. Little or no context could then be recorded in order to expedite the process of identifying the victims, determining the causes of the accident and clearing crash debris from the scene (Dirkmaat et al. 2012). However, we know that a lack of both knowledge of and skills required for aviation accident/outdoor scene processing has led to incomplete wreckage and victim recovery, such as Helios Airways Flight 522, a Boeing 737 that crashed in 2005 (AAIASB 2006). Almost a year after the accident, the remains of a section of the aircraft wing and the remains of several victims were found together in a gorge, outside the original designated search area ("More Helios crash bodies found", 2006). Similarly, the force of impact of the Ethiopian Airlines Boeing 737 MAX Flight 302 resulted in a highly fragmentary and dispersed scene, with commingled aircraft wreckage and human remains, many pieces of which were not recovered by the original investigation. Weeks later, after the investigation was completed, family members visiting the site recognized human bones commingled with aircraft parts and personal effects scattered amongst the debris field. Some also witnessed their loved ones' remains, mixed with personal effects, moved by the use of heavy machinery brought in to clear the debris (Reuters 2019).

These examples highlight the need for both published best practices and personnel trained in their application to be involved in processing an aviation accident scene. Further, both these examples demonstrate failings in the core objectives of any mass fatality scene. These are to locate, define the dimensions and secure the boundary of the scene; identify, document and collect all physical and contextual evidence; and ensure all evidence is transferred to the proper authority without harming the probative value or the chain of custody (Emery 2014). Use of forensic archaeological methods and protocols from the start of the investigation during a mass disaster recovery would ensure that forensic protocols for evidence collection and chain of custody were implemented and maintained (Warnasch 2016). The standard and quality of the work during recovery have been shown to have a direct impact on the success of the victim identification (Emery 2014). This, in turn, influences the outcome of the accident investigation (Warnasch 2016).

The careful analysis of wreckage has been used to correct questionable findings and incorrect accident reports. Ziòlkowski (2017) described the findings of two different investigations into the crash of the Polish Air Force One on 10 April 2010 that killed, amongst others, the President of Poland. The official report, released by the Russian Federation, blamed the cause of the accident on 'pilot error', citing the flight data recorder. However, a subsequent investigation, called an 'academic investigation' by Ziòlkowski, identified elements of 'incorrectness' in the official investigation and determined the cause of the accident to be a midair explosion. The evidence for this vastly different cause included, in part, the work of Polish archaeologists who examined the crash site six months after the accident and recovered around 60,000 pieces of aircraft wreckage, many pieces of which had evidence of petals of explosion (Ziòlkowski 2017). The level of fragmentation identified and the extent of the wreckage scatter were argued to be disproportionate to the amount of damage that would come from the cause of the accident in the official report. The official explanation was considered 'rather unrealistic and contradicting the laws of physics' (Ziòlkowski 2017). The context and stratigraphy of the wreckage were also examined and found not to align with the formal report's explanation. Ziòlkowski (2017) further argued there was no impact crater caused by the wreckage as would be expected if the aircraft had crashed in the way the official report described. Forensically informed analysis of the wreckage highlighted potential falsehoods in the official report provided by the Russian Federation aviation safety investigators (LA_Times 2022), although there were dissenting voices against the Polish investigation finding of a midair explosion (Admiral_Cloudberg 2022). Similarly, the victim identification completed for this accident was also found to be problematic. Errors were found in the forensic autopsy documentation, and as a result, exhumations were conducted, with the commingling of victims' remains evident in many cases (BBC 2017).

The example provided by Ziòlkowski (2017) illustrated that forensic archaeology is not simply a method of data collection. It can also provide a framework for the interpretation of some of the data. As argued by Alfsdotter (2021), following the work of Groen (2018):

> The material record does … not speak for itself but is collected and explained through an interpretative framework that is reliant on the background knowledge of the investigators. An interpretative framework is needed to reconstruct natural and man-made material manifestations at the scene…

It is perhaps not fully appreciated by aviation accident investigators that scene processing and excavation is a destructive process (Blau 2005). As the debris pile is moved and altered, its context is irrevocably lost. The destruction must therefore be controlled to ensure collection and retention of all available evidence. Forensic archaeological techniques can help ensure that the maximum amount of evidence with minimal contamination will be recovered (Blau 2005). Victim identification methodology has progressed, with enhanced morgue protocols and DNA identification having become relatively efficient (Blau 2018). But advances in the recovery of victims and wreckage have lagged behind. Forensic identification work needs to begin as soon as the scene is secured. However, it can be difficult to remove victims' remains without altering physical evidence. This is more likely if those attempting the removal are untrained or unaware of the importance of maintaining provenience, a record of the precise location where an artefact or piece of wreckage was recovered (Wehner and Kernbach-Wighton 2014).

The work of Dirkmaat and colleagues has also shown that evidentiary provenience is extremely important, as it can not only aid victim identification but can provide evidence of the manner of the crash (Dirkmaat 2012; Dirkmaat et al. 2012; Steadman et al. 2014; Dirkmaat and Cabo 2016). They also demonstrated that recordation of all spatial data, including contextual information at a scene, could be collected in a timely manner without adding significantly to overall recovery efforts. The protocols they established allow for more efficient scene management and better evidence collection (Dirkmaat et al. 2012). Investigators and those involved in the recovery of wreckage and victims need to understand the general principles of archaeology, such as provenience and context (where something was found and what else was found near it), features, stratigraphy (layers of formation), principles of supposition (within a series of layers the upper layers are younger, which in lay terms means that the material on the bottom was placed there first) and taphonomy. They also need to understand and appreciate the required techniques of excavating and removing human remains from both surface and buried deposits. Of all factors at a crash site, 'context is the most easily lost of all potentially recoverable information' (Dupras et al. 2011). The maintenance of the integrity of both the temporal and spatial contexts is of paramount importance to any forensic scene (Emery 2014).

Incorporating some training in forensic archaeological theory and methodology into accident investigation techniques would assist in protecting context. While the recovery of the black box (Cockpit Voice Recorder and Flight Data Recorder) is an important aspect of any investigations, the data from the black box needs to be 'ground truth-ed' as evidenced above. 'Ground-truthing' means using direct observation and empirical evidence to compile evidence; in lay terms, 'to see what is really there'. Ground-truthing can be used to support, or contradict as necessary, hypotheses formed as to accident causation. It is also imperative that those rushing to recover the black box do not inadvertently or unknowingly destroy contextual evidence in their often-hurried search.

13.3.4 Established Forensic Archaeological Protocols for Aviation Accident Scene Processing

Depending on the State of occurrence, after an accident occurs, it can take some time to notify the required agencies. Further time is then required for the aviation investigators to arrive at the scene. As such, there is a need for clear and concise, yet flexible, protocols for first responders, such as how to secure the scene. The protocols should be such that, once the investigation team arrived, they could start and continue their particular activities at the current stage of the protocol. This would help ensure the maximum amount of evidence was protected, then collected and retained with the least amount of contamination and evidence loss. Having all agencies operating from published, best practice protocols would provide standardization, improve coordination, and allow for the cohesive collection of evidence (Adamovic et al. 2023). The application of standard forensic archaeological methodology could minimize poor practice and evidence destruction (Oakley 2005).

There are essentially four sequential, though concurrent, steps involved in any thorough forensic scene recovery: (1) initial scene assessment; (2) mapping and excavation; (3) morgue processing; and (4) reconciliation of evidence (Mundorff 2012). The skills of forensic archaeologists and anthropologists could assist with all four areas. Dirkmaat and colleagues trialled and tested two different protocols in terms of forensic archaeological methodologies for air accident investigation: the Weldon Spring Protocol for dispersed scenes and the Clarence Center Protocol for condensed scenes. Dirkmaat et al. (2012) have provided explicit detail of both protocols, and therefore only a brief summary will be provided below.

The Weldon Spring Protocol

The Weldon Spring Protocol was originally formulated following the on-scene documentation of the physical evidence associated with the 1994 crash of the USAir Flight 427 in Pittsburgh and was tested during a Federal Bureau of Investigation

(FBI) training seminar in St Louis, Missouri (Dirkmaat et al. 2012). This new (at the time) protocol involved systematic straight-line pedestrian searches through the crash site by 'search teams', whereby significant evidence (human remains, personal effects, and identifiable aeroplane parts) was flagged and left in place. Following behind the search team, the 'provenance team' used an electronic total station, an electronic instrument/theodolite with integral distance measurement and coordinate measurement capability used in surveying (Allan 2017), to plot the precise location of each flagged piece of evidence. Next, the 'photography team' documented the evidence in situ with digital images. The remains were then collected by the 'collection team' and taken to the intake station and morgue, if required (Dirkmaat 2012).

This protocol was applied in a real accident scene documentation and recovery in 2000, at the site of the Cessna 335 crash that killed Missouri Governor Melvin P. Carnahan and three others (Reinecke and Hochrein 2008; Marx et al. 2014). At this scene, problems associated with the debris and human remains landing in the tree canopy were compounded by the area's steep terrain. The height of damaged and undamaged trees combined with the orientation of aircraft parts on the ground helped to determine the flight dynamics before and after impact, including the attitude (the orientation) at which the aircraft entered the tree canopy. Mapping technology, such as the electronic total station, allowed for the collection of spatial data to assist in identifying patterns in the distribution of otherwise comingled evidence. At this scene, two total stations were used: one mapped the human remains, and one mapped the location of diagnostic aircraft parts (Marx et al. 2014). The 3D spatial processing of commingled items at the crash site offered insights into (1) flight and impact dynamics, (2) peri- or postimpact explosions, (3) passenger and crew positions, and (4) postimpact disturbances from human or nonhuman scavenging (Reinecke and Hochrein 2008). Such data could provide a valuable contribution to any aviation accident investigation.

The Weldon Spring Protocol was devised to ensure thorough and efficient scene processing and evidence recovery at a surface scatter scene where the debris field was relatively wide. However, such a protocol is not usable at every type of air accident scene, which was demonstrated by the crash of Colgan Air Flight 3407.

The Clarence Center Protocol

On 12 February 2009, Colgan Air Flight 3407, a Dash 8–400, crashed into a house in Clarence Center, New York (NTSB 2009). All 49 passengers and crew were killed, along with one individual on the ground. This accident was the first time a civilian-directed accident recovery effort using forensic archaeological methods was undertaken (Dirkmaat 2012). The debris field at this scene was in a much more contained area compared to the crash site for which the Weldon Spring Protocol had been devised. Thus, a different recovery strategy was developed on scene, now known as the Clarence Center Protocol. The team of scene processors, a combination of first responders, air accident investigators, and forensic archaeologists and anthropologists, lined up in a semi-circle around the front end of the fuselage and progressed from the front to the back of the aircraft's wreckage and from outside to inside the debris field until human remains were found. Aircraft and house debris were removed in an orderly fashion, excavated stratigraphically. The goal was to carefully remove all debris overlying the victims so their remains could be recorded by the use of a single total station point, based on the centre of mass, photographed and then lifted straight up and out of the debris and transported. On the third day of the recovery, an area of the crash site within the house, where the gas line had burnt for 12 h, was encountered. The human remains in this area were significantly affected. The recovery process there involved collecting all debris and taking it to the morgue for examination and separation of human remains under better lighting conditions. This careful and considered processing of the scene would directly affect the DVI aspect of the investigation.

The forensic protocols used provided an important benefit in this case when, after the first round of DNA analysis, one individual listed on the flight manifest remained unaccounted for, undiscovered, and unidentified. A second search of the burnt and fragmented remains that had been taken from the gas line area was undertaken and yielded dental remains. Two additional searches of the human tissue assemblage at the Medical Examiner's Office led to the identification of significantly heat-affected bone samples. These eventually led to a DNA profile. The flight manifest with the original passenger seating locations was then compared with the total station map of the identified remains. The seat assignment for the missing individual was determined to be directly in the middle of the 12-h gas fire, which explained the lack of remains first found (Dirkmaat 2012). Due to the extensive recovery and methodical procedure using forensic archaeological protocols, the medical examiner was able to reassure family members that no remains were left behind, maximum efforts had been made to identify all the victims, and that a scientific explanation could be provided for the lack of identifiable remains. The site was cleared of all debris in five days, with close to 100% of recoverable human remains being recovered during this operation (Dirkmaat 2012). The processing of this aviation accident scene demonstrated the benefit of forensic archaeological protocols in both terms of evidence collection and preservation and also the efficiency of processing.

The Clarence Centre Protocol was again used to process the scene of a small business jet crash in Akron, Ohio, on 10 November 2015. This aircraft crashed through an apartment building and continued up an embankment while on approach to landing (NTSB 2015). This was a completely forensic archaeologically directed recovery. Forensic archaeological methods for documentation, mapping, recovery of human remains and reconstruction of past events were used at all times (Dirkmaat, personal communication). Less than an hour after the crash, the Ohio State Highway Patrol Reconstruction Unit responded to the scene. Upon arrival, a decision was made to use multiple devices to initially capture evidence locations, using three total stations and dividing the scene into areas of responsibility. Due to the volatile nature of the scene (fire, structural damage, and human remains), the goal during the first night was to identify as much evidence as possible in case items needed to be quickly moved or recovered. These individual efforts were later merged into a single diagram, using the common target reference points that had been placed throughout the scene to provide a link between the various forensic maps that would be developed during the investigation.

On the second day, electronic total station data of all aircraft parts and all elements around the crashed plane, apartment building, downed wires, all surrounding roads, cars, neighbouring houses, and apartments, etc. were recorded. Victim excavation, mapping, and recovery were organized to ensure the correct association of human remains to assist in the victim identification process. Unlike the Colgan accident site described above, all victim locations at this scene were recorded using multiple points, primarily placed at the main articular joints, to better show the position and orientation of each body within the debris field. The victims' locations were then mapped against the layout of the aircraft seating, providing the aviation accident investigators unequivocal data on where all victims were located within the aircraft cabin during impact. This scene processing illustrated the epitome of an effective and efficient recovery from all perspectives. This included law enforcement, medicolegal and aviation crash investigation, as well as forensic archaeology and forensic anthropology expertise (Dirkmaat, personal communication).

13.4 Summary: What Forensic Archaeology Offers Current Aviation Accident Investigations

Forensic archaeology involves using standard archaeological recovery and interpretation methods to accurately locate, record, and interpret relevant evidence at accident or mass disaster scenes. This analytical approach is critical for the accurate reconstruction of past occurrences by elucidating the relationships and timeline of events (Blau 2005). We are not the first to advocate for the application of forensic archaeology as part of the status quo for forensic investigations of aircraft crash scenes. The primary goal in both air accident investigation and forensic archaeology is the reconstruction of past events based on evidence found in highly altered contexts (Dirkmaat and Cabo 2016). Both Dirkmaat (Dirkmaat 2012; Dirkmaat et al. 2012; Dirkmaat and Cabo 2016) and Blau (2004, 2005, 2015), in particular, have called for the skills of forensic anthropology and archaeology to be used by emergency services and disaster teams for many years. Forensic archaeologists and anthropologists have skills that can be learnt and are based on scientifically proven methods for processing crime scenes. These skills have direct applicability in the realm of air accident investigation (Blau 2005).

The role of forensic archaeology and forensic anthropology has been recognized and systematically deployed for the investigation of outdoor crime scenes, encompassing a range of scenarios such as surface scatters, buried remains, and fatal fires (Schultz and Dupras 2008; Harrison 2019). Agencies are increasingly leveraging forensic archaeological expertise, which has contributed to the advancement of the discipline as an independent profession (Schultz and Dupras 2008; de Leeuwe and Groen 2015). Despite recognition of what contributions forensic archaeological and anthropological skills and methodologies can bring, the expertise of both types of specialists is markedly underused in aviation accident investigation internationally and within specific jurisdictions. Documents supporting aviation accident investigations, including published policies, procedures, and frameworks for scene processing, lack best practices and training requirements for personnel involved in scene processing, data and evidence collection and analysis. These gaps can be closed by adoption of existing forensic archaeological protocols. These protocols can be further adjusted to meet some, if not many, of the specific investigation needs associated with aviation accident scenes. Furthermore, training in these protocols, which include basic forensic archaeological and anthropological methods, should become a basic education component for aviation crash investigators. Lastly, other experts deployed to assist in the investigation and recovery of modern aircraft crash sites should also be adequately trained in these specific aviation standards and should be expected to perform within industry standard guidelines and protocols.

13.5 Conclusion

Currently there are gaps in planning, training, and the application of an evidence-based best practice approach to aviation accident investigation at a global level. We agree with Mundorff that the forensic archaeologists' and anthropologists' expertise for handling unidentified and/or fragmented human remains and their skills in site recovery, excavation and understanding of mortuary operations are needed in the multidisciplinary field of aviation accident investigation (Mundorff 2012). Aviation accident investigators would benefit from a toolkit providing them with an understanding of and training in the application of forensic archaeological and anthropological methods associated with mass disaster. Most aviation accident investigators are aviation industry professionals, such as pilots, engineers, or human factor experts, and thus are subject matter experts in those specific fields. However, successful accident investigation operations require a multidisciplinary approach (Mundorff 2012). While we do not suggest that forensic archaeologists and anthropologists should hold jurisdiction over the aviation accident scene, having investigators use some of their knowledge and skills would augment and refine both victim recovery and accident investigation efforts (Warnasch 2016).

Forensic archaeological protocols already exist for aviation accident investigation and have been used with positive results in different aircraft accident settings, where expert forensic archaeologists were deployed to process the scene and actively collaborated with all other ground personnel and involved agencies. Dirkmaat and colleagues have provided a documented methodology that is easy to follow, does not require expensive equipment and provides high-quality scene analysis outcomes (Dirkmaat et al. 2012). These published protocols should be included in the training that first responders and aviation accident investigators receive.

ICAO reported that a significant number of States had areas of noncompliance in aviation accident investigation. The audit also revealed that even compliant States had deficiencies affecting the quality of their aviation accident investigations. The Weldon Spring and Clarence Center Protocols are clear, concise, practical methodologies based on forensic best practice. Their adoption by aviation accident investigative authorities and first responders, supported by forensic archaeological and anthropological skill training and development, would assist in helping address the noncompliance identified by ICAO.

Forensic archaeological practitioners will recognize the utility of forensic archaeological theoretical approaches and methodologies in aviation accident investigations. However, there appears to be a disconnection between what forensic archaeologists can 'do' and who outside the profession knows of their skills. Forensic archaeology needs to further engage with other agencies that would benefit from their skill sets and methodologies, such as being actively involved globally with ICAO, ISASI and other aviation industry bodies. This would foster further joint development of best practice methodologies for the collection of evidence and interpretation of accident sites.

After an accident, the victims and travelling public deserve to have dedicated, highly trained and competent subject matter experts conducting recoveries and investigations following established best practice, evidence-based guidelines. Methodological competence can be attained through rigorous and specialized training of first responders and aviation accident investigators. However, we recommend that those forensic archaeologists and forensic anthropologists having the necessary knowledge, skills, and experience to assist in aircraft accident investigations be recognized, accepted, and routinely deployed to aviation accident sites. It is time for forensically informed, best practice methodologies, supported by published training standards and competencies, to be implemented for all aviation accident investigations.

References

AAIASB (2006) Aircraft Accident Report: Helios Airways Flight HCY522 on August 14, 2005, in the area of Grammatiko, Athens, 33km Northwest of Athens International Airport, Air Accident Investigation & Aviation Safety Board (AAIASB). Hellenic Republic Ministry of Transport & Communications: Air Accident Investigation & Aviation Safety Board

Adamovic N, Howes LM, White R, Julian R (2023) Understanding the challenges of disaster victim identification: perspectives of Australian forensic practitioners. Forensic Sci Res 8(2):107–115. https://doi.org/10.1093/fsr/owad020

Admiral_Cloudberg (2022) All the President's men: the story of the Smolensk Air disaster and the death of Lech Kaczynski. Medium Retrieved July 18, 2024, from https://admiralcloudberg.medium.com/all-the-presidents-men-the-story-of-the-smolensk-air-disaster-and-the-death-of-lech-kaczy%C5%84ski-590a3977f

Alfsdotter C (2021) Forensic archaeology and forensic anthropology within Swedish law enforcement: current state and suggestions for future developments. Forensic Sci Int Rep 3:100178. https://doi.org/10.1016/j.fsir.2021.100178

Allan AL (2017) Principles of geospatial surveying. Whittles

BBC (2017) Poland air crash probe: remains of ex-president mixed up. BBC. Retrieved 18 July 2024 from https://www.bbc.com/news/world-europe-40130300

Bills K, Costello L, Cattani M (2023) Major aviation accident investigation methodologies used by ITSA members. Saf Sci 168:106315. https://doi.org/10.1016/j.ssci.2023.106315

Blau S (2004) Forensic archaeology in Australia: current situations, future possibilities. Aust Archaeol 58:11–14. https://doi.org/10.1080/03122417.2004.11681775

Blau S (2005) Once chance only: advocating the use of archaeology in search, location and recovery at disaster scenes. Aust J Emerg Manage 20(1):19–24

Blau S (2015) The use of archaeologists at disaster scenes: a reflection 10 years on. Aust J Emerg Manage 30(1):49–50

Blau S (2018) It's all about the context: reflections on the changing role of forensic anthropology in medico-legal death investigations. Aust J Forensic Sci 50(6):628–638. https://doi.org/10.1080/00450618.2017.1422022

Bury A, Saeed F, Khalique A (2020) Simulator-based learning, the Dunning-Kruger effect and the newly- 'qualified' officer of the watch. Seaways Int J Naut Inst

CRICC (2024) CRICC: Cranfield Recovery and Identification of Conflict Casualties team. Retrieved 9 July 2024 from https://www.cranfield.ac.uk/centres/cranfield-forensic-institute/cricc

Davies JM, Steinke C, Flemons WW (2022) Fatal solution: how a healthcare system used tragedy to transform itself and redefine just culture. Routlege

de Leeuwe R, Groen WJM (2015) Forensic archaeology in The Netherlands. In: Groen WJM, Màrquez-Grant N, Janaway RC (eds) Forensic archaeology: a global perspective. Wiley, Ltd, pp 109–120. https://doi.org/10.1002/9781118745977.ch14

Dekker S (2011) The criminalization of human error in aviation and healthcare: a review. Saf Sci 49(2):121–127. https://doi.org/10.1016/j.ssci.2010.09.010

Dirkmaat DC (2012) Forensic anthropology at the mass fatality incident (commercial airliner) crash scene. In: Dirkmaat DC (ed) A companion to forensic anthropology. Wiley, pp 136–156

Dirkmaat DC, Cabo LL (2016) Forensic archaeology and forensic Taphonomy: basic considerations on how to properly process and interpret the outdoor forensic scene. Acad Forensic Pathol 6(1):439–454. https://doi.org/10.23907/2016.045

Dirkmaat DC, Chapman EN, Kenyhercz M, Cabo LL (2012) Enhancing scene processing protocols to improve victim identification and field detection of human remains in mass fatality scenes (2008-DN-BX-K133)

DPAA (n.d.) Defense POW/MIA Accounting Agency. Retrieved July 9, 2024, from https://www.dpaa.mil/

Dunning D (2011) The Dunning–Kruger effect: on being ignorant of one's own ignorance. In: Olson JM, Zanna MP (eds) Advances in experimental social psychology, vol 44. Academic, pp 247–296. https://doi.org/10.1016/B978-0-12-385522-0.00005-6

Dupras TL, Schultz JJ, Wheeler SM, Williams LJ (2011) Applying archaeological methods in a forensic context. In: Dupras TL, Schultz JJ, Wheeler SM, Williams LJ (eds) Forensic recovery of human remains: archaeological approaches, 2nd edn. CRC Press. https://doi.org/10.1201/b11275

Easthope L (2022) When the dust settles. Stories of love, loss and Hope from an expert in disaster. Hodder & Soughton

Eck CR (2023) Broken wings, recovered souls: understanding site formation processes and developing a lexicon for terrestrial military aircraft crash site types associated with the recovery of missing personnel remains. In: Whitehead HW, Lickliter-Mundon M (eds) Strides towards standard methodologies in aeronautical archaeology. Springer. https://doi.org/10.1007/978-3-031-40963-9_2

Emery EB (2014) Forensic anthropology and archaeology in disaster response. In: Smith C (ed) Encyclopedia of global archaeology. Springer, pp 2827–2833. https://doi.org/10.1007/978-1-4419-0465-2

English-Heritage (2002) Military aircraft crash sites: archaeological guidance on their significance and future management. English Heritage, Swindon
ESReDA (2009) Guidelines for safety investigations of accidents. ESReDA – European Safety Reliability and Data Association; ESReDA Working Group on Accident Investigation. https://esreda.org/wp-content/uploads/2016/07/ESReDA_GLSIA_Final_June_2009_For_Download.pdf
Ford J (2006) WWII aviation archaeology in Victoria, Australia. Department of Archaeology, Flinders University
Franklin D, Marks MK (2022) The professional practice of forensic anthropology: contemporary developments and cross-disciplinary applications. Wiley Interdiscip Rev Forensic Sci 4(2):e1442. https://doi.org/10.1002/wfs2.1442
Graser J (2012) From Daedalus to smartphones and NextGen: the evolution of accident investigation tools and techniques. In: International Society of Air Safety Investigation (ISASI) annual conference, Baltimore
Groen WJM (2018) Forensic archaeology: integrating archaeology with criminalistics and criminology. In: Barone PM, Groen WJM (eds) Multidiscplinary approaches to forensic archaeology. Springer International Publishing, pp 1–16. https://doi.org/10.1007/978-3-319-94397-8_1
Harper D (2024) Forensic. Retrieved November 4, from https://www.etymonline.com/word/forensic
Harrison K (2019) The application of archaeological techniques to forensic fire scenes. In: Moran KS, Gold CL (eds) Forensic archaeology: multidisciplinary perspectives. Springer, pp 153–162. https://doi.org/10.1007/978-3-030-03291-3_10
Herkert J, Borenstein J, Miller K (2020) The Boeing 737 MAX: lessons for engineering ethics. Sci Eng Ethics 26:2957–2974. https://doi.org/10.1007/s11948-020-00252-y
Hoppe EA (2020) EES perspective: ethical decision making and the aviation industry. The Bridge 50(2):66–69. https://www.nae.edu/File.aspx?id=234402
ICAO (2011) Document 9756: manual of aircraft accident investigation: part III investigation. International Civil Aviation Organisation. https://archive.org/details/icao-investigation-p3-2011
ICAO (2016) Annex 13 to the convention on international aviation: aircraft accident and incident investigation. ICAO
ICAO (2019) Report on universal safety oversight audit Programme 1 January 2016 to 31 December 2018. ICAO. www.icao.int/safety/CMAForum/Documents/USOAP_REPORT_2016-2018.pdf
ICAO (2022) Report on universal safety oversight audit Programme 1 January 2019 to 31 December 2021. ICAO. www.icao.int/safety/CMAForum/Documents/USOAP_REPORT_2019-2021.pdf
ICAO (2024) Doc 10206, manual on aircraft accident and incident investigation training, First edn. ICAO. https://store.icao.int/en/manual-on-aircraft-accident-and-incident-investigation-training-doc-10206
ICAO (n.d.-a) The history of ICAO and the Chicago convention ICAO. Retrieved July 18, 2024, from https://www.icao.int/about-icao/History/Pages/default.aspx
ICAO (n.d.-b) Welcome to the USOAP continuous monitoring approach (CMA) website. Retrieved July 9, 2024, from https://www.icao.int/safety/CMAForum/Pages/default.aspx
INTERPOL (2023a) Disaster victim identification guide. INTERPOL. https://www.interpol.int/en/content/download/589/file/18Y1344%20E%20DVI_Guide.pdf
INTERPOL (2023b) Disaster victim identification guide – Annexure 3: Phase 1 – Scene. https://www.interpol.int/How-we-work/Forensics/Disaster-Victim-Identification-DVI
ISASI (1999) Guidelines for investigator training and education, 1st edn. International Society of Air Safety Investigators
ISASI (2013) International Society of Air Safety Investigators. Retrieved July 9, 2024, from https://www.isasi.org/
ISASI (2015) Positions on air safety investigation issues, 4th edn. International Society of Air Safety Investigators. www.isasi.org/Documents/ISASI_Positions_Rev7_Adopted_1May2015.pdf
Konieczka R (2017) How to secure basic evidence after an aviation accident. Sci J Sil Univ Technol 94:65–74. https://doi.org/10.20858/sjsutst.2017.94.7

Kruger J, Dunning D (1999) Unskilled and unaware of it: how difficulties in recognizing one's own incompetence lead to inflated self-assessments. J Pers Soc Psychol 77(6):1121–1134. https://doi.org/10.1037/0022-3514.77.6.1121
LA_Times (2022) Russia was behind the Polish president's fatal 2010 plane crash, Polish panel says. Retrieved July 23, 2024, from https://www.latimes.com/world-nation/story/2022-04-11/russia-behind-polish-leaders-plane-crash
Lickliter-Mundon ME (2018) Aviation archaeology: history, theory, practice and direction. Doctor of Philosophy, Texas A & M University. https://www.proquest.com/docview/2671731049?pq-origsite=gscholar&fromopenview=true&sourcetype=Dissertations%20&%20Theses
Marx RB, Hochrein MJ, Fasano AD (2014) More pieces of the puzzle: F.B.I. Evidence response team approaches to scenes with commingled evidence. In: Adams BJ, Byrd JE (eds) Commingled human remains: methods in recovery, analysis, and identification. Elsevier
Michaelides-Mateou S, Mateou A (2010) Flying in the face of criminalization: the safety implications of prosecuting aviation professionals for accidents. Routledge. https://doi.org/10.4324/9781315582559
More Helios crash bodies found (2006) Ekathimerini.com. https://www.ekathimerini.com/news/42506/more-helios-crash-bodies-found/
Mundorff AZ (2012) Integrating forensic anthropology into disaster victim identification. Forensic Sci Med Pathol 8(2):131–139. https://doi.org/10.1007/s12024-011-9275-0
Ng CBR, Bil C, O'Bree T (2021) An expert system framework to support aircraft accident and incident investigations. Aeronaut J 125(1289):1131–1156. https://doi.org/10.1017/aer.2021.11
NTSB (2009) Loss of control on approach: Colgan Air, Inc. Operating as continental connection Flight 3407 Bombardier DHC-8-400, N200WQ Clarence Center, New York, February 12, 2009. www.ntsb.gov/investigations/AccidentReports/Reports/AAR1001.pdf
NTSB (2015) Crash during nonprecision instrument approach to landing execuflight flight 1526 British Aerospace HS 125-700A, N237WR, Akron, Ohio, November 10, 2015. www.ntsb.gov/investigations/AccidentReports/Reports/AAR1603.pdf
Oakley K (2005) Forensic archaeology and anthropology. Forensic Sci Med Pathol 1(3):169–172. https://doi.org/10.1385/FSMP:1:3:169
Reason J (2000) Safety paradoxes and safety culture. Inj Control Saf Promot 7(1):3–14. https://doi.org/10.1076/1566-0974(200003)7:1;1-V;FT003
Reinecke GW, Hochrein MJ (2008) Pieces of the puzzle: FBI evidence response team approaches to scenes with commingled evidence. In: Adams BJ, Byrd JE (eds) Recovery, analysis, and identification of commingled human remains. Humana Press
Reuters (2019) Excavators may be damaging Ethiopoa crash site – diplomats. Reuters. Retrieved July 9, 2024, from https://www.reuters.com/article/world/excavators-may-be-damaging-ethiopia-crash-site-diplomats-idUSKCN1QW2UE/
Schultz JJ, Dupras TL (2008) The contribution of forensic archaeology to homicide investigations. Homicide Stud 12(4):399–413. https://doi.org/10.1177/1088767908324430
Steadman DW, Dirkmaat DC, LeVaughn MM, Miller RG, Regan LA, Vertes D (2014) Recovery and identification of victims of the Colgan air flight 3407 crash. In: Adams BJ, Byrd JE (eds) Commingled human remains. Academic, pp 389–406. https://doi.org/10.1016/B978-0-12-405889-7.00018-6
Thallapureddy S, Sherratt F, Hallowell M, Bhandari S (2024) Effective information collection in incident investigations: a systematic review and narrative synthesis. Saf Sci 171:106404. https://doi.org/10.1016/j.ssci.2023.106404
Ubelaker DH, Blau S, Fondebrider L (2014) Forensic and archaeological analyses: similarities and differences. In: Smith C (ed) Encyclopedia of global archaeology. Springer, pp 2824–2827. https://doi.org/10.1007/978-1-4419-0465-2
Warnasch SC (2016) Forensic archaeological recovery of a large-scale mass disaster scene: lessons learned from two complex recovery pperations at the world trade Centre site. J Forensic Sci 61(3):584. https://doi.org/10.1111/1556-4029.13025

Wehner H-D, Kernbach-Wighton G (2014) Traffic accidents. In: Madea B (ed) Handbook of forensic medicine. Wiley
Whitehead HW, Lickliter-Mundon M (eds) (2023) Strides towards standard methodologies in aeronautical archaeology. Springer. https://doi.org/10.1007/978-3-031-40963-9
Ziòlkowski A (2017) Disasterous air crash and two investigations with different results. Int J Forensic Eng 3(4):277–302. https://doi.org/10.1504/IJFE.2017.10005136

Part III
Heritage Crimes

Chapter 14
Forensic Archaeology and Heritage Crimes

Pier Matteo Barone

Abstract Heritage crimes, including looting, illicit trafficking, and unauthorized modifications of historical sites, pose significant challenges to preserving cultural heritage worldwide. Forensic archaeology, emerging as a distinct discipline in Europe during the 1980s, has become essential in combating these crimes. By employing scientific methodologies within legal contexts, forensic archaeologists assess damage, locate stolen artifacts, and reconstruct events surrounding heritage crimes. This discipline's integration with law enforcement and cultural heritage curators ensures comprehensive strategies to mitigate damages, recover artifacts, and prosecute offenders. Leveraging cutting-edge technologies such as geophysics, 3D modeling, and artificial intelligence, forensic archaeology contributes to proactive preservation and restoration efforts. Despite its proven effectiveness, the field faces challenges in gaining recognition and integration into legal systems in some regions, notably Italy. Case studies like EAMENA (Endangered Archaeology in the Middle East and North Africa) and SHOSI (Safeguarding the Heritage of Syria and Iraq) underscore forensic archaeology's critical role in combating illicit activities and safeguarding cultural legacies. As technology advances, this multidisciplinary approach will continue to shape heritage crime prevention and conservation practices, ensuring the protection of humanity's shared narrative for future generations.

Keywords Forensic archaeology · Heritage crimes · Cultural heritage preservation · Artifact recovery · Geophysical techniques

Illegal activities targeting cultural heritage assets (aka Heritage Crimes) present a major challenge to societies worldwide. These crimes, including looting, illicit trafficking of artifacts, vandalism, and unauthorized modifications of historic sites, deprive us of priceless historical and cultural knowledge and undermine our shared

P. M. Barone (✉)
The American University of Rome—Geoscienze Forensi Italia® Forensic Geoscience Italy, Rome, Italy
e-mail: p.barone@aur.edu

P. M. Barone, WJ M. Groen (eds.), *Forensic Archaeology and New Multidisciplinary Approaches*, Soil Forensics, https://doi.org/10.1007/978-3-031-86308-0_14

heritage. Forensic archaeology, which emerged as a distinct discipline in Europe during the 1980s, has become crucial in the fight against heritage crime. By applying scientific principles and techniques within criminal investigations, forensic archaeology aims to preserve and protect our cultural legacy.

This field involves examining sites to determine and interpret the mechanisms of damage, such as identifying what happened, where, how, and when. Geophysical methods are employed to assess damage and locate hidden stolen items. Artifacts are analyzed to determine their provenance, date and material composition, and to detect trace evidence. This dating process is not only applied to trafficked artifacts but also to modern items made from prohibited materials (like ivory, horn, bone, and turtle/tortoise shell) that are falsely presented as antiquities to bypass legal restrictions (Di Maggio and Barone 2017; Barone and Groen 2018; Vannan and Barone 2024).

Forensic archaeologists play a crucial role in heritage crime investigations. Their expertise in the systematic recovery and analysis of material evidence positions them at the forefront of these efforts. Unlike traditional archaeology, forensic archaeology operates within a legal context, where evidence must withstand rigorous scrutiny in court. This necessitates the use of precise scientific methodologies to piece together evidence from crime scenes, reconstruct activities, and provide objective interpretations that can substantiate or refute legal claims.

Initially focused on crime scene investigation, forensic archaeology's methodologies have been adapted for cultural heritage contexts, where they are used to investigate and mitigate damages to archaeological sites and recover stolen artifacts.

Forensic archaeology's application in cultural heritage is diverse and addresses several critical areas. Forensic archaeologists collaborate with law enforcement agencies to locate and recover artifacts that have been illegally removed from their original contexts. Their expertise is crucial in tracing the origins of these artifacts and providing documented evidence that supports legal actions and prosecutions against traffickers.

This aspect of forensic archaeology involves evaluating the extent of damage inflicted on cultural heritage sites by natural disasters, conflicts, or deliberate acts of vandalism. Forensic archaeologists develop mitigation strategies that aid in the conservation and restoration of affected sites, ensuring that these cultural treasures are preserved for future generations (Vannan and Barone 2024).

By serving as expert witnesses in court cases, forensic archaeologists use their findings to influence policy decisions related to cultural heritage protection. Their testimonies can lead to enhanced protective measures and stronger enforcement of existing laws. Despite its established presence in other European countries, forensic archaeology in Italy faces challenges in gaining recognition and integration into legal and investigative frameworks, attributed partly to the country's slow adaptation to cultural and technological innovations. Here, there is even difficulty semantically accepting the term "forensic archaeology," replacing it with "legal or judicial archaeology" (erroneous both legally and logically): imagine if it would be possible to implement, in a distinctive manner both professionally and scientifically, the specific and intrinsic operations of forensic archaeology in the protection of archaeological heritage! (Barone and Groen 2018) (Fig. 14.1).

Forensic archaeology's effectiveness is highlighted in various case studies. The EAMENA (Endangered Archaeology in the Middle East and North Africa) project employs forensic archaeology to document and combat illegal excavations and looting in the Middle East and North Africa. By using satellite imagery and other remote-sensing data, forensic archaeologists provide actionable intelligence to authorities, helping to curb the trafficking of invaluable cultural artifacts.

In regions like Iraq and Syria, where significant cultural sites have been damaged or destroyed due to conflicts, forensic archaeologists assess the destruction and lead recovery efforts. These activities are crucial for restoring cultural heritage that holds immense historical, cultural, and emotional significance for local and global communities, like the SHOSI (Safeguarding the Heritage of Syria and Iraq) project.

The integration of cutting-edge technologies has significantly enhanced the capabilities of forensic archaeology in heritage conservation. 3D scanning and modeling technology creates precise digital replicas of artifacts and sites, facilitating their study and preservation. For instance, the 3D modeling of Notre-Dame Cathedral before the fire provided a crucial reference for the ongoing restoration efforts, ensuring fidelity to the original architectural details.

Fig. 14.1 An example where the so-called (very erroneously!) "legal or judicial archaeologist" in Italy stumbled into an "unpleasant incident" by reporting a date at the bottom of the expert report (on the left and in the center) that preceded the seizure report (on the right), automatically neutralizing the effectiveness of the expert report itself during the procedural phase. This is just one of the many frequent cases in Italy where the lack of preparation is demonstrated, not just semantically but also professionally and practically, by those who are supposed to oversee the protection of archaeological heritage

Virtual and augmented reality technologies offer immersive experiences that can be educational and deeply engaging. Virtual Reality (VR) reconstruction of the ancient city of Palmyra, for example, allows users to explore the site as it existed before its destruction by ISIS (Islamic State in Iraq and Syria), providing a powerful tool for education and preservation advocacy.

Artificial Intelligence in Conservation is used to analyze large datasets quickly and accurately, identifying patterns and anomalies that may indicate illicit activities, such as unauthorized excavations or sudden changes in landscape. This capability is transforming how cultural heritage sites are monitored and protected against threats, ensuring a proactive approach to conservation (Bilotta et al. 2021).

Forensic archaeologists often employ other advanced techniques, such as remote sensing and geophysics, which include ground-penetrating radar (GPR), magnetometry, and electrical resistivity, to assess damage and locate concealed artifacts. These methods allow for non-invasive investigations, which is essential in contexts where traditional excavation might be too intrusive or damaging (Barone et al. 2019).

Geophysical techniques have become indispensable in modern archaeological investigations and heritage preservation efforts. These methods offer a non-destructive means to explore and monitor archaeological sites, providing valuable data that informs both academic research and conservation strategies (Barone 2016).

GPR has proven particularly useful in various contexts, such as investigating the construction phases of historical buildings, identifying moisture ingress in structures, and locating unexploded ordnance from past conflicts.

The problem of unexploded bombs from World War II presents a unique challenge to heritage preservation. Sites like Pompeii and Vulci have been significantly impacted by wartime bombings, necessitating careful investigation to locate and safely manage these dangerous remnants. Using GPR and other remote-sensing techniques, researchers can create detailed maps of these hazards, ensuring the safety of archaeological excavations and surrounding communities (Barone 2019).

Cultural heritage curators are tasked with the proactive preservation and protection of cultural sites. Institutions like English Heritage and the National Trust exemplify this role, focusing on documentation, public engagement, and the implementation of protective measures against potential threats. Their efforts include site monitoring, risk assessment, and educational campaigns aimed at raising public awareness and deterring criminal activities.

The collaboration between forensic archaeologists and cultural heritage curators is vital in effectively addressing heritage crimes. For example, in response to looting incidents, forensic archaeologists use non-invasive technologies to assess damage and recover stolen items, while curators enhance surveillance and public engagement efforts. This multidisciplinary approach ensures comprehensive strategies that leverage both scientific inquiry and conservation ethics (Fig. 14.2) (Vannan and Barone 2024).

The intersection of archaeology, law, and heritage conservation raises important ethical concerns. Forensic archaeologists and curators must balance the need for thorough investigations with the responsibility to preserve cultural integrity and respect community values. Moreover, the evolving nature of heritage crimes, driven

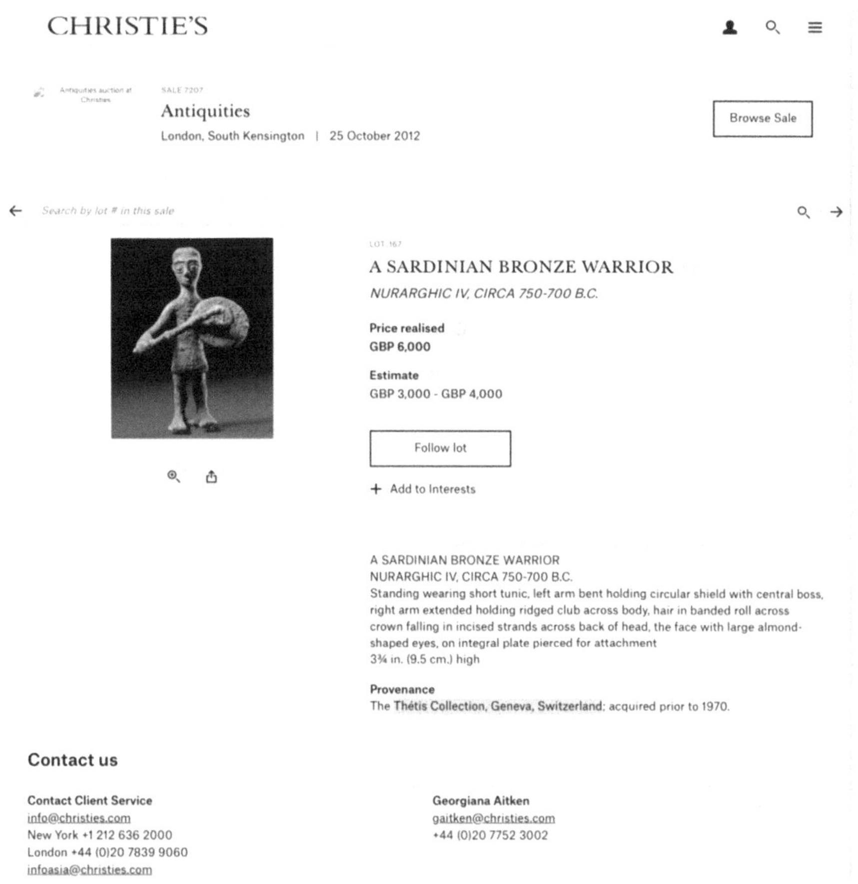

Fig. 14.2 In October 2012, Christie's auction house in London listed a statuette of a Nuragic (ancient Sardinian culture in Italy) warrior in its sales catalog, with an estimated price of £3000/4000. The description includes the object's details and its provenance: Thétis Collection, Geneva, Switzerland, highlighting "not-clear" origin

by technological advancements and changing market demands, requires continuous adaptation and interdisciplinary collaboration.

Forensic archaeology, with its unique blend of scientific rigor and legal acumen, will continue to play a pivotal role in these directions. As the discipline evolves, its contributions to cultural heritage conservation will likely expand, offering new insights and methods for protecting our global heritage. Embracing these innovations responsibly and ethically will be key to navigating the challenges of cultural heritage conservation in the modern world, ensuring that both the physical and intangible aspects of our historical legacies are safeguarded for posterity.

The role of forensic archaeology in heritage crime investigations will undoubtedly expand, driven by technological innovations and an increasing global awareness of the value of cultural heritage. The continued collaboration between forensic archaeologists and cultural heritage curators will be instrumental in devising more effective strategies against heritage crimes. By fostering a culture of respect and appreciation for our shared history, we can ensure that our cultural legacy is preserved for the enlightenment and enjoyment of future generations. The fight against heritage crime is not just a matter of law enforcement or scientific investigation; it is a testament to our collective resolve to honor and protect the narrative of humanity itself.

In conclusion, the integration of forensic archaeology into heritage crime investigations offers a robust framework for addressing the multifaceted challenges posed by these offenses. The collaborative efforts between forensic archaeologists and cultural heritage curators, underpinned by rigorous scientific inquiry and ethical considerations, are crucial in safeguarding our cultural heritage. As the field continues to evolve, embracing new technologies and methodologies, the commitment to protecting our shared legacy must remain steadfast, ensuring that future generations can continue to connect with and learn from the past.

References

Barone PM (2016) Understanding buried anomalies: a practical guide to GPR. LAP Lambert Academic Publishers, Saarbrücken. ISBN: 978-3-659-93579-4

Barone PM (2019) Bombed archaeology: towards a precise identification and a safe management of WWII's dangerous unexploded bombs. Heritage 2(4):2704–2711

Barone PM, Groen WJM (2018) Multidisciplinary approaches to forensic archaeology: topics discussed during the European meetings on forensic archaeology (EMFA). Springer, New York (NY)

Barone PM, Ruffell A, Tsokas GN, Rizzo E (2019) Geophysical surveys for archaeology and cultural heritage preservation. Heritage 2(4):2814–2817

Bilotta G, Nocera R, Barone PM (2021) Cultural heritage and Obia. WSEAS Trans Environ Dev 17:449–465

Di Maggio RM, Barone PM (2017) Geoscientists at crime scenes: a companion to forensic geoscience. Soil forensics. Springer International Publishing, New York (NY)

Vannan A, Barone PM (2024) Heritage crime and forensic archaeology: an integrated approach. The Archaeologist 122:21–23

Chapter 15
Heritage Protection by Local Police and Forensic Archaeologists

Francisco José Rufián Fernández

Abstract There is no doubt that heritage is a crucial element in societies, so it must be protected to allow the next generations to enjoy it. However, its economic value, among other factors like uncontrolled development or climate change, are critical factors that challenge their conservation. In that context, this chapter aims to present a brief proposal for establishing better heritage protection strategies, which will be founded on two specific areas: the Local Police and Forensic Archaeology.

Keywords Local Police · Heritage protection · Forensic archaeology

15.1 Introduction

In order to study the protection of cultural and historical heritage by European police, we must analyze the two main legal areas that constitute its current structure. On the one hand, the laws that make such protection possible within the organization of the police forces must be considered, as they are very different in each state.[1] On the other hand, the configuration of laws for the protection of heritage, among which, according to the very essence of this term, we can include administrative and

[1] Millions of police officers work within Europe and operate in very different and sometimes incompatible ways. Some countries have a single national police service, which is entirely centralized, and others operate within a decentralized model, comprised of various police forces. In the specific case of Spain, the model is composed of two national and centralized police services, which work together in a decentralized model alongside other police services, such as those corresponding to the Autonomous Communities and, on the other hand, the local police, which fall under the authority of the City Mayor.

F. J. R. Fernández (✉)
Local Police and Forensic Archaeologist, Autonomous University of Madrid, Madrid, Spain

P. M. Barone, WJ M. Groen (eds.), *Forensic Archaeology and New Multidisciplinary Approaches*, Soil Forensics, https://doi.org/10.1007/978-3-031-86308-0_15

criminal regulations, will regulate a broad spectrum of areas and, in turn, require a specific specialization on the part of the police services, as will be shown below.

These laws will be different in each State. Despite the European Union's (EU) efforts to achieve legal and judicial cooperation that is as effective as possible, there is still a great deal of work to be done and a broad margin for improvement in police work to protect heritage. In this sense, both European Union Agency for Law Enforcement Cooperation (EUROPOL) and European Union Agency for Criminal Justice Cooperation (EUROJUST) have been working to bridge these gaps to try to overcover these discrepancies, particularly those affecting judicial police investigations, which are also plagued by differences between the EU Member States, for example, in the role held by prosecutors and their relationship with the police.

Another critical aspect to be considered is the large volume of crimes (together with administrative infractions) that affect heritage in current times: vandalism, illegal trade, looting, smuggling, and other similar offenses committed concerning heritage, such as receiving stolen items, fraud, money laundering, organized crimes, and even terrorism financing. It is not difficult to imagine the complexity of covering so many areas, which makes police work in this field extremely challenging. This is the primary reasoning for creating specialized units within different police forces, which will be highlighted more thoroughly throughout the chapter.

In this context, it should be noted that ordinarily, local police forces (those working within a city's specific territorial area) have not traditionally specialized in the protection of heritage, as opposed to national or federal police forces. Therefore, this chapter aims to emphasize two different points. The first point aims to showcase the advantages of having a local police force specialized in heritage protection, using some case studies, such as the Spanish model for police organization, as examples. The main problems currently facing dedicated units of this nature will be presented to highlight these issues. The second point aims to formulate a plea regarding the need to implement research in the field of forensic archaeology through a brief and succinct summary, by way of example, of the research that is currently being employed to assist law enforcement in its fight against looting and the illicit trafficking of cultural goods.

15.2 Heritage Protection by the Police: An Overview

Most cities boast significant heritage, representing the cultural values and history of different regions. These assets also play a crucial role in attracting tourists and generating income for residents. As such, it is easy to see how national, federal, and municipal governments have been working to develop administrative structures focusing on the protection of heritage over many years. However, such dedicated structures have not been so common within the frameworks of European police forces or public prosecutor's offices. As the most prominent agencies and studies have pointed out (Boz 2018; European Commission et al. 2019; Interpol 2019), having specialized units dedicated to heritage protection is essential. However, the reality is quite different, and we can observe huge differences between European nations. Italy, for example, represents the best example of the commitment to police specialization, as the Carabinieri Corps has an extensive network of heritage protection police officers stationed throughout the country. Nevertheless, these police units in other states can encompass a force ranging from a single police officer to 20, or in some areas of the country, there may be no unit present at all. In any event, those specialized units almost always belong to a state or federal police corps; it is very uncommon to find examples of these units being created within the scope of local police forces.

Practically, all of these dedicated units focus their resources on fighting the illicit trafficking of cultural goods. This is a logical course of action due to how relevant the fight against the illegal trafficking of cultural goods has been in the protection of heritage assets, as we can see (i) manifested across all relevant international legal instruments which are constantly being updated; (ii) in the volume of global projects funded by the European Commission or other institutions of note,[2] focusing on various crucial aspects linked to the illegal trade, as well as international cooperation; (iii) in academic research into the matter, an area of expertise which has grown exponentially over the past decade, together with; (iv) an enormous increase in the availability and consumption of news media. In that sense, as interest in the matter has grown, questions regarding how this type of illicit activity is undertaken, and even more significantly, how to fight it, have grown louder.

Here, we can find the first critical point in the system: illicit trafficking involves many crimes or administrative offenses and has an international organizational component. Bearing in mind the point raised above with regard to the significantly differing legislation and law enforcement structures in different countries, together with the few dedicated police units and prosecutors, the difficulties facing those working to fight the trade day by day are plain to see. This chapter does not aim to explain the problem of illicit trafficking of cultural goods,[3] but will provide a

[2] Below are some of the European projects related to the subject that are currently being implemented:

PITCHER—Preventing Illicit Trafficking of Cultural Heritage is a project that aims to provide open educational materials for teachers to use in new learning courses to prevent the illicit trafficking of cultural goods.

AURORA—Artwork Unique Recognition and Tracking through chemically encoded data, miniaturized devices, and blockchain alliance.

ANCHISE—Applying New solutions for Cultural Heritage protection through Innovative, Scientific, social, and Economic engagement.

ENIGMA—Endorsing safeguarding, protection, and provenance management of cultural heritage.

RITHMS—The project intends to boost the operational capacity of Police and Customs/Border Authorities in addressing the increasingly organized and poly-criminal nature of the trafficking in cultural goods through research, technological innovation, outreach, and training.

[3] For further information on the consequences and characteristics of international trafficking in cultural property, please consult Mackenzie et al. (2020), Brodie et al. (2022), or Rufián Fernández and Sabrine (2020).

concise list of its more relevant characteristics to facilitate the presentation of the argument.

The extent and specific features of such criminality could be studied from three perspectives closely related to its characteristics, and as will be explained, in all cases, an increase in the functional capabilities of local police forces would greatly facilitate anti-trafficking measures. The first perspective refers to the international dimension involved, which has traditionally meant that local administrations have been left out of the studies of the problem and the solutions proposed. This has been primarily the result of a lack of in-depth research that has focused efforts on customs and countries where the objects were initially obtained. In order to maintain that assertion, it is essential to understand how the trade operates and to detect similarities that could help prosecute the illegal actors involved. In this context, the classical division of roles involved in unlawful trafficking establishes some categories depending on the function developed in the trade, especially of archaeological items. Based on the study of patterns within this type of market, some researchers, such as Balcells (2018, 2021) or Mackenzie et al. (2020), together with some reports compiled by international organizations like United Nations Educational, Scientific and Cultural Organization (Boz 2018) or the European Commission et al. (2019), have identified similar patterns and, based on these patterns, have tried to dissect their operations. As a result, some countries will be classified as source countries, those from which cultural objects originate, and others as transit or destination countries, depending upon which stage of the journey those objects can be found.

In this functionality model, different countries are shown as different steps followed by the objects before arriving at the buyer. These steps exhibit significant similarities to other illegal markets, which enable us to deduce that organized crime is involved, or put simply, those involved use the same methods that have been proven safe for other illegal networks. In that regard, Nellemann et al. (2018) elaborated on a study that provides a comprehensive global representation of the international network of organized crime in general, not concerning cultural goods specifically. The study shows that certain countries seem to act as connectors, and a lot of actors are strategically located in tax havens, which is striking (for example, in Spain). It is also easy to see those similarities with the illegal trade of cultural goods, especially concerning money laundering. In that sense, in a report coordinated by the European Commission et al. (2019), an exciting summary of some of the most significant police cases was drafted; it is plain to see the similarities throughout.

Bearing in mind that, logically, the first legal and academic attempts to reduce illicit trafficking were conducted by means of customs control and in countries where the objects were initially obtained. That international component may also be one of the driving forces behind the fact that local police forces have traditionally not been equipped with this kind of unit, this being a situation that has made it even more difficult for police to engage in this type of work.

The second perspective has been introduced before, pointing out that illicit trafficking, as such, is not included in any applicable regulations, hindering enforcement. The term describes a global activity comprising a series of actions that separately constitute crimes or administrative offenses under the different legislations involved in the entire process from start to finish. This is perhaps one of the main characteristics that has made it so difficult to control the trade, as the same crimes are infrequently committed together or within the same territory (bearing in mind the different laws that exist within different territorial entities). As Suárez-Mansilla (2018, 2019, 2020) points out, explaining the position taken with some real-world examples, the illicit distribution networks of this type of object take advantage of the broad variety of existing legislation regarding the international trade of works of art or antiques. When any action taken is solely focused on customs, detecting those kinds of loopholes can be extremely difficult, which is why international cooperation between dedicated units is essential. However, to detect this kind of illegal behavior, it is critical to conduct regular inspections of the market, which is a task that usually exceeds the capacity of those dedicated units within the national and federal police forces.

All the above ultimately leads us to the third perspective to be considered. This perspective is characteristic of the illicit art and antiquities trade and is closely related to the previous perspectives, something that distinguishes it greatly from other legal and illegal international markets. This characteristic is that the objects subject to trade are not, in essence, illegal because there is a legal market for them that has been operating for decades. In other words, a legal market coexists alongside an illegal one, and the objects traded are of mixed provenance. Researchers have studied this perspective in great detail (Mackenzie 2011; Mackenzie and Yates 2016; Mackenzie et al. 2020), and they summarized the concept using the idea of a "gray market". This feature of the trade complicates the detection of illicit objects and the prosecution of the perpetrators even further, so advances in knowledge regarding the illegal market and new methodologies to disrupt it are necessary, particularly due to the difficulties involved in providing evidence for such investigations.

15.3 The Role of Local Police Forces

After analyzing some of the more challenging problems in heritage protection regarding illicit trafficking, a few proposals will be posited to strengthen the role of law enforcement based on an improved specialization within local forces. As mentioned above, having structures put in place within public administrations to care for heritage is essential, but it is also crucial in terms of criminal investigations. Only with the complete system in place will we be able to ensure that professionalism is streamlined throughout the entire process, from the investigation to the final judicial ruling. As previously mentioned, within the various models of police organization that we see across Europe, the Spanish model opted to recognize the capacity of local police forces to act in the same manner and with the same powers as police forces at the national or regional levels. The distinction between the competence of one or another force to act is made based on criminal and territorial parameters.

Therefore, based on this model and on the actions that are currently being carried out in Spain, a series of proposals will be listed below, which, if they were expanded to other countries and their police forces, would greatly improve police work across the continent.

As mentioned above, controlling the international trade of cultural goods is undoubtedly one of the main problems that we now face. However, since the 1970s, when the first regulatory texts were drafted to try to control it, all efforts have been directed toward interstate activity and border control. In that sense, some of the actions that specialized units used to conduct were, for example, recording criminal practices or maintaining a national database of stolen or missing objects (INTERPOL 2019). As previously mentioned, cooperation between law enforcement is essential for the system to function. There must be fluid mechanisms for collaboration and exchange of information between all law enforcement entities investigating such crimes. It must be borne in mind that two factors converge at this point. On the one hand are the reports of stolen objects, which are entered into certain databases, and on the other are the details of the objects that are traded and are subject to authorizations by cultural administrations or to administrative oversight by the police, such as the existing system of logbooks used in some countries. It is compulsory to guarantee the operability of this entire system and that the police forces that work within said system are deployed appropriately on the ground, meeting the needs of the country. In the countries where it is implemented, the logbook mechanism is a compulsory system in which all art and antiquities dealers must fill out official records with the details of the objects and the actors involved in the purchase and sale thereof, which are subject to inspection by the police.

The standard operating procedure is that the specialized units of the national or, in some cases, federal police are responsible for maintaining these databases and carrying out inspections of the logbooks. Moreover, taking into account that they must be checked to ensure that these are consistent with the objects and with the documentation that supports the purchases, sales, or imports and exports. If these inspections can be carried out by the local police within the establishments located within their territory, the quality and speed of the work would improve exponentially compared to how it is normally done across all countries, carrying out coordinated work with the rest of the police forces on the continent and the administrations involved, through a computerized system of logbooks and interoperable databases. (Rufián Fernández 2024).

Enhancing this type of oversight involves another important improvement within the system, which is related to a better understanding of the problem of illicit trafficking and, from that point, proposing evidence-based solutions. This would result in a large amount of data that could be analyzed. The actual scale of the illicit trade is not well known, and the exchange of information should flow better (Yates and Brodie 2023). These problems could be resolved to a significant extent if we could establish a data-gathering model in which the market actors and law enforcement participate. We must remember that those systems already function in several European states, but not with such capabilities, and only with the collaboration of the national or sometimes even just federal police services. The challenge is to adapt the system to a European level and turn it digital to make sure that real control of the market is developed (Rufián Fernández 2024).

On the other hand, the capacity of local police forces to monitor archaeological sites or heritage elements in the countryside is so obvious that they will not be developed much further here. Real preventive work against looting cannot be carried out without the people who provide security in these areas. However, for this to be effective, these local forces must be specialized and trained, something that is currently merely anecdotal. We can find an excellent example of this in the local police services in England, where local police and Historic England have been developing initiatives to prevent heritage-related crime for many years.[4]

Efforts like these should be applied in combination with preventing vandalism, especially in cities. Poorly designed public spaces or abandoned areas, coupled with vandalism, are the perfect mix for creating an unsafe environment for inhabitants, as well as a situation of insecurity for cultural heritage sites. In addition, it has been demonstrated time and time again that failure to improve such situations over time will lead to greater levels of insecurity. In that sense, local police work is essential, and an excellent example of how to combat this trend has been the creation of a specialized unit within the Municipal Police of Madrid.[5] This unit was created to protect the city's urban heritage but has been assigned to combatting graffiti due to its negative impact on habitability and the damage it causes to local heritage.

We can find other indirect improvements that would make the state police system much more sustainable. Local police are bound to a specific area and work under the command of the city mayor. This allows economic effort and resources to be distributed among administrations. In those situations, state services could focus on the supranational component of specific cases while preventing and investigating other related crimes committed within their given territory and overseeing the local police. In the case of the Carabinieri Corps in Italy, their specialized heritage protection unit has an extensive presence throughout the country, which can be held up as an excellent example of how to work through a single police force. However, the capacity to achieve any similar specialist distribution would require considerable economic resources and effort for any single public administration. In the opposite direction, we can take a look at the case of Spain, where both police units specialized in heritage protection exist within the two national police authorities present throughout the national territory (namely, the Civil Guard and the National Police) and within the police forces of the Autonomous Communities, which are currently well established. Despite the fact that this can be done, and some examples are seen, there is still a long way to go in training specialists working for local police forces.

Finally, it is important to highlight another consequence of the implementation of this model, which would be the achievement of an enormous preventive work, which, as has been stated, is the basis of any modern police service. There is little

---

[4] https://historicengland.org.uk/images-books/publications/heritage-crime-prevention-guide/heag319-heritage-crime-prevention/

[5] https://www.elmundo.es/madrid/2024/02/21/65d4f4a021efa00a138b45a7.html

need to stress the practical impossibility of implementing such preventive models, based on the vast amounts of resources that would be required of specialized units with greatly restricted human resources, working throughout the territory of an entire state, pursuing crimes of an international nature.

15.4 Archaeology's Role in Prosecuting Heritage-Related Crimes

We have explained some of the particular characteristics of the trade that make a heritage crime challenging to prosecute. Unfortunately, some other specific traits in archaeological heritage make it even more difficult. When we analyze past judicial proceedings related to archaeology, it is all too common for cases to be dismissed without any penalties being handed down to defendants. In addition, the justification provided by the judge or tribunal presiding over such cases is regularly based on the lack of evidence and, consequently, on the application of the judicial principle of *in dubio pro reo* (when in doubt, rule for the accused).

Essential advantages have been developed in recent years to make the evidence of a crime easier to prove when the case concerns archaeology in general. A significant volume of research is currently being conducted into criminology, judicial matters, and forensic sciences regarding this issue; yet, it is still necessary to work on preparing the appropriate conditions to guarantee the applicability of results and the helpfulness of this type of study to police forces and prosecutors.

Traditionally, the branch of Forensic Archaeology has been mainly associated with its more traditional application, which is supporting the police, forensic medicine, and other related disciplines in searching for, excavating, and studying human burials (Groen 2018). However, forensic archaeology has much more to contribute, for example, to heritage crimes, illegal trade, and looting, among others, especially if we consider the problematic issues regarding providing archaeological evidence in courts. These kinds of archaeologist professionals have much greater knowledge surrounding heritage from a broad perspective. In that sense, universities and specialized training centers must conduct more research and begin training new archaeologists in fields like advisory roles regarding heritage protection laws, forensic archaeology applied to heritage crimes, criminology, and expert court witnesses, among other options (Barone 2018).

This kind of research arises from different perspectives due to the compulsory multidisciplinary approach needed, and we want to mention some of them as examples. Regarding the use of archaeological methodology itself in forensic scenarios, we can find the work of Rufián Fernández and Fernández Díaz (2017) that focused on the application of the new planimetry and recording techniques that are habitually used in archaeology to the collection of data in visual inspections conducted by police.

However, we can also find other related fields that are applied alongside archaeology. One of the most significant developments has been the research conducted by Alesia Koush in her doctoral thesis. The study is based on using liquids to deter looting of archaeological sites, making it easy for law enforcement to prove the provenance of objects, even when they have been smuggled (Koush 2023, 2024).

In a similar vein to that research objective, we can find another study conducted by a multidisciplinary team focused on using archaeometry to prove the provenance of archaeological objects. They suggest investigating where an object has been looted from by analyzing the biological remains associated with it and comparing it with the earth in suspected archaeological sites (Rodríguez Temiño et al. 2018). It is currently a marginal issue for judicial proceedings to prove the time frame that an object remained in the ground and the site from which it was extracted.

However, many more lines of investigation are being developed, most focused on prosecuting crimes against archaeological heritage due to the evidentiary difficulties mentioned above. We can also cite other research in which the objective was to prove the provenance of objects using geographical data and archaeological information. One such example is the research by Romeo Marugán (2022), in which the author analyzes the geographical distribution of very well-known archaeological items within the Aragón region of Spain. That work enabled the author to create distribution maps in which different archaeological objects are marked. Using those maps, when the police find looted archaeological objects, it is possible for them to see an important range of likely sites from which the objects could have come.

From a similar perspective, we can find other research in which archaeological methodology is combined with other fields of knowledge, such as criminology. When applied to archaeological protection, the use of other sciences allows us to open the functionalities of the methodology to different objectives. In such a way, the use, for example, of criminological profiles has allowed Alay i Rodríguez (2021, 2021b) to create a methodology for investigating the looting of archaeological sites, especially looting committed using metal detectors. In so doing, patterns can be established based on their capacity for damage and the methods used to prevent and detect them. Going further, those methodologists could extend their objectives to other related areas, such as security. The same author elaborated on a study system that measures the risk of an archaeological site being looted. That is the first step toward establishing the correct measures when we talk about protection, as it allows us to plan the surveillance of these sites, a typically difficult task due to their geographical situation.

On the other hand, few research works have been found within the context of security itself. One example is that penned by Clark et al. (2019), in which the team, which specializes in the field of security, evaluated the physical security of the site under study and its surroundings in order to identify the risks and to propose new protective measures based on the resources available. As in most sites of this type, the main risk to which it is exposed is plundering, and it is particularly striking that an essential element of this risk factor is the lack of appreciation and understanding of the site's true value by the population surrounding it.

Other areas of expertise are more closely related to archaeology as a science, such as geology, which, when combined, offer a myriad of attractive possibilities. One of the options is to study the risks intrinsic to the areas where heritage assets are located through geological studies aimed at detecting risks in the deposits. This enables the actors involved to develop customized prevention strategies and to design protection protocols adapted to the specific needs identified. The methodology for this study has been based primarily on detecting major natural events that led to a catastrophe in the past in order to extrapolate them to the present and obtain a risk prediction. Among the works that can be found on the subject are those of Jiménez Sánchez and Ballesteros, who defined the concept of geoarchaeological risk as "the relative probability, expressed in spatial terms, that an archaeological site, with a certain degree of conservation, is potentially threatened by an active geological process" (Jiménez Sánchez and Ballesteros 2017: 60).

On the other hand, there are works aimed at the study of archaeoseismology and its application to the prediction of the potential repeat processes of seismic events, with the goal of predicting the seismic hazard of an area and deducing the consequent risk planning required, even for the adjacent areas (Giner-Robles et al. 2011). Pier Matteo Barone et al. (2021), Barone and Di Maggio (2023) have probably conducted the most advanced work regarding the forensic uses of geoarchaeology. They demonstrate how geoarchaeology provides a comprehensive and interdisciplinary approach to investigating crime scenes and provides practical examples of using it.

To conclude, we would like to highlight Spain's efforts to achieve a multidisciplinary and holistic approach to the fight against heritage crime. In this regard, we can find a variety of research based upon the work of the police or the forest guards regarding heritage protection and the judicial police. Some examples include the work done by Rabadán Retortillo (2015), creating a protocol to investigate this kind of crime; the research conducted by Picón (2018), creating that specialization among forest guards in Catalonia; and finally, the doctoral thesis of Rufián Fernández (2024), based on the work of local police forces.

15.5 Conclusion

It can be concluded that the specialization of the police and other bodies that directly or indirectly monitor historical heritage is essential in order to guarantee its conservation. Looking back, the measures taken to combat the problems have been geared in the same direction for decades, but unfortunately, significant improvements have not been observed. It is time to try new measures, to incorporate new actors, even those working within the art and antiquities market itself, and to establish modern criteria for protecting heritage. In this sense, there is still much work to be done. However, the relevant number of projects and people working on them, as well as the increasingly apparent awareness of society and political decision-makers regarding the issue, suggest that substantial improvements could be achieved in the coming years.

In addition, the specific characteristics of these crimes make their investigation very complicated, especially those related to archaeological heritage. Therefore, it can also be concluded that archaeology, as a science and as a profession, is still a field undergoing development and has a vast amount of room for improvement. In that sense, universities and training centers, including those belonging to the police forces, have a long way to go, both in terms of assistance regarding forensic techniques and in the fight against crimes related to historical heritage. Scientists, legal experts, and law enforcement are obliged to collaborate with the aim of achieving efficient protection of cultural and historical heritage.

Bibliography

Alay i Rodríguez JC (2021) Arqueofurtivismo: tipología, perfilación criminológica y protocolos de actuación. In: Guisasola Lerma C, Periago Morant J (eds) Tutela de los bienes culturales. Una visión cosmopolita desde el derecho penal, el derecho internacional y la criminología. Tirant lo Blanch, Valencia, pp 29–64

Alay i Rodríguez JC (2021b) Arqueofurtivismo. Manual sobre el estudio de las intervenciones arqueológicas ilegales. Sèrie Vària del Seminari dÈstudis i Recerques Prehistòriques, 2. Barcelona University. ISBN 978-84-944730-9-8

Balcells M (2018) Aspectos criminológicos del expolio y del tráfico ilícito del patrimonio arqueológico. In: Yáñez A, Rodríguez Temiño I (eds) El expoliar se va a acabar. Tirant lo Blanch, Valencia, pp 335–357

Balcells M (2021) El expoliador en la Torre de Babel. Apuntes para un estudio empírico de la figura del saqueador de antigüedades. In: Guisasola Lerma C, Periago Morant J (eds) Tutela de los bienes culturales. Una visión cosmopolita desde el derecho penal, el derecho internacional y la criminología. Tirant lo Blanch, Valencia, pp 65–96

Barone PM (2018) Not just body and decomposition: forensic archaeology preventing antiquity crimes. In: Barone PM, Groen WJM (eds) Multidisciplinary approaches to forensic archaeology. Soil forensics. Springer, Cham, pp 219–230. https://doi.org/10.1007/978-3-319-94397-8_16

Barone PM, Di Maggio RM (2023) Exploring the growing importance of forensic Geoarchaeology in Italy. Forensic Sci 3:533–543. https://doi.org/10.3390/forensicsci3040037

Barone PM, Di Maggio RM, Mesturini S (2021) Forensic Geoarchaeology in the search for missing persons. Forensic Sci 1:8–15. https://doi.org/10.3390/forensicsci1010003

Boz Z (2018) Fighting the illicit trafficking of cultural property: a toolkit for European judiciary and law enforcement. UNESCO. Available at: http://www.unesco.org/new/fileadmin/MULTIMEDIA/HQ/CLT/movable/pdf/Toolkit.pdf. Accessed 10 Feb 2024

Brodie N, Kersel M, Mackenzie S, Sabrine I, Smith E, Yates D (2022) Why there is still an illicit trade in cultural objects and what we can do about it. J Field Archaeol 47(2):117–130. https://doi.org/10.1080/00934690.2021.1996979

Clark JH, Sanz Marcos R, Carotenudo R (2019) Archeological site of Clunia Sulpicia. In: Kalam & EKABA Foundation (ed) Seguridad en el Patrimonio. Simposio Científico Internacional, pp 103–108

European Commission, Directorate-General for Education, Youth, Sport and Culture, Brodie N, Batura O, Hoog G, Slot B, Wanrooij N, Yates D (2019) Illicit trade in cultural goods in Europe: characteristics, criminal justice responses and an analysis of the applicability of technologies in the combat against the trade: final report. Publications Office. Available at: https://op.europa.

eu/en/publication-detail/-/publication/d79a105a-a6aa-11e9-9d01-01aa75ed71a1/language-en. Accessed 18 Feb 2024

Giner-Robles J, Silva PG, Pérez-López R, Rodríguez-Pascua M, Azcárate T, Garduño M, Lario J (2011) Evaluación del daño sísmico en edificios históricos y yacimientos arqueológicos: aplicación al estudio del riesgo sísmico, proyecto EDASI, Serie Investigación. Fundación MAPFRE

Groen WJM (2018) Forensic archaeology: integrating archaeology with criminalistics and criminology. In: Barone PM, Groen WJM (eds) Multidisciplinary approaches to forensic archaeology. Soil forensics. Springer, Cham, pp 1–18. https://doi.org/10.1007/978-3-319-94397-8_1

INTERPOL (2019) Creating a national cultural heritage unit. Available at: https://www.interpol.int/Crimes/Cultural-heritage-crime/Protecting-cultural-heritage. Accessed 12 Feb 2024

Jiménez Sánchez M, Ballesteros D (2017) Metodología de evaluación del riesgo geoarqueológico en castros marítimos: El Castiellu (Asturias, España). Geogaceta 62:59–62

Koush A (2023) Forensic traceable liquid for deterring trafficking in cultural property: pilot implementation in Iraq. J Field Archaeol 49(1):59–73. https://doi.org/10.1080/00934690.2023.2291237

Koush A (2024) Towards *malum prohibitum*: crime deterrence strategies for reducing illicit antiquities trade. Crime Law Soc Change. https://doi.org/10.1007/s10611-024-10169-3

Mackenzie S (2011) The market as criminal and criminals in the market: reducing opportunities for organized crime in the international antiquities market. In: Manacorda S, Chappell D (eds) Crime in the art and antiquities world: illegal trafficking in cultural property, pp 69–85. https://doi.org/10.1007/978-1-4419-7946-9_4

Mackenzie S, Yates D (2016) What is Grey about the "Grey market" in antiquities. In: Beckert J, Dewey M (eds) The architecture of illegal markets: towards an economic sociology of illegality in the economy. Oxford University Press, Oxford, pp 70–86. https://traffickingculture.org/publications/what-is-grey-about-the-grey-market-in-antiquities/

Mackenzie S, Brodie N, Yates D, Tsirogiannis C (2020) Trafficking culture: new directions in researching the global market in illicit antiquities. Routledge

Nellemann C, Henriksen R, Pravettoni R, Stewart D, Kotsovou M, Schlingemann, Shaw M, Reitano T (eds) (2018) World atlas of illlicit flows. A RHIPTO-INTERPOL-GI assessment. RHIPTO -Norwegian Center for Global Analyses, INTERPOL and the Global Initiative Against Transnational Organized Crime. Available at: https://globalinitiative.net/analysis/world-atlas-of-illicit-flows/. Accessed 17 Feb 2024

Picón A (2018) Expolio arqueológico en Cataluña y la implicación del cos D'Agents rurals de la Generalitat de Catalunya. In: Yáñez A, Rodríguez Temiño I (eds) El expoliar se va a acabar. Uso de detectores de metales y arqueología: Sanciones administrativas y penales. Tirant lo Blanc, Valencia, pp 103–129

Rabadán Retortillo T (2015) Delitos contra el patrimonio histórico. Metodología policial. TREA

Rodríguez Temiño I, Yáñez A, Jorge Villar S, Reyes Mateo A, Rufino Rus J, Salas Álvarez J, Lavín Berdonces A (2018) Forensic Archaeometry applied to antiquities trafficking: the beginnings of an investigation at the Frontiers of knowledge. Arts 7(4):98. https://doi.org/10.3390/arts7040098

Romeo Marugán F (2022) A new method of forensic archaeology identification of the origin of archaeological materials seized in police proceedings. In: Oostrman N, Yates D (eds) Crime and art. Sociological and criminological perspectives of crimes in the art world, vol 1. Springer, pp 79–99

Rufián Fernández FJ (2024) La protección del Patrimonio Histórico por las Policías Locales. Doctoral Dissertation. Autónoma University of Madrid. https://repositorio.uam.es/handle/10486/715328

Rufián Fernández FJ, Fernández Díaz M (2017) Técnicas fotogramétricas aplicadas a la planimetría pericial. In: II Anuario Internacional de Criminología y Ciencias Forenses, pp 439–446

Rufián Fernández FJ, Sabrine I (2020) Illicit trafficking of antiquities and its consequences on the SDGs. Peace, justice and strong institutions. In: Encyclopedia of the UN sustainable development goals. Springer, pp 1–8. https://doi.org/10.1007/978-3-319-71066-2_124-1

Suárez-Mansilla M (2018) Blood antiquities: a net acting in Spain helped to finance DAESH through illicit trafficking of cultural goods. Art World Law Bull Chronicles Themis Athenea 4:1–32

Suárez-Mansilla M (2019) ≘Es España un buen país de paso para el tráfico ilícito de bienes culturales? Anuario Iberoamericano de Derecho del Arte 2019:417–492

Suárez-Mansilla M (2020) ≘Sirve el tráfico ilícito de bienes culturales para financiar el terrorismo? Revista d'arqueologia de Ponent 30:309–336. https://doi.org/10.21001/rap.2020.30.17

Yates D, Brodie N (2023) The illicit trade in antiquities is not the world's third-largest illicit trade: a critical evaluation of a factoid. Antiquity 97(394):991–1003. https://doi.org/10.15184/aqy.2023.90

Chapter 16
The Human Remains Trade in Spain

Damien Huffer, Nicholas Márquez-Grant, Elena Ruiz, Carlos Andrés Cristóbal, Teresa Cabellos, Enrique Dorado, José Ignacio de Miguel Moro, and Elisa Ruiz-Tagle Fernández

Abstract Over the last several years, academia, law enforcement, and the public have become increasingly aware that private commercial collecting of a wide range of human remains has found a ready home on numerous e-commerce and social media platforms and online live auctions. This is in addition to brick-and-mortar auction houses and stores through which all kinds of antiquities are sold. The growing human remains collecting community can find and sell to each other through the internet due to the generally poor moderation of black and grey market activity on most platforms. Here, we present and discuss examples of human remains trafficking pertinent to Spain, i.e., the buyers, sellers, or middlemen based in Spain (importing, exporting, or internally circulating shipments). A quantification of the number

D. Huffer (✉)
School of Biological Science, University of Adelaide, Adelaide, SA, Australia

Department of History, Carleton University, Ottawa, ON, Canada

The Alliance to Counter Crime Online, Washington, DC, USA

School of Social Science, University of Queensland, Brisbane, Australia

N. Márquez-Grant
Cranfield Forensic Institute, Cranfield University, Bedford, UK

E. Ruiz
Identification Central Unit, General Headquarters of Forensics, National Police, Madrid, Spain

C. A. Cristóbal
Illicit Trafficking Service of Cultural Heritage, General Directorate of Cultural Heritage and Fine Arts, Ministry of Culture, Madrid, Spain

T. Cabellos
Instituto Nacional de Toxicología y Ciencias Forenses, Madrid, Spain

E. Dorado · E. R.-T. Fernández
Institute de Medicina Legal de Madrid, Madrid, Spain

J. I. de Miguel Moro
Consejería de Sanidad de la Comunidad de Madrid, Madrid, Spain

P. M. Barone, WJ M. Groen (eds.), *Forensic Archaeology and New Multidisciplinary Approaches*, Soil Forensics, https://doi.org/10.1007/978-3-031-86308-0_16

of cases investigated or prosecuted in Spain, total annual prices, or the potential amount of human remains moved through the system has not been attempted to date. Therefore, we focus on the particulars of each case to the extent known, as well as how trafficking human remains tests current cultural property and human remains legislation, and how forensic anthropology and archaeology are vital tools in the fight against this trade. We conclude with recommendations for how professionals and the public can respond when online trade is encountered and how the public can help to push back against its continued proliferation.

Keywords Human remains trade · Forensic anthropology · Illicit trafficking · Cultural heritage crimes · Online marketplaces

16.1 Introduction

Forensic archaeology is typically understood as the excavation of clandestine graves whether in more domestic police cases or human rights contexts; however, the wider role of forensic archaeology (e.g. see Groen et al. 2015) includes the protection of cultural heritage. In fact, many Federal law enforcement agencies worldwide (e.g. Carabinieri in Italy, Guardia Civil in Spain) as well as the military (e.g. Rush 2014, 2023; Solly 2018) have teams that deal with the protection of cultural heritage and crimes against heritage, in addition to region-wide collaborations, such as the Heritage Crime Task Force, headquartered at the Organization for Security and Co-operation in Europe (OSCE) in Vienna. At locations where heritage crime, especially looting or site vandalism, occurs, forensic archaeologists will often assist law enforcement investigations. Forensic anthropologists will get involved when human remains, and particularly skeletonized remains, are seized or recovered via excavation, whether due to attempted illicit trafficking or the discovery and mitigation of in-progress looting.

This chapter provides an opportunity to explore the role of forensic archaeologists and anthropologists in policing and preventing a specific aspect of heritage crime, the illicit human remains trade, by discussing the general background and context underpinning these types of investigations, describing specific examples of online trade, and presenting a case derived from an apprehended shipment (Dorado et al. 2022).[1] Over the last several years, academia, law enforcement, and the public have become increasingly aware of the private and commercial collecting of a wide range of human remains as seen on numerous e-commerce, social media platforms and online live auctions. This is in addition to the brick-and-mortar auction

[1] This focus on Spain derives from the presentation of this work on the trade of human remains presented at the EMFA meeting in Madrid, Spain, in 2023. The work presented by D. Huffer and N. Márquez-Grant was entitled *The Human Remains Trade To, From, and Within Spain: Socio-Legal Context and Case Studies*. European Meeting of Forensic Archaeology, Madrid. 29th September 2023.

houses, antique stores, and "oddities" shops through which all manner of antiquities are sold, both on and offline. This collecting community can find and sell to each other through the internet and the generally poor moderation of black and grey market activity on most platforms. Indeed, whilst revising this chapter, a story broke regarding the attempted online auction by an auction house in Oxfordshire (Davies 2024; Gudge 2024; Panwar 2024). The 22 lots of Indigenous human remains from numerous cultures on offer in this case all first entered Western markets via colonial-era trade, theft, or violence. Through concerted action by numerous parties, especially descendant community representatives such as the Forum for Naga Reconciliation (FNR), the auctioneer was persuaded to withdraw these specific listings. What their fate will be going forward is unknown at the time of writing, but we hope that repatriation can occur quickly.

Recently, heritage crime research, often in aid of frontline law enforcement efforts, has markedly increased what is known about the depth and breadth of cultural heritage trafficking online, including human remains. Plumbing the depth of this ever-changing online 'ecosystem' is complicated, made further challenging by the fact that local markets in many countries and the online human remains trade outside of the English-speaking world have barely begun to be mapped. It is understood that content moderation failures plague many platforms (thus allowing posts that violate platform Terms of Service). For those global platforms headquartered in the United States of America, the 'legal liability shield' against even criminal user content that the U.S. Communications Decency Act § 230 provides has allowed a wide variety of crimes to flourish and cross platforms (e.g. Allison and Martin 2024; Carvalho et al. 2023; Elkhazeen et al. 2022; Harrington et al. 2023; Hodgson 2024). Nevertheless, some other platforms (such as the Oxfordshire example above) have stopped the selling of human remains due to pressure on the ethical (not necessarily illegal) aspect of selling human remains, as stated by professional biological anthropology associations such as BABAO's (British Association of Biological Anthropology and Osteoarcheology) *Trading and Sale of Human Remains Task Force* in the UK (of which the first author, DH, is a member and co-founder).

16.2 Background: The Human Remains Trade Goes Global

The current human remains trade is known to include a very wide variety of archaeological, historical, and anatomical human remains. Whole or partial skeletons and other soft tissues (referred to as "wet specimens") are sourced from archaeological sites, allegedly defunct museums or deaccessioned teaching collections, documented repositories such as tombs, catacombs, church ossuaries, and cemeteries, and the "medical bone trade" that mostly emanated from India and China from the mid-late 1800s until the 1980s, generally speaking (e.g. Carney 2011; Agarwal 2024a, 2024b). From our current knowledge and investigations, human remains are privately bought and sold for a multitude of reasons, including personal use as house decoration, drinking vessels, and even lampshades, as well as commercial use as decoration in shops, bars, tattoo parlours, etc. Whilst many collectors are primarily interested in skulls, there are those seeking individual disarticulated elements or complete skeletons, in addition to a wide variety of organs and tissues, preserved foetuses, blood, alleged cremation ash or cemetery soil, and even hominin fossils (Huffer and Graham 2023; Huffer et al. 2022; Huffer and Charlton 2019; Kjaergaard 2012; Seidemann and Hawkins 2019). Furthermore, the ongoing trade may also include antiquities or ethnographic objects that are made of human bone or those that incorporate bone, teeth, or hair (e.g. Brown 2020). Niche collectors pay higher prices for human remains bearing clear evidence of once having passed through a museum collection, or those with a "story" that may allege the remains were exhumed from an archaeological site, catacomb, or ossuary (e.g. Rose 2021).

The ability for dealers and collectors to easily connect, or for prominent dealers to influence other individuals to begin collecting, has markedly expanded since the 1990s with the rise of e-commerce and social media platforms. Today, the private collection and sale of human remains occur primarily online (see e.g. Huffer and Graham 2023; Daniels and Shiffman 2018; Pester 2022). Simultaneously, crucial steps in each transaction occur offline via brick-and-mortar stores or more informal trades or transactions made in person, likely in cash and without receipts. Whilst the scope and extent of this global trade have increased and new collecting communities have formed, the desire to own human remains (as well as antiquities, historic artefacts, ethnographic items, etc.) is as old as antiquity itself. Whilst it is on occasion legal, it certainly is not ethical and is arguably highly immoral. Other steps in the transaction, such as online advertisement or shipment across borders, are potentially illegal in certain jurisdictions.

16.2.1 The Combination of Bioarchaeology, Forensic Anthropology, and OSINT

Given how extensive trafficking networks can become when allowed to proliferate across the internet, how readily they can spread across platforms, and the general size of the internet ecosystem itself, combatting the human remains trade requires interdisciplinary effort. Here, as with other categories of cybercrime research, aspects of digital forensics and the use of 'OSINT' (Open-Source Intelligence) are well-established methods that even low- or no-budget civilian-led projects can utilize. OSINT and the application of social network analysis to uncover insights into how trafficking networks operate and connect are increasingly relied upon to gather intel that can illuminate a buyer or seller's history of online trafficking activity.

OSINT is defined by its reliance on publicly available data and information, on both the surface and 'deep' webs (Borges 2024). The information obtained should be treated as time-sensitive and address a specific intelligence requirement (whether requested by the prosecution or defence in a case, or to answer a specific question in a research project). Courts in the United States and many other jurisdictions maintain that acceptable open-source information must be for a public audience, available by request, subscription, or purchase; able to be seen or heard by a casual observer; presented in a public forum; or obtained by visiting a public place or event (Borges 2024). Sales posts on public social media and e-commerce platforms are born-digital, accessible from nearly anywhere on earth, and increasingly multimedia in nature (including text, photographs, quantifiable metadata, and sometimes video). The development of OSINT as a method has been ongoing since at least the Second World War (e.g. Block 2022). Some scholars (e.g. Hatfield 2023) attest that OSINT is not separate from other forms of intelligence gathering, like HUMINT (Human Intelligence; intelligence gathering by interpersonal contacts) and GEOSINT (Geospatial Intelligence; intelligence gathering by means of satellite tech). Regardless, OSINT efforts using social media and e-commerce data, at least in part, continue to find ready application in trafficking and cybercrime research (e.g. Gondhali et al. 2024; Duncan and Inch 2024; Clément and Inglis 2022).

16.2.2 The Ethical Responsibilities of Civilian Researchers

Civilian researchers have a clear responsibility to collect data, analyze, and publish about online illicit trafficking networks (and the people, guilty or innocent, that comprise them) following the highest ethical standards. This applies to not just human remains trafficking, where the rights of the dead and of potentially innocent individuals 'lurking' within the spaces where trafficking occurs, but not necessarily participating in it themselves, are both at play. Scientists, especially bioarchaeologists, archaeologists, and forensic anthropologists, are not, for the most part and in most countries, law enforcement agent. However, they often collaborate with law enforcement, and there is arguably a 'duty to report' evidence of in-progress or recent site disturbance or vandalism (especially if it relates to a potential crime scene). This collaboration comes about through police forces in Italy and Spain that liaise with medico-legal institutes or forensic anthropologists working in collaboration with police forces in the UK, amongst other examples. Simultaneously, conducting online trafficking research ethically also requires eliminating or at least minimizing risks to the researcher by never using one's personal account to observe or scrape data within spaces where trafficking occurs, such as private social media groups or forums. Negotiating 'duty to report' responsibilities can be complex and is often at the discretion of the researcher.

Ethical conduct in research using public or private social media data, as commonly defined by Institutional Review Board (IRB) committees or research funders (see discussion in Graham et al. 2024; Davidson et al. 2024), also requires full anonymization of posts to avoid sharing the handles or profile pictures of both the original poster and commentors. Especially given that many commentors on a sales post might not actually intend to purchase or bid. Conducting ethical research into online crime also carries the responsibility to ensure that no further harm is done to depicted individuals or that unnecessarily traumatic images are made public. This includes cases in which the depicted individuals are dead. For that reason, the figures presented and discussed below have all the identifiable information blacked out, associated text paraphrased, and any images of human remains blurred. The exception to this best practice can be seen in instances when law enforcement officers or investigators approach civilian subject-matter experts with evidence from a seizure, specifically requesting advice, impromptu 1st-level analysis from photographs, or information about the potential on- or off-line collecting history of a suspect. That is not the case with this review chapter.

16.3 The Human Remains Trade to, from, and Within Spain

The above demonstrates that the number of cases being investigated and countries from and to which human remains continue to be sent continues to grow. However, law enforcement involvement usually depends upon whether a clear and unmistakable crime has been committed.

In Spain, the Ministry of Culture has a section on the Illicit Trafficking of Cultural Heritage, which coordinates any investigation against an illicit act that involves cultural heritage, such as illegal trade, vandalism to an archaeological site, financing of terrorism, and fraud through the sale of cultural heritage items, thefts, fakes, etc.[2] These investigations apply to collaboration with law enforcement agencies that specialize in Cultural heritage, mainly the Heritage section (*Sección de Patrimonio Histórico)* of the Civil Guard (*Guardia Civil)* and the National Police (*Brigada de Patrimonio Histórico de la Policía Nacional).* Other agencies are the Spanish Border Agency (*Departamento de Aduanas),* as well as other national ministries within Spain, foreign affairs, and regional police forces. Within this collaboration, the section that investigates illicit trafficking of cultural heritage within the Spanish Ministry of Culture is responsible for:

- Addressing any allegations or charges pertaining to illegal activities involving national or international cultural heritage.
- Liaising between law enforcement agencies/police and heritage institutions.
- Addressing any questions or allegations regarding illegal trade posed by museum curators, police, art dealers and collectors and the general public.
- Controlling the antiques trade (online and offline).
- Officially requesting expert witness reports and possible monetary value assessments, if required.
- Revising any requests for import and export of cultural heritage that are presented to the Ministry of Culture.

[2] It must be borne in mind that the definition of historical or cultural heritage in Spanish legislation (see also Márquez-Grant et al. 2011) is broad, including historical objects, archaeological artefacts, artistic, ethnographic, paleontological, documents, etc.

- Exercising the duty to assist the police in searching for suspect addresses during an investigation.
- Managing the transport and curation of cultural heritage whilst a judicial process is being carried out.
- Coordinating the return of Spanish cultural property to Spain as well as the return to other countries if they are required by authorities.
- Maintaining professional development through meetings organized by the Ministry of Culture, Guardia Civil, Policía Nacional, Borders, Organization for Security and Co-operation in Europe (OSCE), United Nations, Europol, and Operation Pandora and representing Spain at International United Nations Educational, Scientific and Cultural Organization (UNESCO) meetings relating to illegal trafficking of cultural heritage.[3]

Indeed, Spanish law enforcement such as the National Police Heritage Team or *Brigada de Investigación de Patrimonio Histórico*, and the Civil Guard's [4] heritage team (Historical Heritage Investigation Team Central Operative Unit or UCO) and the Service for the Protection of Nature (*Servicio de Protección de la Naturaleza* or SEPRONA), have investigated many aspects at or destruction of archaeological and historic sites (e.g. see Policía Nacional 2023). These police units deal with theft of cultural property, fakes and forgeries, and vandalism to cultural heritage, and their work has often been visible in the news. Moreover, on occasion, photographs have been used to assess evidence of looting or online sales otherwise unavailable. One such example relates to a National Police investigation, which was sent to the Central Identification Unit (*Unidad Central de Identificación*) which includes forensic anthropology. Here, images of archaeological artefacts were seen being held by a person. The question was whether the person could be identified from the photograph, as their fingerprints could be observed. An identification was made in this case (Jara San Miguel et al. 2021). The potential for this as well as other types of evidence, such as vein pattern analysis (Hackman and Black 2023), applied to these crimes and others is huge.

More recently, these units have been tasked with investigating cases involving human remains. In Spain, illegal activities related to human remains trafficking, which later require a medico-legal investigation, often relate to graverobbing from cemeteries so that bodies or body parts can be sold nationally or internationally, those taken to be used in rituals, sale for purposes of anatomical education, or just for private collection. According to Spanish legislation, human remains ('*restos humanos*') involve those body parts derived from amputations, mutilations, surgical intervention, autopsies, abortions, or anything related to teaching and research. Another term used in Spanish legislation for human remains is '*restos cadavéricos*',

[3] Convention for the Protection of Cultural Property in the Event of Armed Conflict, The Hague, 1954; the Convention on the Means of Prohibiting and Preventing the Illicit Import, Export, and Transfer of Ownership of Cultural Property, signed in Paris in 1970; and the UNIDROIT Convention on Stolen or Illegally Exported Cultural Objects, Rome, 1995.

[4] See news items: https://www.guardiacivil.es/es/prensa/noticias/8605_0.html

which refers to human remains that are older than five years post mortem (*Guía de Consenso sobre sanidad Mortuoria Aprobada por la Comisión de Salud Pública de 24 de julio 2018*), whilst human bones ('*restos óseos*') refer to bodies that have become skeletonized without any soft tissue remaining (*Decreto 129/2023, de 31 de agosto, de sanidad mortuoria de Galicia*).

The legislation does cover whether ultimate disposal is either cremation or inhumation within an authorized location, as well as how the remains should be transported (*Guía de Consenso sobre sanidad Mortuoria Aprobada por la Comisión de Salud Pública de 24 de julio 2018; Decreto 2263/1974, de 20 de julio*). This also applies to organs and tissues that have been used for transplants or for education and research. The importation of human remains into Spain has its own legislation and conditions. Any lack of respect to the memory of the dead, any damage to graves, and any damage to human remains that are buried can lead to criminal charges (*Artículo 526 del Código Penal español, Ley Orgánica 10/1995, de 23 de noviembre, del Código Penal*). *Referencia: BOE-A-1995-25444*). According to Castro Liñares (2022), between 2011 and 2019, approximately 20 court proceedings relating to death or the dead occurred, which only accounted for 0.09% of all penal proceedings in Spain during that period.

Some of the cases involving human remains were covered by the press, including Operation 'Osarium',[5] involving human remains from a Minimum Number of Individuals (MNI) of 200, as well as hundreds of artefacts, all dating to *c.* 4000 years B.P. The artefacts and human remains were claimed to be part of the primary suspect's inheritance, but the case was nevertheless investigated by the *Guardia Civil* in November 2022. Whilst this example is an archaeological/historical case, others include the more recent dead, such as the stealing of corpses from hospitals to then be sold to universities by a criminal network including members who worked at two funeral homes.[6] Other cases relate to members of the general public who have human remains and do not want to keep them, so they dispose of them in the rubbish or elsewhere. This is problematic, as the origin of the remains is unknown, the chronology is unknown, and it may be costly to undertake DNA or other identification techniques.

One case that came to the attention of the Institute of Legal Medicine in Madrid in 2022 and was investigated by forensic anthropologists (Dorado et al. 2022) was the case of a calvarium (missing the maxillo-facial region and mandible), wrapped in newspaper and with the outermost wrapping painted similarly (but crudely) to Mexican Day of the Dead *calavera* sugar skulls. The parcel was destined for an undisclosed recipient in the USA but was intercepted by Customs and sent to a museum to confirm its authenticity as a human skull (rather than a plastic or resin replica). Curators then recommended it be sent to the Institute of Legal Medicine in Madrid. The skull still retained some soft tissue and hair, and its appearance,

[5] https: //www.elespanol.com/alicante/cultura/20221230/investigan-herencia-ilegal-piezas-arqueologicas-restos-humanos/727927614_0.html

[6] https://m.sundayworld.com/crime/world-crime/body-smuggling-gang-busted-by-spanish-police-after-selling-corpses-to-universities/a1872548509.html

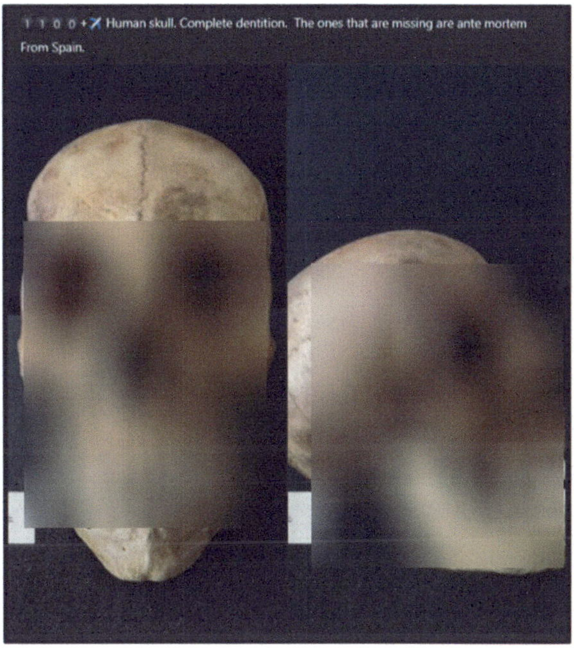

Fig. 16.1 An anonymized screen captureg from the public profile of a dealer offering numerous, primarily adult, skulls via Facebook in early 2018. All posts alleged that shipments were sent from Spain but did not indicate whether the remains themselves originated from Spain. Image blurred by the authors

morphology, and age meant it was classifiable as cadaveric remains under Spanish law (Dorado et al. 2022). Figures 16.1 and 16.2 show two c. 2018 examples of what the online human remains trade from or within Spain can look like, both identified and screen captured by DH.

One of the examples above (Fig. 16.1) shows one of several posts from a Facebook profile operating from at least 2018. This individual posted publicly and within several "oddities" collectors' groups regarding numerous, primarily adult, skulls that they were offering for sale. All posts were in English despite the claim that shipment would occur from an undisclosed location in Spain. The original poster implied that global shipping was possible. At the time of writing this paper, however, the profile has not been relocatable for several years, so it is unknown what happened to the original seller or the remains allegedly in their possession, nor whether the profile name was in fact a pseudonym.

16.4 Discussion and Conclusion

The information presented above is just a snapshot of a global phenomenon to which buyers and sellers actively contribute, including those shipping within, to, or from Spain, as well as other countries. Highlighting cases from within jurisdictions not frequently discussed in the international heritage crime research community, such as Spain, is important not only to demonstrate that the human remains trade is

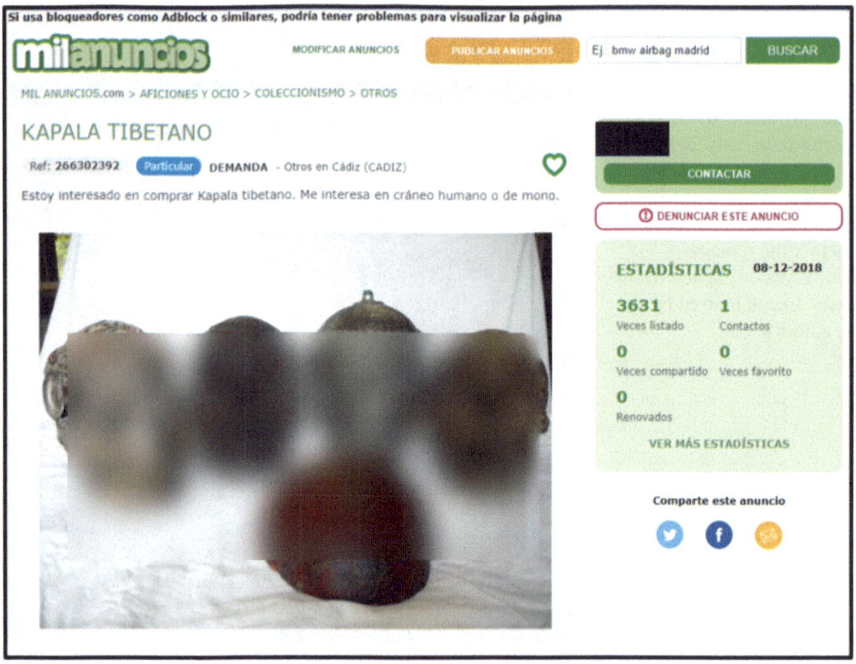

Fig. 16.2 A public post on the e-commerce platform Milanuncios.com from a user in Cadiz. They state their interest in buying Tibetan Kapala (elaborately decorated human skulls or calvaria), as well as an interest in human or monkey skulls in general. The announcement potentially displays items already in their collection

indeed global but that it exists in many countries (that can be the source, transit point, and market simultaneously) precisely because of the loopholes and lack of uniformity seen in regional and global legislation surrounding the disposition of human remains (Seidemann and Hawkins 2019; Huffer 2024; Scovazzi 2024; O'Neill 2024).

Since there is still much unknown about the human remains trade, and how and where it operates at the margins of national and regional-level legislation, and how buyers and sellers knowingly exploit platform moderation failures, we conclude this chapter by asking law enforcement and heritage professionals to recognize three main points:

1. The antiquities and human remains trade has moved primarily online. To reflect that reality, it is imperative that 'intel' from e-commerce and social media platforms be more readily treated as valuable evidence suitable for prosecutions as long as the digital chain of custody can be preserved and documented. Whilst not every aspect of a sale will be visible to civilian researchers given end-to-end encrypted messaging, the posting of human remains online is often the only evidence we have that the remains exist and are currently on the market.

2. More clearly acknowledge that the international human remains trade is evolving and that 'niche' collectors of such material specifically seek real or alleged remains from archaeological sites, museum storerooms, etc. We can clearly demonstrate that, in Spain, as well as the wider European Union (EU), and globally, the market for human remains contains much more than just "medical specimens", as certain collectors like to proclaim to the media and the public. More importantly, the online 'ecosystem' that allows so-called "medical specimens" to be bought and sold is the same system that allows many other categories of human remains to circulate.
3. In Spain and within the wider EU, the sale of human remains between private collectors often falls within legal gaps, especially when conducted online. Beyond that, the human remains trade stands as a clear example that what is "legal" might not arguably be called ethical or moral. Thus, professional bioarchaeologists and forensic anthropologists have an ethical responsibility to not authenticate the market by assisting collectors with demographic profiles, laboratory analyses, or anything else. In some jurisdictions, ignorance of the laws or the 'duty to report' Customs violations if a civilian researcher becomes aware of them is not enough to avoid complications or reputational damage should human remains be seized and a dealer or buyer investigated.

Ultimately, disrupting the on- and off-line human remains trade and applying our expertise in aid of law enforcement is a task worth pursuing by both forensic archaeologists and anthropologists. Especially for forensic archaeologists, it is an aspect of the job that can stretch the utility of their training far beyond the search for and excavation of clandestine graves. Therefore, awareness of the existence of these and methods by which today's human remains trade operates within, to, and from Spain and other countries should encompass part of the specialized training all forensic anthropologists and archaeologists receive.

References

Agarwal SC (2024a) The disposability and inclusion of Brown bodies. Am J Biol Anthropol. https://doi.org/10.1002/ajpa.25003

Agarwal SC (2024b) The bioethics of skeletal anatomy collections from India. Nat Commun 15:1692. https://doi.org/10.1038/s41467-024-45738-6

Allison C, Martin X (2024) Police concerned about rise in TikTok 'crimfluencers' in Alice Springs and youth crime curfew continues. Retrieved May 2024, from https://www.abc.net.au/news/2024-04-03/alice-springs-nt-youth-curfew-social-media-impact-tiktok/103657084

Block L (2022) The long history of OSINT. J Intell Hist 23(2):95–109. https://doi.org/10.1080/16161262.2023.2224091

Borges E (2024) What Is Open Source Intelligence (OSINT)? Retrieved from https://www.recordedfuture.com/blog/open-source-intelligence-definition

Brown M (2020) Tibetan objects made of human remains to go on show at British Museum. Retrieved August 2024, from https://www.theguardian.com/culture/2020/feb/23/tibetan-objects-made-of-human-remains-to-go-on-show-at-british-museum-tantric-buddhism

Carney S (2011) The red market: on the trail of the World's organ brokers, bone thieves, blood farmers, and child traffickers. Harper Collins US, New York

Carvalho AF, de Morais IOB, Souza TB (2023) Profiting from cruelty: digital content creators abuse animals worldwide to incur profit. Biol Conserv 287:110321. https://doi.org/10.1016/j.biocon.2023.110321

Castro Liñares D (2022) El respeto debido a los difuntos: Exhumación político-criminal del bien jurídico protegido del artículo 526 CP. Revista de Derecho Penal y Criminología 27:13–43. https://doi.org/10.5944/rdpc.27.2022.30768

Clément T, Inglis S (2022) Vietnam's virtual landscape for illicit wildlife trading. A snapshot of e-commerce and social media. Global Initiative Against Transnational Organized Crime Trend Report. Retrieved from https://globalinitiative.net/wp-content/uploads/2022/10/GITOC-MMFU-Vietnams-virtual-landscape-for-illicit-wildlife-trading-A-snapshot-of-e-commerce-and-social-media.pdf

Daniels SM, Shiffman J (2018) Businessman who sold diseased human body parts gets nine years in prison. Retrieved August 2024, from https://www.reuters.com/article/us-usa-bodies-sentence-idUSKCN1IN2PA/

Davidson K, Graham S, Huffer D (2024) A protocol for when social media goes private: studying archaeological or heritage discourses in closed Facebook groups. Internet Archaeol 67:10.11141/ia.67.11

Davies C (2024) UK auction house cancels sale of shrunken heads and skulls. Retrieved from https://www.theguardian.com/culture/2024/oct/09/uk-auction-house-cancels-sale-of-shrunken-heads-and-skulls

Dorado E, Carrillo M, Ruiz-Tagle E (2022) El singular caso de un cráneo decorado. Revista Internacional de Antropología y Odontología Forense 5:93–98

Duncan S, Inch S (2024) Riding the digital highway with the Mongols and the Vagos: applying OSINT techniques to assess member criminality and connectivity. In: Blokland A, Von Lampe K, van Deuren S (eds) Outlaw bikers as organised crime. Routledge, London, pp 248–270

Elkhazeen A, Poulos C, Zhang X, Cavanaugh J, Cain M (2022) A TikTok™ "Benadryl challenge" death—a case report and review of the literature. J Forensic Sci 68(1):339–342. https://doi.org/10.1111/1556-4029.15149

Gondhali U, Merzon A, Nunphong T, Lo T-Y, Liu Y-H, Petrossian GA (2024) Crime script analysis of the illegal sales of spiny-tailed lizards on YouTube. Crime Sci 13(8). https://doi.org/10.1186/s40163-024-00206-w

Graham S, Davidson K, Huffer D (2024) Behind closed doors: the human remains trade within private Facebook groups. Internet Archaeol 67:10.11141/ia.67.14

Groen M, Márquez-Grant N, Janaway R (eds) (2015) Forensic archaeology: a global perspective. Wiley-Blackwell, Chichester

Gudge E (2024) Nagaland, India: CM demands end to auction of sacred Naga skull in UK, calling it dehumanizing. Retrieved from https://www.bbc.com/news/articles/cy4dwg0e0m2o

Hackman L, Black S (2023) Forensic examination of the hand. J R Anthropol Inst 29:116–131. https://doi.org/10.1111/1467-9655.13999

Harrington LA, Elwin A, Paterson S, D'Cruze N (2023) The viewer doesn't always seem to care—response to fake animal rescues on YouTube and implications for social media self-policing policies. People Nature 5(1):103–118. https://doi.org/10.1002/pan3.10416

Hatfield JM (2023) There is no such thing as open source intelligence. Int J Intell Count Intell 37(2):397–418. https://doi.org/10.1080/08850607.2023.2172367

Hodgson E (2024) Exposed: The sick world of TikTok animal abusers using catapults to kill wildlife in Kent. Retrieved May 2024, from https://www.kentonline.co.uk/kent/news/exposed-the-sick-world-of-tiktok-animal-abusers-306137/

Huffer D (2024) Buy one get one: the legal and socio-cultural context of 'gifting' within the Australian human remains trade. J Comp Appl Archaeol 7(1):115–125. https://doi.org/10.5334/jcaa.137

Huffer D, Charlton N (2019) "Serious enquiries only, please": ethical issues raised by the online human remains trade. In: Squires K, Errickson D, Márquez-Grant N (eds) Ethical approaches to human remains: a global challenge in bioarchaeology and forensic anthropology. Springer, Cham, pp 95–129

Huffer D, Graham S (2023) These were people once: the online trade in human remains and why it matters. Berghahn Books, Brooklyn

Huffer D, Simons J, Brughmans T, Graham S (2022) 'Alleen voor studiedoeleinden' (for study purposes only): the human remains trade on Marktplaats.nl. Anthropologica et Praehistorica 131(2020):179–194

Jara San Miguel JC, Cuadrado Piñas J, Miralles Mosquera S, Ruiz Mediavilla E (2021) An identification case study from fingerprint photographs. Forensic Sci Int 324:110826. https://doi.org/10.1016/j.forsciint.2021.110826

Kjaergaard PC (2012) The fossil trade: paying a price for human origins. Isis 103(2):340–355

Márquez-Grant N, Rissech C, López-Costas O, Alemán I, Caro Dobón L (2011) Spain/España. In: Márquez-Grant N, Fibiger L (eds) The Routledge handbook of archaeological remains and legislation: an international guide to laws and practice in the excavation and treatment of human remains. Routledge, pp 423–438

O'Neill M (2024) Trafficking and organs, tissues, and cells: an examination of European and UK legislation and gaps. Eur J Crime Crim Law Crim Justice 32(1):32–57. https://doi.org/10.1163/15718174-bja10051

Panwar S (2024) Nagaland, India: CM demands end to auction of sacred Naga skull in UK, calling it dehumanizing. Retrieved from https://thedailyguardian.com/nagaland-india-cm-demands-end-to-auction-of-sacred-naga-skull-in-uk-calling-it-dehumanizing/

Pester P (2022) Desecrated human skulls are being sold on social media in U.K.'s unregulated bone trade. Retrieved August 2024, from https://www.scientificamerican.com/article/desecrated-human-skulls-are-being-sold-on-social-media-in-u-k-s-unregulated-bone-trade/

Policía Nacional (2023) Intervenidas en Madrid 11 piezas de oro valoradas en más de 60 millones de euros pertenecientes al patrimonio histórico de Ucrania. Retrieved August 2024, from https://www.policia.es/es/comunicacion_prensa_detalle.php?ID=15929

Rose J (2021) The Hythe church, a wall of skulls and the appalling crime that 'disturbed' an entire town. Retrieved August 2024, from https://www.kentlive.news/news/kent-news/hythe-church-wall-skulls-appalling-4881973

Rush LW (2014) Introducing cultural heritage management to the US military. In: Albro R, Ivey B (eds) Cultural awareness in the military: developments and implications for future humanitarian cooperation. Palgrave Pivot, London

Rush LW (ed) (2023) Archaeology, cultural property, and the military. Boyden & Brewer, Martlesham

Scovazzi T (2024) Human remains as cultural heritage. In: Lixinski L, Morisset LK (eds) The Routledge handbook of heritage and the law. Routledge, London

Seidemann RM, Hawkins WT (2019) Acquisition and disposition problems and experiences policing the online marketplace for human remains. In: Moran KS, Gold CL (eds) Forensic archaeology. Springer, Cham, pp 313–326. https://doi.org/10.1007/978-3-030-03291-3_19

Solly M (2018) British Army revives monuments men to salvage art in war-torn countries. Smithsonian Magazine. October 16, 2018. Retrieved August 2024, from https://www.smithsonianmag.com/smart-news/british-army-revives-monuments-men-hopes-salvaging-art-war-torn-countries-180970563/

Index

P. M. Barone, WJ M. Groen (eds.), *Forensic Archaeology and New Multidisciplinary Approaches*, Soil Forensics, https://doi.org/10.1007/978-3-031-86308-0

The manufacturer's authorised representative in the EU is Springer Nature Customer Service Centre GmbH, Europaplatz 3, 69115 Heidelberg, Germany. If you have any concerns regarding our products, please contact ProductSafety@springernature.com

Printed and bound by CPI Group (UK) Ltd, Croydon, CR0 4YY
30/09/2026
02225596-0005